John Gilbert

Also by Eve Golden

Platinum Girl:
The Life and Legends of Jean Harlow
(1991)

Vamp:
The Rise and Fall of Theda Bara
(1996)

Anna Held and the Birth of Ziegfeld's Broadway
(2000)

Golden Images:
41 Essays on Silent Film Stars
(2001)

The Brief, Madcap Life of Kay Kendall
(2002)

Vernon and Irene Castle's Ragtime Revolution
(2007)

Bride of Golden Images:
Essays on Stars of the 1930s–60s
(2009)

JOHN GILBERT

The Last of the Silent Film Stars

Eve Golden

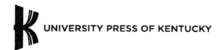

University Press of Kentucky

Scholarly publisher for the Commonwealth,
serving Bellarmine University, Berea College, Centre College of Kentucky, Eastern Kentucky University, The Filson Historical Society, Georgetown College, Kentucky Historical Society, Kentucky State University, Morehead State University, Murray State University, Northern Kentucky University, Transylvania University, University of Kentucky, University of Louisville, and Western Kentucky University.

Editorial and Sales Offices: The University Press of Kentucky
663 South Limestone Street, Lexington, Kentucky 40508–4008
www.kentuckypress.com

17 16 15 14 13   5 4 3 2 1

Library of Congress Cataloging-in-Publication Data

Golden, Eve.
John Gilbert : the last of the silent film stars / Eve Golden.
pages cm
Includes filmography.
Includes bibliographical references and index.
ISBN 978-0-8131-4162-6 (hardcover : alk. paper) —
ISBN 978-0-8131-4163-3 (epub) — ISBN 978-0-8131-4164-0 (pdf)
1. Gilbert, John, 1897-1936. 2. Motion picture actors and actresses—United States—Biography. I. Title.
PN2287.G517G65 2013
791.4302'8092—dc23
[B]   2012051380

This book is printed on acid-free paper meeting the requirements of the American National Standard for Permanence in Paper for Printed Library Materials.

Manufactured in the United States of America.

Member of the Association of
American University Presses

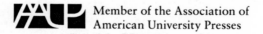

To my Aussie pals

Mark Johnson and Ross Trevelyan

Contents

Introduction

October 1929, "If I Had a Talking Picture of You"

> It's all very well to make pictures of these heroes and villains of the past, but are they honestly and truthfully any more romantic than the man who fills my gasoline tank? How do you know what emotions the man across the street from you is experiencing? How do you know what love has come into his life, what he feels?
>
> —John Gilbert, 1927

> I wish I could tell you, in a few words, the whole story of those dreadful years, these years that the locusts have eaten. . . . So many things, so many reasons, they would fill a book.
>
> —John Gilbert, 1933

Honeymooners John Gilbert and Ina Claire were among the more eye-catching American tourists in Europe in the summer of 1929. Fortyish Ina Claire was Broadway's leading light comedienne, and as for John Gilbert—in his early thirties, he was the screen's hottest heartthrob, the top male sex symbol of the late 1920s and one of MGM's box-office champs. Handsome, mercurial, and very talented, he had already married and divorced one star (Leatrice Joy) and had famously taken movie newcomer Greta Garbo as his lover—"Jack" Gilbert (as he was known to friends and enemies alike) would go on to marry another actress (ingénue Virginia Bruce) and become the lover of Garbo's chief competitor as a glamour queen, Marlene Dietrich. Indeed, there were few leading ladies who were not pursued by him (the list would include Lillian Gish, Lupe Velez, Mae Murray, and Barbara La Marr).

He and Ina Claire had wed—after a swift courtship—that May in Las Vegas. The brittle, sophisticated Ina Claire and the emotional whirlwind John Gilbert were an unlikely couple, and few friends gave their marriage much chance. A probably apocryphal exchange pretty much summed up their relationship:

> Reporter: "Tell me, Miss Claire, what is it like being married to a big star?"
>
> Ina Claire: "I don't know, why don't you ask Mr. Gilbert?"

Although he'd been a star at MGM for four years, with such hits as *The Merry Widow, The Big Parade, Flesh and the Devil,* and *Love,* John Gilbert had many worries as he and his new wife embarked on the *Ile de France* for Europe, trailed by fans, reporters, and photographers. He had recently completed his first two talking films, but his relationship with MGM management was increasingly strained. In May he had made *Redemption,* a dark, heavy Russian drama—despite his early stage training, John Gilbert had no microphone experience, and was nervous and floundering. Being coached by his wife only made him feel more inadequate. In July, while *Redemption* was still being edited, he filmed a Ruritarian romance, *His Glorious Night,* directed by actor Lionel Barrymore and costarring newcomer Catherine Dale Owen. He knew neither project was much good, and suspected that *His Glorious Night* might be a real stinker. He was not sure which would be released first, as his feature talking debut. For reasons long debated, MGM led with *His Glorious Night.*

John Gilbert was still on his leisurely way home from his honeymoon when *His Glorious Night* opened on October 5, 1929—a première that would find its way into Hollywood legend. To this day, many believe that John Gilbert's "high, squeaky, effeminate" voice sent his career into an instant tailspin, that he skulked off to drink himself to death. The talkie failure of John Gilbert (and, to a lesser extent, Clara Bow) became an emblem of the era: kazoo-voiced Lina Lamont in *Singin' in the Rain* is based partly on John Gilbert's sudden fall. Gloria Swanson's Norma Desmond (*Sunset Boulevard*) and Jean Dujardin's George Valentin (*The Artist*) have more than a little John Gilbert in them. Norma Desmond even rages, "They took the idols and smashed them, the Fairbankses, the Gilberts, the Valentinos! And who've we got now? Some *nobodies!*"

Like many rumors, it contains a little bit of truth and a lot of myth making. The *New York Times* review of *His Glorious Night* was not as dire as legend will have it: "Both Mr. Gilbert and Catherine Dale Owen contribute competent performances to this production," Mordaunt Hall wrote. "Mr. Gilbert . . . is to be congratulated on the manner in which he handles this speaking rôle. His voice is pleasant, but not one which is rich in nuances. His performance is good, but it would benefit by the suggestion of a little more wit. He, as one might presume, wears his officer's uniform as if he were bred in the army traditions." But Hall also noted something that would come to haunt Gilbert even beyond his death: "The actor constantly repeats 'I love you' to the Princess Orsolini as he kisses her. In fact, his many protestations of affection . . . caused a large female contingent in the theatre yesterday afternoon to giggle and laugh." *Variety*'s review was even deadlier: "A few more talker productions like this and John Gilbert will be able to change places with [comedian] Harry Langdon."

The New York American wrote, "John makes the grade with ease. . . . The picture leaves no doubt as to his continued popularity as a star." *Los Angeles Times* critic Edwin Schallert said, "The intelligence of his work is even more marked in sound than in silence." The *New York Review* called *His Glorious Night* "John Gilbert's first all-talking triumph."

But, like most overly sensitive people, Jack processed only the bad reviews. Ina Claire later told his daughter that MGM sent emissaries brandishing the worst reviews to meet them as they docked in New York. "He'd told me about his trouble with the studio and now they'd come all the way to tell him *that*."

John Gilbert was a huge star in 1929—one of the biggest, at the biggest studio—but he was not bulletproof. A nasty *Vanity Fair* profile in 1928 had prompted him to write a multipart defense and memoir in *Photoplay*. His recently ended romance with Greta Garbo had made both of them objects of tabloid and fan-magazine gossip. His drinking, his womanizing, his larger-than-life personality: all made him a target for moralizers and journalists out for a scoop. And the inevitable coming of talking pictures was making movie fans rethink their loyalties—stage stars like Ina Claire might very well displace the old favorites.

He seemed realistic and upbeat when interviewed in late October. He wanted to make an epic version of Stephen Vincent Benét's Civil War poem *John Brown's Body.* He had a story about a scheming, lascivious chauffeur he wanted to film. Still, he admitted that the mixed reviews for *His Glorious Night* were "like a slap in the face. . . . I looked forward to seeing it well received. And now this! Oh, well."

By the end of 1929, his marriage to Ina Claire would be over, and there would be no lifeline thrown by MGM. His coworkers Greta Garbo, Norma Shearer, and Joan Crawford would be nurtured through good talkies and bad, but John Gilbert would soon find himself unemployable.

Part 1

The Climb

Chapter One

So much of my youth was spent praying for a good season.
—John Gilbert, 1927

John Gilbert was—perhaps literally—born in a trunk. He was born John Cecil Pringle in Logan, Utah—about eighty miles north of Salt Lake City—on July 10, 1897, the son of a small-time stock-company manager and his young actress bride. Jack's father, John George Priegel, had been born in Missouri in 1865; by the 1890s he was known as "Johnnie Pringle" and was barnstorming around the country, managing (and acting in) his own stock company. Jack's mother, Ida Adair Apperly, had been born in 1877 in Colorado. She was living in Utah when Johnnie Pringle blew into town and swept her off her feet: the stolid, no-nonsense Apperlys were appalled when she announced that she wanted to go on the stage and that she had just married into "the show business."

Small traveling theater companies did not leave much behind in the way of press clippings; their shows were heralded by posters—torn down or covered over within days—and if they were reviewed at all, it was in tiny local papers that are now long since out of business. We get only a few glimpses of Jack's parents. The *Spirit Lake (Iowa) Beacon* of January 24, 1900, announced a presentation of "the great comedy success *A White Elephant,* headed by the popular favorites, Johnnie and Ida Pringle, and an excellent company. Everything new and up-to-date. Reserved seats now on sale at the City Drug Store. Prices, 25, 35 and 50 cents." In

Baby John Cecil Pringle with his mother, Ida, 1898 (Wisconsin Center for Film & Theater Research).

1903 Ida—billed as "Ida Adair"—was "especially engaged for the role of Anne of Austria" in the Edward F. Albee Stock Company's production of *The Three Musketeers.* By 1905 Ida was the leading woman with the Empire Stock Company of Columbus, Ohio ("It has enjoyed a run of nearly two years, and its popularity is ever increasing," said *Theatre* magazine). Adair had "wide experience and unusual talents . . . extremely popular with Columbus theatergoers," giving the lie to later descriptions of Jack's mother as a failed actress. In 1907 she turns up in Cincinnati: "Miss Ida Adair, as Miss Harriet Fordyce [in *The Earl of Pawtucket*], was extremely good," said *Billboard.*

Jack's* parents had divorced by then; the boy stayed with his mother while his father continued to travel the country with the Johnnie Pringle

*Biographers fall into two camps: first-name users and last-name users. I am of the former group—I wrote biographies of Anna, Kay, and Vernon, not Held, Kendall, and Castle. I feel it is more appropriate for show-business biographies. This presented a dilemma here, as John Gilbert was universally referred to as "Jack" by his coworkers, family, and friends, and often by reviewers and fan-magazine writers. Calling him "John" seemed awkward and wrong somehow. I hope readers will not think it presumptuous and overly familiar of me, but I opted to go with "Jack."

Stock Company. Pringle could be seen in 1906 at the Seattle Theater, "greeted by an enthusiastic and appreciative audience. It is seldom the patrons of this theater have had the pleasure of witnessing such a well balanced and finished performance." Articles written at the time of his death, in the 1920s, had him running his own stock companies in "Chicago, New York and other eastern cities," though this cannot be confirmed.

Johnnie and Ida Pringle belonged to an old, if not revered, tradition: the traveling players. The first-known theater troupe in America predated the United States; there was a professional acting company in Virginia in 1752. Before the Civil War, companies traveled by horse and carriage or plied the rivers. But the railroads gave new life to the business—though not comfort or luxury. The trains of the Pringles' day were bumpy, they tended to derail or get stuck behind felled trees or fallen rocks, and schedules were so lax that connections were missed as often as they were caught. Train seats were not always padded, and windows had to be opened to let in fresh air (along with dust and cinders).

Rooming houses were sometimes not to be had at all, in which case actors had to beg rooms from the locals or sleep in the depot atop their luggage. The theaters themselves could be a trial if the booking agent was not to be trusted. Scenery sometimes didn't fit onstage or there *was* no "backstage" for entrances and storage. Small-town dressing rooms were notorious. Sol Smith, in the late nineteenth century, wrote that in Nashville his "dressing room" had been dug into the ground behind the theater. "Human bones were strewn about in every direction. The first night, the lamplighter being a little pushed for time to get all ready, seized upon a skull, and, sticking two tallow candles in the eye sockets, I found my dressing room thus lighted."

Not everyone slept on luggage or dressed in graves; sometimes it *could* be a lark. Some people thrived on the travel, the excitement, and the *acting*. The fact that John Gilbert's parents—and later his stepfather, Walter Gilbert—never gave up show business indicates that it was all worth the bother, at least in their eyes. Ida could have returned—with her babe in arms, like the classic melodrama heroine—to her solidly settled farming family, but she never did.

Other silent movie stars grew up on the road, among them John Gilbert's future costars Mary Pickford and Lillian Gish. "Actors, like soldiers, can bed down anywhere," Gish wrote in her memoirs. She recalled her troupe squeezing as many people into one hotel room as possible: "They would lie crosswise on the bed and sleep or sew or, if the water was hot, do their laundry. I would curl up in a chair or go for a walk alone and watch the children of the town playing." Sometimes there was no hotel, or a missed train necessitated a long wait in the town's depot. "My bed was usually the sloping desk that was used for writing telegrams," Gish recalled. "I often napped on a stone floor, with papers underneath my body."

It sounds Dickensian, and often was, but Gish also remembered happy times on the road, feeling sorry for children stuck in their schools and churches and dull, repetitive lives. Jack often bitterly recalled his childhood as loveless and impoverished, but in a calm, happy mood in 1927 he told Alma Whitaker of the *Los Angeles Times* that "we were often very poor, all right, but we often had intermittent luxuries. Mother would take me around with her. When we had good seasons we stayed at the best hotels and swanked it. When it was a poor one, we migrated to the cheap and nasty sections of the towns. So much of my youth was spent praying for a good season. I wouldn't like to be poor again, you understand, but if I ever were I could dramatize it for myself and see myself as a life's adventurer."

The late nineteenth century was the golden age of the touring company, and talented hard workers like the Pringles and Walter Gilbert could make a decent living, with a little luck. "Even in the one-night towns, there could be as many as 228 different shows through the winter and it was difficult and exciting to decide which you wanted to see," wrote theater historian and actor Philip Lewis. In those pre-movie, pre-radio days, one form of theater or another was the primary source of entertainment. Vaudeville, musicals, dramas, church revivals, lectures (sometimes with magic-lantern slides), circuses; even the smallest town *had* to have access to at least some of these. Broadway hits had three or four companies touring the country, with the "A" company boasting the original stars (Ida Gilbert toured in a "B" company version of *Madame X*, starring Marjorie Rambeau, in the early 1910s).

The December 1906 issue of the *Theatre* magazine contains contributions from local critics across the country, telling what shows were landing in their towns. Philadelphia, Boston, Chicago, and their like, of course, got major Broadway companies with big stars (Henry Irving,

Marie Cahill, Julia Marlowe, Maude Adams). But stars were dragging their plays and their companies of struggling, hopeful supporting players all over the United States that month: Anna Held in Baltimore, Clara Bloodgood (who would kill herself while on tour in Baltimore a year later) in Cleveland, the black musical-comedy team Williams and Walker in Lincoln, Nebraska, Mrs. Fiske in Pittsburgh, French soubrette Yvette Guilbert in Oklahoma City.

The smaller towns were heard from, too. M. J. Wiggins reported to the *Theatre* that Oswego, New York, had "the best and most prosperous" season in history, with Porter J. White in *The Proud Prince* and such stars as Nance O'Neil, Eva Tanguay, and Helena Modjeska passing through—as well as motion pictures every Sunday at the Richardson Theater. Morgantown, West Virginia, saw the lesser-known Mildred Holland in *A Paradise of Lies* and John E. Henshaw in *Captain Careless* as well as offerings of melodrama and vaudeville. This was the world of Ida Gilbert—although she generally appeared not with the big stars in classic shows remembered today by theater aficionados but with the likes of Hans Roberts in *Checkers,* Max Figman in *The Man on the Box,* and Sadie Raymond in *The Missouri Girl.*

Whatever company Jack's parents were in at the time—their own or someone else's—the manager would book the season through a guide like Julius Kahn's, which listed some seventeen hundred theaters throughout the United States and what kind of shows they took (also their size, ticket prices, and so on). After the booking manager had a tour set up, the advance man would paper the town with posters and newspaper ads, make sure the theater actually existed, and usually hightail it to the next stop before the company overlapped him. Actors "could not *afford* to get sick," Lewis wrote. "The show had to go on, because otherwise there would be no salary."

Ida Pringle "married up" when she wed Walter Gilbert, an actor with slightly better connections and prospects than her hardworking first husband—Gilbert went on to enjoy a respectable, if not stellar, career. Gilbert also proved to be a more sympathetic father—he never discussed why, but young John Cecil Pringle began calling himself John Cecil Gilbert by his early teens. He mentioned his birth father only in unpleasant terms and referred to Walter Gilbert as his "father." He had a reliable grandfather to fall back on, too: when she was unable to take him on the road, Ida farmed her son out to her parents, the stable, if rather disapproving, Apperlys in Utah.

When he was old enough, Jack was shipped off to the Hitchcock Military Academy in San Rafael, northern California. Founded in 1907 by Reverend Charles Hitchcock, it consisted of five buildings, including dorms and a gym. Today the school is co-owned by the Marin Ballet School, the Marin Tennis Club, and Trinity Community Church. Scrawny, undernourished, and wary of boys his own age, Jack began to develop his social skills during these years, as well as his athleticism. He was never a big, muscular man—he grew up to be a very slim five foot nine—but given access to the sports facilities at Hitchcock, Jack discovered a love for tennis, swimming, horseback riding, and golf, all of which he enjoyed for the rest of his life. In the ninth grade, when he was about fifteen, Jack left Hitchcock—in later interviews, he never made clear whether he'd graduated or had needed to go to work to help support his mother.

Ida Gilbert's presence simply cannot be ignored in a discussion of her son's future life. Armchair psychologists—most of them fan-magazine writers—dragged poor Ida from her grave again and again trying to diagnose John Gilbert's tortured love life. "Lovely Ida, as profligate as a Winter wind, as vivid as a sunset," wrote Katherine Albert in a particularly purple magazine piece of 1930. The queen of the sob sisters, Adela Rogers St. Johns, brought out the heavy artillery in 1936: "Jack loved her—and bitterly resented things she had done to him. He never quite trusted love nor life. . . . And he never found in the women he loved, the mother he was always seeking." It's always easy and convenient to blame the mother (Jack had a father and a stepfather, too, but they were rarely mentioned).

Jack's daughter Leatrice, in her memoirs, quotes actress Marie Stoddard—later Leatrice's acting coach in Hollywood—as saying that Ida was "a good trouper . . . but she had a blind spot about that boy. She hardly knew he was there. And he was such a nice little fellow, always polite, but his face was pinched-looking, too old for his years. You wanted to hug him and make him laugh." Leatrice Gilbert also claims Ida left Jack with a New York seamstress whose flat also served as a whorehouse for her own daughter: "I was only seven but I knew more about the world than many people ever discover," she quotes her father as recalling.

The young Jack Gilbert, ca. 1905 (author's collection).

If travel was sad and lonely for little John Pringle—later Gilbert—it was sad and lonely for his single mother, too. Often on the road without a husband—or between husbands—she was still young and pretty and no doubt aching for company. Theater historian (and former trouper) Philip C. Lewis wrote movingly of life on the road: "The players were briefly the best-known people in town and yet they were lonely. Under the focus of lights and the spectators' concentrated gaze, they became vividly familiar in the short time between overture and final curtain. Yet no one knew them and they would be gone before they knew any of those who had been so close and friendly in the auditorium dark."

Filtered through Jack's dark memories told to wife Leatrice Joy and passed down to their daughter Leatrice Gilbert, Ida Pringle comes off as a monster: "His mother had not wanted him, his mother paid no attention to him," Leatrice Gilbert told film historian Kevin Brownlow in the fascinating, invaluable John Gilbert segment of his 1980 documentary series, *Hollywood: The Pioneers*. "She would lock him in closets for hours, all day, just to get him out of the way. She had many lovers, and would wake him up in the middle of the night to introduce him to his new 'daddy.'" "He hardly ever went to school, there would be two weeks here, three weeks there," his daughter added. "He never had toys. He was never allowed to carry toys or books with him."

Different people react differently to challenging childhoods, of course. Jack grew up to become an easily hurt, thin-skinned young man who needed badly to be loved and accepted. He also used his tough luck to educate himself, to mold himself into the person he wanted to be: smart, funny, accomplished, devil-may-care. But he always felt he was putting on an act, one that everyone could see through.

Around 1905, when John Gilbert was eight years old, the whole touring business began to slide downhill. A group of New York producers had banded together into a Theatrical Syndicate in the late 1890s, and by 1905 they controlled so many theaters nationwide that if you weren't under contract with the Syndicate, you had a terrible time finding work. Many star performers rebelled (Minnie Maddern Fiske, Richard Mansfield, Sarah Bernhardt, and others played in tents rather than buckle under). Given that there were fewer houses for independent companies, Ida Gilbert had to get herself cast in Syndicate shows or she was out of luck. Audiences were sparser, too, as the twentieth century rolled on: automobiles, record players, and moving pictures stole interest away from traditional theater. Philip Lewis wrote that there were 339 theatrical companies on tour in 1900; by 1910 that had dropped to 236—and by 1915, only 124. Still, Ida Gilbert, John Pringle, and Walter Gilbert all worked more or less steadily—supported themselves and their son, if not in style—and that in itself was an accomplishment and a testament to their talents and professionalism.

On September 29, 1913, thirty-six-year-old Ida Gilbert died in Salt Lake City, Utah. The cause was probably tuberculosis—at least, that's what her son recalled years later. She was buried in the family plot in

The teenaged "Jack C. Gilbert," ca. 1915 (author's collection).

Logan, and if sixteen-year-old "Jack C. Gilbert," as he called himself, felt any grief or regrets about her, he never let on. For the rest of his life, he recalled his mother and birth father with an unrelenting bitterness.

There followed a year of odd jobs, which he later claimed included working as a salesman for the B. F. Goodrich Company and as a copy boy at the *Oregonian* newspaper, the latter job giving him an appreciation for the press not common among film stars.

By early 1915 the teenaged Jack was working as stage manager for the Baker Stock Company in Spokane, Washington (not to be confused with the more successful Baker Stock Company in Portland, Oregon). Other Baker veterans included such future movie pioneers as screenwriter and director Melville Brown and actor Howard Russell. Jack later recalled his duties: "Ringing the curtain up and down, calling the overtures and warning to the actors that their cues for entrance are approaching, holding a manuscript at rehearsals, making out stage settings and property plots, and seeing to it that every prop or article used during each act is in its correct position. If, during the action of the play, a white-faced, suffering little mother says to the swarthy villain, 'Here is the will,' and there is no will—God help the stage manager." (The author, who worked as a stage manager for several productions when just a little older than John Gilbert was in 1915, can attest to the truth of these duties.)

Jack recalled that the company shut down in March 1915. He took a train for Portland, where Walter Gilbert (to whom he pointedly refers as "my father") was directing a stock company. According to his 1928 *Photoplay* memoirs, Jack bent his ambitions toward becoming a movie actor. This might seem odd, considering the financially and emotionally impoverished childhood show business had handed him. Perhaps he wanted to do his parents one better, or perhaps it was just all he knew.

Chapter Two

> A young world mad with ecstatic life, a fifteen dollar a week world, but—swell!
>
> —John Gilbert, 1928

Walter Gilbert obligingly sent a letter to a former coworker, Walter Edwards, a longtime director who was currently working for producer Thomas Ince at the newly opened Triangle Film Corporation in Culver City, California. Edwards had entered films in 1912, but there is no telling how far he would have gone, as he died in 1920, still working steadily at the time. His career shows that there were other successful silent directors besides D. W. Griffith, Erich von Stroheim, and Cecil B. DeMille. He directed more than one hundred movies, yet he and every one of his titles have fallen into oblivion. He worked with the biggest stars of the day (Wallace Reid, Alma Rubens, and Marguerite Clark as well as Constance Talmadge and Harrison Ford, whom he directed in a series of romantic comedies), but he was pretty much forgotten by the end of the silent era. Two professional headshots of the skinny, teenaged "Jack C. Gilbert" were sent off to Edwards. Amazingly, Jack recalled, a letter came in return: "Mr. Ince says he can give the boy fifteen dollars a week if he cares to come down." Such career breaks were almost unheard of, even in 1915.

The film industry had sprung up so quickly since its inception in the 1890s that by the 1920s people were already looking back nostalgically at its early years. We think of 1915—when John Gilbert made his first movie—as the toddler years of the business, but even then it was hard to break into the profession. In the spring of 1916, *Motion Picture* magazine sent out a pretty young reporter, Suzette Booth, to try her luck in the acting business with no contacts to ease her way. "It is not the great stars that can give advice," she warned. "When they broke in, it was very easy." Booth managed to sweet-talk her way into work as an extra at Balboa Studios in the "dusty village" of Long Beach, but her very first assignment was as a background dancer wearing "a few inches of cheesecloth, with a garland of roses." When she refused, she was told, "Either put on that costume or go to the office and get your money." She did the latter: "Thus ended my career at Balboa."

Next Booth tried buttonholing director Christy Cabanne at Fine Arts; he ducked out on her, and the following day he waved her away with "Can't see you today, Miss Booth; come around next June." She was unable to track down the great and elusive D. W. Griffith, but an assistant sent her in to see the "ogre" Frank Woods, a screenwriter, who yelled, "*We don't want anybody!*" so loudly he scared her out of the studio.

So John Gilbert was very lucky indeed to have a stepfather and a family friend who could talk Triangle into hiring him. Researcher Richard Kukan, who has recently completed a survey of American films in the years 1896–1915, says that Jack picked the best possible year to make his entrance into the industry. "In 1914, the American studios start batting out one terrific feature film after another. And at the same time cameras are often placed much closer to the actors than was normally the case in previous years, so the viewer becomes much more involved in the action. A lot of these films seem as fresh today as the day they were issued. The advent of talents like Maurice Tourneur and William S. Hart and Cecil B. DeMille means that a filmmaker couldn't just stumble through a mess like Frederick Warde's *Richard III* and Helen Gardner's *Cleopatra* anymore and expect anyone to put up with it. The only explanation I can devise for this is that Tourneur, et al., were more talented than their predecessors (Griffith apart, and for a time you can see even him struggling to catch up with the newcomers)."

By 1915, Kukan notes, "An actor can now count on being visible. Many directors are confidently, routinely producing work which would have seemed incredibly innovative even five years previously. Now that many famous actors are making movies, there's no shame in joining in. You watch movies of 1906, and they're mostly an exercise in antiquarianism. You hunt for a good shot, a well-edited moment, a brief glimpse of good acting. You don't get much for your troubles. Even around 1910, when Griffith is working wonders, there are still lots of stodgy, dull movies by people who haven't yet 'got it.' But by 1914 the dull, clumsy movies are largely gone."

The teenaged John Gilbert—completely naïve and unfamiliar with films—could not possibly have arrived at a better place, at a better time, and with better contacts than he did. The Triangle Film Corporation had just been created, the brainchild of theater manager and movie executive Harry Aitken. Aitken had formed the Western Film Exchange as early as 1906, going on to create or manage several motion-picture production companies: American, Majestic (briefly the home of rising star Mary Pickford), and Reliance, which in 1913 boasted D. W. Griffith as production chief (Aitken would play a major role in financing *The Birth of a Nation* and *Intolerance*). Aitken also founded one of the most powerful distributors of the era, the Mutual Film Corporation, which handled productions by the New York Motion Picture Company, including both Thomas Ince's westerns and Mack Sennett's Keystone comedies.

Aiken battled with the board of Mutual over funding and artistic freedom (his adversaries quite rightly contended that Aitken the distributor tended to favor the releases of Aitken the producer), and through 1914 he scrambled to find financing for a new company that would produce, distribute, and exhibit films—foreshadowing the structure of the later, larger Hollywood studios. The formation of Triangle Film Corporation was finalized in July 1915, just after Jack Gilbert had shown up at the doorstep of one of its three "angles," Thomas Ince's Inceville Studios in the hills of Santa Monica.

The other two Triangle principals were D. W. Griffith and Mack Sennett. The studio was essentially a combination of Aitken's assets (notably his existing relationship—and contract—with Griffith) and those of the New York Motion Picture Company (Sennett and Ince). Triangle's aim was to provide its exhibitors with four films a week: one feature each from Griffith and Ince and two short comedies from Sennett. Not necessarily *directed* by Griffith, Ince, or Sennett, mind you—they worked as producers and had their own stable of directors under them. By the mid-1910s features tended to be about three to six reels in length, a reel running about twelve minutes. Comedy shorts were either one- or two-reelers.

Thomas H. Ince was only thirty-three years old in 1915, but he was a big, beefy, prematurely gray-haired man, looking every inch the imposing studio head. His brothers John and Ralph were also in the business, both boasting lengthy acting and directing careers. Much like Jack, Thomas Ince had grown up in stock companies and was suffering from the lack of reliable stage work when he threw his lot in with the movies. Ince got his feet wet as an actor at Independent Movie Pictures (IMP) and Biograph, returned to IMP as a director, and in very short order rose to the position of supervisor of the New York Motion Picture Company's western unit. He proved to be an innovative production chief, and his films (particularly westerns starring William S. Hart) were hugely successful with critics and audiences alike.

Historian Kalton Lahue notes in his book about Triangle that Ince was all business, and a frenzied workaholic: "Ince demanded and received absolute obedience from everyone on the lot, but most especially from his directors. Once a property had been developed or acquired for filming, his script writers developed a detailed continuity and Tom went over each and every scene with them, disapproving or recommending changes. . . . The finished product was an extremely detailed shooting script calling out scenes, sets and sequences over which Ince maintained control at all times."

The studio town of Inceville began to take shape near Santa Monica in late 1911—four hundred employees, eighteen thousand acres, "most of it foothill country and beach," an "upright farm." The star character actor of their stock company was J. Barney Sherry, who told the *Los Angeles Times,* "There have been some great changes in moving picture work and in methods of production. In the first place, the fellow that ranted and swung his arms around most was the best actor." Inceville was as much a community as a studio, off on its own in the hills. In November 1914 Incevillians (including cowboy star William S. Hart) banded together to help fight a Sepulveda Canyon brush fire. As an example of how free and easy the nonunion Inceville sets were, when director Charles Miller needed more extras than he could find for a 1916 Bessie Barriscale film, he was told by a higher-up, "Go and get the scenario department, and everyone who is not working, and put them in your set." Stars, other directors, cameramen, and an art director were drafted.

Director King Vidor, who arrived in Hollywood in 1918, recalled in

The man who got Jack into the film industry, director and producer Thomas Ince, late 1910s (author's collection).

his memoirs how unprofessional some of the early studios were in those days before unions and résumés. "Men who had never been inside a studio were given directing assignments on pure bluff," he wrote. "Some of these ne'er-do-wells would turn out several pictures before being discovered; by the time busy executives got around to viewing their initial efforts, they would be well into their third film." Vidor also recalled the outdoor sets used in not-always-sunny California: "Heavy tarpaulins were used to cover the sets on rainy days. They were supposed to keep the rain off upholstered furniture, actors, and arc lamps, but the result instead was a highly charged soggy mess. . . . The great expression of the day was, 'Go ahead and shoot. It won't pick up.'"

Jack had no idea where Inceville was or how to get there. He later claimed he called the studio as soon as he arrived in Los Angeles and got into a fight with whoever was manning the switchboard:

> "How do I get out there?"
> "Walk."
> "Don't get fresh!"
> "Go to hell." [*click*]

He finally found his way ("God knows how") to the studios via train and streetcar, "far up the beach beyond Santa Monica. There lay the studio of my dreams, under two feet of dust," he wrote some fifteen years later. "Inceville resembled nothing more than a sleepy, dirty Western town—scattered buildings, of plain boards, and rut-worn roads leading up into the hills."

The gatekeeper refused Jack entrance, and there was no phone, so he leaned against the front gate and looked anxiously at the other early-morning arrivals. Happily, among them was an old friend: Herschell Mayall. Jack already knew Mayall worked at Inceville (indeed, one suspects he rode out there with him and the whole "they wouldn't let me in" story was invented for dramatic effect). Mayall, in his fifties, had a long stage and film career behind him by 1915.

Mayall ushered Jack in and took him to Walter Edwards's office. Edwards—who had just started working at Inceville himself—in turn, accompanied Jack to see Thomas Ince and studio manager E. H. Allan. The newcomer was given a cordial greeting, shown around, and went out to dinner with Edwards. The next day he showed up at work happily expecting to be cast in something.

E. H. Allen did not know what to make of this new acquisition; Jack had seemingly been under the wing of Ince himself and Walter Edwards when they met. For a week or so he wandered about unnoticed, made friends with a screenwriter, played with Rags, the studio dog, "and drank Coca-Cola." Finally he was classified—as an extra—and led off to wardrobe, where he was given both a blue Union soldier uniform and Indian getup ("a breech-clout, a black wig, two feathers, a pair of Indian moccasins, and a can of brown paint called bol-Armenia"). He spent the morning riding around as an Indian, "giving vent to occasional war-whoops and firing old rusty muskets at imaginary blue soldiers," and the afternoon as his own enemy, "firing the same rusty muskets at imaginary Indians. . . . A young world mad with ecstatic life, a fifteen dollar a week world, but—swell!"

This movie—if he did not invent it for his memoirs—cannot be traced. Indeed, John (often billed as "Jack") Gilbert probably appeared in the background of many films in 1915–17 that have fallen off the face of the earth. Internet databases, magazine and newspaper reviews, even studio records, simply do not list extras. Jack himself probably did not know the titles or release dates of most of his early projects. Another supposed film that may not have existed was a drama about a mine disaster in which Jack claimed to have been an extra. He was playing a dead body when one of the fires set for dramatic purposes got too close: "I opened my eyes and discovered that my shoes were burning briskly. Then my pants burst into flames." Jack leaped up to put himself out, while director Stanford Richman yelled, "You've killed the scene, you yellow rat!" But Jack's pants may have indeed been on fire: there was no director named Stanford Richman, and he neglects to tell us the title of this movie.

Jack later recalled the social caste system at Inceville, which probably held true at all movie studios (at least those specializing in westerns). There were the hams, "that is, the actors who played parts. Even the bit men or small part artists came under that category, and they rarely mingled or conversed with the lesser lights." The cowboys were royalty at Inceville: "Their arrival seemed to electrify the air, and with oaths and shouts they took command." But Jack was one of the lowly "bushwa," a term he guessed derived from "bourgeois." These were the extras, who "constituted the background of scenes, the mob, the atmosphere; they were just as clannish as the 'hams,' and did not attempt to mingle with their superiors."

The low-rent, homespun theatrical atmosphere at Inceville could be pleasant and inviting; Jack recalled sunny Santa Monica days, the ocean breeze blowing, and "people in various costumes [running] about the place like ants, full breech Indians, blue-uniformed soldiers of the 1860 period, plainsmen, Irish peasants and Spanish troubadours, Chinese coolies and Hindu priests."

Inceville, way off in the hills, was not Ince's corporate headquarters—in 1915 Ince had constructed what would become a landmark in Culver City, in western Los Angeles. The community was still in its earliest pioneering days (being promoted, not surprisingly, by one Harry Culver, real-estate developer). Ince was convinced of Culver City's future and it was certainly more convenient to downtown L.A. than Inceville. On a large lot at 10202 West Washington Boulevard, Ince opened his new studio in 1915. The Washington Boulevard entrance to the facility was an imposing line of Greek-style colonnades—not only one of Los Angeles's few architectural survivals from those days but an instantly recognizable one: the Triangle Studios were later the home of Metro-Goldwyn-Mayer and, today, of Sony Pictures Studios.

The Culver City lot had eight stages, administration buildings, prop rooms, a restaurant, dressing rooms, and garages. Ince eventually convinced Triangle to buy thirty-one acres of land adjoining the Culver City headquarters, as Inceville was not proving to be large enough even after its two original stages (each fifty by eighty feet) were supplemented with new, larger shooting stages—both glass-walled and permanent sets.

Jack took a cheap room at the grandly named Waldorf Hotel in Santa Monica. The Waldorf was not as bad as Jack later made out: it was a sturdy five-story hotel right on the beach on Ocean Front Walk, and was in the news during Jack's residency when famous "Human Fly" Archie Crisp climbed its edifice in November 1916.

Jack's earliest-known Triangle film was the well-received Civil War drama *The Coward,* directed by Reginald Barker and starring character actor Frank Keenan and the up-and-coming Charles Ray as a young man who tries to weasel out of serving in the military. Jack was a "bushwa" in this. It did well, helping to launch Ray's career: *Variety* called *The Coward* "a step forward in the moving picture art. . . . Ray's performance is really a revelation in picture acting" (though the review notes that Keenan had too many close-ups and was too theatrical). The *New York Times* agreed: "Not only is the picture photographically excellent, but the atmosphere of the South has been preserved in the smallest details." This reviewer also noted that "there is a bit too much of Mr. Keenan standing point-blank before the camera, turning his head slowly from left to right, breathing visibly the while."

Jack was again an extra in *The Corner* (filmed in late 1915), "a corking story of capital vs. labor," according to *Variety*—plant closings, runs on banks, hungry children, and a wife taking the Easiest Way because "I could not bear to see the children starve." Jack went on to play a bit part in another Charles Ray drama, the 1917 society melodrama *The Weaker Sex,* of which *Variety* said, "There is a wallop, a punch, and a heap of suspense . . . a thriller that will get over in great shape."

Through 1915 and '16, Jack had small roles in two dramas starring Louise Glaum, a stage star who had been having quite some success in movies of late. Glaum later broke through in vamp roles, but in the 1910s she was starring in domestic dramas and westerns. Jack was an extra in Glaum's *Matrimony* (released late in 1915), a drama about marital infidelity. It "reopens a thoroughly thrashed-out subject for those who are interested," wrote *Variety.* He had a more substantial part in Glaum's 1917 western *Golden Rule Kate.* It was "a big dramatic western play of the Bill Hart type," noted the *Los Angeles Times,* whose reviewer was impressed that "all the exteriors were filmed at the Santa Monica ranch studios of the Triangle, where a complete western town has been built for productions of this nature." Jack also got one of his earliest press mentions for *Golden Rule Kate,* as small as it was: "Jack Gilbert, Jack Richardson, Mildred Harris, William Conklin, Gertrude Claire and J. P. Lockney form a strong supporting cast."

The first two reels of *Golden Rule Kate* still exist, and show Jack enthusiastically throwing himself into the role of the Heller, a young troublemaker in a Nevada mining-camp town. Looking like a sullen juvenile delinquent, he drinks, fights, and—as his name implies—raises hell in the bar run by the title character, played by Glaum (he's "a good kid when he's not drinking," Kate says of the Heller, a line Jack himself was to hear repeatedly over the years). He also has a moment of quiet charm when he goes back to his cabin and fondly caresses a photo of his sweetheart, Kate's sister (played by sixteen-year-old Mildred Harris, who would, the following year, become the first Mrs. Charles Chaplin).

Two dramas starring Bessie Barriscale followed in early 1916—a pretty blonde, she was one of Triangle's most reliable female stars. Jack was an extra in Barriscale's costume drama *Bullets and Brown Eyes,* described by *Variety* as a film much better than its title, a "dashing romantic love and action story. . . . Miss Barriscale has never done better work before the camera." The *Los Angeles Times* wrote, "It's safe to say every Film Fannie will take a peep at beautiful Bill Desmond in his regimentals." In *The Last Act,* an already-old plot point was dragged out: struggling actress Barriscale goes on for the star, who has sprained her ankle. She also has an affair with a married man, then (like Claudette Colbert decades later in *The Smiling Lieutenant*) selflessly advises his prudish wife to jazz up her lingerie. Jack, again, was a faceless extra.

By far the biggest moneymaker at Inceville in 1916 was rough-hewn, fifty-one-year-old cowboy star William S. Hart. He'd had a very respectable Broadway career, which included such huge hits as *Ben-Hur, The Squaw Man,* and *The Trail of the Lonesome Pine.* By 1914 he recognized that movies were the coming thing, and that westerns were going to make his career. From the earliest days of American movies, westerns were cheap, exciting profit machines. Indeed, *The Great Train Robbery* (1903) was one of the earliest "story" films in the United States. Nearly all studios turned out westerns in the pre-1915 years; Broncho Billy Anderson became the first cowboy star, making countless one- and two-reelers from 1906 through the 1910s. Hart was lured to Triangle by Thomas Ince in 1915 and pretty much given carte blanche to be in charge of his own films, choosing the director, cast, and story.

Jack appeared in three William S. Hart films, all in 1916, and he began to feel his foothold at Triangle getting stronger. He was only a background player in one of Hart's best-remembered vehicles, *Hell's Hinges,* the story of a rough but noble gunfighter (Hart, of course) protecting the town's new preacher and his lovely sister. In Hart's *The Aryan* Jack was in the background again (Hart played a vengeful fleeced prospector who is softened up by a charming settler).

But his first sizeable role came next, in the Hart mountain melodrama *The Apostle of Vengeance,* released in the summer of 1916. Jack, billed fifth, later recalled, "I shall never forget the thrill of having successfully played my first [sizeable] part in pictures. By successfully I mean that Cliff Smith, my director, and William S. Hart seemed satisfied." *Variety* raved about the film: "A photoplay thriller that will live long and prosper . . . one of the best scenarios that Mr. Hart has seen in some time . . . without a doubt one of the best pieces of work he has done before the camera. . . . Mr. Hart's supporting company is entirely adequate."

Jack felt more than "adequate" and thought he was over the hump—but for the rest of 1916 he found himself bouncing back and forth between extra work, tiny bits, and the occasional small supporting role. Assigned to play a background extra in *Aloha Oe,* he "sulked through the Hawaiian picture, and returned home each night to brood over the lack of appreciation of my work." (*Aloha Oe* was riding the coattails of the successful 1912 Broadway play *The Bird of Paradise;* it involved a lawyer turned South Seas castaway and was mostly notable, said *Variety,* for good locales and excellent courtroom photography.)

Jack was again invisible as a background extra in *Civilization,* one of the year's biggest, most expensive epics. An antiwar drama, it featured Christ coming back in the body of a count and giving a warlike king what for (the reincarnated Christ, complained *Variety,* "smacks strongly of Catholicism"). The film, *Variety* went on, "ranks with the world's greatest cinema productions"—not so leading lady Enid Markey, though, who, thought one critic, looked ready to drop off to sleep throughout. Sets for *Civilization* began going up as early as May 1915; shooting started in earnest in June and it was not ready for editing till the beginning of 1916.

When *Civilization* opened nationwide in the summer of 1916, though, it was greeted unenthusiastically by audiences already fed up with war talk. The film cost $100,000 (a fairly huge outlay for a 1916 movie) and brought in $800,000, but it took a lot of critical flak. Many isolationists wanted to keep America out of the war; many interventionists wanted the country in. But no one wanted to be preached at by Thomas Ince, as he himself admitted. "I have learned," he said, "that there is a certain type of play that the public loudly demands, but never pays to see. In this class may be placed the allegorical, the symbolical, the diabolical, and those pictures which are so obviously moral that they cease to be interesting."

In late 1915 or early '16, according to Jack's account, he was swept up in a youthful, tragic romance. While filming *Civilization,* he went on a double date to the Ship Café in Venice, California. He was paired with fellow bit player Effie Stuart, "small and fresh and feminine," a few years older than the eighteen-year-old Jack. "Effie's smile reminded me of sixteen babies in a row" was his delightful phrase. The two hit it off, and "carefree days at Inceville played an obligato to love-filled nights." They quarreled occasionally: about work, money, affections, whatever young lovers quarrel about.

During one of their "time-out" sessions, Effie was working in a crowd scene on the balcony of the king's palace in *Civilization* when the movie set collapsed. "Agonized shrieks, rearing horses, dust, curses, shouts, bedlam, hell!" Jack joined the crowd to see Effie—white faced, eyes closed, blood on her cheek—dragged out unconscious and put in an ambulance. She died on her way to the hospital. "Something froze within me," wrote Jack in 1928. "The silence which followed seemed an eternity. . . . I fell, sobbing, upon the sand."

Very sad and moving and tragic—and probably absolute nonsense. There never was an actress named Effie (or Ephemia) Stuart (or Stewart). No one was killed or seriously injured while filming *Civilization*—indeed, careful study of newspapers and industry publications show no actress of her description dying in an accident between 1915 and 1917. These things were not hushed up at the time; stories of extras, stunt people, and bystanders being killed or injured were not uncommon in the press, and an accident of that magnitude would certainly have gotten coverage.

If there was no Effie, perhaps there was some tragic love affair around 1917; maybe Jack hypothetically killed off a still-living ex-lover, knowing she would read the piece. Perhaps Jack—or his ghostwriter (probably Adela Rogers St. Johns)—simply figured that a tragic love affair would read well in his life story. In any event, the mythical Effie Stuart became a stock character in the John Gilbert Story, repeated for decades.

During the last half of 1916 we know that Jack worked in at least five films at Triangle, though he probably did background work (writing,

A headshot by pioneering Hollywood photographer Albert Witzel, late 1910s (Wisconsin Center for Film & Theater Research).

props, stunt or extra work) in others. At least one hopes he did, as he was hard pressed to support himself at this time. Movie work paid very little; he was paid only when he worked, and some of these supporting roles may have taken less than a week to complete. Certainly, 1916 was his hardest year financially since the leanest days of his childhood. He had a small supporting role in the Frank Keenan crime drama *The Phantom* ("All the elements that go toward making a successful picture production. There is suspense, atmosphere and above all it is well acted" wrote *Variety*). He was down to a background extra in the drama about a lighthouse keeper *Eye of the Night* ("the sort of 'sob stuff' that rings true. . . . It is one of the best"). A larger role (as a British spy) followed with the war drama *Shell 43,* starring H. B. Warner, and he had another part supporting Frank Keenan in *The Sin Ye Do* ("One of the strongest stories of modern times yet screened. . . . The acting of the entire cast is a rare treat"). Back to the background again—as Frank Keenan's son—in *The Bride of Hate,* an antebellum slavery drama (*Variety* felt it "sure to offend some of the people of the South").

Jack was not the only one on shaky ground—by early 1916 Triangle's financial position was dire. Ince, Griffith, and Sennett were unable to produce enough good films to make exhibitors happy, and through mismanagement, whatever profits existed were going astray. A year after founding Triangle, Harry Aitken was scrambling for refinancing. "I believe that our capacity for the preparation of the highest class motion picture plays to be unsurpassed," he bluffed to *Moving Picture World* in April 1916. "Griffith, Ince and Sennett are in frequent conference, and . . . I found them most enthusiastic over the outlook." But at the same time, Aitken was trying to arrange a merger with Adolph Zukor's Famous Players; it fell through.

Jack's career took a turn for the better in 1917—and remember, he had been in the movies for only a year and a half and was just turning twenty. He got his first really meaty role, as the hunchbacked son of the town drunkard (Jack's character was named, embarrassingly, "Crip" Halloran), in *Princess of the Dark.* This was Enid Bennett's debut as a Triangle star, but Jack stole the show: "The general impression audiences will carry away after seeing the feature," wrote *Variety,* "will be of Jack Gilbert . . . rather than of the performance of Miss Bennett."

The film did well enough to be serialized in the April 1917 issue of *Photoplay,* along with photos of Jack and the rest of the cast. Crip Halloran was the kind of role Jack would always enjoy, the tormented outsider: he loves the blind girl, who works as a slavey in his mother's boarding house. But when a rich mining executive pays for an operation

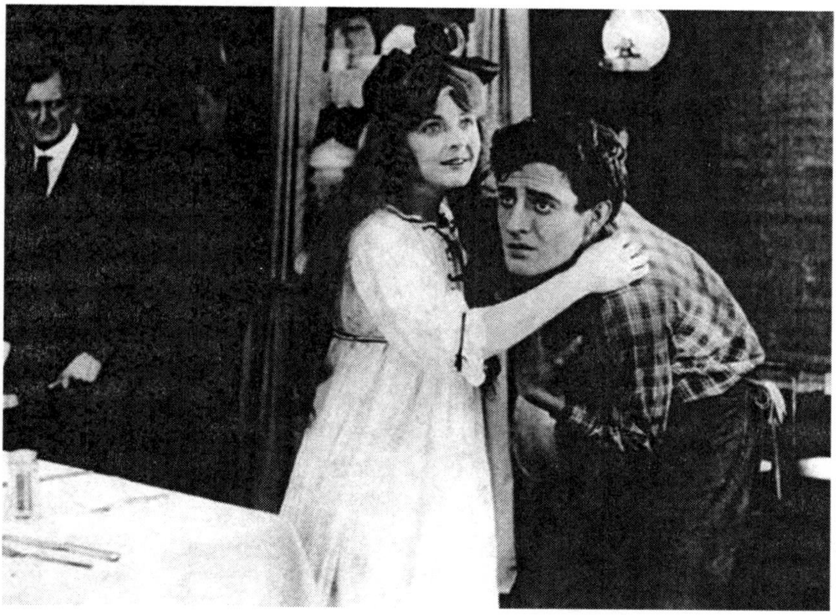

A good early character role: *Princess of the Dark,* with Enid Bennett, 1917 (author's collection).

restoring her sight, Crip sees the pity in her eyes, runs off to their favorite hideaway, and kills himself, leaving the path open for her rich suitor.

According to Jack's daughter—who must have heard it from her mother, his future wife Leatrice Joy—Jack and Enid Bennett had a brief romance. Making the relationship easier was the fact that both lived at the Engstram Apartments on West Fifth Street in Los Angeles, where he had moved once he could afford to leave the Waldorf. Bennett was a sweet-faced Australian whose sisters Catherine and Marjorie also acted (indeed, Marjorie lived, and worked, long enough to appear on TV's *The Twilight Zone, F Troop,* and *Barney Miller*). Jack mentions Bennett in passing in his *Photoplay* memoirs but doesn't speak of a romance—she was very much alive and married in 1928; she wed director Fred Niblo in 1918 and continued working in films into the 1940s. Perhaps Enid Bennett was "Effie Stuart," and the on-set accident was Jack's way of pseudonymously ending their affair.

After the success of *Princess of the Dark,* Jack was given a two-year contract at Triangle, starting out at $30 a week and advancing to $40.

"I had found my place at last!" he rejoiced. "No more time clock to punch, a leading part to play and a contract in my pocket." Despite his excellent reviews (and those of Bennett), Jack downplayed *Princess of the Dark* in retrospect: "We wailed and suffered all through the filming of the production, imagining we were performing great dramatics." He claimed to have been demoted back to extra work afterward and told by studio manager E. H. Allen that "I should feel damned well lucky I had a job." He also recalled overhearing Triangle director Irvin Willat turn down a chance to work with him: "My God, no—he's terrible! Besides, his nose looks Jewish." Again, that does not quite jibe with the facts: *Princess of the Dark* was released early in 1917, and for the rest of that year Jack played good supporting and costarring roles.

Jack had another good—or at least big—role in the war drama *The Dark Road,* released in March 1917. He played the callow victim of vamp Dorothy Dalton—she tricks him into carrying war secrets, he is killed in battle, and her perfidy is discovered (Dalton dies a satisfyingly horrible death in the final reel). A small supporting role followed in the "exceedingly slow" (as per *Variety*) *Happiness* (May 1917); he had another brief role in *The Millionaire Vagrant* that same month, in which rich lawyer Charles Ray lived among the poor to show they could stay on the straight and narrow without money (Ray, of course, learns some Valuable Lessons).

Happiness survives, showing Jack in a rare comic role. It's a college romance: sheltered Philadelphia society girl Enid Bennett (who is lovely, in a Lillian Gish–like way) goes off to a coed school and is courted by a poor but honest boy (Charles Gunn, a charming actor who died the following year from the Spanish flu) and the college snob, played by Jack—complete with tight, vulgar suits and a silly little moustache that made him look like a refugee from a Keystone comedy. "Money + a slight social standing – brains = one hopeless cad," reads his introductory title, and Jack threw himself into the role engagingly, with goggle-eyed stares, pouts, and unctuous flirting. He and Charles Gunn had a rousing fight scene, during which Jack was dunked into a washtub and thrown into a rubbish bin—his little comedy moustache, impressively, stayed stuck on. *Happiness* is a cute little film, stolen by Andrew Arbuckle (cousin of the better-known Roscoe) as Enid Bennett's sympathetic uncle. And it shows how being part of the Triangle stock company was paying off for Jack—he was thrown into all kinds of roles (as well as into rubbish bins) and was getting invaluable on-the-job training while earning his paycheck.

Another good role in an Enid Bennett vehicle, *The Mother Instinct* (released in the summer of 1917), followed—the tortuous plot involved missing children, Paris models, mistaken identity, and murder but "nothing thrilling about it in any manner," shrugged *Variety*. That same summer saw *The Hater of Men,* with Bessie Barriscale as a girl reporter so dismayed by what she sees in the divorce courts that she drops nice reporter fiancé Jack and becomes a free-living bohemian: her pals "are welcome at all times to come eat or drink," noted *Variety,* "and they manage to do the latter to perfection."

Jack was bumped up to male lead in *The Hater of Men,* a print of which survives at the Library of Congress. Bessie Barriscale gives a wonderful performance as the anti-marriage feminist; though, rather matronly at thirty-three, she looked more like Jack's mother than his fiancée. Jack—still with his little comedy moustache from *Happiness*—had not grown into his looks yet. At twenty, he looked all of sixteen and appeared to weigh ninety pounds soaking wet. His lean face was all nose and chin and huge eyes; the "John Gilbert" of the 1920s was not yet visible, except when he smiled.

The Hater of Men is an interesting film: very modern in stating that women can lose their individuality and (certainly in 1917) their independence when they marry. But it is also very conventional as Barriscale discovers she does not like being seen as "one of the boys" or as a free, loose woman by her male friends and coworkers. In the end she rushes back into Jack's arms, her title voicing a slang gag that it is startling to see was already in common use by 1917: "Oh, Billy, a girl's an awful fool to get married—*NOT!*"

One of Jack's costars in *The Mother Instinct* was Rowland Lee, who later became a busy film director (*Zoo in Budapest, Tower of London, Son of Frankenstein*). Lee told Jack's daughter Leatrice that Jack "was a very lonely kid" and that Lee invited him home for dinner with his family: "I don't think he had ever tasted home cooking before and he tried not to show how hungry he was. After that, we more or less adopted him."

Jack's first real starring role, and a good character part to boot, came in October 1917 with the dark western *The Devil Dodger.* He played an ailing, suicidal parson who tries to goad the town bully into killing him—but he winds up saving the life of the local gambler with a heart of gold and even finds true love with dance-hall girl Fluffy (played by starlet Carolyn Wagner). It was an interesting part, and Jack no doubt brought all his training and intensity to it—sadly, like most of his early work, it is long vanished. Another good role came with *Up or Down?* (November 1917), a western with a comic twist: Jack played a hopeful novelist whose cowboy friend arranges fake robberies, kidnappings, and other Wild West adventures to inspire his work. Jack gets his book published and wins the hand of leading lady Fritzi Ridgeway.

But just as Jack was really getting his footing at Triangle, the studio was continuing to sink. Even as Thomas Ince was telling reporters, "It has been rumored out here that Triangle is about to disband. I cannot imagine where such twaddle came from, but I can say that Triangle has never been in better financial condition," the studio was indeed facing bankruptcy.

Triangle's three "angles" saw the writing on the wall and soon deserted the company; Griffith quit in March 1917, going first to Paramount, then First National, and finally to United Artists, which he cofounded in 1919 with Mary Pickford, Douglas Fairbanks, and Charlie Chaplin. Ince followed him in June 1917, taking William S. Hart with him and leaving no reliable moneymaking western star to take his place. Mack Sennett, whose cheap, popular Keystone comedies were a huge moneymaker for Triangle, decamped a few weeks after Ince, leaving behind the Keystone brand name and forming his own Mack Sennett Comedies Corporation.

As Triangle product fell off in quality and star power, bookings fell off, and of course corners were cut even further. Aitken sold Triangle's distribution arm to W. W. Hodkinson in a last-ditch effort to save what was left of the company. Hodkinson was something of a rogue and pacesetter in the 1910s: he was an early advocate of the feature-length film and played a major part in establishing nationwide feature-film distribution on a workable basis. He cofounded Paramount in 1914, which distributed films from Famous Players and other production companies. In 1916 Hodkinson had been booted out of Paramount by Zukor—he was no luckier with the Triangle Distributing Corporation and resigned after a few months. He went on to form the W. W. Hodkinson Corporation (later renamed the Producers Distributing Company).

Shortly after Hodkinson's departure, H. O. Davis, who had been vice president and general manager of Universal, was named Triangle's general manager. Universal's business manager, G. E. Patterson, accompanied Davis. "As businessmen and persons they were efficient and charming," said Jack. "As motion picture producers I thought they were duds."

During the waning days of Triangle, in 1918, Jack had a small supporting role in *Nancy Comes Home,* a comedy about a neglected rich girl (Myrtle Lind) who hobnobs with the fast-living criminal element to teach her parents a thing or two. His last film for Triangle was *The Mask,* the tale of a poor girl who becomes a nouveau riche snob. Claire Anderson—a slumberous-eyed Mack Sennett bathing beauty recently (and briefly) graduated into features, had the lead. It was a typical little programmer, but Jack made an impression as Anderson's poor boyfriend, who still loves her: "John Gilbert adds the comedy touches and is always amusing," said *Variety.*

So far, *Princess of the Dark* had given Jack a good character role, he played weak and tragic in *The Devil Dodger,* and he had good light-comedy parts in *Up or Down?* and *The Mask:* Triangle had proved an excellent school for him. Lillian Gish and Bette Davis, late in their lives, admitted that being tossed into one role after another—sometimes large and sometimes tiny—was the reason they became lasting stars. And that is what Triangle had done for John Gilbert.

In a scenario that would be replayed at studio after studio, Jack did not see eye to eye with the people who had taken over his studio. Monte Katterjohn—who had written *Golden Rule Kate*—tipped Jack off about a new company, Paralta Plays, Inc., which was raiding Triangle stars, crew, and writers. Paralta offered Jack a $60 a week screenwriting contract. Jack, in an appalling display of unprofessionalism, told his new bosses at Triangle that he had been underage when he signed with them, and "thumbed my nose at their contract."

By late 1918, Triangle's Washington Boulevard studios in Culver City had been leased to rising producer Samuel Goldwyn, and the few remaining directors and crew slunk back to Inceville in Santa Monica, from which they had sprung. By 1920, Triangle had passed away.

Perhaps it is poetic justice, then, that Paralta Plays, Inc., for which Jack decamped, managed to stay in business for only one year. The company did manage to reel in such stars as Bessie Barriscale, J. Warren Kerrigan, Henry B. Walthall, and Louise Glaum as well as several reliable Triangle directors. Jack was the male lead (to his old Triangle costar Louise Glaum) in *Wedlock*—he played a millionaire unfairly sent to jail, and Glaum was the girl who stuck by him. But in *One Dollar Bid*—a hillbilly drama—he was reduced to a background player. And he was no happier with Paralta than he had been at the end of his Triangle days.

Chapter Three

I stared at a woman sitting opposite me in my apartment. I discovered that she was my wife.

—John Gilbert, 1928

Freelancing as a film actor was perilous in the late 1910s, but not as unusual as it would become later, when stars and bit players alike so often enjoyed being in the safe rut of a long-term studio contract. From 1918 through 1921, Jack had films produced and/or released through companies big and small, some still in business today, others long forgotten: the large, France-based Pathé, the once-mighty but now ailing Vitagraph, Paramount, Haworth Pictures Corporation, Universal, Tyrad Pictures, Jesse D. Hampton Productions, First National, and Metro—which would play a huge role in his future. Nearly all of his directors in those years have long since faded from history and can be named only by the most fanatic of film-history buffs (Reginald Barker, Ernest Warde, Kenean Buel, Thomas Heffron, Charles Sealing, William Worthington, Lynn Reynolds, Park Frame).

Jack had a sizeable role in a Robert Brunton–produced project of early 1918: in *More Trouble* he played the clean-cut collegiate son of rich mill owner Frank Keenan, who is accused of wild spending sprees and embezzlement (turns out his college pal is to blame). But Jack must have hated this part: "Goody-goodies like Harvey [Jack's character] may exist," wrote *Variety,* "but no one has discovered them." It was exactly the kind of role he spent a lifetime complaining about.

Through 1918 Jack was getting just enough work to keep him from quitting altogether but not enough to decently feed and clothe himself. He claimed he tried to enlist in the navy, "but they would have none of my five feet eleven and one hundred and fifteen pounds" (actually five feet nine by most accounts, though the 115 pounds looks right). He did not like the idea of the army (trenches) and the aviation section of the U.S. Army Signal Corps was closed to applicants. He moved from the Engstram on West Fifth Street to a less expensive boarding house (two meals a day and a small room for $7 a week) and was able to keep his little car running.

It was here that Jack met the woman who would become his first wife.

Twenty-year-old Olivia Burwell was living in the boarding house with her mother, a sister, a brother, and her brother's wife—they had come to California from their native Mississippi after the elder Mr. Burwell had died and the brother got a job in a fruit-packing company. (Olivia was neither an actress nor the daughter of the boarding house owner, as has sometimes been written.) Down and out and with too much time on his hands, Jack found himself enchanted by the petite Olivia Burwell, her soft southern accent, and her ladylike, unactressy ways.

What followed seems to have been a panic marriage: Jack got his draft notice and was to leave for Kelly Field in Texas in ten days. They married on August 26, in a Methodist church and moved into a tiny apartment. Troop movements were halted because of the Spanish flu epidemic, which unfortunately also slowed studio employment. Jack sold his car and wrote to his stepfather Walter Gilbert for financial help: the answer he got, Jack recalled, "was to pray and believe—and, in closing, [he] reprimanded me for not having saved my money." He added bitterly (this was in 1928), "I have not wasted postage stamps on him since." Jack's annoyance did not last forever; he later remembered his stepfather in his will.

Jack made four more films in the summer and fall of 1918 for Paralta Plays, distributed by W. W. Hodkinson's eponymous company. He submitted a script to Hodkinson, for an underworld drama starring Henry B. Walthall; it was accepted, and director Howard Hickman put it into production with so many changes that it "bore no resemblance to

The first Mrs. Gilbert, Olivia Burwell (Wisconsin Center for Film & Theater Research).

my scenario." When he complained, Jack recalled, Hickman told him, "You got your money for your story, didn't you? You've still got your job, haven't you? All right—beat it!" Howard Hickman didn't actually direct Walthall during this period, but perhaps Jack muddled the facts or the names for the sake of a good story.

Jack continued working, slowly but steadily. He had leading—or at least supporting—roles in several 1918 films. In *Shackled* (produced by Paralta and released through Hodkinson) he played a college boy who loses his fiancée when he enlists in the war (she later sees the error of her ways and takes him back). "The parts of Cosgrove [Jack's rival] and Ashley are excellently taken by Charles West and John Gilbert," noted *Variety*. In *Three X Gordon* he played a friend of J. Warren Kerrigan, who runs a kind of dude-ranch rehab for rich wastrels. He had a supporting role in the Bret Harte–based western *The Dawn of Understanding*, which starred up-and-coming actress Bessie Love. Jack played "a primitive sort who has two Chinese servants," according to *Variety*—which called him "Jack Williams" in its review.

The most important thing to come from these otherwise minor films for Paralta-Hodkinson was the woman who would become Jack's second wife—and, some feel, his great love—Leatrice Joy (in *Wedlock* he had been billed second and Joy seventh; they both had supporting roles in *Three X Gordon*). Leatrice Joy was several years older than Jack—twenty-five to his twenty-one in 1918. A New Orleans native, she had a surprisingly deep, melodious voice, pert, sharp little features, and lustrous black curls (which she eventually cut into a very becoming bob). She'd entered movies the same year that Jack had, working her way slowly up through bits and supporting roles by the time they costarred in *Three X Gordon*. "I came out from New Orleans with a small company," she recalled. "It went broke, and I was left stranded, I might have written home for money, but I was too proud. I lived in a funny little hall bedroom downtown, and cooked my meals myself over a gas heater—that is, when I had something to cook, or any gas."

Joy's early days were as tough as Jack's had been. She told the *Los Angeles Times*'s Grace Kingsley, "I actually went hungry. When I ate at all, it was at some funny little joint down on Main Street. I found a place where you got more beans and coffee for 10 cents than any other place. Bread and butter, I remember, were thrown in. . . . When I got a bit or an extra part to do, I earned $3 to $10 a day." Jack recalled seeing her for the first time in the casting offices of Jesse D. Hampton Productions. "I almost stumbled over a figure huddled in a chair in a gloomy corner. . . . She had been in silent prayer, entreating a distant deity to land this job for her." They thought they may have appeared together in a Canadian picture directed by Reginald Barker; one of four Jack made with him in 1916–17. Jack treated Leatrice to lunch, they became casual friends, drifted apart, then met again briefly from time to time.

The Great War ended on November 11, 1918, and demobilized servicemen returned home in waves over the next few years. Studios found themselves overwhelmed with job applicants, many of them ex-employees hoping to be taken back. Jack had more competition on his hands, and he also had a wife to support. There followed an encouraging part in *The White Heather*—the first of six projects he would work on with director Maurice Tourneur. Though Jack admired Thomas Ince and was grateful to him for giving him a start, Ince had no real creative or artistic influence on him. Tourneur was the first director whom Jack really admired and learned from.

Maurice Tourneur was a stiff-looking and imposing forty-six-year-old when he and Jack first worked together. He had been a successful theater and movie director in his native France before relocating to the United States in 1914. When Eastman film millionaire Jules Brulatour—

Jack's first mentor, director and producer Maurice Tourneur, late 1910s (author's collection).

whom we shall meet again in 1920—founded Paragon Films in Fort Lee, New Jersey, in 1915, he brought Tourneur in as a partner/director/production head, but the company failed rather quickly. Tourneur bounced around from partner to partner, but in 1919 was filming for his own Maurice Tourneur Productions, again bankrolled by Brulatour, releasing through Paramount.

Tourneur—like Jack—was an artistic perfectionist, someone who believed in going all out to get the very best effects, no matter what time and money had to be expended, and whose feelings were trampled on. Director Clarence Brown—who started as one of Tourneur's apprentices—said years later, "He was more on the ball photographically than any other director. . . . Whenever we saw a painting with an interesting lighting effect, we'd copy it. We had a library of pictures. . . . Tourneur was great on tinting and toning. We never made a picture unless every scene was colored. . . . The most beautiful shots I ever saw on the screen were in Tourneur's pictures."

But although Brown called Tourneur "my god. I owe him everything," he also prided himself on being a better director of performers than Tourneur had been, bragging that he invariably improved on the master's scenes: "He had only one failing in his pictures," said Brown. "He was cold. He had no heart. . . . I'd get the actors in a corner of the set and we'd talk and kid around awhile. Then we'd take the scene again, the same way as he'd taken it. But now it had a little something that it didn't have before—warmth."

Tourneur was a vocal advocate of art in movies, which perhaps is why he never succeeded for long as a producer and distributor. He told *Motion Picture* magazine in September 1918, "The time has come when we can no longer merely photograph moving and inanimate objects and call it art. We are not photographers, but artists—at least, I hope so. We must present the effect such a scene has upon the artist-director's mind, so that an audience will catch the mental reaction." And he seemed to be anticipating some of Jack's own complaints about the star system and the production-line quality of production that same year in *Motion Picture World*. "The star system of today is proving its fallacy," said Tourneur. "Consider the problem of the producer with a chain of stars. He must manufacture films regularly, using these stars at systematic intervals, in order to succeed. The independent producer, on the other hand, can afford to select the star to fit his photodrama."

The White Heather, produced and directed by Tourneur, was Jack's first Paramount project; a silly, old-fashioned melodrama based on a London hit of the 1890s. "The sublime but forbidden love that prompted a man to risk his life in a desperate undersea battle for a woman will rest in your memory always," Paramount's publicity hyperventilated. "The sheer beauty of the scenes photographed on the ocean's floor will leave you gasping in amazement!" Jack had only a supporting role—no desperate undersea battles for him—but "Jack Gilbert did a corking fall after a shootup in the slum scene," wrote an admiring *Variety* reviewer.

Tourneur was happy with Jack's work—and Jack enjoyed working with Tourneur—but there were no follow-up offers. "Day after day after day the rounds of the studios, and agents' offices—and night after night after night the return to Olivia," he recalled years later. As usually happens, the partners in the panic marriage began to regret it rather quickly. "That night I stared at a woman sitting opposite me in my apartment," Jack wrote. "I discovered that she was my wife." Jack never had a bad word to say against Olivia Burwell, and she never gave any interview about him. They were just young (both of them twentyish), inexperienced, and had no business being married to each other. "Soon there was no speech between us," wrote Jack. "She would not complain. Never did she whine—nor cry out at my worthlessness."

The marriage just petered out quietly. Olivia went back to Mississippi sometime in 1919, and they didn't even bother filing for divorce until 1921 (a fact that would prove inconvenient for Jack and the next Mrs. Gilbert). "I corresponded with Olivia, but my letters were empty of everything but platitudes. I was writing to an utterly strange person." Olivia Burwell vanished quietly and contentedly back into private life, though she showed signs of being as clever as all of the future Mrs. John Gilberts. By 1936 she had married court reporter Joseph Morgan, and in 1939 she applied for a patent for a folding bed screen "to protect either children or adults while sleeping out of doors from insects and animals." Olivia Gilbert Morgan died in Arizona in 1982.

The Busher—Jack's second Paramount film, produced by his old Triangle boss, Thomas Ince—is one of his few early works that survives and is easily available to modern viewers. It starred Charles Ray as a small-town ("bush-league") baseball player, and a pre-flapper Colleen Moore (unusually coy and girlish, for her) as the girl he loves. Jack played Jim Blair, Ray's wealthy rival. The beautifully photographed Booth Tarkington–like small-town atmosphere of 1919 is charming, with little everyday touches that passed unnoticed to contemporary audiences but provide a delightful time machine today. Jack, all bounding self-confidence as a banker's son, with his slick roadster and tweed cap, looks underweight and all of sixteen years old (he also looks Arrow-collar handsome next to Charles Ray's cherubic hero). Ray is signed by a visiting manager for the "St. Paul Pink Sox," gets a swelled head, flirts with a vamp, and is humiliatingly bumped back down to the minors. He comes home a ragged bum to find Jack romancing Colleen Moore—Jack takes a villainous turn when, to pay off a gambling debt, he "fixes" a hometown game. The disgraced Ray comes through, wins the game (and Moore)—and, sadder but wiser, he turns down yet another major-league offer. It was a cute little movie, and while it gave Jack virtually no acting to do, it exposed him to audiences in a high-budgeted star vehicle.

The summer of 1919 saw Jack at a variety of studios, large and small (and playing parts large and small): for Haworth he played a supporting role in the silly melodrama *The Man Beneath*. This was a confusing, badly edited film about "a Hindoo who has been educated in England and become a famous scientist," played by dashing Japanese leading man Sessue Hayakawa. The "Hindoo" falls for a white girl but nobly forsakes her at the end—Jack and Pauline Curley played the appropriately mated, lily-white romantic friends of the leads. Curley also played romantic lead to Jack offscreen, if only briefly. She recounted to author Michael Ankerich in 1993 that the two found themselves attracted to each other. Jack asked out the sixteen-year-old, who knew her mother would be opposed. She told her mother that "Jack" had asked her out, knowing she would think of another family friend. "When Jack Gilbert arrived, my mother was horrified, but it was too late to do anything about it. We got to go out on one date, but that was it."

For Universal Jack had a small role in the society drama *A Little Brother of the Rich*. Based on a scandalous 1908 novel, it was "fit only for second grade houses, if even for them," sniffed *Variety*. Poor Jack, as one of the rich, was "dressed so ridiculously, considering that he was supposed to be the son of a millionaire, that those who went to the trade show had difficulty keeping their laughter from being overheard outside." He went on to work his way through Tyrad Pictures' *The Red Viper* (a social drama) and Fox's *Doing Their Bit,* a war film starring child actresses Jane and Katherine Lee.

He finished out 1919 playing second leads. In *For a Woman's Honor* he was the trouble-prone brother of the female lead who is helped out of scrapes by her heroic boyfriend. The *Variety* review was downright painful: "Loose ends are such at the finish that the audience at Loews New York started to kid the last 200 feet of the picture with mock applause." *Widow by Proxy* (from an old May Irwin stage hit) was a bit better; it involved two ingénues and two spinsters, and Jack played the missing "handsome hero lover" of one, who reappears in the last reel.

A real break came late in 1919 when he was chosen to support the biggest star in films, Mary Pickford. In *Heart o' the Hills* Jack (and he was, again, billed as "Jack Gilbert") was by no means Pickford's leading man, though he played a sizeable supporting role. The project was a Kentucky hillbilly drama starring Pickford as a tough Annie Oakley type who vows to "git" the unknown man who killed her father. The plot veers through crooked land speculation, a murder trial (Mary Pickford, somewhat startlingly, takes part in a Ku Klux Klan–like lynch mob, complete with white robes and hoods), and bucolic romance (and yes, she does finally find the man "what killed her pap").

Jack played Gray Pendleton, a "bluegrass aristocrat" visiting the mountains. He flirts innocently with Pickford and does a creditable jig during a "shin-dig" (which ends with someone's grandpappy hollering, "Hol' on thar, I done lost me teeth!"). Jack pops up several times through the film as his brotherly affection for Pickford's character deepens into love, to the consternation of Pickford's boyfriend and Gray Pendleton's girlfriend. He wasn't given all that much to do, but he looked handsome and fresh faced and provided a credible romantic partner to America's Sweetheart.

As his career picked up (and so did his bank account), likewise Jack's spirits and social life improved. He joined the Los Angeles Athletic Club on West Seventh Street, often staying overnight in its members' rooms, and moved out of his tiny apartment—with its unhappy memories of Olivia—into the Garden Court Apartments on Hollywood Boulevard.

It was a lovely residential hotel with a private courtyard and suites paneled in teak and mahogany. The ballroom hosted Saturday-night dances, where stars and attractive hopefuls mingled flirtatiously.

The jovial atmosphere of the Athletic Club brought Jack out of his funk. "The gymnasium and swimming pool would put on much-needed weight," he reasoned, and "One's residence there leant certain prestige to one's name." He met famous stars who would become lifelong friends, particularly comic superstar Charlie Chaplin and clean-cut leading man Richard Barthelmess. "They seemed so gay and rich and successfully happy," Jack said. "I hoped that I would one day attain their lack of self-consciousness. I never have."

In 1920 Jack was rehired by Maurice Tourneur, with whom he'd worked on *The White Heather.* Tourneur produced about a dozen films between 1918 and 1921, most of them released through Paramount. Jack signed a two-year contract with Tourneur and stalked him in a manner that was both flattering and annoying. Jack worked as actor, screenwriter, and assistant director, soaking up every bit of advice from his new idol.

In 1920 Jack wrote or adapted scenarios for Tourneur's *The White Circle, The Great Redeemer, Deep Waters,* and possibly a few other films that have slipped between the cracks of history. "I have never been so happy," he recalled. "Working eighteen hours a day—writing, co-directing, titling, cutting, and, least of all—acting." This did provide an excellent schoolroom for the budding actor, just as Triangle had broken him in via the stock-company route. It also gave him just enough knowledge and experience to tell other directors and screenwriters how to do their jobs.

In 1920 he met another director who would have a big effect on his career: Clarence Brown. Brown, born in 1890, would go on to become one of the busiest directors in Hollywood and would helm three of Jack's biggest films. By 1920 he had been working as an editor and assistant director for several years. He and Jack first worked together on *The Great Redeemer,* which Jack claimed to have rescued from an unusable script by Jules Furthman (a prolific screenwriter of such later titles as *Blonde Venus, Shanghai Express, Bombshell, Only Angels Have Wings, The Big Sleep,* and *Nightmare Alley*—and of numerous, lesser, John Gilbert–starring movies of the early 1920s).

Clarence Brown recalled *The Great Redeemer*—released through Metro Pictures—as a traumatic wake-up call for Jack. Brown himself was a neophyte director, and this was one of Jack's first scripts; the cameraman, assistant director, and art director were all new to the business. After seeing the finished film in a screening room, Jack got hysterical: "My God! He's ruined my story! This is the worst thing I've ever seen in my life!" Brown did not disagree: "I think I lost my cookies. Tears were in my eyes, and my career was ended." Then Maurice Tourneur—perhaps trying to calm everyone down or with a better notion of what sold tickets—patted Brown on the shoulder: "Mr. Brown, that is a wonderful picture." Brown admitted that it indeed "made a great hit. It was the first Metro picture to play on Broadway. I got the award from Sing Sing for the best picture of the year!"

In 1920 Tourneur, Thomas Ince, Mack Sennett; directors Allan Dwan, George Loane Tucker, and Marshall Neilan; and producer/director J. Parker Read Jr. formed Associated Producers Inc. They hoped to both produce and distribute their own films, always a very risky undertaking, as Triangle had proved. Tourneur explained, "I should like to make pictures that dealt simply in humanity, but I always hear the distributor asking, 'What's the big punch in your picture?' or 'Has it got a ballroom scene in it, or something else that will get 'em?'"

Both Tourneur and Ince believed in Jack, and he was given a contract to direct four movies for the new company (Clarence Brown was also taken on as a director). Jack was paid an impressive $400 a week, plus 10 percent of profits. Jack also played star maker: he spotted a young extra on the set of *The White Circle* and recommended her to Tourneur. Her name was changed from Violet Rose (which was odd, for that would have been a perfect silent-movie-star name) to Barbara Bedford, and she went on to a very respectable career (including two films with Jack and character work right through the 1940s). In 1920 he cowrote and costarred with Bedford in the adventure *Deep Waters,* based on the play *Caleb West, Master Diver* (which was, in turn, loosely based on the real-life Thomas Scott, who built the Race Rock lighthouse off Long Island).

But there's always a catch, and in this case it was moneyman Jules Brulatour and his protégée, actress Hope Hampton. Brulatour and Hampton were the road-company William Randolph Hearst and Marion Davies. Brulatour had made his fortune selling the French Lumière brothers' and then Eastman Kodak's raw film stock to U.S. movie producers; he invested in various moving-picture companies through the 1910s and married actress Dorothy Gibson (who was already semifamous as a *Titanic* survivor). By the late 1910s Brulatour was involved with beauty queen and budding actress Hope Hampton, a twenty-something working as an extra for Maurice Tourneur. Their New York–based company, Hope Hampton Productions, released through Tourneur's Associated Producers Inc.

Like Marion Davies, Hampton was a smart, funny, and agreeable woman; unlike Davies, she was not a brilliant actress (her nickname, inevitably, was Hopeless Hampton). In 1920 Brulatour and Hampton turned out *A Modern Salome,* to little effect. Late that year Jack was hired to adapt the play *The Bait* for Tourneur to direct and Hampton to star in. Hampton, said Jack, was "self-conscious and had no knowledge of timing, but such were my efforts that after two weeks had gone by, Brulatour was bidding for my future services." Unwisely, Jack gambled on Brulatour, who obtained his release from Tourneur and Associated Producers and hired him to write, direct (with some unacknowledged help from Henri Ménessier), and edit (again, with help, from Katherine Hilliker) a drama called *Love's Penalty.* Jack was to get $1,000 a week, his own production unit, and a six-year contract—he was on top of the world, and saw himself finally branching out from acting and becoming another Tourneur, Griffith, or DeMille. He headed for New York to begin his great new career. "Jack Gilbert has left for New York to megaphone Hope Hampton," the *Los Angeles Times* reported in the summer of 1920.

Love's Penalty told the story of Janis Clayton, who takes a job with the man she believes caused her sister to commit suicide. Janis loses her fiancé, her wealth, and her self-respect in an effort to avenge her sister, but she wins out in the end, as the cad loses his own family in a shipwreck and is shot by another one of his victims. It's a tale that might have made a corking 1940s film noir, but *Love's Penalty* bombed spectacularly. "It's so bad it's funny," wrote the *Los Angeles Times.* "Nothing in the old barrel of situations has been overlooked. . . . Although you are a milliner, become a stenographer on the spur of the moment! Easiest thing in the world! The author lays down on the job." As for star Hope Hampton, "Her beauty is a pleasing asset, but it requires exactly the

Jack's disastrous experiment as a director: Hope Hampton and John O'Brien in *Love's Penalty,* 1921 (The Everett Collection).

right lighting. She has learned some picture technique, but she does not put over any subtleties nor thought or feeling."

But the disaster of *Love's Penalty* forever put paid to Jack's writing and directing ambitions. After his death friends pointed to the failure of his early talkies *His Glorious Night* and *Redemption* as the Waterloo of his career. But had *Love's Penalty* turned out differently, he might have veered off into a behind-the-camera career—one that he always regretted not pursuing more energetically.

"What a picture I made!" Jack later recalled. "It was unbelievably horrible." *Love's Penalty* no longer exists—which, from all accounts, may be a blessing. "The story was awful," said Jack. "I wrote it! I was responsible for the direction. It was ghastly! The cutting was incalculably bewildering. I did it! It is inconceivable that the thing could have been so bad." Leatrice Joy later told her daughter by Jack that *Love's Penalty* "wasn't bad." She later worked with one of its cast members, Percy Marmont, in *The Marriage Cheat,* and Marmont told Joy that

"Jack wouldn't stop talking about how awful it was, and it was really a nice little picture. I'm not ashamed of it."

For the rest of his life, Jack talked, over and over, of wanting to write and direct again. He finally did, toward the end of his life, sell a story for an excellent film—but the screenplay was written by someone else; and he never again directed. "I had no more right at that time to undertake the making of a motion picture than I now have of assuming charge of the Standard Oil Company" (though one has the feeling that if John D. Rockefeller had offered Jack the chance at Standard Oil, he would have jumped right in with both feet).

Screenwriter Frances Marion, though, felt that he was never cut out to be a writer: "Jack, gregarious by nature, resented the isolation imposed upon anyone who chooses writing for a profession," she recalled in her memoirs, "and [he] listened to the insidious flattery of friends: 'If you would only become an actor, you could give Valentino a run for his money.'"

Jack was not the only ship to founder on the rocks of Hope Hampton's career: Clarence Brown recalled that Maurice Tourneur refused to go near her after directing her in *The Bait* and that he himself made *The Light in the Dark* (1922) with Hampton and Lon Chaney: "It was awful," he moaned to historian Kevin Brownlow decades later. "Don't let's talk about it." "Hopeless Hampton" had a happy ending of sorts, even if she never became a star: she made a few more silents and the 1938 musical *The Road to Reno;* exhibiting an unexpected talent, she also sang with the Philadelphia Grand Opera. Unlike Marion Davies, she wed her mentor: she and Jules Brulatour were married from 1923 till his 1946 death—after which Hampton embarked on a second career, as an over-the-top New York society fixture. Almost till her death in 1982, she appeared at every Broadway and opera first night, swathed in the latest designer gowns (she was among Norell's first supporters)—Hope Hampton was even named Miss Twist of 1962 after throwing herself into the new dance craze at the Peppermint Lounge.

But back in 1920, Jack wanted out of his contract, and Brulatour (and no doubt Hope Hampton) wanted to be rid of Jack. He later claimed he impetuously tore up his contract and did himself out of a $10,000 settlement, though the paperwork on that is long gone. Arriving back in Los Angeles with his tail between his legs, he was told that he was still a good bet to get acting roles but that no one was going to touch him as a director. Jack resisted for about five minutes—"I would not act. I was rotten on the screen. No one could force me to act"—before accepting small roles in two films. *Ladies Must Live* was a society drama from Paramount, featuring Leatrice Joy in a bit part. *The Servant in the House,* a religious drama from FBO, directed by future great Jack Conway, may actually have been a late Triangle production, held on the shelf for as long as a year and released in 1921.

Then, in early 1921 Jack was offered a three-year contract at Fox Film Corporation. He took what can only be considered the sensible path and signed on as an actor. He was to do this again in a few years—grab the brass ring and then curse himself (and his employer) for what he felt were lost chances at artistic freedom and integrity.

When Jack had first entered the industry in 1915, the field was crowded with film companies—some of them producing, some distributing, some doing both. But the most famous names of the silent era had surprisingly short lives: Brooklyn's Vitagraph Studios, the Philadelphia-based Lubin, Chicago's Essanay Studios, New York's famed Biograph, Thanhouser in New Rochelle, Edison, Kalem, Mutual, New Jersey's Nestor, Selig Polyscope—all were born and died within the silent era. Some were folded into larger studios (Warner Bros., for instance, eventually bought Vitagraph). But some simply could not compete with the huge Wall Street–funded corporations that emerged by the late 1910s.

By the 1920s the industry was coalescing around several larger studios, some of which are still going strong today: Fox, founded by William Fox in 1915 and still producing movies and TV under various subsidiaries; Universal, formed by Carl Laemmle in 1912; Paramount, founded by Adolph Zukor (initially as Famous Players) in 1912; Warner Bros. (formed, of course, by the Warner brothers, in 1918); United Artists, formed by Mary Pickford, Douglas Fairbanks, Charlie Chaplin, and D. W. Griffith in 1919; and Jack's future home, MGM, which we will discuss at length later.

Fox Film Corporation was at loose ends when Jack joined in late 1921. Its first and biggest star had been Theda Bara, whose vamp films brought in huge profits in the late 1910s—but Bara, sick of playing the same sort of role endlessly, left (with bad feelings on both sides) in 1919.

Fox's only big star then was Tom Mix, so the studio poured its resources into his westerns—cheap and easy to produce, always reliable moneymakers.

There were other handsome leading men already at Fox in 1921, but none of them ever broke through from reliable working actors into lasting stars: the tough guy Maurice "Lefty" Flynn; the now-forgotten Albert Ray, Harold Goodwin, and Tom Douglas; the strong-jawed Johnnie Walker. Fox's only real male stars in the early 1920s were cowboys Tom Mix and the up-and-coming Buck Jones; the company badly needed a romantic lead and was anxious to build up Jack.

Fox's West Coast studios were located in the old Selig Polyscope building at 1845 Allesandro Street (now Glendale Boulevard) in hilly and tree-lined Edendale (northwest of downtown Los Angeles, the neighborhood is now known as Echo Park). "Sadly," writes historian Allen Ellenberger, "the site is now an empty lot in a mostly industrial area. The community that surrounds the spot and the people who pass by are most likely unaware of the historical significance of the site. It's unfortunate that an archeological dig could not be done there before a warehouse or some other industrial building is constructed."

Jack, looking back from his perch at MGM in the late 1920s, had nothing nice to say about Fox. "I was unhappy most of the time. My pictures were cheaply made and badly done. When I begged for such stories as *Seventh Heaven* and *The Sea Hawk* I was adjudged insane and temperamental." (*Seventh Heaven* was produced at Fox after Jack's tenure, but no doubt he did complain, a lot.) He admitted that from a business standpoint, "their policy at that time was to make as many pictures in as short a time as possible and profit on the quantity"—pretty much the operating mode of most studios. "But such a condition was not conducive to happiness nor to intensity of purpose."

His first Fox release—it hit theaters in July 1921—was a starring role in the romantic drama *Shame*, adapted from a magazine story. "Stardom is to be conferred on that favored leading man, John Gilbert, by the Fox Corporation," wrote the *Los Angeles Times* after *Shame* opened, noting that this stardom was "the result, 'tis said, of Mr. Gilbert's performance in the picture *Shame*, William Fox himself being convinced that the young actor is star material." It was a very silly tale of a man who is made to think he is half Chinese (N.B.: he really isn't). "We'd love to see

The second Mrs. John Gilbert, Paramount star Leatrice Joy, mid-1920s (author's collection).

a story in which the hero or heroine really was half-caste—and see what they'd do about it," the *Times* sensibly noted, adding darkly that "Jack Gilbert is master of too fine and vivid a method to be made to overact as he does in this play. Remember the work he used to do for the old Ince directors?"

By 1921 Jack and Leatrice Joy were beginning to get serious about their relationship. Her star, too, was rising: she was working for Goldwyn and by the end of that year was signed to a contract with Cecil

B. DeMille at Paramount that would shoot her to the top of the heap (*Manslaughter,* a 1922 DeMille film starring Joy as a thrill-seeking flapper, cemented her stardom). "My mother really loved being a star," Jack and Leatrice's daughter told writer Jimmy Bangley. "She just adored the recognition and praise and, believe me, she never got tired of the paparazzi." John Gilbert, she felt, "was the direct opposite of mother. He hated being recognized, and the press," though he did befriend many reporters and even critics. "He tried to avoid photographers."

On February 25, 1921, John Gilbert and Leatrice Joy announced their engagement. "Mr. Gilbert is one of the most talented and promising of the younger male stars," noted the *Los Angeles Times*. "Miss Joy is not only one of the most beautiful of the Goldwyn stars, but she makes a very fine impression of possessing unusual dramatic powers in every picture in which she appears." "Whatever I achieve in the future or whatever I will ever be able to do I owe to Miss Joy," Jack beamed happily.

Decades later, an elderly Leatrice Joy was still visibly smitten, as she spoke to film historian Kevin Brownlow. She recalled a photo Jack had inscribed to her: "Modesty should prevent my saying it, but I have no modesty, so I'm gonna say it," she laughed to Brownlow. He inscribed it "to my beloved wife, after whom God patterned the angels." "I'm a little ham at heart and I loved it, and I wouldn't have changed a word," Joy happily admitted. "He was always an enigma, I never solved him. I wish I had. Many people have been likened I guess to mercury, but Jack Gilbert *was* mercury. You'd touch him, and he'd vanish."

Like Jack, Leatrice Joy was smart and funny and adventurous, and the stories she later told show how bracing and fun their relationship must have been at its best. "Jack and I had a little game we used to play called 'I do, you do,'" Joy told historian William Drew. "It was testing our courage and all that. He'd do crazy things, and then I'd do them too. . . . One day, we were walking along Hollywood Boulevard by the barber shop and he said, 'I go in, I do, I get a haircut.' So I said, 'I do, too,' and with that, I went into Wellman's Barber Shop. The barber cut my hair exactly like Jack's so from the back we both looked like two men."

All of John Gilbert's marriages were spur-of-the-moment affairs, and this one was true to form: he and Leatrice Joy took off for Tijuana—the movie capital's quickie-marriage getaway—and wed sometime in

Jack and Leatrice Joy, ca. 1922 (author's collection).

November 1921. "Both are numbered among the most promising film stars of the day," said the *Los Angeles Times* when the marriage was finally admitted early in 1922. "Her rise in the screen world has been built on a genuine basis of talent and hard work. Jack Gilbert is the star of a number of Fox features, and is considered one of the finest of the younger actors."

The bride came complete with a problematic mother-in-law. Leatrice Joy told film historian William Drew in 1983 that "my mother didn't particularly care for him. She'd always say, 'I don't see how you can marry a man who paints his face, period.' She always called him Mr. Gilbert and that made it a little bit difficult for me because I adored my mother, I simply adored her."

The newlyweds first moved into a house in Laurel Canyon, then to a small, cozy cottage on the corner of Sweetzer Avenue and Fountain Avenue in Hollywood. According to some sources their cook was future actress Louise Beavers (*Imitation of Life, Bombshell, She Done Him Wrong, Holiday Inn,* TV's *Beulah*). The Gilberts happily planned a European honeymoon (which never took place). In a 1922 interview with the *Los Angeles Times,* Leatrice Joy said, "All our lives long, both of us, I found after I had met Jack, have longed for a trip to Europe. We talked of it the very first time we met. . . . Oh, of course not together—then. But we both said how much we wanted to go abroad. Jack wants to see France, the sad old battlegrounds, as well as Paris, once more trying to be gay. And he wants to see Monte Carlo, too! But he promises just to look."

The Gilberts lived around the corner from comic stars Charlie Chaplin and Max Linder, and Linder "and Jack hold long conversations about the war," wrote the *Times*'s Grace Kingsley, "in which Max Linder served, you remember, and for which Gilbert trained, but did not go, as his orders to leave were rescinded just two days before he was to start for France."

Before Jack and Leatrice married they had a long talk about his previous—and current—affairs. One rift in their long engagement came in the glamorous form of Barbara La Marr, who would have a supporting role in his 1922 film *Arabian Love* and would later have a costarring role in *St. Elmo.* La Marr was only twenty-six in 1922, but had already been married four times. Her beauty has not aged well, mostly because of heavy makeup and a tendency (shared with Mae Murray) to purse her lips and make "movie-star faces" for the still camera. But her surviving films show La Marr to have been a surprisingly good, low-key actress.

Jack's daughter Leatrice Fountain told writer Jimmy Bangley that Jack had a "torrid affair" with La Marr. "Even though my mother was jealous of Barbara, she liked her very much, so she must have been very charming." Fountain quoted her mother in her memoirs as saying that La Marr continued to call Jack even after his marriage. "The phone rang at about two in the morning," Leatrice Joy recalled. "I answered it and it was Barbara La Marr. She said, 'Oh, Leatrice, darling, may I speak to Jack, please?' I said, 'of course, dear,' and then threw the phone under the bed and went back to sleep."

La Marr's career continued upward after she and Jack split up—she worked at Metro, Goldwyn, First National, and Jack's alma mater, Maurice Tourneur Productions—with such costars as Ramon Novarro, Lew Cody, and Conway Tearle, before dying at the age of twenty-nine, in 1926. The official cause was tuberculosis, though there were rumors of drugs, alcohol, and anorexia. La Marr was not Jack's only romance on the side: Joy claimed that he also was courting—seriously or not—actresses Lila Lee (a cute little flapper nicknamed Cuddles) and Bebe Daniels (a huge star in the 1920s, best known today for breaking her ankle in *42nd Street*).

The newlywed Jack was doing pretty well for himself in the spring of 1922, during which he had three films in theaters. In the melodrama *Gleam O'Dawn* he costarred with his own discovery, Barbara Bedford; the unfortunately titled *The Yellow Stain* was a small-town drama, with Jack as an idealistic young lawyer fighting off the town's evil political boss, much as Jimmy Stewart was to do in later years. He "certainly handles the role," was *Variety*'s oddly bland compliment. *Arabian Love* rode the coattails of the 1921 hit *The Sheik,* starring Jack as a young American who joins a band of Arabian nomads and falls for a white hostage (Bedford again). While shooting *Arabian Love* in the Mojave Desert, the company ran low on water, and when Jack's character had to sip from a flagon of poisoned water, he was given what the camels had been drinking. "You may notice, if you are very keen," wrote the *Los Angeles Times,* "John Gilbert's peculiar expression in that particular scene in *Arabian Love* as he takes that irresistible sip."

What *The Sheik* did for Valentino, Fox reasoned, maybe *Arabian Love* could do for their new acquisition. The film itself may have been a standard programmer, offering nothing in the way of acting opportunity, but it did provide a good showcase. *Variety* noted an "interesting actor in the person of John Gilbert, who stands out as a comer. In a great many ways [he] physically reminds of Wallace Reid. There is also the ability to ride and put up a corking fight. Gilbert looks as though Fox had picked a good screen bet and he should develop, provided that he is given the right material."

In the 1922 drama *Honor First,* Jack played identical twins (one cowardly and one noble, as is always the case in the movies, though presumably not in real life). Cowardly Twin accidentally dies while trying to murder Noble Twin, who—in a somewhat creepy "happy ending," winds up with former sister-in-law Renée Adorée.

Then came a real star showcase, *Monte Cristo,* based on Dumas (père)'s novel about an imprisoned young sailor who plots revenge after escaping and recovering a hidden treasure (on the island of Monte Cristo). It was translated into a stage play, most notably acted by James O'Neill for more than three decades. *The Count of Monte Cristo* had already been filmed several times, including a French serial of 1918 and a rather primitive 1913 American version starring O'Neill himself. But an epic remake was due, and Fox began creating sets on his lot as early as September 1921. *Monte Cristo* was noted for its underwater photography, and Jack was called upon to swim, in what proved to be a brief but very exciting escape scene from his prison (he claimed he had learned to swim while at the Hitchcock Military Academy from a Hawaiian classmate).

When it was released in September 1922, Adele Whitely Fletcher of *Motion Picture* magazine was not impressed by the movie or the cast: "Seldom do you feel any vital regard for the future of the characters. . . . The inspiration for their acts was missing." The *Los Angeles Times* critics, though, felt that "John Gilbert . . . might well be proud of his work. . . . The star accomplishes his delineations with thorough artistry."

Monte Cristo was long thought to be a lost film, but a nearly complete copy was found in the Czech Republic, and a restored, rescored version is available for viewing today. *Monte Cristo* is obviously an expensive film in terms of sets, costumes (early nineteenth century), and cinematography. It's an enjoyable, well-crafted adventure, but hardly one of the classics of the silent screen. It provides a nice showcase for Jack in that he looks attractive and is in nearly every frame of the film. Only in the second half does he really get a chance to act, when his delightfully evil vengeance is enacted—here, Jack shows the subtle character actor he would become late in his career. Slightly villainous, cold eyed, and mad suited him.

Monte Cristo was his second film with a woman who would become his most frequent leading lady, the tiny, dark Renée Adorée, who was startlingly lovely in a bit part as the daughter of one of the hero's betrayers. One year younger than Jack, she was born into a French circus family and came to the United States in 1919. She was signed by Fox in 1922; *Monte Cristo* was only her fourth movie. Jack enjoyed working with her—she was an instinctive, delicate actress, always professional and easy to work with.

With his first big starring vehicle in theaters, Jack was already sounding off about roles. "He believes in giving the hero character," said Edwin Schallert of the *Los Angeles Times*. "I don't say, of course, that he intends to wish on his hero all the scum of wickedness that can be scraped from the villain's evil mind. But he thinks that there should be some relief from too much goody-goodyness." Which is just what he did with *Monte Cristo*—here was a hero who was also more than a little creepy.

He told Schallert that he would like to direct or write or produce in a way that had held sway ten years earlier, during the early days of filmmaking: "working out your play without the aid of scenario, just allowing it to develop from point to point, from situation to situation. I believe it could be done, and the results prove very effective on the screen, even with a serious theme. I would delight, for instance, in . . . putting three or four men in a set and endeavoring to find something for them to do. It really is astonishing how much can be found for them to do. I believe that the same method could be used for the serious drama. I would have a theme in mind, of course. I would know in a general way how the plot would work out, but I would let the situations develop themselves." Experiments in improvisation did not lend themselves to big studio productions, of course: time (and film) was money, and such ingenuous, fuzzy-headed artistry had to be confined to neighborhood improv groups, not the Fox lot.

Jack's first-released 1923 film was *While Paris Sleeps,* an interesting precursor to *Mystery of the Wax Museum* and *House of Wax*. It had actually been shot in 1920 by Maurice Tourneur as *The Glory of Love,* but Paramount hated it and put it on the shelf. By 1923, though, its lead actors—Jack and Lon Chaney—showed some signs of becoming marketable stars, and Hodkinson snapped it up for release. *While Paris Sleeps* starred Chaney (still known as a character actor; this was one of his first horror roles) as a sculptor in love with his model. Jack played Chaney's young rival, who is kidnapped and tortured in a wax museum, certainly one of the earliest uses of this now-classic horror plot.

In May 1922 rising star Rudolph Valentino had been briefly jailed for bigamy: his divorce from bit player Jean Acker had not been finalized when he married set and costume designer Natacha Rambova in a Mexican ceremony. It didn't hurt Valentino's career in the long run, but embarrassing headlines resulted; no one likes to spend the night in stir, and Famous Players–Lasky would have had cause to cancel his contract had they wished. Jack and Leatrice Joy took the hint: their own Mexican marriage might not be quite legal, and to avoid scandal, Leatrice moved out of their home and was interviewed and photographed in her own respectable bachelorette pad. Contacted for a legal divorce in January 1923, Olivia Burwell sued for a property settlement in addition to the $5,000 lump sum and $225-a-month alimony settlement she had obtained in December 1921. With all that squared away, Jack and Leatrice remarried, their Mexican marriage quietly annulled by Leatrice's studio (the same as Valentino's, Famous Players–Lasky). At 5:30 p.m. on March 3, 1923, the couple was remarried at the home of Judge Summerfield, with future producer Paul Bern in attendance. The two had now moved back into their home at 1275 Sweetzer Avenue.

Through the spring of 1923 the newly re-wed actor had numerous films in the theaters. *Variety* dismissed *The Love Gambler* as "just a western," adding insult to injury by misnaming Jack "John Gilmore" in their review. Another "just a western" was *A California Romance*—but in this case *Variety* suspected that the film had been made as a straight western drama, then Fox—realizing how hopeless it was—added comedy titles, along the lines of *Fractured Flickers* or *Mystery Science Theater 3000*. It worked: "It's hoak pure and simple, and good for a laugh anywhere." *Truxton King* was a costume drama, with Jack as an American who rescues a boy king from revolution ("Gilbert gives an interesting performance that will please the fans," wrote *Variety,* making up somewhat for "John Gilmore"). And in *Madness of Youth* he costarred with rising young actress Billie Dove. *St. Elmo* costarred Jack with two rising young Fox starlets, comic character actress Bessie Love (still in her ingénue phase) and his former flame Barbara La Marr. *St. Elmo*—based on a wildly popular nineteenth-century novel—told the story of a scapegrace who is "saved" by the love of a Good Woman.

Jack's marriage to Leatrice Joy followed a pattern that cut a depressingly steady rut through his life: fall madly in love, marry impetuously, and within three months become impossible to live with. By June 1923 Jack and Leatrice had separated, after he reportedly slapped her during an argument. She went back to him almost right away when he promised to give up drinking—which, of course, he didn't. For the rest of their brief marriage, they were on-again, off-again; Jack occasionally found a friendly spare bedroom with friends Carey Wilson and Paul Bern at their house on North Kings Road in Beverly Hills.

Monte Cristo had been successful enough for Fox to try another Douglas Fairbanks–type action role and star Jack in *Cameo Kirby,* released in 1923, one year after *Monte Cristo.* Based on a Broadway show of the 1910s by Booth Tarkington, it takes place in 1850s New Orleans. *Cameo Kirby* was Jack's only film with the great John Ford, then at the dawn of a long career. Ford had been in movies since 1914, as an actor, writer, and director, and by the time of *Cameo Kirby* he was already specializing in two-fisted action and western films. Jack starred as a Mississippi riverboat gambler of unusually honest and upright demeanor who falls in love with the daughter of a man he'd unintentionally pushed into suicide. Duels, fleeing from the law, and much derring-do ensue—Jack's leading lady was Gertrude Olmstead, and future star Jean Arthur made her debut in a small role. This was also the first film in which director "Jack Ford" was billed as "John Ford" (it had only been a year since the last time "John Gilbert" had been billed as "Jack Gilbert," in *Calvert's Valley*).

Cameo Kirby opened in Los Angeles in November 1923. The papers printed some publicity nonsense about Jack having known Mark Twain as a boy: "In those days the shaggy-haired Twain would sit with Gilbert on his knee, telling him stories of the old days on the river. . . . 'I'll never forget the stories Mr. Clemens used to tell me. . . . He would recount his own experiences as a pilot and add others about picturesque men with whom he came in contact. His stories were so colorful that they created a lasting impression on my childish brain, which served me well in this picture.'"

Cameo Kirby was the only Fox film Jack liked—"the only fine thing I was associated with at the studio." It's easy to see why Jack was so proud of *Cameo Kirby*—though with so few of his Fox films surviving, we can't really compare it to, say, *Shame* or *The Wolf Man.* John Ford is the driving hand behind *Cameo Kirby,* and he was certainly more adept than Jack's previous Fox directors, the likes of John Francis Dillon, Joseph Franz, Edmund Mortimer, and Jerome Storm.

Cameo Kirby is a pre–Civil War romance, following the adventures of the world's only honest riverboat gambler, John "Cameo" Kirby (nicknamed for the good-luck jewelry he wears). Through the course of the film, poor Kirby fails to save a wealthy landowner from ruin; he is blamed for the landowner's suicide; he is shot right off a riverboat by a villain (the always entertaining Alan Hale Sr.); and he falls in love with the suicide's daughter (an excellent Gertrude Olmstead). *Cameo Kirby* is an expensive, atmospheric, and thoroughly charming movie, with gorgeous antebellum costumes and plenty of location scenery—rivers, plantations, weeping willows. There is even an exciting (and very dangerous) riverboat race, in the days when the old paddle steamers were viewed with both nostalgia and scorn (they did tend to catch fire or explode).

Jack's Kirby is not a dashing, smile-flashing rogue—thanks to Ford reining in the actor the character is quiet and thoughtful. This is not the Douglas Fairbanks– or Rudolph Valentino–style John Gilbert soon to be groomed by MGM but a laid-back character actor showing off few tricks or quirks. The almost grim performances Ford got in later years from Henry Fonda, John Wayne, James Stewart, and Victor McLaglen can be seen here in John Gilbert's down-turned eyes and calm body language.

Jack befriended brothers Kenneth and Howard Hawks while at Fox—Howard Hawks, an assistant director and editor in the early 1920s, would go on to become the colorful director of *Scarface, Bringing Up Baby, His Girl Friday, Ball of Fire,* and many other screen classics. Younger brother Kenneth would also become a promising director, till his death in a 1930 plane crash. Both Hawks brothers told Jack he was too good for the projects he was being given, and that *Cameo Kirby* was proof that he needed to get out and find a studio that would nurture his career.

His last 1923 release was *The Exiles,* based on a story by real-life swashbuckler Richard Harding Davis. It was the story of a "terribly earnest" young New Yorker who travels to the debauched Far East, gets some of the rough edges knocked off him, falls in love with a young blackmail victim, and is "brought face to face, and for the first time in my life, not with principles of conduct, not with causes, and not with laws, but with my fellow men." *Variety* panned the film, calling Jack "a capable leading man of the matinee idol hero type," a description that must have infuriated and frustrated him.

By early 1924 he was itching for a way out of Fox, with his contract coming up for renewal. Several of his last Fox films, though, were unusual and provided good showcases. Particularly *Just Off Broadway,* which had much in common with one of his better talkies, *The Phantom of Paris* (Jack played a detective faking amnesia). *Variety* was impressed: "Gilbert, who heretofore has been seen usually in heavy roles, proves an adept farceur and puts a good deal of character into his rather light-waisted role."

The Wolf Man was notable for several reasons: for one thing, it introduced Jack to a lifelong friend, his costar Norma Shearer. It also might have been a good, serious study of alcoholism, but that seems to have been a lost opportunity. Jack played a character who "gets rough when in liquor, and every time he places a monocle in his eye, it's a sign of trouble"—*The Lost Weekend* it wasn't.

Twenty-two-year-old Norma Shearer had entered films as an extra in 1920 and had all the drive and steely-eyed ambition of her future rival, Joan Crawford. Unlike Crawford, Shearer was no great beauty (Mrs. Patrick Campbell once reportedly said of her, "Such pretty little eyes—and so close together, too!"). But Norma Shearer was smart and hard working and talented (much better in drama than in comedy, where she tended to go all arch). She was freelancing at Fox, and spent 1924 hopping from studio to studio, making eight films that year before landing, along with Jack, at Metro-Goldwyn-Mayer. John Gilbert and

Norma Shearer never were a romantic pair; they were a nice example of how a man and woman could be platonic pals (his nickname for her was "Auntie"). She was one of the few leading ladies he did not fall in love with, and she soon had her eyes on bigger fish, anyway.

A Man's Mate reteamed Jack with Renée Adorée in a tale of the Parisian Apache underworld. Adorée stole the show: she "displays real talent as one of the Parisian gamines," while Jack "appears to be miscast. He has been seen to more advantage in lighter roles." *The Lone Chance* teamed Jack with the rather hard-boiled Evelyn Brent in an almost *Monte Cristo*–like plot about a young man who escapes after being wrongfully jailed. Jack's last film for Fox was *Romance Ranch* (released in the summer of 1924), which *Variety* dismissed as a "casual western of the well-known type. . . . Gilbert is a passive personality in this instance, who fails to demand definite consideration." All in all, the film must have made him glad to see the end of that contract and look forward to what Metro had in store.

Jack had befriended Paul Bern, who was working as an editor and screenwriter at Fox. Bern was smart, funny, sympathetic, and a rising star within the studio system. He also had the misfortune of looking rather like an earthworm in a suit, so his passionate crushes on actress after actress ended in heartbreak (what few knew was that Bern had a common-law wife stashed away at the Algonquin Hotel in New York). Bern, who prided himself on being a good talent scout, introduced Jack to a rising young producer named Irving Thalberg.

The puppy-eyed "Boy Wonder of Hollywood" was twenty-four years old when he and Jack met in late 1923, and he looked all of sixteen. Physically frail and pampered by his mother, Thalberg was sweet, friendly, and funny—but also as dogmatic and cold-blooded as the most terrifying studio heads. But Thalberg used a sugar-coated stiletto to kill, rather than a bludgeon. He started his career as sweet, avuncular studio head Carl Laemmle's assistant at Universal, working his way up to producer within a couple of years. Some feel it was Thalberg who tipped the scale of power from director to producer: his iron-fisted handling of Erich von Stroheim amazed studio executives and made directors quake in their puttees.

In 1923 Thalberg left Universal and joined Louis B. Mayer Productions as vice president and head of production—he and Mayer had a strained, wary relationship for the rest of Thalberg's life. They respected each other's talents and both wanted what was best for the studio and for the individual films, but they were jealous of each other's power and did not trust one another for a moment. When MGM was formed in 1924, Thalberg became vice president and head of production (executive titles were as confusing and meaningless then as they are now). Paul Bern said he overheard Thalberg telling Louis B. Mayer of Fox that in Jack the studio doesn't "know what they've got." Bern got Thalberg and Jack together to talk business: joining Metro—soon to become Metro-Goldwyn-Mayer—"would be a great chance for a growing boy."

In early March 1924 Jack's current Fox contract ran out—he was offered the lead in *The Man Who Came Back* to re-sign, but he said he wanted to freelance (George O'Brien was given the part). "I greatly appreciate everything which the Fox people have done for me, however, and I realize they have done a great deal. However, my wife, Leatrice Joy, and I want to take some trips later, and I cannot do this when tied up on a contract. The first seven weeks vacation we have, we mean to take a trip to Europe."

But Jack signed with Metro-Goldwyn-Mayer on April 30, 1924. "Despite his resolution to sign no more contracts, taken when he completed his Fox contract, John Gilbert apparently just could not resist the lure of a nice fat salary held out to him in consideration of his affixing his John Henry to a contract with the Metro-Goldwyn-Mayor [*sic*] company, and therefore the dashing Jack is once more a slave to art." "I consider my present engagement a very excellent one," Jack said. "I had hoped to free lance in order that my wife, Leatrice Joy, and myself might have some time to travel; but she signed a new contract, and that delays our travel days for a while. But we surely mean to go to Europe at the first opportunity." Actually, Leatrice had signed with Paramount in 1922 and had just had a hit with Cecil B. DeMille's *The Ten Commandments* in 1923. In 1925 she followed DeMille to his new Producers Distributing Corporation.

Chapter Four

Liquor was provided by the host for everybody, and morphine and cocaine, with hypodermic syringes, for those who craved them.

—*New York Herald,* 1922

Just as Jack was getting a foothold in the early 1920s, the movie industry was struck with an unprecedented series of deaths and scandals that brought not only worldwide press coverage but the wrath of religious, political, and censorship groups. The movies had been subject to the usual sad events in the early years: deaths in the Great War and from the 1918 flu epidemic, car crashes and illnesses. The experience of going to the movies to see a favorite star who was now dead was a new form of schadenfreude. But the early years of the 1920s brought headline after headline: some merely sad, others reinforcing the theory that show people were harlots, riffraff, and tramps who needed to be watched carefully and kept in their place.

In 1920 alone, four rising young stars died in eyebrow-raising ways. D. W. Griffith protégée Clarine Seymour, a charming proto-flapper, died at twenty-one after a sudden illness ("strangulated intestines" was the official cause, but of course abortion was darkly hinted at). Ormer Locklear, a dashing stunt pilot recently signed by Fox, died in an on-set crash. Griffith star Bobbie Harron—a brilliant young actor who starred in *Intolerance* and *Hearts of the World,* among others—shot himself in a New York hotel room (accidentally, it was claimed). And Olive Thomas, a Ziegfeld *Follies* beauty who had moved successfully into films, died after taking poison in a Paris hotel—to this day, no one knows if it was suicide, accident, or murder (the fact that her husband—Mary Pickford's brother, Jack—was with her at the time added to the newsworthiness).

The deaths continued through the early '20s, not all of them terribly mysterious: child stars Breezy Eason Jr. (car accident) and Bobby Connelly (bronchitis), ingénues Martha Mansfield (on-set fire) and Lucille Ricksen (tuberculosis). The 1924 death of Jack's first boss, Triangle producer Thomas Ince, turned into a scandal only after the fact. Ince—just forty-two years old—took ill while a guest on William Randolph Hearst's yacht. He was taken ashore in San Diego and died at home, the official cause heart failure. But so many people hated Hearst that rumors started up immediately—it was bad booze that had killed Ince, or (even juicier) Hearst had shot him after finding him with his mistress, Marion Davies. No coroner's inquest was held, and Ince was cremated, which only made people more suspicious. The San Diego district attorney held a desultory inquest, and Ince's doctor testified that he had long suffered from heart palpitations. End of inquest, but not end of rumors, which have been churned about in books and movies ever since. In short, there is not one shred of evidence that Thomas Ince's death was anything but natural, but that has never slowed down a good rumor.

That testifying doctor, Daniel Carson Goodman, by the way, was quite a character himself: he was with his fiancée, action-serial star Florence LaBadie, when she was in a fatal car accident in 1917; he later married actress Alma Rubens, who died a drug addict. Besides Rubens, among the top-tier actresses known to be drug users were Mabel Normand and Juanita Hansen. Normand was featured in a blind newspaper item after director William Desmond Taylor's murder: "A noted actress who tried the cure, but who was forced back into 'slavery' by the dope peddlers, has had a love affair with Taylor. There have been quarrels and at least one fight, as a result of which the actress went to a hospital." Mabel Normand was later caught up in another front-page story, when her chauffeur shot and seriously wounded millionaire playboy Courtland Dines while she and Charlie Chaplin's leading lady Edna Purviance were guests at Dines's home. Dines never testified and the case was dropped—but it is not coincidental that the careers of Normand and Purviance took a downward turn afterward.

In a 1922 *New York Herald* investigative series, reporter Thoreau Cronyn went to Hollywood in search of "'orgies,' narcotics, alcohol, vice, extravagant living," but what he found was "no worse than similar things indulged in by persons of the same moral stripe in other parts of the country, notably New York." Cronyn did tantalize with stories of occasional naughty parties: "Liquor was provided by the host for everybody, and morphine and cocaine, with hypodermic syringes, for those who craved them. . . . Some of the more intoxicated revelers disrobed as they danced. . . . Bathing parties on the beaches at which some of the 'ladies and gentlemen' who had forgotten to bring their bathing suits were not prevented from going into the water comfortably." A federal agent told Cronyn, "There really are a good many drug addicts in the motion picture crowd, but most of them are among the low class, roustabout actors, and the extra people who are not working steadily but call themselves actors. However, the stories have been wildly exaggerated." He added, "It's the Mexicans and negroes who bother us, not the movie folk."

As for alcohol—Jack's drug of choice—Cronyn found that "in parts of Los Angeles it is sold openly, notably at soft drink counters. . . . Every thirsty burgher has his list of bootleggers' telephone numbers. He swaps telephone lists with his neighbor, just as he used to trade home brew recipes. He phones his order to the bootlegger and the stuff is delivered at the back door."

Jack's drinking was just becoming worrisome as Prohibition was enforced. Jack was probably not wealthy enough to stockpile liquor—good, drinkable liquor, anyway—between the time the Volstead Act was passed in October 1919 and the time it became the law of the land in January 1920. But for the next thirteen years, he was one of its most enthusiastic opponents. Jack's drinking did not interfere with his professional life—not till the very end—but by the early 1920s he was becoming a binge drinker, especially when depressed or angry.

California wine still sold well despite the illegality. "My impression," wrote Cronyn, "is that movie people, taken collectively, have in the past given and attended more 'booze parties' than most other communities of the same size, and that reckless indulgence has been more frequent." In November 1923 federal agents busted several large-scale L.A. bootlegging rings and found customer lists of major film players and executives.

The five bootleggers' clients included Jack, Viola Dana, actor William Desmond, Art Acord, Lloyd Hamilton, Bryant Washburne, Mabel Normand, Henry B. Walthall, and many others.

The *New York American* claimed in 1921 that "Nero . . . would have turned his head in shame at some of the modern-day ribald gatherings in which certain members of the Hollywood motion picture colony gave their passions and impulses unrestrained play." At one party—hosted by "a prominent male actor of the screen," a hostess wheeled around a snack tray laden with "an assortment of needles, opium pipes, morphine, cocaine, heroin and opium . . . the excesses proved of so extreme a nature as finally to nauseate even some of the participants and impel them to leave the party in disgust."

Movie Weekly blamed jaded Jazz Age New Yorkers for infiltrating poor innocent Los Angeles, particularly "innumerable . . . chorus girls who have come to Hollywood to live the easy, moneyed life that the position of leading woman in film productions offers. These women are not in pictures because of their love of Art. They, for the most part, belong to the ultra-fast set and can be seen in the various cafes dancing hilariously and exploiting their personal charms with utter abandon."

The Big Three scandals—the ones that finally brought down serious censorship and governmental schoolmarms—were the deaths of Virginia Rappe, William Desmond Taylor, and Wallace Reid.

The first great—or terrible, if you were personally involved—scandal of the 1920s was the Fatty Arbuckle case. Roscoe Arbuckle (he reportedly hated his stage name Fatty) was a huge comic star in every sense: his 1910s comedies are still a delight. Arbuckle's movies with Mabel Normand were more romantic comedy than slapstick, showing off both stars' acting gifts and real charm. By the 1920s Arbuckle had graduated from two-reelers and was making feature comedies for Famous Players–Lasky. Then disaster struck over Labor Day weekend 1921 in San Francisco.

The tragedy was not Arbuckle's, though, it was Virginia Rappe's. Today she is best known as "the dead girl" in the Arbuckle case, a failed starlet. Researcher Joan Myers has uncovered a more nuanced picture of Rappe: she was actually a fairly successful model and fashion designer, and although her film career was minor, she got excellent reviews. That all came to an end on September 9, 1921, when Rappe died in a San Francisco hospital four days after taking ill at a St. Francis Hotel party hosted by Arbuckle, actor/director Lowell Sherman, and director Fred Fischbach—Rappe was left to linger painfully in the St. Francis for several days before being hospitalized, which might leave everyone at the party open to negligent homicide charges. To this day, no one knows exactly how or why Virginia Rappe died; after three widely covered trials Arbuckle was found innocent of any blame. But the damage was done: Arbuckle was dropped by his studio (though he worked steadily for the rest of his life, as a director and eventually acting again).

While Arbuckle's reputation has rebounded—many of his films are available on DVD—Virginia Rappe has long been the victim of a smear campaign. "What Arbuckle's defense maintained is that Virginia's bladder ruptured spontaneously because she was a diseased whore," says Myers. Arbuckle champion Adela Rogers St. Johns spent the next fifty years bad-mouthing Rappe: "I wouldn't call her a *tramp,*" she said to Kevin Brownlow in the 1970s, eyebrows arched, "but she was an extra girl who made her way as best she could, and she had a habit of taking off all her clothes, prance around, see what trade she could drum up, I guess."

In trashing Rappe to boost Arbuckle, his champions also damaged the industry. The *New York Evening World* noted that the Arbuckle scandal threw a scare into the community: "Since [then], the Hollywood film colony has 'gone to bed' at 11 o'clock, while formerly this was the time when lights were brightest in the homes of many high salaried stars."

In February 1922, Paramount director William Desmond Taylor was shot to death in his Westlake Park bungalow—a murder that is still unsolved and that has been the subject of countless books, theories, and Bruce Long's excellent Taylorology website. Not only was the murder of a top director juicy enough in itself, but layer after layer of awfulness arose during the investigation, making headlines nationwide. Taylor's pal Mabel Normand was the last to see him alive, and it came out that he had been helping her quit her drug habit (scorned dealers were among the suspects). Teenaged Paramount ingénue Mary Miles Minter left a number of embarrassing love notes in the home of the forty-nine-year-old Taylor (Minter's mother, a real crackpot, has long been the chief suspect). And Taylor himself turned out not to be what everyone had thought: his real name was William Deane-Tanner, and he had run out on a bankrupt business, a wife, and two children in New York.

None of this was reflecting well on the film community. "There should be some effective way to remove the garbage element from the producing end of the motion picture business," wrote the Motion Picture Theater Owners' Association of America shortly after Taylor's death. "Now we have the Taylor murder with its . . . multiplicity of actresses, and other scandalous circumstances involving well-known stars. The possibility of a well-known producer being mixed in confronts us and the whole mess of tragic obscenity is nauseating." Actress Dorothy Gish—a rather fun-loving flapper—said in 1922, "When I walk down the street nowadays and someone recognizes me, I feel like turning my head so that I won't hear them say: 'Oh, there's another one of those picture actresses. I wonder when her story will be told on the front pages of the newspapers.'" Joe Webb of the *Austin American* sarcastically wrote that Hollywood stars needed their huge salaries: "Dope is expensive and how could they afford to stay hopped-up if they didn't make big money?"

And speaking of dope, the third great scandal came along later that same year—toward the end of 1922 it was leaked to the press that handsome, clean-cut leading man Wallace Reid was fighting morphine addiction. Reid had gotten hooked on the painkiller after a 1919 train accident and had been in and out of rehab ever since. In January 1923 he died in a clinic from respiratory and renal failure, in one last attempt to go cold turkey. His widow, actress Dorothy Davenport, became an antidrug crusader, producing (with Thomas Ince) *Human Wreckage*. All very well and good, but this brought still more attention to Hollywood's drug intake.

Oddly enough, John Gilbert kept his nose clean and was never involved in any major scandal or lawsuit—his studio bosses should have been thanking their lucky stars. His downfall was liquor, not drugs, and his drinking never interfered with his work—his opinions, yes, but not his drinking. Despite his tendency to fall madly in love with his costars with an almost tedious regularity, he never broke up a marriage (not even his own) and was never brought to court by either a furious husband or a jilted lover. Also, Jack's lovers were female—the homosexuality of MGM stars William Haines and Ramon Novarro made the studio slightly nervous about blackmailers. As long as Haines and Novarro were bringing in profits, MGM executives and stockholders couldn't care less about their orientation, but a gay scandal would have been disastrous.

When scandal did strike Jack, it was indirectly: through his brother-in-law. In January 1924 Leatrice's brother, Bill Joy, was accused of attempted rape. Bill and Leatrice's manager had cut out of a party and gone on a moonlight ride with sisters Margaret and Jeanette Monteith. Bill Joy tried to get Margaret to drink from his flask—she refused, jumped out of the car, and ran; he chased her down and "attempted to attack the girl." She fought him off, returned to the car, and the next day filed charges with the Los Angeles police. Joy escaped prosecution "when corroboration of her story could not be obtained."

Up till now, state censorship boards had held sway over movies, with regulations and phobias varying from state to state (some were tougher on showing crime, others sex, others drugs and liquor, and so on). Movies were chopped and changed as prints were shipped to Kentucky, Pennsylvania, Ohio. Now with religious groups (chiefly the Catholic Church—though their feared Legion of Decency was not formed till 1933) weighing in, it looked as though a national government censorship board was around the corner. To forestall this, former U.S. postmaster general Will Hays was called upon in 1922 by several studio chiefs to head the Motion Picture Producers and Distributors of America, a "voluntary" ratings and censorship board. "Voluntary" is in quotes because this scheme was by no means a popular or even a feasible one—many studios denounced Hays and his board, as did state censors who thought him the bought rent boy of the movie industry.

Will Hays loved the movies, and in some ways he was the industry's rent boy. The first tentative Hays Code of 1927 proscribed such subjects, "irrespective of the manner in which they are treated," as nudity, drugs, "any inference of sex perversion," "sex relationships between white and black races," poking fun at religion, guns, theft and robbery (which would pretty much eliminate all gangster films), "man and woman in bed together," "excessive or lustful kissing," and on and on. Happily, no one paid the slightest attention to any of this, and with the Motion Picture Producers and Distributors of America providing cover, filmmakers continued wrecking morals till the real clamp-down in mid-1934.

Part 2

The Peak

Chapter Five

It's so great to be a part of anything like this. I just can't believe I'm really here.

—John Gilbert, 1924

When Jack reported to work at the new Metro-Goldwyn-Mayer studios, he was actually stepping back into his own past: the production headquarters, at 10202 West Washington Boulevard, in Culver City, was the colonnaded old Triangle Studio building. Fellow freshmen starting out at MGM in 1924 and '25 included leading ladies Aileen Pringle, Blanche Sweet, Anita Stewart, Mae Murray, Norma Shearer, Eleanor Boardman, and Joan Crawford. His competing leading men were Ramon Novarro, William Haines, Lloyd Hughes, and Conrad Nagel—as well as character star Lon Chaney, comic Buster Keaton, and child wonder Jackie Coogan. MGM also had a stable of star directors on hand, including King Vidor, Erich von Stroheim, Clarence Brown, and Tod Browning.

Metro-Goldwyn-Mayer was the result of a three-company 1924 merger brainstormed by movie executive Marcus Loew that combined Metro Pictures Corporation, Goldwyn Pictures, and Louis B. Mayer Pictures Corporation. In 1920 Loew had purchased Metro, which had been founded by Richard Rowland and the boisterous, opinionated workhorse Louis B. Mayer in 1915. Mayer had left that company to open Louis B. Mayer Pictures Corporation in 1918, but Loew kept his eye on him. In 1924 Loew also bought Goldwyn Pictures, which was the 1916 brainchild of Samuel Goldfish and the Selwyn brothers (the joke around town being it either had to be called "Goldwyn" or "Selfish"). Sam Goldfish liked the name so much he wisely changed his own. Goldwyn had lost control of his own studio in 1922, which was now floundering under the management of Frank Joseph Godsol. Loew, who ran the huge Loew's Theater chain, combined the three organizations, and thus—on May 16, 1924—was born Metro-Goldwyn-Mayer (though its releases were still billed as "Metro-Goldwyn" pictures as late as 1926).

Louis B. Mayer was such a colorful character that it seems in retrospect that he was solely in charge of the studio, but this was far from the case. Nicholas Schenck—Marcus Loew's money manager—ran the financial end of the business from New York. Mayer was named first vice president and head of studio operations. Production heads were former Warner Bros. general manager Harry Rapf, and Irving Thalberg. By no means did Mayer have final say on everything. Mayer and Schenck, who cordially hated each other, coexisted (happily, on separate coasts) till Schenck controversially ousted Mayer in 1951.

MGM announced in June 1924 that in its first year of production it would spend at least $15 million making more than fifty movies. The studio planned to add four more stages to the lot, three more administration buildings, a prop building, $200,000 worth of equipment, and "a small fortune" in costumes and furniture.

Jack was signed at $1,500 a week—he made less than Lon Chaney and Alice Terry (a now-forgotten dramatic actress), but slightly more than Ramon Novarro and Conrad Nagel. Novarro, two years younger than Jack, was a boyishly handsome, ingratiating actor who had been rising steadily since his 1922 breakthrough as a dashing villain in Metro's *The Prisoner of Zenda*. Smart, funny, and likeable, Novarro got to play few villains; he was soon typecast as the lovelorn boy next door (his Mexican accent no impediment in silent films). He had three movies in release in 1924, and in 1925 would star in the year's blockbuster, *Ben-Hur.*

MGM's other early male star, Conrad Nagel, never really clicked with audiences and is largely forgotten today. A cooperative team player, the rather bland, blond Nagel (born the same year as Jack, also in the Midwest), was a reliable leading man, able to gaze longingly at the star without really getting in her way. In 1924 he had an impressive eight films in release, supporting Aileen Pringle, Alma Rubens, Blanche Sweet,

Jack's MGM bosses Irving Thalberg and Louis B. Mayer, seen here in 1933 (The Everett Collection).

Eleanor Boardman, and—along with Jack—Norma Shearer, in *The Snob.* Nagel went on to become president of the Academy of Motion Picture Arts and Sciences, and he hosted several early Oscars ceremonies; he lived long enough to appear on TV's *Gunsmoke* and *Perry Mason* in the 1960s.

Jack's first project to be produced at MGM was the circus thriller *He Who Gets Slapped,* directed by Victor Sjöström, the Swedish great who had been acting and directing for some ten years by this point. Brought to the United States in 1923 by Goldwyn, he was grandfathered in to the new corporation (his name anglicized to Seastrom). The film was budgeted at $172,000 (an average "A" budget for those days) and costarred Jack's friend Norma Shearer and Lon Chaney, who had recently burst into real stardom with Universal's *The Hunchback of Notre Dame.*

It was a very weird film, an odd one with which to inaugurate the new company. Based on a Russian play (which also ran on Broadway in 1922), it told the story of a brilliant scientist who goes mad when betrayed by his wife and business partner. He becomes a circus clown, one who "desired only to be slapped" (clowns are pretty hard to deal with under any circumstances, but insane S & M clowns reach a whole new level of creepy). Jack played Bezano, a young bareback rider, looking very fetching and youthful in circus garb. *He Who Gets Slapped*—which, happily, survives—is fast moving and entertaining (with, clown-phobics be warned, *lots* of clowns). Chaney gives his usual superb performance (and, unexpectedly to fans of his horror films, he looks quite handsome in the early scenes, in mussed hair and trim goatee). The plot moves quickly, as everyone falls in love with poor Norma Shearer: the mad clown, Jack's callow bareback rider, the evil former business partner. It all ends satisfyingly with vengeance, blood, and a hungry circus lion.

Jack had little to do (though he did some of the easier riding and trapeze work, of course the dangerous stunts were left to professionals). And he was pretty angry about it. In fact, he was angry about a lot: Jack later recalled that he was infuriated at seeing the size of his role in *He Who Gets Slapped:* "Any one of fifty men could have played the part. What was the angle? What were they trying to do with me? Were they dissatisfied with my work? That was it. They were sorry they had signed me."

A major part of Irving Thalberg's job was calming down actors and

Jack with Norma Shearer and Lon Chaney in *He Who Gets Slapped,* 1924 (The Everett Collection).

playing diplomat. He told Jack, "This part, as small as it is, will do you more good than anything you have ever done"—which was absolute nonsense, but it worked.

Filming continued through June and July 1924; the *Slapped* set was not a particularly happy one. The older, more serious Seastrom and Chaney paired off, leaving youngsters Jack and Norma Shearer to fend for themselves—this only strengthened their friendship. They went to parties and nightclubs together, but there was never a serious romance between the two—Norma Shearer already had her eye on Irving Thalberg, one of Hollywood's most eligible bachelors. While Jack and Norma Shearer were great friends, Lon Chaney did not get on with his second lead at all, according to an anonymous tipster, who told writer Jim Tully years later that Jack had asked that Chaney's visiting wife not watch while he was filming. "Chaney was disgusted," Tully quotes this source. "For Gilbert to do this to an outsider, Chaney thought, might be all right, and a fine gesture. But to do it to someone in the business . . . that both disgusted and amused the older actor."

Released in November 1924, *He Who Gets Slapped* proved to be a big moneymaker for the new young studio (it made an impressive profit of $349,000), and it helped set MGM on its feet. This was not yet the glamorous Dream Factory of the 1930s and '40s: Mayer biographer Scott Eyman notes that the offices were still "small, shabby and jury-rigged," and the lot was dubbed the Triangle Shirtwaist Factory, in honor of both the notorious sweatshop death trap and the old Triangle Studios. "Everything was piled on top of everything else," writes Eyman. "The portrait studio was three rooms on the third floor of the editing building, and could only be reached by [an] exterior iron staircase; even the grandest stars had to lug their own costumes up the stairs for sittings."

Jack's second Metro-Goldwyn-Mayer film (though his first to go into release) was the bodice-ripping romance *His Hour,* which began shooting in May 1924. Jack's sponsor for this film was the bizarre author Elinor Glyn, who arrived in a cloud of veils, perfume, and emeralds to exclaim, "Ah—behold the black stallion," much to Jack's embarrassment. *His Hour* was based on Glyn's 1910 novel about a heavy-breathing Russian nobleman who makes mad, passionate love to a sweet British woman. It was the sort of thing Glyn turned out in her sleep. She'd begun her career writing such smart, funny books as *The Visits of Elizabeth,* but soon discovered there was more money in unintentionally funny trash like *Three Weeks* (1907), her best seller about a mysterious, tragic noblewoman who seduces a young Englishman on a tiger-skin rug. Elinor Glyn novels were begging to be made into films, and many of them were, through the 1920s: *His Hour, Three Weeks, Beyond the Rocks, The Only Thing, Red Hair* and, most famously, *It,* which starred Clara Bow in her signature role.

But Elinor Glyn's most remarkable creation was Elinor Glyn. Sixty years old in 1924, she was as glamorous as any Hollywood starlet. With her red hair, ultra-fashionable clothes, and an air of three grand duchesses gone haywire, she both terrified and amused Hollywood. Glyn purportedly had casting approval on *His Hour* (the leading lady, Aileen Pringle, was a dead ringer for Glyn circa 1900), but it's just as likely the media-savvy author was told, "John Gilbert is going to be in your film, he's your 'black stallion.'"

After his first reaction ("This is trash!" he said of *His Hour*), Jack grew to like and appreciate Elinor Glyn. For all her aggressive weirdness, she was smart and insightful and "got the joke"—she was happy to play the part of Elinor Glyn as long as it increased book sales and movie attendance.

His Hour was directed by thirty-year-old King Vidor, a raffish, elfin man who would become one of Jack's closest friends—and who would direct him another four times, including in his career-changing favorite role. Vidor had entered films in 1913 and had worked as a producer, director, and screenwriter; his biggest hit so far had been the Irish romance *Peg o' My Heart,* for Metro, starring the Broadway version's lead, the troubled and brilliant Laurette Taylor. Vidor had one of Hollywood's longest directing careers, beginning and ending with documentaries: *Hurricane in Galveston* (1913) and *The Metaphor* (1980). His career eventually included such classics as *The Crowd, Show People, Stella Dallas,* and *Duel in the Sun,* and such stinkers as the risible *Beyond the Forest.*

Jack was right: *His Hour* was indeed trash. But it was beautifully gilded trash, already showing the lush MGM style. Gorgeous sets and costumes, talented cast, great camerawork. The film took place in czarist Russia, with Aileen Pringle playing a visiting British widow and Jack as Prince Grichko, "a wild young man . . . interested in three things: women, wine, and sport." The plot made no sense whatsoever, and the two leads had no chemistry; it was not their fault, as Aileen Pringle's character was chilly and disinterested from beginning to end, and Jack's Prince Grichko was little more than a stalker and a rapist.

This being an Elinor Glyn story, though, there was a lot of eroticism; two scenes in particular were red-hot. In one, Jack encounters Aileen Pringle feigning sleep in a train's upper berth; he flirtatiously brushes his moustache against her hand and lightly bites her. Later, the two are seen in an open carriage in the dead of winter: wrapped in voluminous fur coats, hats, and gloves, only their faces bare; they writhe and kiss and snuggle in a scene much sexier than half nudity. Jack got little opportunity to act in this film, but it was a star-making part: he looked impressive in his Russian military garb, he showed off his riding and dancing skills, and it was impossible to see anyone else while he was onscreen (though costars Carrie Clark Ward, as an old gossip, and handsome Bertram Grassby, as Grichko's friend, steal what scenes they can).

The *New York Times* found the film "not displeasing," adding, "John Gilbert, who indulges in lots of hand kissing as the Prince, is re-

On the set of *His Hour,* with (from left) director King Vidor, technical advisor Mike Mitchell, author Elinor Glyn, and costar Aileen Pringle, 1924 (The Everett Collection).

ally thoroughly capable in this part." At least one reviewer felt that *His Hour* effectively "glorified" Jack from a pleasant actor into a full-fledged star: Previously, wrote the unnamed critic, "we have seen Mr. Gilbert, but never has he made our heart beat one count the faster. Now, all that has changed! He is an eager lover, a fine dancer, a good rider, an intelligent actor and he has 'it'—that quality which Elinor Glyn makes a specialty of having in her heroes. Also, he wears the most alluring garb a costumer can find—the fitted basque and circular skirt effect of the Russian prince." Budgeted at $197,000, *His Hour* brought in a profit of $159,000 on its September 1924 release.

In early August 1924 Jack was happy to be cast as *The Snob*'s snob for director Monta Bell, produced by Harry Rapf. Early rushes of his romantic scenes with Norma Shearer in *He Who Gets Slapped* were so impressive that Shearer was cast as his leading lady in this film, too. Jack played the title role: a small-town college teacher, married to Shearer, too eager to advance socially. He cozies up to Conrad Nagel ("one of the

One of Jack's better MGM roles: *The Snob,* with Norma Shearer and Conrad Nagel, 1924 (author's collection).

Boston Appletons") and a local heiress (played by the always wonderful Phyllis Haver)—little suspecting that his now-dissatisfied wife is actually wealthy herself. The plot—from a popular novel—sounds awful, and the *New York Times* was not impressed with Bell's direction ("Mr. Bell drums home his ideas, when it would have been well for him to remember that Ernest Lubitsch is content to give only a few feet to a masterly stroke").

Movie Weekly reviewer Alma Talley did not think much of the movie or the role as written, but added, "All the more credit, then, to John Gilbert, who not only plays it, but is simply merciless in its interpretation. Every disagreeable curve of the lip, every fatuous gesture—Mr. Gilbert spares nothing in making the man a thorough-going cad. Never for a moment does he consider, 'My fans won't like me in this.' It is a marvelous performance." Another reviewer agreed that "Jack Gilbert carries off the acting honors in the title role. It is the finest piece of work he has done. There are original bits of characterization that are so refreshing that we have the feeling that Gilbert could be a success at whatever he lays his hand."

Jack talked happily about his role and what the *Los Angeles Times* called "a rare opportunity to demonstrate he is something more than a handsome leading man." "The stage doesn't have the same hard and fast rules of heroes never being unpleasant, or villains always being sinister," Jack said. "Why should we stick to these rules in pictures? I think the public would rather see an actor vary his screen character than forever witness the same personality. The character of the snob is the most interesting I have ever done. It is a complex personality—a psychological study of a selfish man who will do anything to advance himself. It is a portrait of a tremendous conceit. I'd rather play it and play it well than do a hundred typical roles."

The Snob opened in November 1924, right after the delayed *His Hour.* "The presence of Jack Gilbert in a picture is evidently good insurance nowadays for much joy and gladness in the vicinity of the box office," wrote the *Los Angeles Times,* calling it "a character study rather than a story. . . . Although it isn't a film that by the very nature of things would seem destined for an overwhelming popularity, there is just enough of comedy running through it to engage the casual entertainment seeker." Jack "does attain a cleverness in his characterization and a lightness that will make the boob eccentricities of *The Snob* thoroughly pleasurable. It is, indeed, a creditable attainment for him."

A month after the release—the film had done only middling well, bringing in a profit of $96,000—Jack told the *Times,* "A good many of my friends criticized my judgment in playing an unsympathetic character. To my mind it is the best of judgment, for a leading man has almost no opportunity to show the slightest versatility. I do not believe people who go to see pictures want always to have their heroes spotless, and their heroines chaste dumbbells. This part of *The Snob* provides a great opportunity for real characterization. He is likable in many ways for all his selfishness and conceit, and the character, with its changes of emotions and poses, gives a chance for real psychological study of a complex personality."

This was the first of Jack's three films with Monta Bell, and the two men hit it off immediately. They both had newspaper backgrounds—however brief and unprofitable—and both enjoyed batting around new twists and depths in the characters and plot lines of their projects. Bell, who had worked briefly as an actor, sympathized with Jack's temper and anxiety while trying to do his best. Bell was a great raconteur, and he was soon a member of Jack's band along with Paul Bern and occasionally Irving Thalberg—shy, but eager to be one of the boys. Bell also shared Jack's sense of humor: he had his dog trained, when told, "Do '*Hollywood,*'" to lie on its back and spread its legs.

As Jack's and Leatrice's careers continued to skate along, their marriage did not. After scoring in Cecil B. DeMille's melodrama *Manslaughter,* Joy had appeared in such hits as *The Ten Commandments* and *The Marriage Cheat,* and was nearly as big a draw for Paramount as Jack was for MGM. But in August 1924 she filed for separation from Jack through her lawyer, Edward Gray, charging "habitual intemperance." "Miss Joy asserted in her complaint that she had been unable to work for some time and was out of money, and that her husband had an engagement at $1500 a week. She asks alimony, counsel fees, costs and money to pay hospital bills of her impending confinement. Gilbert, she said, spent much of his income for liquor and insisted on having large quantities in the house at all times." The breaking point was a recent party at his house.

"The fault was ninety-nine and nine-tenths mine," Jack admitted. Years later, he elaborated to reporter Gladys Hall that their careers were to blame: "When Leatrice and I were married she would be working when I was between pictures. I'd be working and she would be idle. We were always conflicting like that. We never had any time together." And back to her mother's, suitcases in hand, went Leatrice.

In 1983 Leatrice Joy told historian William Drew about a previously unknown affair Jack had with theater great Laurette Taylor. She was in Los Angeles making three movies in the early 1920s, all of them for Metro and two directed by Jack's friend King Vidor. Taylor was thirteen years older than Jack—she turned forty in 1924—and she was married to writer J. Hartley Manners (who was hovering nearby, having written the screenplays for her three 1920s films). Nonetheless, said Leatrice Joy, the lovely, big-eyed Taylor "was the straw that broke the camel's back because when I left Jack, she said she was going to marry him."

Jack's drinking, his temper, their careers, faded into the background in hindsight, and by 1983 Joy felt that "with most divorces it's an aggressive woman because men don't leave their wives, honest to goodness they don't." Taylor, she said, was staying at Pickfair—Mary Pickford and Douglas Fairbanks Sr.'s cozy country home—and "Jack used to go out there every weekend. . . . Laurette would say, 'Come on, Jack darling. Remember you sit here, sweetheart, come on, Jack.' I didn't need an elephant to knock me down to know that something was going on." Fifty years later, Joy was still jealous of "this Laurette Taylor who was old enough to be his grandmother"—she caught herself and laughed to Drew, "I don't mean that. Why do I say that? She wasn't old."

Making the divorce all the more painful was the fact that Leatrice Joy was about to give birth to Jack's first child: Leatrice Gilbert was born at 10:40 a.m. on September 6, 1924, at the Good Samaritan Hospital in Los Angeles, with her mother's mother and Dr. Titian Coffey in attendance—the father was nowhere to be seen.

In these early days, Jack was still happy with his career and with his new studio. Writer Victor Heerman recalled coming by the set on a Sunday to pick up a script and finding John Gilbert wandering around the deserted studio. "What are you doing here? Don't you take Sundays off like the rest of us?" he asked. Jack told him, "I just can't stay away from this place, Victor. It's so great to be a part of anything like this. I just can't believe I'm really here." These upswings were few and far between, though, and would vanish entirely within a year or two.

"When we all began at MGM, after the big merger—Louis B. Mayer, Irving Thalberg, myself, all the others—we were friends," Jack later recalled. "We worked together during working hours. We played together after working hours. We were afire. We had tremendous things ahead of us. Then the tremendous things began to happen. We went, all of us, higher and higher and as we sky-rocketed, we drifted apart. We began to be too stupidly successful. Or I did. We were on the same lot but not akin."

Jack's final 1924 release was *The Wife of the Centaur,* a domestic drama costarring Eleanor Boardman, Aileen Pringle, and the rising young star-in-training William Haines. Based on a recent best seller by Cyril Hume, it was directed by *His Hour*'s King Vidor; Jack played a poet torn between a party-girl vamp (Pringle) and the sweet ingénue

(Boardman). (P.S. He ends up with Boardman.) Jack grew back his dashing moustache for the role, having shaved it off for *The Snob* and *He Who Gets Slapped.*

This was his first of three films with Eleanor Boardman, an odd figure of the silent era. A top star, a lovely and quietly talented actress, married to two leading directors (first King Vidor, and later Harry d'Arrast) and star of one of the era's most famous films (Vidor's *The Crowd,* 1928), she is virtually forgotten today. A successful model, she entered movies in 1922 and—like Jack—was signed by Metro in 1924. But her career ended in the early 1930s—not coincidentally, around the same time that her marriage to King Vidor also ended. Boardman lived into her nineties and gave many charming, amusing interviews about her friends and costars; she also spread, perhaps inadvertently, several questionable stories about John Gilbert.

Jack was excited about the chance to create the character of the fickle, shallow poet in *The Wife of the Centaur,* but he spent the whole production butting heads with Vidor. "I had retained my own ideas as to how certain emotions should be expressed," Jack admitted. "King won out, nine-tenths of the time, much against my will."

The results were mixed, though Jack himself came off well. One reviewer raved that Jack was "the kid himself. Jack with his sly eyes, his spoiled mouth, his Prince-of-Wales slouch. He's the sort who can break a girl's heart twenty times a day—and patch it up each time." The film itself—plot, titles, direction—came in for some harsh notices, though, the same reviewer chiding, "Jack—or *Jeff*—sees his lady of the moment in the swimming pool and jumps in after her with all his clothes on. That's the spirit of the picture. He's always doing things like that. He talks like that in his titles. He marries one girl when he wants another."

Another critic praised both Jack's performance and his director. "It is a keen character study of a charming pagan. Mr. Vidor has carefully kept him away from heavy emotional scenes; there are no fireworks, there is no heavy acting. And yet the conflict in the Centaur's nature is handled dramatically and effectively. It is by far the best thing that Mr. Gilbert has done." In a line that must have given Leatrice Joy a turn, the same paper called Jack's character in *The Wife of the Centaur* "one of those attractive men that no sane woman would ever dream of marrying." Budgeted at a modest $116,000, Centaur made a profit of $104,000.

Chapter Six

Sequence after sequence was good. . . . No love has ever enthralled me as did the making of this picture [*The Big Parade*].

—John Gilbert, 1928

While Jack may have been a prickly perfectionist, he was also social and likable, able to draw many friends into his circle. He was an enthusiastic partygoer and host, and he spent much time with directors: King Vidor, Clarence Brown, Jack Conway, Victor Fleming, Edmund Goulding. Jack's daughter Leatrice Fountain felt that he and King Vidor were what would today be termed "frenemies." Jack treated women like "queens and ladies," she said (though his four ex-wives may have disagreed, and divorce charges include some very ungentlemanly conduct). Vidor, said Fountain, "used them, was ruthless and went on to the next. He was jealous of John Gilbert and the way women went after him. I guess those two were sexual rivals."

He was also drawn to screenwriters: Douglas Doty, Frank Dazey, Carey Wilson, and a number of female writers, Anita Loos, Agnes Christine Johnston, Bess Meredyth—even Elinor Glyn became a friend. He was particularly close to actors Richard Barthelmess and Ronald Colman (who was a regular tennis partner) and the couples Cedric Gibbons (MGM's star scenic designer) and his wife, actress Dolores Del Rio, as well as the married stars Edmund Lowe and Lilyan Tashman.

Among his other friends were MGM's head of publicity, Howard Strickling, well known for sweet-talking the press and smoothing over scandals; and Edwin Schallert, movie critic for the *Los Angeles Times* for more than forty years (he was sympathetic and fair to Jack, but never coddled him or let him get away with a bad performance). He was also friendly with Gladys Hall, a writer just a few years older than Jack, who had been covering the movie industry since 1910. She wrote for numerous fan magazines through the years and had a column in the 1920s, "The Diary of a Professional Movie Fan." Jack had Hall's home phone number, and on more than one occasion called her up to invite her over for a scoop—usually to complain about his latest project or his bosses.

One of his closest female friends—to hear her tell it, anyway—was Adela Rogers St. Johns, the very model of the fan-mag sob sister. With prose as purple as a three-day bruise, St. Johns spent her very long life (she died in 1988, aged ninety-four) extolling her love/hate relationship with Hollywood. The daughter of notorious criminal-defense attorney Earl Rogers, she wrote for the *San Francisco Examiner, Cosmopolitan,* the *Saturday Evening Post,* and—most influentially—*Photoplay.* She also wrote a number of novels and several highly imaginative "nonfiction" works, and contributed to several screenplays (though none of Jack's). In countless interviews, St. Johns showed that she was a fascinating conversationalist who never let the truth get in the way of a good rousing story. She loved and hated hard, and fortunately for Jack, she loved him.

Jack, Paul Bern, Irving Thalberg, and Jack Conway also drew writer John Colton into their boys' club, which spoke volumes about them and about 1920s Hollywood—the scenarist (for Jack's *Man, Woman and Sin* and *The Cossacks* as well as the Broadway hits *Rain* and *The Shanghai Gesture*), Colton regaled his curious heterosexual friends with tales of gay nightclubs.

Often, Jack and Irving Thalberg would join Paul Bern and screenwriter Carey Wilson for boisterous Boys' Nights. Adela Rogers St. Johns—whose word should never be taken as gospel—Wilson's next-door neighbor, claimed that "they played records all night. I had three children and two shepherd dogs and no one of us could sleep." Poor Paul Bern was always falling for one actress or another—Joan Crawford, Barbara La Marr, Mabel Normand. Lovely, sexual girls who looked up to him as a father or older brother, but who had no interest in him romantically. Understandably, Bern was often in despair. "He has a Magdelene complex," a sympathetic Jack—who rarely had a woman say no to him—told Irving Thalberg. "Paul does crazy things for whores." One of St. Johns's most notorious tales was of Paul Bern's suicide attempt, purportedly over Barbara La Marr. According to St. Johns, Bern had begged La Marr to marry him. Turned down, "Paul had put his head in the toilet to drown himself," said St. Johns. "When it didn't work, he couldn't get out of the bowl. Thalberg took a screwdriver and got him out of the bowl. But the seat was still around Paul's neck." In addition to the sheer unlikelihood of this scenario, it doesn't even sound physically possible (though this writer's dedication to research goes only so far).

And Irving Thalberg—was he a friend? It's debatable if *anyone* was Irving Thalberg's "friend." For all his soft-spoken, courtly ways and big puppy-dog eyes, Irving Thalberg was Business First, as many unsuspecting employees (Jack included) would find to their shock. Certainly Jack was pals with Norma Shearer, and he frequently socialized with the Thalbergs after Norma and Irving married in 1927.

The nights Jack spent at home alone, he spent with books. Like Marilyn Monroe, another self-conscious, self-educated poor kid, Jack was a voracious reader of classics, poetry, history, biography, philosophy. He went Monroe one better by becoming an opera fan: "He scarcely ever missed the opera when he was really enjoying life," recalled Edwin Schallert, and Jack numbered singers Grace Moore and Helen Jepson among his friends. Writer Gene Markey told Jack's daughter Leatrice of talk-filled evenings at Jack's—talk of books, films, politics, art, love affairs. "Jack would put a glass of Scotch-and-soda on the mantelpiece of his long living room," Markey said. "His manservant would put another glass at the far end of the room, and Jack would stride between them, talking, warming up to his themes, sipping the liquor he liked best, on into the night."

Jack's first 1925 release was to be *The Merry Widow,* based on Franz Lehár's wildly popular operetta that had swept the world at the dawn of the century. The catchy, hummable melodies ("The Merry Widow Waltz" in particular) and the romantic plot made the play a sensation, and the *mittel*-European setting unleashed a decades-long plague of fey operettas. On stage and screen, uniformed princes and coy princesses trilled and mingled with gypsies and commoners: Nelson Eddy and Jeanette MacDonald were still at the old stand into the 1940s.

Jack in *The Merry Widow,* 1925 (The Everett Collection).

It had been filmed before, but none of the versions had really made an impression. Certainly translating a musical into silence posed problems: but if the title was popular enough and the plot and characters sufficiently interesting, many a musical comedy or operetta was snatched up for screen adaptations. Even musical numbers were filmed, accompanied by a piano or orchestra playing from studio-issued sheet music.

MGM's *Merry Widow* was in pre-production talks in October 1924;

Mae Murray—one of the few MGM stars who could really dance—was the only choice for the title role. Fan favorites for the male lead were Jack, Norman Kerry (remembered today as the handsome leading man of *The Phantom of the Opera*), Ronald Colman, and Allan Forrest (totally forgotten today, he was married to Mary Pickford's ill-fated sister Lottie and appeared in numerous 1920s films). "It has at times been quite a close race between Gilbert and Norman Kerry, though Gilbert's performances in *His Hour* and *The Snob* did all but establish him as the first choice," wrote the *Los Angeles Times*. Kerry was certainly pumped for the film and kissed every backside in sight: "I'd rather play the part . . . than anything else in the world," he said in the summer of 1924. "Von Stroheim, I think, is one of the greatest, if not the greatest, director in the entire picture industry. . . . His understanding of his work makes it a joy just to come in contact with him." Of Mae Murray, Kerry said, "One of the most beautiful women upon the screen, she will be the dazzling widow to perfection."

Despite all this apple polishing, Jack was selected over Norman Kerry for the part. And so MGM found itself with a major production on its hands featuring three of the most talented, troublesome, and emotionally unstable characters in Hollywood: John Gilbert, Mae Murray, and director Erich von Stroheim.

Mayer, by the way, was forced to use von Stroheim, or at least cajoled into doing so. His first choice for director had been the reliable Robert Z. Leonard, Mae Murray's husband. Leonard had shepherded his wife through many a film—but by late 1925 their marriage was on the rocks, and anyway Thalberg preferred the dangerous but talented von Stroheim. Mayer, though, was still smarting from *Greed*. That film is more famous today for its production dramas than for its inherent qualities as a movie.

Von Stroheim had started *Greed* at Goldwyn, and two agonizing years later he and the movie had landed at Metro. It was more than nine hours long, and it was grim and uncompromising—a scene-by-scene transcription of the Frank Norris book upon which it was based. Von Stroheim reluctantly cut it down to five hours; his friend, director Rex Ingram, cut about another hour; and then Thalberg had studio editors further cut it, to about two hours. To this day "the lost reels of *Greed*" are the holy grail of movie buffs. *The Merry Widow* would be von Stroheim's first film for MGM, and the studio knew it was in for a fight—but that von Stroheim's films were also brilliant, like hard-edged diamonds. Thalberg had already crossed swords with von Stroheim, but admired his work enough to take the chance.

Mae Murray, thirty-six at the time of *The Merry Widow,* had been a star since she'd entered films in 1916. She was a talented dancer, with several Broadway revues and the Ziegfeld *Follies* under her belt. She was also quite an odd duck, hard to classify: not a sex symbol, not a flapper, certainly not a dramatic star. Tiny (barely five feet tall, if that) with assisted blonde curls and a quirky heart-shaped face, she was one of those actresses capable of giving marvelous performances when she had a strict director at the helm (George Fitzmaurice had elicited some of her best-reviewed work). But too often she was directed by her husband, who let her get away with murder: posing, pouting, and Mae Murraying all over the place (some color footage of her shot in 1922 has recently been made public—it shows her at her loveliest and most affected). Von Stroheim would certainly whip a good performance out of Mae Murray, but the process would not be pretty.

Jack's memory was that Irving Thalberg wanted him for *The Merry Widow,* but von Stroheim still hoped for Norman Kerry. "I am forced to use you in my picture," Jack claims the director told him. "I do not want you, but the decision was not in my hands. I assure you that I will do everything in my power to make you comfortable." Things started out chilly but professional, everyone on good behavior. By the third week, said Jack, a fifteen-minute screaming battle on the set had him stalking off to his dressing room. Von Stroheim followed and apologized, and "that disagreement cemented a relationship which for my part will never end. Von Stroheim is not only one of my dearest friends, but he retains my admiration and respect for being the greatest director we have and the greatest expressionist in motion pictures."

Jack, of course, fell in love with Mae Murray, at least to hear her tell it. He sent her roses and a note reading, "I will have no trouble giving my best. I will adore you. Jack." The roses continued to arrive, and the notes got more passionate: "Let me fall in love with you! Then I will no longer be—Bad Boy Jack." Mae Murray, of course, was a shameless tale-teller, but this does sound exactly like Jack's usual routine—fall madly in love with the leading lady and play it to the hilt.

"He had a spark toward me in the beginning," she recalled, "but we worked that out, because I said, 'Jack, put whatever emotion you have to me in the picture. I'm your buddy.' John was so insulted by that man [von Stroheim], and he just couldn't take it—he didn't have what I have, I *fight*. . . . He was *super*-sensitive."

Murray, in a 1934 interview, recalled some of those battles: "Von Stroheim yelled at Jack. It wasn't just an ordinary call-down, either—a little unnecessary, I think. Jack suddenly disappeared from the set. Very quietly. And for hours we searched for him. And where do you suppose he was discovered? Upstairs in his dressing-room—in the clothes closet, sitting in a melancholy huddle on the floor."

In her 1959 memoirs, Murray concocted one of Hollywood's most delirious legends about another incident. The book—ghosted by veteran writer Jane Ardmore—was written in the third person, which made it even odder. She recalled Jack stalking out after an on-set blowup. Told in her dressing room that Jack had "left for South America," third-person Mae "ran out of the dressing room, off the set, down the street out across Washington Boulevard, in her diamond buckled shoes and paradise topknot, not knowing she was naked, faster than she'd ever run in her life. . . . 'Jack!' she screamed, rushing up to him, throwing herself on him. 'Come back, please come back.' . . . 'What the hell's going on here,' yelled a policeman. 'Lady, look here, you can't run around this way.'"

Now, Mae Murray lived in a little pink bubble all her life, reality rarely intruding. But even ignoring her penchant for fanciful tales, this scenario is hugely unlikely. Even if she had forgotten that she was stark naked, it's hard to imagine a major star making it down the outdoor dressing-room steps, all the way across the MGM lot, out the guard-patrolled front gates, and down Washington Boulevard without being stopped by someone (or at least being photographed by a lucky tourist).

In her earlier, 1934, version of this tale, Mae had said, "And another time, when everything seemed to go wrong, when after many petty arguments over the famous waltz routine . . . [he] disappeared again. I don't blame him. One of the stage carpenters yelled that Gilbert had ducked out a side door and was running down Washington Boulevard. I was in my costume. But I rushed out of the place, ran breathlessly down the street yelling for Jack to come back. He had thrown his bath-robe over his Prince's costume and was on his way—to China—when he was caught and talked into coming back." No nudity, just breathless and "in my costume." The clothes came off much later, to help sell her memoirs.

For all her wackiness, Mae Murray gave reporter Virginia Maxwell a perceptive view of Jack in 1934: "Jack is terribly sensitive," she said. "He is easily hurt. But instead of lashing back like most of us do when we are hurt, he goes in for bravado—some gesture which is merely an emotional outlet. That's why his troubles are always headlined, I think. It's the reason he seems to be in difficulties constantly."

But it was Mae Murray and von Stroheim who caused the most fireworks—Jack was, comparatively speaking, a model of professionalism and even temper. Mae Murray wanted, of course, a Mae Murray film: lovely and sparkly and gay and full of flattering close-ups of Mae Murray being adorable. Von Stroheim wanted a von Stroheim film: a dark indictment of the moneyed upper classes full of orgies, sexual fetishes, and hideously deformed characters. It's amazing the movie got made at all. Some of von Stroheim's reputed sadism is visible; when Prince Danilo spills a bowl of hot soup on Sally O'Hara in order to get her out of her dress, one can clearly see that the soup Jack pours over Mae Murray's lap is indeed steaming hot, and she reacts accordingly.

"Each day's work was a duel of wills," Mae Murray recalled in her memoirs. "It was a strange world, the domain of von Stroheim." She was horrified by what she saw in the daily rushes: "the most lurid scenes: degenerate parties, orgies . . . royal women with hair on their faces and chin supporters. . . . Kissing people's bottoms and kissing feet, the old man behaving obscenely with a closet full of shoes!" She recalled him storming at her on the set, "You are a self-conscious and mannered actress. I yell at you, I hammer until we knock away all that conceals your real capacity for feeling. We want no cutey-cute mouth, Miss Murray." Which is—whether she realized it or not—exactly what she needed; von Stroheim did indeed get one of her better performances out of her.

It all came to a head toward the end of the production with the famous waltz scene, which was a highlight of the original operetta: Prince Danilo and the widow meet at a ball, now torn between their former love for each other and their hurt feelings and jealousies. As the crowd parts, Danilo takes the widow from his rival, Crown Prince Mirko. For Mae Murray, a dancer, this was to be the high point of the film—of course, von Stroheim wanted no part of it. Forced to include the scene,

The scene that caused all the trouble: Jack waltzing with Mae Murray in *The Merry Widow*, 1925 (author's collection).

he wanted to downplay the dance and concentrate on the set and character details he so loved.

The huge ballroom set was crowded with extras (including twenty-four-year-old Clark Gable and, reportedly, Jack's father, John Pringle, who was reduced to extra work). Murray recalled in her memoirs that Jack tripped on the first take, and von Stroheim had yelled, "Louse-y, just as I knew it would be. The show girl and the rank amateur." She then—by her own account—attacked him screaming, "Hun! You dirty hun!" (odd language from a woman whose real name was Koenig).

Historian Kevin Brownlow tells a somewhat more likely version, obtained from Don Ryan, who had a small role in the film. Murray had wanted all action focused on her and her partner, extras standing aside. "This is not a Mae Murray Production," von Stroheim objected. "You don't have to have a pathway to the star. Act like human beings." Acting like a human being was the last thing Mae Murray wanted to do, so von Stroheim told cameraman Oliver Marsh to shoot it and walked off the set. He called Harry Rapf in New York and quit—much to Rapf's delight, as that shut von Stroheim out of his share of the profits.

Monta Bell was brought in to direct the waltz scene, but then the unexpected happened: the extras rebelled. "We want von Stroheim!" they chanted, which must have been awfully hard on poor Monta Bell. "They were taking their jobs in their hands and hurling them right in Mayer's face," Ryan told Brownlow. "They were carried away by emotion, true enough. They knew it was a hundred-to-one shot they would never work again in any movie studio in Los Angeles." Production halted, the extras sent emissaries to Mayer pleading for the reinstatement of von Stroheim—and, amazingly, MGM buckled. Mae Murray, Erich von Stroheim, and Louis B. Mayer had it out, and the scene was shot to everyone's grudging satisfaction.

Astonishingly, the shoot lasted only fourteen weeks. Thalberg refused to let von Stroheim edit it, and von Stroheim angrily walked out—again—on MGM. When the film was released in September 1925, he skipped the première, but later snuck into a theater where it was playing: "They applauded. They laughed and thought it was great," he said. "But I'm shrinking in my seat because I'm ashamed."

The Merry Widow became a huge hit (costing $592,000, it brought in profits of $758,000), enough so that in 1927 one Prince Danilo of

Montenegro decided to cash in and file a lawsuit, claiming the film libeled him: "I am unspeakably pained to see myself travestied by a cheap cinema star," he huffed. "The film constitutes a serious libel on myself, my family . . . and on my late lamented country, Montenegro." Von Stroheim wrote a scathing letter to the prince's lawyers: "We can only reply that these charges are so silly and asinine that the only real answer to these charges should be a laugh and a wink with the eye." Refuting the comparisons between real life and the movie point by point, von Stroheim also noted that if the film version of the prince were insulting, "The peoples from all over the world would not have acclaimed Jack Gilbert as the most beloved actor on account of the part of Prince Danilo which he portrayed so masterly." Nonetheless, the prince cashed in to the tune of $4,000 (when MGM remade the film in 1934, they demoted Danilo to captain and changed the country's name to Marshovia).

The Merry Widow, happily, exists in a lovely restored version, with musical score, and one can see every cent of that $592,000 onscreen. In this film version of the operetta, Mae Murray portrays dancer Sally O'Hara, "of the *Manhattan Follies,*" on tour in the not-mythical-enough country of Castellano, "capital of the kingdom of Monteblanco—embraced eternally by the encircling White Mountains." She is pursued by the country's three leading citizens: creepy foot-fetishist millionaire Baron Sadoja (Tully Marshall), creepy death's-head grinning Crown Prince Mirko (Roy D'Arcy, in a role von Stroheim himself considered playing), and dashing, non-creepy second in line to the throne Crown Prince Danilo (Jack).

The Merry Widow is a long film: it was even longer as von Stroheim finished it, and although his version was cut down by MGM, it still ran well over two hours on release. Two long hours: von Stroheim lingered over set pieces and character vignettes to the point where the plot dragged. Some of these vignettes were marvelous, though, such as the three men focusing their opera glasses on Sally O'Hara's *Follies* dance according to their interests: Sadoja on her feet, Mirko on her crotch, Danilo on her face.

For all his obsessions and tantrums, though, von Stroheim really was an actor's director (being an actor himself), and much footage was given over to lingering close and medium shots of the two leads exhibiting sadness, fear, fury, and generally showing off their considerable talents (the overacting was handled by Roy D'Arcy, whose comic-strip villain all but twirled his moustache and tied Mae Murray to the train tracks).

Richard Watts Jr. wrote in the *New York Herald Tribune* that "John Gilbert has never before done anything to compare. . . . Here at last is the role of a romantic hero played with grace, charm, and humor, rather than the customary insipid heroics. Here at last is a screen lover you can watch without the danger of becoming seasick." Another critic called Jack "the most promising star since Valentino," adding that "elderly ladies will not like him and very young girls won't, but for that vast majority in between I predict he will be the *raison d'etre* for the Better Movie Season."

The Merry Widow opened in early September 1925. "There is just one bright spot in Broadway's film world this week, and that is the little Embassy Theater, where *The Merry Widow* is playing," wrote Helen Klumpe in the *Los Angeles Times*. "It is the most glorious entertainment that has come to our screens in a long time. *The Merry Widow* is a masterpiece of direction and it is a triumph for John Gilbert and Mae Murray. If her work in this picture is the result of quarreling with her director, as has been said, then she ought always to work with a director who disagrees with her. Every characteristic fault has been removed from her acting, and a charmingly sincere and natural performance is the result. As for John Gilbert . . . he seems much more than a handsome, ingratiating young man: he is a skilled, adroit actor, whose methods are occasionally reminiscent of von Stroheim. Not that I think his performance is in any way modeled after von Stroheim's. It merely seems that von Stroheim brought out the best in him."

In the beginning of May 1925 Jack bought what would be his last home, on a winding hilltop road in the Beverly Estates subdivision. The home was situated on three and a half acres at 1400 Tower Grove Drive. (The house is long gone, sadly. After Jack's death, actress Miriam Hopkins lived there, then David O. Selznick and Jennifer Jones, who completely gutted and remodeled it into an airy, paneled suburban bungalow. It was demolished and replaced by the 1990s seven-bedroom home that stands there today.) Jack's house was quite small compared with today's suburban McMansions but, like many movie-star houses from the 1920s on, it was as much a set as a home. These were the homes of people who found themselves swimming in money, often after a lifetime of scrimping. Told by their studios to live like stars, they did so with gusto, often with a delightfully naïve lack of taste, and their homes—pointed out on bus tours—made a statement about how they wanted to be perceived by their fans and their coworkers alike.

There was the English country-house charm of Mary Pickford and Douglas Fairbanks's Pickfair in Beverly Hills; Jean Harlow's white-marble colonial in Holmby Hills; the farmhouse getaways of Clark Gable and Carole Lombard, and Joel McCrea and Frances Dee. Ramon Novarro and art director Cedric Gibbons (along with his wife, Dolores Del Rio) went for stark art moderne mansions, Novarro's designed by Lloyd Wright (the more famous Frank's son). Darryl Zanuck's, William Holden's, and Lana Turner's homes were almost quaint suburban cottages. Rudy Vallee's unremarkable home on Sunset Boulevard was remodeled by Jayne Mansfield and Mickey Hargitay in the 1950s into the deliciously vulgar Pink Palace, the apotheosis of the movie-star mansion.

Jack's Tower Grove Drive home was Spanish style, in white stucco with rounded archways and tile roof—typical for Southern California. The interior looked like a set from *Monte Cristo:* timber beams, big, dark furniture, a large ballroom, and a "man cave" living room with fireplace (indeed, his huge canopied bed, with heavy brocade draperies, had been bought from the *Monte Cristo* set). He lavished great love and care on his home: red-tiled floors, stained-glass windows, Oriental rugs, his collection of books and records (the records could be heard all over the house and even outside, thanks to his state-of-the-art speaker system). There was an airy, wicker-furnished sun room, a backyard swimming pool and tennis court, and a breathtaking view over Los Angeles all the way to the ocean and Catalina. He regularly had his friend Harold Grieve (set designer for such films as *Ben-Hur* and *The Thief of Bagdad*) redesign rooms, often for a new wife or live-in lover. Daughter Leatrice remembered a bookshelf with a secret stairway leading to a basement bar.

"I've a lovely place way up high, oh, miles high and a way, way back up in the Beverly Hills," he told Mona Gardner of the *Los Angeles Times*. "One of those places where you can see everything and yet there isn't a sound to disturb. By Jove, when you get up there and look around you get so many feelings, just all tumbling over each other until I don't see how a person can help expressing some of them."

The hilltop home where Jack lived from 1926 till his death (Wisconsin Center for Film & Theater Research).

The Spanish look was (and is) ubiquitous in Southern California: W. C. Fields, Thomas Ince, cowboy star Tom Mix, Leslie Howard, Paul Muni, Colleen Moore, Wallace Beery—all had stucco, red-tiled homes with arches and dark, beamed ceilings. Coincidentally, Rudolph Valentino was moving into his hilltop mansion in Beverly Hills, dubbed Falcon Lair (Jack never named his house) at exactly the same time, in 1925. Falcon Lair was a slightly larger and more spread-out version of Jack's house: Spanish tiled roof, wrought iron details, stuffed with antiques bought on European travels and pilfered from movie sets. He had horse stables and a huge painting of himself in his *Blood and Sand* costume. Valentino's house, like Jack's, was off in the hills, secluded and difficult for guests and fans alike to find. He didn't live in it long—Valentino died a year after moving in. Falcon Lair, like John Gilbert's Tower Grove Drive house, is gone, having been bulldozed in 2006.

One of Jack's closest neighbors was King Vidor, who also lived on Tower Grove Drive (in yet another Spanish-style house). Vidor's house was just below Jack's on the hill, and Jack bragged that he could throw

Jack spent too much time brooding in his living room (Wisconsin Center for Film & Theater Research).

dead bottles "and other tributes" onto his neighbor's roof. "We were the first residents to venture so far up into the hills, and we felt like pioneers," said Vidor. In 1927, a year after his marriage to Eleanor Boardman, Vidor sold the house to John Barrymore, who over the years expanded it with an aviary, guest houses, patios, and pergolas, making Jack's home next door look modest in comparison. Barrymore, like Jack, loved the hilltop view of Los Angeles: "I may have to paint my face for a living," he said, "but isn't it wonderful I can look down on the place where I have to do it."

On May 28, 1925, Jack's divorce from Leatrice Joy became final; the *Los Angeles Times* cited "a drunken debauch asserted to have been staged by her husband and a number of his friends" as one of the causes. Leatrice showed up at court "visibly nervous . . . simply clad and without the trace of makeup about her." She said that on August 9, 1924, "Gilbert informed her that he was going on a party, and that she could either go with him or stay home alone. It was just one month prior to the birth of her baby and she didn't care to do either one. She went to her mother's home for the night." Judge Summerfield asked her if it was possible they might reconcile, and she said, "No. The love I had for him is dead, quite dead." She received $15,000 and $50 a week child support.

In late 1924 director King Vidor had told Irving Thalberg that he wanted to do a big important film, "about any one of three subjects: steel, wheat, or war." Thalberg wisely chose war, and the result was *The Big Parade*. War films had never really experienced a lull—Hollywood cranked them out before the United States entered the Great War (both pro and con), and of course during the war itself. Through the early 1920s, a slow but steady trickle of war films continued to be released, although many in the audience were sick to death of it. *The Four Horsemen of the Apocalypse*, which provided Rudolph Valentino with his first great role, was the best of them.

Vidor, who had not yet directed a really big hit, "wanted it to be the story of a young American who was neither over-patriotic nor a pacifist, but who went to war and reacted normally to all the things that happened to him." Irving Thalberg brought playwright (and war veteran) Laurence Stallings west from New York to write a treatment, which infuriated executives at Fox: they had purchased film rights to Stallings's *What Price Glory?* which was currently running on Broadway (Fox's version would be released late in 1926). They contemplated a lawsuit, but the storyline itself was so generic (young boy becomes a man at war) that one writer pointed out that *The Big Parade* was closer in plot to Charlie Chaplin's 1918 comedy *Shoulder Arms* than it was to *What Price Glory?*

Vidor recalled in his memoirs that he accompanied Stallings by train back to New York, where he felt he could get more writing done. Kept awake in his lower berth by Stallings's horrifying war stories, Vidor told himself, "This is all too fantastic and unreal. It never happened." One night Stallings's wooden leg—hanging outside his berth on a hook—swung with the motion of the train and caught Vidor "hard in the chin. . . . I could never again say to myself that the horrors of war didn't happen; I accepted the facts." He also resolved to have his hero similarly lose a leg.

King Vidor initially did not want Jack for *The Big Parade*. He thought he was the wrong type—too sophisticated—and remembered with dismay the fights they'd had on the set of *The Wife of the Centaur.* But Thalberg insisted, and Jack was cast in what began as a run-of-the-mill six-reel war picture. Jack had to shave off his *Merry Widow* moustache for his role as a callow midwestern boy; he also went without any screen makeup. Vidor recalled that Jack refused to read ahead in the script, taking it day by day: "He wanted to be ready to do the scene as the director required and he didn't want his mind to be cluttered up with a mass of preconceived ideas. . . . It made good sense and it worked."

Shooting on *The Big Parade* was humming along better than anyone had hoped—for once, even Jack had no complaints. "Sequence after sequence was good. We knew it," he recalled in 1928. "There was no doubt in our minds, nor any display of ego. We simply knew we were photographing honest action. . . . As I was adjusting my gas mask, King approached, his hand outstretched. Through a grin, he uttered prophetic words, the ultimate inspiration for movie makers, 'Grauman's Egyptian, baby.'" Thalberg and exhibitor J. J. McCarthy saw a preliminary rough cut of the film and recognized that this was worth putting even more time and money into. "Thalberg was the first to sense an underlying greatness in our story," said Jack, "which imbued Vidor and the rest of us with knowledge of our responsibility."

Vidor's direction, he later told the *Los Angeles Times,* amounted to telepathy. The much-loved scene where Jack introduces French farm girl Renée Adorée to chewing gum (she chews and, unimpressed, swallows it, to Jack's chagrin) was largely improvised, according to him. "Renee Adoree . . . never knew that she was even going to chew gum when we sat down together. . . . I had the gum, and as we looked at each other I pulled it out and gave her some. She didn't think beforehand of swallowing it, but we discovered afterward that she was expected to do so by Vidor. There is something like an electrical current running between that director's mind and the players . . . he inspired us to do that which he wanted."

Like many performers, Jack sometimes enjoyed mood music on set: during *The Big Parade,* said Vidor, Jack liked to hear the romantic pop tune "Moonlight and Roses" (presumably during the love scenes and not during battle).

The Big Parade remains one of Jack's best movies, and best performances, as well as probably the best silent film about the Great War.

Jack teaching Renée Adorée to chew gum, *The Big Parade,* 1925 (The Everett Collection).

Jack played Jim Apperson, a spoiled young mill owner's son who, carried away by patriotic excitement, impulsively enlists in 1917. He ships off to France, where he befriends a bartender (Tom O'Brien) and a steelworker (a wildly overacting Karl Dane) and falls in love with a farm girl (Renée Adorée)—it's a coming-of-age tale, as most war stories are. The first half is a buddy and love movie, with nice touches of light comedy (or not so light, in Dane's case); the second half includes some harrowing battle scenes.

Jack convincingly plays a naïve twenty-something, and his love scenes with Adorée are worlds apart from his later heavy-breathing make-out sessions with Greta Garbo. He and Adorée are unaffected, tentative, and very sexy. While the scene where Jack introduces Adorée to chewing gum is more famous, another moment—when he admits to her he has a sweetheart back home—is a brilliant bit of silent-movie acting. No hysterics or melodrama, just quiet heartbreak. His comic scenes show the kind of timing and facial expression that he did not get a chance to use often enough (one bit, where he tries to convey a barrel

Jack's greatest role: as James Apperson in *The Big Parade,* 1925 (The Everett Collection).

back to camp by wearing it over his head, was worthy of Buster Keaton or Harold Lloyd).

The film takes a darker turn in its second half as the troops go to the front: the battle scene builds slowly from a tense advance through the woods (and we gradually notice they are stepping over bodies). Snipers cut down the soldiers one by one, and it all builds to full-scale warfare, with bombs, gas, grenades, machine guns, mass slaughter on both sides. One scene that made an impression on Jack had his character, shot through the leg, in a shell hole with a dying German soldier. It's similar to the "enemies in a shell hole" scene in *All Quiet on the Western Front,* but is darker and more bitter: there is no "We're all really brothers" epiphany. As the German lies dying, Jack gives him a cigarette but also angrily pushes his face away from him again and again, obviously muttering obscenities. Vidor later said the scene was largely improvised: "I didn't have a big voice, I might say, 'more,' 'now,' 'that's wonderful,' 'that's great.' . . . I wouldn't talk all the time and I'd get silent as quickly as possible. It was hypnotism."

Jack loved doing these "guy scenes," as he found his Great Lover tag a little embarrassing. He also enjoyed being deglamourized. In a hospital scene, flies hover around his face. When his mother (Claire McDowell, in a terrific performance) first sees him with his left leg gone, it's shocking both to her and to audiences, not used to seeing their dashing movie heroes crippled.

The Big Parade, sadly, resulted in the first death on the MGM lot: electrician Carl Barlow was killed when a Cooper-Hewitt bank light broke away from its cast-iron support, crushing him and seriously injuring fellow worker Cecil Hart. If MGM was ever able to hush up such accidents, as was later claimed, this was not one of those times; the death was widely reported in the press, giving the film some unwanted advance publicity.

The Big Parade opened in Los Angeles on November 5, 1925. Jack was unattached at the time, and ex-wife Leatrice Joy agreed to accompany him to the première, of course igniting remarriage rumors. Joy later told Jack he had ripped two handkerchiefs to shreds during the movie. Other viewers must have as well—the war, remember, had ended only seven years ago, and the veterans in the audience were still young men (and the widows and nurses young women). This was not yet nostalgia; it was a harrowing look back at the day before yesterday.

Jack later said of his character, "He was real and honest. There was no flamboyant, unnatural heroics about that boy. He was what he was, like all of us." Vidor himself felt that "it proved successful not because it was a war drama, or because there were big scenes, but because the audience saw the reactions of an every-day young American and an every-day girl, just human folks, under certain circumstances."

Working with King Vidor on *The Big Parade* prodded awake Jack's desire to direct, which had been pretty much killed off by Hope Hampton. He was full of ideas and ambitions that summer of 1925: "I would rather direct than eat, write, paint or compose. I have long desired to direct and now I have discovered why my desire is so strong for this work. I think I have absolute proof of what the director of the future will be. . . . We have today about one, two, or three directors who have passed the point of merely directing and really become screen authors. King Vidor writes his stories on the screen: not *for* the screen, mind you. He doesn't attempt to put words to use in telling the story, but, on the contrary, develops a physical manifestation or a mood."

"No love has ever enthralled me as did the making of this picture," Jack later said. "No achievement will ever excite me so much. It was the high point of my career. All that has followed is balderdash." Unusually for him, he was pleased with the film as a whole; there was a bad moment when the studio wanted to shoot an alternate happy ending in which Jack's character comes home whole and uninjured. But the heartbreaking ending we see today—he loses a leg, his mother embraces him tearfully, remembering him as a child—was the only one filmed. "We never made it," Jack said gratefully, "because the overhead was running up into the hundred thousands—had been ever since we decided to make a 'special' out of an ordinary program picture—and our first hurried previews showed us that the great American public didn't want it! Jim Apperson, we found, could stand against the world on one leg."

The Big Parade was not only the height of Jack's artistic career—by his valuation, anyway—it made more money than any of his films. It was theatrically rereleased several times over the years (later with sound effects and music added), and of course was later available on video. It made more money for MGM than any other film until *Mrs. Miniver,* released in 1942 (*The Big Parade* cost $382,000 and made a profit of $3.5 million).

Release of *The Merry Widow* and *The Big Parade* established John Gilbert as one of the biggest male stars in Hollywood, neck and neck with Rudolph Valentino and Douglas Fairbanks. In early June, just as his divorce from Leatrice Joy became final and he was glowing with the excitement of just having finished shooting *The Big Parade,* he gave a revealing and heartfelt interview to Mona Gardner of the *Los Angeles Times.* "I don't want to be labeled 'star,'" Jack claimed. "It doesn't mean a thing, except maybe as a guarantee that you flop twice as hard as you otherwise would. You know, you can't cram a person down an exhibitor's throat, or down the public's either. No producer can simply tack that onto an actor's name and then expect that everyone is going to accept it without batting an eye."

He saw the danger of carrying a whole production on his shoulders, which sometimes happened when a studio over-relied on a star to bring fans to the theater regardless of the vehicle or director. "If the story is good and the cast is good, it makes the work of everyone stand out that much more," Jack recognized. "But if they put a lot of second-rate people in support of one high-priced star, it won't be long before Mr. Exhibitor is going to say, 'Damn this John Gilbert, damn all stars.' But what can a person do about it? It seems they're dead set on starring several people out here and for some reason or other they picked on me."

He tried to be philosophical, or at least give that impression: "If I do make an awful flop, I won't be so very surprised. . . . It will shorten my time upon the screen by one and a half to two years. But then, I don't care. I'll be making a lot of money in the meantime and just think what I can do with it!" But in reality, Jack was having too grand a time being a Great Big Movie Star. In fact, he seems to have given up his ambition of screenwriting. "I don't seem to be able to write anymore," he told Gardner. "Somehow nothing seems to come. You know that feeling, when thoughts are just coursing through your mind, turning circles and somersaults and just bustin' to get out. Well, you know then it's never work to write, everything just comes to you so easily that you can hardly write it down fast enough. That's the way I used to feel, but now I have to work and labor over each sentence and before I get anywhere I'm disgusted and pitch it to one side.

"During this last picture, *The Big Parade,* they tell me I have done better work than I ever have done before. I don't know, but if I have, it has been because of these things. I go to bed at a certain set hour every night. I allow nothing to interfere with that, friends' dinner parties or the like. I have thought nothing, lived nothing, but that picture. Go to bed at 9 or 10 o'clock and then up early in the morning with the mind as clean as a whistle—that is, as clear as this mind of mine *can* be." Jack even rationalized his divorce in terms of his career: "Married men can't do those things. There's always the family to be thought of, and their pleasures, and the minute a person dabbles a little in both, both are going to be neglected and jealous, the wife of the work, while the work suffers because of attention to the wife."

The *Los Angeles Times* recognized what an amazing year Jack had had: "'Lucky Break' has become John Gilbert's middle name. No male star—nor feminine star, for that matter—has ever been given such a succession of 'plums' as has Gilbert in the past year. . . . To the envious, it might be whispered that such 'luck' is the culmination of years of hard labor, of obscurity, of unrealized worth." Indeed, John Gilbert ranked as one of MGM's top four money-making stars of 1925, the others being Marion Davies, Ramon Novarro, and Norma Shearer.

Winding down from the high of *The Big Parade,* Jack participated in the Silly Season in Hollywood—all stars were expected to take part in public ceremonies, to show themselves to the fans and be photographed for the fan magazines. It went along with being a star, and Jack agreeably dove in. On July 31, 1925, the Greater Movie Season Parade snaked through town, from Sunset Boulevard through Broadway Place to Main Street, then west on Adams to Vermont. Floats and cars and veterans' bands and a huge turnout of stars, either happy to get the day off from work or annoyed at having to make monkeys of themselves on the studios' orders: Jack took part, along with the Costello and Talmadge sisters, Irving Thalberg, Jack's past and future costars Renée Adorée, Eleanor Boardman, Joan Crawford (still billed as Lucille Le Sueur), and Norma Shearer as well as Charles Farrell, Ramon Novarro, Marion Davies, William Haines, Harry Langdon, the teenaged Douglas Fairbanks Jr., his father, Doug Sr., and his stepmother, Mary Pickford, Buster Keaton, and head movie censor Will Hays.

The studios also held golf tournaments that summer: MGM vs. Paramount (Jack was soundly thrashed by Paramount's head, Jesse Lasky, though MGM came out ahead overall). And by October 1925, he and Leatrice Joy were amiably socializing again. She was having a big success with *Made for Love,* and Jack for the first time met his baby daughter.

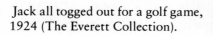

Jack all togged out for a golf game, 1924 (The Everett Collection).

Early in 1925 Lillian Gish signed a two-year, six-picture contract with MGM. The twenty-nine-year-old Gish had been a movie star for more than ten years—impressive, in so young an industry. She'd served her apprenticeship as a brilliant dramatic actress under D. W. Griffith in such films as *The Birth of a Nation, Broken Blossoms, Way Down East,* and *Orphans of the Storm.* She had recently had successes with *The White Sister* and *Romola,* and now Irving Thalberg wanted her at MGM.

Her first film under her new contract was to be *La Bohème,* based on an episode in Henri Murger's delightful 1851 book *Scènes de la vie de Bohème.* It was the inspiration for Puccini's 1896 opera *La Bohème* (and, much later, for Jonathan Larson's Broadway musical *Rent*). Murger's original book is well worth picking up; it's not just the story of poor consumptive Mimi and her unreliable lover. The chapters rove over the whole band of brawling, eccentric artists and their lovers, friends, and enemies, and many of the stories are hilarious (one, of poor little seamstress Francine and her fur muff, is just as sad as Mimi's tale).

Thalberg showed Gish a rough cut of *The Big Parade* as an audition for director King Vidor: "I asked Irving for its director and entire cast," she recalled, and thus Jack was signed to play the love-struck Bohemian Rodolphe (Renée Adorée, costar of *The Big Parade,* was reduced to a small supporting role in this Gish vehicle). If John Gilbert was a world-class perfectionist and complainer, he met his match in Lillian Gish. According to her own memoirs, she didn't like anything about MGM's methods or *La Bohème*'s production. From August through November 1925, Lillian Gish threw her weight around and tried to remake MGM in the old stage-trained D. W. Griffith mold.

She hated the lack of rehearsal and the use of mood music on the set, but sighed, "I could not impose my kind of rehearsal on the others, nor could I object when they wanted music for their scenes. I had never had music before, and I simply had to close my ears and continue working. The music was fine," Gish allowed, "when I wasn't trying to concentrate on a scene." She hated the costumes created by famed designer and illustrator Erté: "I found that all the costumes looked like brand-new dresses. I explained that Mimi was being put out of her attic because she could not pay her rent." Erté argued that he used only cheap calico, but Gish said they still looked too nice, and she designed her own with old worn silk. Gish and Erté both lived into their late nineties, and neither of them ever quite got over their spat.

The huge, expensive MGM sets also worried Gish. She rightfully balked at her attic dwelling, which looked like the mansion-sized apartments on many TV sitcoms. "'These are poor Bohemians,' I protested. 'They can't live in a big, beautiful house.' 'How are we to get exhibitors to pay big prices for your pictures if they don't see productions values?' the front office demanded." They finally settled on airplane-hangar-sized garrets with suitable mood lighting and shabbiness built in. "I couldn't accustom myself to their strange set of values," sighed Gish, as though she had not been in show business her entire life. With King Vidor in charge, shooting proceeded on schedule, even with Gish's roadblocks.

And, of course, Jack was rumored to have fallen in love with his leading lady. Indeed, Gish's secretary, Phyllis Moir, recalled that "both King Vidor and John Gilbert fell in love with Lillian. . . . [Jack] started writing her love letters and quarreling with King Vidor." Gish later claimed that Jack proposed to her, and Marion Davies wrote that Jack cornered Gish in her dressing room, violets in hand.

Gish was determined to keep herself sexless both onscreen and off. Despite rumors of her involvement with D. W. Griffith, drama critic and magazine editor George Jean Nathan, her business manager, Charles Holland Duell, and her lifelong friend photographer Nell Dorr, Lillian Gish never married and was never seriously linked to anyone romantically. She extended this to her screen persona: Gish was lovely, in a Watteau watercolor kind of way. She never bobbed her hair, and although she dressed in chic modern fashions in private life, during her youth she played only untouchable icons (her one slip was 1916's *Diane of the Follies*). Through the 1910s she was the Edwardian good girl (even when wronged by cads); in the 1920s she played historical figures or—in her great *The Wind*—a gingham-gowned farm girl. Not till middle age had safely "desexed" her did Gish take on strong, modern characters.

This did not bode well for the romance of Rodolphe and Mimi, or for John Gilbert's onscreen love making. "It seemed to me that, if we avoided showing the lovers in a physical embrace, the scenes would build up suppressed emotion and be much more effective," said Gish—whereupon jaws dropped all over the MGM lot, and Gish was forced to shoot some (rather demure) love scenes. "Oh, dear, I've got to go through an-

Jack and Lillian Gish in *La Bohème,* 1926 (The Everett Collection).

other day of kissing John Gilbert," she sighed heavily to unsympathetic friends.

She also shied away from her director. "When I would take her hand when talking about the part," Vidor wrote in his memoirs, "she would slowly but deliberately withdraw it from my grasp. If Jack, in rehearsing or walking across the studio lawn, would lightly put his arm over her shoulders, she would easily twist away." Whether Gish was in character and "playing the part of the delicate flower, the unapproachable virgin," as Vidor suspected, or whether Gish herself was just not a touchy-feely type, it put off her director and costar.

La Bohème is a beautiful piece of work, the sets and costumes perfectly evoking 1830s Paris (those huge sets Gish complained about could pass for artists' lofts). But the cast, one and all, overacts enthusiastically, either permitted or encouraged by Vidor. Gish's Mimi is virginal to the point of absurdity: Murger's Mimi was "the mistress of one of [Rodolphe's] friends . . . very taking, not at all prudish, and could stand tobacco-smoke and literary conversations without a headache." The literary Mimi and Rodolphe move in together right away, and Mimi repeatedly leaves him for richer pastures—in the movie, the two act like virginal teenagers. The book's version of Mimi's demise was too sad and squalid for the movies, but Gish's agonizing death march through Paris to be with Rodolphe at the end was the film's tragic high point. It also led to one of those unintentionally ironic movie scenes, as Renée Adorée's Musette sits at the bedside of Lillian Gish's Mimi as she dies of tuberculosis (Gish, of course, lived to be a hale and hearty ninety-nine, while Adorée succumbed to tuberculosis at thirty-five).

The most startling moment in the film is Gish's death scene, for which she did an impressive amount of research and self-mortification. "I went to a hospital to observe the progress of tuberculosis in its terminal stages," she recalled. She allowed herself to be dragged through a street set by a horse, trying to get to her lover's rooms. Vidor later claimed that Gish starved and dehydrated herself for her death scene, even putting cotton into her mouth to dry it out further. But she herself scoffed, "That's nonsense! How could you keep working seventy-five years, and do ridiculous things like that?" Nonetheless, her death scene is shocking and unlovely.

La Bohème opened in Los Angeles in May 1926. Lillian Gish was in London with her ailing mother and couldn't be at the Forum Theater at the première. But the rest of the cast showed up, along with fellow MGM players Mae Murray, William Haines, Lon Chaney, Conrad Nagel, and Eleanor Boardman. Also at the première was Jack, whose "appearance to a group of flappers caused such palpitation that at one time his very coat threatened to leave its wearer. Girls crowded around him as he passed through the way made by the striped awning above and the carpeted aisle below." Also in attendance were Norma Shearer ("trig and smart in a street costume which was the last word in style and cut"), Carmel Myers ("wearing a gown of creme-colored Spanish lace trimmed with French flowers"), and the newly renamed Joan Crawford ("in pink chiffon").

The film cost $632,000—one of Jack's most expensive movies—and made a profit of $377,000. It cemented both stars' places at the top of the studio heap. Lillian Gish went on to make several more silents for MGM till leaving in 1928—possibly in a huff about *The Wind*'s happy ending, or possibly just because of the looming of talkies.

Reviews were positive, but not unreserved raves. Edwin Schallert of the *Los Angeles Times* wrote, "It is not a great production in the sense that it is deeply convincing, but it offers moments of effective charm and picturesqueness." He felt that "the production as a whole has been jazzed and livened up with subtleties and bits of business that do not ring true" and noted of its female star that "some of the potentially loveliest scenes have been spoiled by the too frantic efforts of Miss Gish to give them lightness. . . . There is not the least doubt in the world that Miss Gish dies beautifully." As for Jack, Schallert wrote that he "discloses as dashing a presence as in any picture that he has made since *His Hour*. Yet it is the sort of dash in this instance that does not at times seem quite free from conscious effort. . . . He also is successful in suggesting some unusually subtle shades of feeling in the later episodes." Jack himself felt that *La Bohème* was "artistic and delicate, but never believable."

In February 1926 Jack took a brief vacation—a working one, as he was accompanied to New York by King Vidor and Irving Thalberg while they hashed out their next project together (a big-budget adventure called *Bardelys the Magnificent*). Eleanor Boardman, who had just been signed to a new MGM contract, was decided upon as his leading lady—Vidor had his eye on her for his leading lady offscreen as well. Jack enjoyed his trips to Prohibition-era New York: he told Gladys Hall in 1927, "I never go to bed. . . . I simply can't. I go from one idiotic night club to another and I hate them and think they are a waste of time and money, but I simply do not seem to be able to refuse invitations."

Some of those invitations, happily, were from the fabled Algonquin Round Table set of writers and critics, who loved palling around with—and mercilessly teasing—movie and stage stars. Screenwriter and playwright George Oppenheimer told Jack's daughter Leatrice that Jack and Dorothy Parker "took to each other immediately. I have seldom seen anyone, let alone an actor, have as good a time as he had with Dottie, Donald Ogden Stewart, and Bob Benchley. They gave him hell, too. They never addressed him as John or Jack. It was always 'Great Lover of the Silver Screen.'" Jack, thank goodness, took the joke in good humor, accompanying the hard-drinking crew to every speakeasy in Manhattan. Oppenheimer also told Leatrice that Jack later wired Parker $2,500 when she was—as she too often tended to be—flat broke and in the hospital.

Back in Los Angeles, Jack threw himself back into community activities, playing the part of the gracious star: he took part in the groundbreaking for the new (still-extant) Carter DeHaven Music Box Theater on Hollywood Boulevard along with DeHaven himself, Rudolph Valentino, Viola Dana, Colleen Moore, and others. Then he sat back and waited for his next project, a run-of-the-mill romantic triangle to be filmed while *Bardelys* was being prepared. Jack was in a perverse mood in the summer of 1926 when the *Los Angeles Times* asked various stars their dream roles. "Peter Pan," he answered. The reporter played along, noting that "before I left the Metro-Goldwyn lot Mr. Louis B. Mayer assured me that plans were being made to star John Gilbert in *Peter Pan*. I sincerely hope that he will be as successful in interpreting that part as he was in playing Cleopatra in *A Fool There Was*."

Chapter Seven

> She is capable of doing a lot of damage. . . . Upsetting thrones, breaking up friendships, wrecking homes—that sort of thing.
>
> —John Gilbert, 1927

In late June 1926 it was announced that Clarence Brown would delay filming *The Trail of '98* so he could do *Flesh and the Devil* first. One little line at the very end of the article mentioned in passing that "Greta Garbo will play the leading role opposite the star."

The Greta Garbo whom Jack met in the summer of 1926 was lonely, scared, and pretty sure she had made a terrible mistake leaving Europe. The twenty-year-old had been a rising starlet thanks to her mentor, director Mauritz Stiller. Louis B. Mayer had snapped up both of them on a 1925 talent-shopping trip (it was never confirmed who he really wanted—the actress or the director). With barely a schoolgirl's mastery of English, Garbo was forced to pose for cheesecake photos, conduct interviews, and portray silly, one-dimensional vamps onscreen.

In her first American project, *The Torrent,* she was directed not by Stiller but by Monta Bell; she had no chemistry (onscreen or off) with leading man Ricardo Cortez. Stiller was assigned to, then fired from, her next film, *The Temptress:* Fred Niblo directed, and Antonio Moreno costarred. Both films were competent but unexciting melodramas that gave her little chance to really act.

Not only was she separated from Stiller (he returned to Sweden in late 1927 and would die the following year), but Garbo now suffered

Greta Garbo in a portrait by Ruth Harriet Louise, late 1920s (author's collection).

a personal loss. Her younger sister Alva—herself a great beauty and promising young actress—died of lymphatic cancer on April 21, 1926, while Greta was filming *The Temptress*. What little socializing she did was with Hollywood's Swedish community: Stiller, Lars Hanson, Nils Asther, Einar Hanson, Karl Dane. She skulked sullenly around, too shy to speak to people and plotting her escape back to Sweden.

Garbo and Gilbert had already met, and the portents were not promising for friendship, let alone romance: Jack walked past the newcomer one day on the MGM lot and shouted out cheerily, "Hello, Greta!" She froze up and replied, "It's *Miss* Garbo." Jack laughed, "Imagine upstaging *me!*" Even naïve starlet Anita Page, signed by MGM in the late 1920s, knew that "you just didn't go up to Garbo and say hello!" Groucho Marx once reportedly spotted Garbo at MGM, peeked under her slouch hat, and told her, "Pardon me, madam, I thought you were a guy I knew in Pittsburgh."

Flesh and the Devil was based on a 1906 novel by Hermann Sudermann: the story of two boyhood friends caught in a romantic triangle and torn apart by an amoral vamp. Joining Jack and Garbo was handsome blond actor Lars Hanson—a fellow Swede who had already appeared with Garbo in the 1924 Swedish release *Gösta Berlings Saga,* directed by Mauritz Stiller. Cinematographer William H. Daniels assured that everyone looked fabulous—in fact, he became Garbo's favored cameraman, shooting nearly all of her films, through *Ninotchka.*

The costars' official introduction came on the set around the beginning of August 1926, when they shot the scene where Jack's character (earnest young military cadet Leo von Harden) meets Garbo's (the mysterious Felicitas von Rhaden). In retrospect, everyone saw "love at first sight," as Garbo's interpreter, actor Sven Hugo Borg, put it. "Some instant spark, some flash seemed to pass between them the instant they looked into each other's eyes," said Borg years later. Of course, Garbo and Gilbert were acting the parts of two people who fall in love—you can see this spark and flash today in the film, and it *is* tempting to put it down to more than just professional ability.

Director Clarence Brown told historian Kevin Brownlow, "At first Gilbert didn't know if he wanted to work with her." Shortly after that first train-station introduction, they filmed an outdoor love scene: Brown, in hindsight, felt that "it was the damndest thing you ever saw. It was the sort of thing Elinor Glyn used to write about. When they got into that first love scene, well, nobody else was even there. Those two were alone in a world of their own."

Which was par for the course with Jack, who threw himself into his scenes and his characters 100 percent. Garbo, however, tended to hold back—though this was not generally known about her as early as 1926. If she really was as lost in the moment as Brown said, it was indeed remarkable.

A light moment on the set of *Flesh and the Devil,* 1926 (The Everett Collection).

By the summer of 1926 it was open news about the Garbo and Gilbert love affair. "Neither Gilbert nor Miss Garbo would deny the report when questioned yesterday on the set where they are appearing in a film together for the first time. 'Please ask Mr. Gilbert,' Miss Garbo said. . . . It is common gossip in the Metro-Goldwyn-Mayer lot that the screen pair are much in love and that there is more than acting in their love scenes together. Gilbert, when pressed as to the truth of the engagement rumor said, 'I wish I could say more, but you must ask Miss Garbo.'"

Barbara Kent—the twenty-year-old who played Jack's childhood sweetheart—told author Michael Ankerich in 1997 that Clarence Brown "had a style that allowed us to rehearse and to find our own characters. He was a very quiet man and would talk to us in the softest voice. He was especially careful with Garbo and would almost whisper his instructions to her."

The film looks lovely; the cast is set off like jewels, and the snowy winter scenes are especially atmospheric and lovely. *Flesh and the Devil* takes place in a *mittel*-European setting and incorporates duels and

The great love affair with Garbo begins: *Flesh and the Devil,* 1926 (The Everett Collection).

castles, but the studio wisely opted for modern dress (Jack looked particularly fetching in trim military garb and a dashing overcoat). The film ages well; the performances are not overdone (with the exception of one breakdown by Garbo); the only real false step comes when Jack's character is racing back home from Africa and hallucinates giant floating Garbo heads everywhere, which must have been pretty hilarious even in 1926. John Gilbert is definitely the star of this movie, getting more screen time than Garbo or the third point in the triangle, Lars Hanson. Garbo's vamp is mostly acted in an effective, low-key style; indeed, she comes off as more weak willed than evil. Jack is alternately boyish and boisterous (early in the film, with pal Hanson), then pained and suffering (after falling prey to Garbo's wiles). But his suffering is never overdone in a melodramatic way; sometimes he acts showing only the back of his head and his shoulders.

Flesh and the Devil was held over for three weeks in New York before even opening in Los Angeles in January 1927: "It has broken all records for audience attendance," noted the *Los Angeles Times.* "Mr.

Gilbert . . . goes at his not disagreeable task with a fine fervor, and manages to be as thoroughly engaging as he was in *The Merry Widow*. . . . There are instances of superb cleverness in the construction of pictorial effects, and instances of stupidity in the development of dramatic interest." The *Santa Monica Outlook*'s critic called *Flesh and the Devil* "the first German picture made in America. It has all the settings of Europe; all the technique of the old world; it is a drama from one of Europe's mightiest dramatists." *Flesh and the Devil* cost a middling $373,000 and made $466,000 profit.

Jack's opinion of it: "Mildly exciting because of its brazen display of sex lure," he sniffed, "but only important for me because of my meeting with a glorious person named Garbo."

By the time *Flesh and the Devil* had finished filming, Garbo was spending a lot of time at Jack's Tower Grove Drive home. Jack decided to remodel the guest room for her; it had been almost comically spare: bare walls, narrow bed, a crucifix on the wall the only decoration. In short, the perfect Garbo room. But Jack took it into his head that she would want something girly and froufrou, and had Harold Grieve whip up a surprise for her: a Louis XVI extravaganza with black marble guest bath. According to Hedda Hopper, he even carved a crown to hold the canopy over her bed. Predictably, Garbo hated it, and moved out to a small cabin on the estate grounds, where Jack had a waterfall and pine trees installed to make her feel even more secluded.

On Sundays—the only day off in those six-day workweeks—Jack would have his friends and neighbors over for swimming and tennis. Sunday brunch at John Gilbert's was one of Hollywood's greatest pleasures in the late 1920s: a genial host, he provided food and drink (legal and illegal) and a mixed crowd of performers (Norma Shearer, Charlie Chaplin, Richard Barthelmess, Ronald Colman, Colleen Moore, Mae Murray), executives (Paul Bern, Irving Thalberg, Howard Strickling), and writers (Carey Wilson, Donald Ogden Stewart, Adela Rogers St. Johns, Anita Loos). "Jack lived like a prince of the realm . . . he was the master of all he surveyed—all but the elusive Miss Garbo," recalled Norma Shearer. "She came and went like an amusing child, sometimes swimming and playing tennis with us, but just as often hiding in her rooms." King Vidor recalled, "Tennis and other games would scarcely be under way when it would be discovered that Greta had mysteriously disappeared, leaving Jack in a fever of frustration."

But Garbo's shyness was of a particular Swedish type, which did not include the American shyness about the human form. Eleanor Boardman recalled Garbo walking "around Jack Gilbert's garden perfectly nude, with her dressing gown over her back like this, and the Japanese gardener would *look* at her." Garbo was, sighed Boardman, "man, woman and child. You can't pigeonhole Garbo. She was fascinating. *Extremely* selfish. Beautiful. Strange."

If Jack was a good dramatic coach for her, he was also slowly bringing her out of her shell. Shy to the point of phobic, still unsure of her English, and highly distrustful, Garbo was forced by her social boyfriend to attend premières, go to house parties (at least once to William Randolph Hearst and Marion Davies's famed San Simeon) and picnics. If ever Greta Garbo was going to become a normal, all-American girl, this was the time. Carey Wilson recalled her swimming and hiking and taking tennis lessons from King Vidor (grasping the racket well up toward the throat, she would smack the ball so heartily that there wasn't much to be done about it in the event it happened to land in the court). Wilson once found her doing headstands on a sofa cushion: She still contained so much physical exuberance that standing on her head, on a sofa pillow, seemed to be the simple and desirable thing to do.

Songwriter Howard Dietz—himself three times married—recalled Jack's frustration with Garbo and his attempts to tease her into some kind of reaction. "When I said, 'I'm going out,' the only thing she said was, 'I'll leave the door open, Jack!'" he complained to Dietz. "I said, 'I'm going out to sleep with Anna May Wong!' 'I'll leave the door open, Jack,' was all she said. What in the hell do I *do?*"

The events of September 8, 1926, have been hashed over endlessly in the past eight decades—among old movie fans, anyway. This may have been the day that Louis B. Mayer vowed to destroy John Gilbert and the day that the Garbo/Gilbert romance ended. Or it may simply have been an awkward social event with no real import. It all depends on whom one believes.

It was the wedding day of Jack's friend and frequent director King Vidor and Jack's occasional costar Eleanor Boardman. Boardman told

Jack's frequent costar Eleanor Boardman and frequent director King Vidor, seen here a year after their 1926 wedding (The Everett Collection).

author Michael Ankerich in 1988 that it had all started at an August 1926 dinner at Vidor's house, down the street from Jack's. Vidor, recently divorced from actress Florence Vidor, told guests Jack and Greta Garbo that he and Eleanor Boardman were planning a big splashy wedding at Marion Davies's Beverly Hills home the following month. Boardman claimed that during the dinner, Jack asked Garbo to make it a double ceremony and "much to everyone's surprise," she said yes. Garbo's biographer Karen Swenson notes that Jack and Garbo had known each other only three weeks by then, and while he was apt to rush into ill-planned marriages, it would be remarkable indeed for the standoffish Garbo to accede to such a proposal.

September 8 was a Wednesday, so everyone showed up after work. Swenson says that Jack and Garbo had filmed a dramatic love scene for *Flesh and the Devil* that day. According to Boardman (King Vidor mentions none of this in his memoirs, despite lengthy chapters on Jack and Greta Garbo), Jack showed up on time and nervous, along with such guests as Louis B. Mayer and his wife and daughters, Irving Thalberg, Sam Goldwyn, Elinor Glyn, William Haines, and of course hosts Marion Davies and William Randolph Hearst. But no Garbo. "Gilbert kept getting drunker and drunker," Boardman told Ankerich, "and he kept phoning, but there was no answer. Finally, we went on with the wedding."

Then came the fabled confrontation: "I was upstairs," Boardman recalled in the 1970s. "Gilbert was getting rather violent. Seems that Mayer . . . was in the men's room with Gilbert, and Gilbert was crying about this thing . . . and Mayer said, 'sleep with her. Don't marry her.' Gilbert socked him, knocked him down, and he hit his head on the tile. That was really the beginning of the end of Gilbert's career." Boardman told Jack's daughter Leatrice that Mayer raged, "'I'll destroy you.' From that point on, you can see Jack's career going like this [making a downhill gesture]. He's pulling in one direction, and there's some absolute force pulling him back."

There are several problems with this story—for one thing, the sole source is Eleanor Boardman who, one assumes, was not lurking in the men's toilet when the fight occurred. Fellow guest Irene Mayer—Louis's daughter—denied any of it ever happened, and fellow guest Joseph Cohn, an MGM executive, scoffed, "If Gilbert would have hit Mayer, Mayer would have killed him. Mayer was a brutally strong man." Not to mention that if Mayer (hardly the sort to suggest, "Can't you just sleep with her?" in the first place) had been struck hard enough to hit his head on a tile floor, some kind of medical attention would have been called for—indeed, he would have legal grounds for firing an employee who did such a thing.

Eleanor Boardman was a smart, well-spoken woman, not given to flights of fancy or gossip. But no one else at the wedding—none of John Gilbert's or Louis B. Mayer's friends or enemies, not King Vidor—ever mentioned this remarkable occurrence (except for Sam Marx, in a different version we shall encounter shortly). Boardman later admitted flat out to historian William Drew, "I think Mayer was a bastard and I haven't anything good to say about him," which may have colored her memory of long-ago events.

Swenson also did some ace detective work in deconstructing this story: she discovered that, while Vidor and Boardman had taken out marriage licenses, neither John Gilbert nor Greta Garbo (or John Pringle or Greta Gustafsson or any of their other possible names) had applied for marriage licenses in Los Angeles, Riverside, or Orange counties. Swenson also uncovered the unpublished memoirs of Jack's friend, actor and newsman Harry Crocker, who wrote that Jack indeed proposed to Garbo at each and every opportunity, but that far from accepting, "she always kept him at arm's length." Crocker's view of the Vidor/Boardman wedding was simply that "the sight of his friends' happiness threw John Gilbert into a fine frenzy of despair. It is no exaggeration to say that he actually soaked the lapels of his male friends with bitter tears."

Crocker also claimed that Jack felt that MGM was keeping the lovers from marrying, though there is no evidence of this (stars married all the time, though Mayer would certainly not have liked to see his rising new actress linked to John Gilbert). Whether or not that is true, it is not unlikely that an unhappy Jack, thrown into a social situation with Mayer, had sharp words with him. Any situation that put those two men in the same room was asking for trouble. Anyway, everyone went to work the next day and filmed the church scene in *Flesh and the Devil.*

As for Mayer's threats ("You're finished, Gilbert!"), Gilbert was hardly finished. This supposed fight took place in late 1926: for the next three years, Jack was MGM's biggest male star, appearing in another nine profit-making silents, and he was re-signed to a hugely remunerative contract in 1928. Those who feel Mayer used talkies to put the skids under Jack can hardly think he saw that opportunity coming three years away—Mayer couldn't even see talkies coming when they were right on top of him. If Mayer vowed to "finish" John Gilbert in September 1926, he was the most inept adversary in Hollywood. Indeed, three years later, MGM proudly listed its "stars" (as opposed to featured players) as Jack, Lon Chaney, Joan Crawford, Marion Davies, Greta Garbo, William Haines, Buster Keaton, Ramon Novarro, and Norma Shearer.

Whether or not Garbo stood him up at the September wedding, *something* happened late in 1926 to shipwreck their relationship—their "great romance of the century" lasted maybe four months. Thereafter, it was a year or so of Jack pursuing a retreating Garbo and then, finally, a polite friendship.

Agnes Smith interviewed Jack for the February 1927 *Photoplay* (the article was given the hugely insulting title "Up Speaks a Gallant Loser").

Smith wrote, "A great many stories have been broadcast concerning the romance of Greta Garbo and John Gilbert. . . . And then, when everyone was all set for another Hollywood wedding, Greta walked out." A month earlier, that same magazine had said flat out that "Jack Gilbert was in love. And you have never seen a man in love until you have seen Jack in the throes of the delicate passion. . . . He was all set to ask her to marry him, and he had intimated that he loved her. But then something happened and the romance went up in the air. . . . Alas for the course of true love!"

One cannot discuss the Greta Garbo/John Gilbert affair without touching on the lady's much-analyzed sexual and gender issues. Was she straight? Gay? Bisexual? Transgender? Asexual? No one knows—it's possible she did not know herself, which would explain her lifelong solitude. According to her biographers, Garbo frequently referred to herself as male, as a child calling herself "Gustafsson's youngest boy." She preferred men's clothing and hated the makeup and coiffures required for her career. She asked Mayer to cast her in male roles, as Hamlet, as Pierrot—which he laughed off. She was never able to maintain a romantic relationship with either men or women—indeed, no one knows for sure if she and Jack ever actually *had* sex. It's unknown if her later close friendships with Leopold Stokowksi, Cecil Beaton, Gayelord Hauser, Mercedes de Acosta, or George Schlee were platonic or romantic. Both Beaton and de Acosta claimed sexual relationships with her, but both were notorious self-promoting storytellers (of de Acosta's memoirs, *Here Lies the Heart,* actress Eva Le Gallienne added, "and lies, and lies . . .").

Jack spoke admiringly and lovingly of Garbo to *Photoplay*'s Agnes Smith—though as friends learned to their dismay, the surest way of being cut dead by Garbo was to say anything about her to anyone, let alone to the press. Jack's quotes to *Photoplay* may indeed be his, though they have a whiff of fan-magazine hyperbole: "She is like a statue. There is something eternal about her. Not only did she baffle me, but she has baffled everyone at the studio. . . . She is capable of doing a lot of damage—unconsciously, of course. Upsetting thrones, breaking up friendships, wrecking homes—that sort of thing." Jack did indeed talk in such overblown phrases at times, but this is just the sort of florid praise that made Garbo take off for the hills.

Or, in one case, the beach: being stood up once again, Jack was told by Garbo's maid that she had gone to the beach. "I jumped in my car and motored for miles," he told Smith, "way out beyond Santa Monica. I found her at last. She was all alone and just coming out of the surf. She didn't see me, so I watched her to see what she would do. She stood on the beach, all by herself, and just looked out at the ocean. And she remained so, without moving, for fifteen minutes." This does indeed sound like Garbo—and very unlike the social, bumptious John Gilbert of the 1920s (though in the 1930s he did his own share of solitary brooding).

Comic actress Beatrice Lillie was in town in 1926 to make the movie *Exit Smiling* for MGM. "I hadn't much time to sample the local joie de vivre," she wrote in her memoirs, "but I was determined to give it a try." She was, by her own admittedly exaggerated account, eager to stir up trouble: Garbo and Gilbert, she noticed, "were making eyes at each other. . . . They took themselves *so seriously,* and I'm always tempted to puncture solemnity wherever it appears."

Lillie claimed she sent Jack an anonymous red rose every day she worked at MGM—and again, it is important to take Bea Lillie's stories with a grain of salt. She said she then suffered a minor car accident on Tower Grove Drive and staggered to King Vidor's house, asking for Jack—the Vidors' butler drove her to his house, where "Jack opened the door, dazzling in a blue brocade dressing gown and open-necked silk shirt." Lillie was deposited on a divan, and "I started to sit up, but he got to me first. With tears streaming down his cheeks, he threw his arms around a set of shaking shoulders and pinned me with a great big kiss."

Well, maybe. Garbo's biographer Karen Swenson notes that Lillie's car accident occurred on August 24, 1926, when she was on her way home *from* John Gilbert's, where a private memorial for Rudolph Valentino had been held. But Lillie was discerning enough to notice that "Jack really believed the studio press releases that dubbed him 'The Great Lover,' and he did his damndest to live up to his reputation. Whatever his latest role on the screen, he continued to act it off screen. . . . Jack had a talent for backing into trouble."

Chapter Eight

> John Gilbert is the current sensation. Quick money and heavy will be his. How long will he last?
>
> —*Los Angeles Times,* 1925

As early as December 1925, Herbert Howe of the *Los Angeles Times* was looking over the upcoming class of performers and wondering who the next big stars would be. "Valentino won't have his clothes torn off his back anymore, thanks to Mr. John Gilbert, whose broadcloth now maddens the flapper to clawing frenzy," wrote Howe. "John Gilbert is the current sensation. Quick money and heavy will be his. How long will he last? As long as any one of the other great lovers. It doesn't make any difference how great an actor he is, he'll have to play hot lovers. Gilbert is brilliant, flashing, temperamental, a blade and a bomb. He'll burn things up. . . . Gilbert is infinitely more dexterous and has a far more reliable future on the Metro-Goldwyn lot than Valentino had following The Rajah."

Howe went on to emphasize that Jack had the honor of being the biggest star at the biggest studio, that "the Metro-Goldwyn lion had them all [other studios] terrified. They all meander around their lots wishing they could borrow Novarro or Gilbert or Norma Shearer or Monta Bell or King Vidor. They'd have to borrow Irving Thalberg to know what to do with them. . . . King Vidor is the most valuable director in pictures. Were I a producer low enough to think of money (most of them talk only about being soldiers or artists in a great cause) I'd rather have Vidor than any six junked together. He'd make me money without making me ashamed of myself."

On August 23, 1926, Rudolph Valentino died in a New York hospital, about a week after being felled by a gastric ulcer—the same malady that was just beginning to trouble Jack, largely due to his drinking. Valentino was thirty-one and had been a major star for five years: he was known chiefly as a heavy-breathing sex symbol, which pained him no end. Valentino actually showed great promise as a dramatic actor (his performances in *The Four Horsemen of the Apocalypse* and *The Conquering Power* show off his talents in that direction), and he also brought a great light-comedy touch to nearly all of his roles (in *Cobra* he is almost Cary Grant–like in his approach). But it was the dashing sex roles that brought in the money: *Blood and Sand, The Eagle, The Son of the Sheik*. By the time he died, Valentino was beginning to despair of ever proving himself as an actor.

Of course, death turned out to be a very good career move for him: had Valentino lived another few years he would have wound up as a Latino character actor, as did Ricardo Cortez, Gilbert Roland, Rod La Rocque, Antonio Moreno. Dying in 1926, before ever making a talkie, ensured his immortality as one of the greats of the era: to this day fans gather at his graveside on the anniversary of his birth and death, and the occasional Lady in Black leaves roses for him.

Jack was an usher at Valentino's funeral on September 7 at the Church of the Good Shepherd in Hollywood. He released a statement: "The death of Valentino is a terrific loss to the screen . . . a great artist and one of the finest gentlemen it has ever been my privilege to call a friend." Jack's supposed reminiscences about Rudolph Valentino sounded like—and probably were—the work of his friend Adela Rogers St. Johns: "In the midst of my fame, I have studied Rudy carefully, envying the ease with which he wore his crown. He possessed a quality which I nor any other star will ever attain."

In early September 1926, with Valentino barely cold in his grave, Herbert Howe of the *Los Angeles Times* was already musing on who would inherit his crown: Ronald Colman, Ramon Novarro, John Barrymore, or Jack? "Jack Gilbert is a flashing, daring, swashbuckling cavalier. Yet there are human depths as revealed in *The Big Parade*. But it is as the

Jack comparing moustaches with Ramon Novarro (left) on the MGM lot, 1926, while Jack was shooting *Bardelys the Magnificent* (Wisconsin Center for Film & Theater Research).

ebullient lover of *The Merry Widow* that he has taken his pedestal, I think. In that, as in *La Bohème,* he is champagne, than which there is no better. But champagne is not for breakfast, lunch and dinner. Gilbert, above all, must vary his characterizations, holding in leash his too striking manner, or there'll be surfeit. He can easily overplay Gilbert: give too much of his own heady effervescence."

Valentino's fall from the top of the ladder gave Jack the opportunity to scramble to the top. With *Flesh and the Devil, La Bohème,* and *Bardelys the Magnificent* all being released in 1926, and another four films in the works for 1927, there was really no other male star as big, as successful at the box office, as lusted after by fans all over the world.

At MGM Jack's biggest competitors were Ramon Novarro and William Haines. Novarro turned twenty-seven in 1926. Like Jack, he had entered movies in the mid-1910s and worked his way up through bit and supporting roles; he became a full-fledged star in 1925 with MGM's big-budget *Ben-Hur.* Though this film's success was partly due to luscious glimpses of Novarro's loincloth-clad physique, he was promoted as a boy next door, not an action hero. His button eyes and shy smile made him look younger than his years and unthreatening: in such mid-1920s films as *The Student Prince in Old Heidelberg* and *The Midshipman,* he could have been Jack's younger brother, rather than his rival in love.

William Haines, too, was more collegiate than sophisticated. Born in 1900, he'd had a supporting role in Jack's *The Wife of the Centaur;* by 1925 he was supporting such stars as Mary Pickford, Lon Chaney, and Norma Shearer. Haines's breakthrough year was 1926, when he played a wise-cracking young college boy in *Brown of Harvard* and a wise-cracking young recruit in *Tell It to the Marines.* His forte was the brash, jazzy young fellow who needs to be taken down a peg or two (and always was by the final reel, either by a sweet starlet or a brusque character actor).

One of the biggest male stars of the 1920s was United Artists' Douglas Fairbanks Sr.—a Broadway star of the early 1910s, he made his screen debut in 1915 and continued at the top of the heap through the end of the silent era. In the 1920s he leaped athletically through a series of wildly popular action films, with Jack's *Bardelys the Magnificent* an obvious homage. Jack was never a serious rival to Fairbanks as an action star. He could ride, swim, and parry swords well enough, but his physique and his personality were more suited to the boudoir than the deck of a pirate ship. Indeed, few actors could take on Fairbanks at his own game, though some tried.

One aspect of Douglas Fairbanks Sr.'s career that has been overlooked was his appeal as a sex symbol, easily rivaling Jack and Valentino. In the 1910s he usually played comic businessmen, cowboys, and college boys. But through the 1920s, Fairbanks's public image morphed more and more into wild sexual fantasy, and in his publicity stills he often looks like a male stripper or a participant in the Greenwich Village Halloween parade: sexy half-naked pirate, sexy half-naked Arab, sexy half-naked gaucho. Particularly in *The Thief of Bagdad* and *The Black Pirate,* his impressive physique was set off by wisps of chiffon and lamé, torn bits of black leather, and high boots. His marriage to America's Sweetheart Mary Pickford only helped to cement his status as a sex symbol (and, for what it's worth, it gave Mary's image a little frisson of sexuality, too).

John Barrymore went through an action-hero period in the 1920s, having won his fame through playing the classics. Barrymore was forty-four in 1926 and had not yet destroyed his looks and health through drink and fast living. That year he appeared in *The Sea Beast* (an adaptation of *Moby Dick*) and *Don Juan*, looking hale and healthy—in *The Beloved Rogue* (1927), Barrymore very creditably appeared in nothing but a torn loincloth. He was certainly a major rival to John Gilbert as a Great Lover—his reputation as a serious actor had been proven onstage in the 1910s and early '20s, and through the silent era he starred in such enviable roles as *Dr. Jekyll and Mr. Hyde, Sherlock Holmes,* and *Beau Brummel.*

One of the newer stars in Hollywood was also one of Jack's most worrisome rivals (though a close friend offscreen): Ronald Colman. Although six years older than Jack, he didn't really become a Hollywood player till 1923, when he costarred with Lillian Gish in Metro's *The White Sister.* Through the mid-1920s Colman established himself as a handsome, gentlemanly lover and a subtle actor, most often opposite leading ladies Constance Talmadge and Blanche Sweet. In 1925 he met his Garbo: blonde Hungarian actress Vilma Banky. They costarred in five films between 1925 and '28, becoming one of the hottest romantic couples of the late silent era.

Screenwriter Frances Marion recalled that in the mid-1920s Samuel Goldwyn was asked, "How come you're not putting Colman in a picture like *The Big Parade* that's making such a hit for Gilbert? Aren't you afraid Gilbert will beat him to the draw?" Goldwyn was said to have answered, "Ever hear the fable about the tortoise and the hare? It's no fable. The one who runs too fast loses his breath." Ronald Colman never did lose his breath: with his perfect bone structure and big brown puppy-dog eyes, Colman in his mid-thirties was one of the fastest-rising male stars of the late silent era. And his velvety British voice would carry him to leading-man status well into the 1950s.

Jack's friend Richard Barthelmess had reached the height of his career in 1921 with the drama *Tol'able David.* Barthelmess had been raised to stardom by D. W. Griffith in the late 1910s and had since struck out on his own: square-jawed and clean-cut, he starred in three or four films a year. Some of them were big hits (most notably *The Patent Leather Kid* in 1927). But he never really broke through to top-rank stardom, and after talkies hit, he reinvented himself as a reliable character actor.

All studios had a corral full of second-tier leading men as well. Largely forgotten today except by real film-history buffs, these actors worked steadily, appeared in big-budget films as well as Bs, and played opposite the biggest female stars of the era. At MGM Conrad Nagel and Norman Kerry were the threats used when Jack did not want a role. Nagel, who had played opposite Jack in *The Snob,* was a competent, reliable contract player. In the 1920s he ably supported such female stars as Norma Shearer, Marion Davies, Eleanor Boardman, and Renée Adorée—without distracting from their charms with excess sex appeal or personality. Nagel never rose beyond "leading-man" status, as he was handsome and talented without being exciting. The peculiar star quality that Jack (and Valentino and Douglas Fairbanks Sr.) had been blessed with was absent.

Norman Kerry, another handsome MGM contract player, looked a bit like Jack and was first choice for the lead in *The Merry Widow.* A bit older (he turned thirty in 1924), he was born Norman Kaiser but wisely changed his name with the start of the First World War. Kerry was playing leads by the 1920s, and through the decade he appeared in an impressive array of hit films: his three with Lon Chaney (*The Hunchback of Notre Dame, The Phantom of the Opera,* and *The Unknown*) have made him more widely seen today than many bigger stars of his era. But Kerry, like Nagel, was stalled at second-string leading man and never really broke through (he retired from film in the 1940s).

Both inside and outside MGM, Hollywood was teeming with young character actors, "male starlets," and charming young (and not-so-young) supporting players, some of whom were on their last legs in the mid-1920s, some of whom were yet to rise to stardom: handsome Milton Sills had been a leading man in the 1910s, and in the mid-1920s was still good-looking enough to play leads and even action heroes (*The Sea Hawk*). Dark, dreamy Warner Baxter seemed to be idling in the 1920s as a second lead till talkies made him one of the busiest actors onscreen through the 1940s. Tough-guys Richard Dix, Victor McLaglen, and Thomas Meighan worked steadily in westerns and action films, also playing romantic leads when called upon.

Then there were the puppies yipping at Jack's heels: rising young contract players of the mid-1920s, some of whom would go on to lasting stardom or respectable character or western careers—or who would crash and burn. There were the second-string Latin Lovers (Ramon Novarro was far too big a star to be classed with them): Ricardo Cortez, Gilbert Roland, Antonio Moreno, Rod La Rocque, Don Alvarado. There was also a new class of promising young leading men, all born within a year of 1900: Richard Arlen, James Murray, James Hall, Neil Hamilton, George O'Brien, Charles Farrell, Gary Cooper. John Gilbert may have been the biggest male star at MGM in 1926, but he was smart enough—and neurotic enough—to know that there were hundreds happy and able to take his place.

Nineteen twenty-six also saw the exit from MGM—and the American movie industry—of Jack's former mentor Maurice Tourneur who, like Jack, could not get along with Louis B. Mayer. Tourneur had been directing *The Mysterious Island* at MGM, but Mayer insisted that the film's producer be present to monitor his progress. Insulted, Tourneur walked off the set and out of MGM four days into production. The film was eventually released as a part-talkie in 1929; Tourneur went on to a successful directing career in his native France (his son, Jacques Tourneur, directed such dark classics as *Cat People, I Walked with a Zombie,* and *Out of the Past*).

Gladys Hall quizzed John Gilbert, twenty-nine and at the height of his career in 1927, about how stardom had changed him—he half-jokingly whined about "the price of fame." "My tragedy is the tragedy of all the cinema people, really," he said. "We have everything—too soon. I've travelled. I have more money than I ever dreamed I'd have in a lifetime. I've had love affairs. I've been married. I have the kind of a house I want. I have cars and dogs and horses and pleasures. What can life offer me when I am forty-nine? What will there be left for me to want? Nothing that I can imagine."

He could not picture retirement or old age—even middle age: "After living at top speed," he told Hall, "after eating thrills and excitement for breakfast, luncheon, tea and dinner, I won't be able to settle back and tend flowers and play a round of golf and smoke a contemplative pipe. I know that. I don't fool myself. That's one thing I haven't come to yet—fooling myself. The easiest person in the world to fool is yourself and I try to keep clear of it."

Even at his happiest, when he was working on a good film and was "absolutely wrapped up in it," he was frustrated by his ambitions: "I'm like a kid who has graduated from drawing pigs and cats on his slate—I'm in for doing portraits now. I'd rather do one or two *big* pictures a year and have them *matter.*" And yet he could still say depressing things like "Sometimes I think poor [dead] Valentino may be the happiest of us all. I don't *know,* that's all. It's so easy, so infernally easy, to make a mess of your life, and if you mess it up after a certain age it isn't easy to straighten it out again."

But as much as he complained about being saddled with stardom and his Great Lover persona, he enjoyed the hell out of it, too, and played it up to the hilt. He *became* whatever character he was playing, sometimes to the chagrin of friends, wives, and lovers. "If a new assignment were a dashing Cossack officer," wrote King Vidor, with perhaps a touch of exaggeration, "Jack would hire Russian servants in his household, and guests would be entertained with a balalaika orchestra while they were served vodka and caviar. I began to worry over the intensity with which Jack lived each part."

And Jack was as much a sex symbol as an actor, which both annoyed and secretly tickled him. He loved women, he loved sex, and couldn't help but be flattered by the attention even as he shrank away in self-consciousness. Jack had a hard time thinking of himself as handsome, and indeed his looks were not of the classic Arrow-collar model sort. He was generally a little underweight—but in the 1920s few men had the sort of body-builder physique that seems to be required of male stars today. He had wonderful eyes and a great smile, but his nose was a bit too big and too long for "perfection" ("Jewish," it was often called, to his annoyance). And he never quite lost the gawkiness that is so obvious in his earliest films, when he was all pencil-neck and flailing, skinny limbs. Even when Jack was in a smart military uniform or white tie, gliding insinuatingly toward his leading lady, he gave a slightly sidelong look of "I'm just playing, now." Had he not been quite so handsome, Jack might have been a great physical comic along the lines of Harold Lloyd or Stan Laurel.

Jack was reteamed with King Vidor's bride Eleanor Boardman for his next film, *Bardelys the Magnificent,* based on a 1906 novel by Rafael Sabatini (whose works also inspired such hits as *Captain Blood* and *Scaramouche*).

Decked out in an unflattering hairpiece, upturned moustache, and triangular "soul patch" (all of which were revived seven years later for *Queen Christina*), Jack played the marquis de Bardelys, a womanizing rogue in the court of Louis XIV. *Bardelys* is a funny, charming inconsequential movie (though, budgeted at $460,000, definitely an A film). Jack roisters his way happily through the film, which gave him little chance for deep acting or character development—but he did get a chance to show his light-comedy skills, which were so underused. Amid a plot featuring mistaken identity, too many tiresome swordfights, Bardelys romancing Boardman and alternately kissing up to and rebelling against the king (that plot point is never really clear), Jack seemed to be enjoying himself playing his charming character. Roy D'Arcy and George K. Arthur were terrific villains, and a final-reel escape from the gallows is shot as a parody of—rather than homage to—Douglas Fairbanks Sr.'s escapades (a joke that was lost on most reviewers).

One scene in particular stays in viewers' minds, thanks to Vidor and cinematographer William Daniels. As Jack and Eleanor Boardman drift in a small boat over a lake, the low-hanging tree branches pass languidly between the two leads, between the audience and the camera. It's a lovely effect, and Vidor said decades later that fans who had long forgotten the film's title asked him about it.

When *Bardelys* was released in September 1926, the *New York Times*'s Mordaunt Hall described the character as "a composite of d'Artagnan, Don Juan and that millionaire cowboy, Tom Mix," adding, "By his dashing portrayal of Bardelys, John Gilbert leaps into the active realms of Douglas Fairbanks, John Barrymore and Mr. Mix."

"Jack Gilbert's most elaborate starring feature during his career," wrote Edwin Schallert in the *Los Angeles Times*. "To say that *Bardelys the Magnificent* will be recognized as one of King Vidor's distinctive achievements of the screen would be undoubtedly giving too roseate an estimate of his accomplishments in this production. . . . Jack Gilbert's role is one that everybody will find more than favorable to him, and he plays it easily and cleverly. His love making, exceptionally well done in this case, will win unusual appreciation. His acting is otherwise very splendid." Alma Whitaker admired Jack's "masterly Doug Fairbanks stunts of acrobatic miracles," adding, "Valentino himself never surpassed John's love-making in pictures."

Not everyone—not even everyone at the *Los Angeles Times*—was impressed. Whitney Williams sniffed at both *Bardelys* and at John Barrymore's new *Don Juan.* "John Gilbert's attempt to duplicate a feat which only Doug Fairbanks can get away with was a pitiful play for a hand," he wrote. "Gilbert is not the type, and the sooner both he and his directors realize it the better it will be." Jack himself told Alma Whitaker of the *Los Angeles Times* that he was unhappy with the film, a major breach of company policy then and now: "I don't want to be portraying this incredible 'magnificent' stuff," he complained. "Whenever they talk 'costume picture' to me again, I am going to mentally translate all the characters into modern clothes and see how they would work out in say, Pasadena, today. If they don't ring true, they are out." Another critic disagreed: "Gilbert's acting is of the smooth, restrained sort that makes the spectators feel that they are witnessing the intimate development of a genuine romance."

The film cost $460,000 and brought back a profit of $135,000. Jack's own final word on it: "Applesauce. With one John Gilbert contributing most of the sauce." *Bardelys* was nearly a lost film: MGM destroyed the negative in 1936, when its rights to the Sabatini novel expired (ironically, *Bardelys* had not been filmed before and has not been since). In 2006 a nitrate print was found in France, missing only the third reel (which in its recent release was filled by stills and title cards).

Chapter Nine

> I became arrogant, of course. I admit it. I was John Gilbert, the supreme, the untouchable.
>
> —John Gilbert, 1933

At the end of 1926 Jack was awarded *Photoplay*'s annual best-acting medal, one of the highest honors in those pre-Oscars years, for *The Big Parade*. Riding high on his success, he traveled to New York, where he was reported to be in talks with Famous Players–Lasky, which "is more than keen to annex Gilbert at the expiration of his Metro-Goldwyn-Mayer contract, but that of course might be said with equal truth of all the producing companies," as the *Los Angeles Times* wrote. "The role of Clyde Griffiths in *An American Tragedy* has been promised Gilbert if he will but sign. . . . He said in several published interviews that he would like nothing better than to play the Dreiser role on the screen and furthermore, as it seems definitely certain that Monta Bell will direct it when the time comes, the sympathetic relations existing between Gilbert and Bell are adduced as evidence of what is in the wind."

But the talks with Famous Players–Lasky fell through; dejected from losing his shot at *An American Tragedy,* Jack had to make do with a dark carnival tale, *The Show.* He promisingly told the *Los Angeles Times,* "I am a low-down bum of a sideshow barker in a traveling show, a mean little whelp who treats women shamefully and I beat up Renée Adorée." But by the end of filming he was disenchanted: "We had to get some reclamation in the end," he complained. "Apart from that, it is honest, all right."

Renée Adorée gives French lessons to director Tod Browning, Jack, and Lionel Barrymore on the set of *The Show,* 1927 (The Everett Collection).

The Show was Jack's first project with the eccentric director Tod Browning. A former actor (and circus clown and acrobat), Browning took up directing in the late 1910s. At Universal and later with MGM, he specialized in dark, quirky projects, including nine starring vehicles for Lon Chaney. Browning is best known today for his terrifying early-1930s classics *Freaks* and *Dracula,* and he brought some of this toughness and creepiness to *The Show.* Browning was also a prickly character. "He was very difficult to work with," recalled film editor Basil Wrangell. "Very sarcastic, very unappreciative of any effort, and very demanding."

Jack had wanted to appear in a film version of the Ferenc Molnar play *Liliom,* about an abusive, tragic carnival barker who commits suicide and comes back to earth to look after his daughter. The play was, of course, reincarnated as Rodgers and Hammerstein's *Carousel* in 1945 (as *Liliom,* it had been shot in 1919 and would be again in 1930 and '34). Instead, the 1910 Tenney Jackson novel *The Day of Souls* was optioned and this movie was ostensibly based on it—but *The Show* had nothing whatsoever to do with Jackson's novel about the denizens of pre-earthquake San Francisco.

Perhaps to placate Jack, bits of *Liliom* were indeed used: Jack portrayed Cock Robin (!), a womanizing, thieving barker at a Hungarian carnival. A romantic triangle simmers between Cock Robin, hoochie-coochie dancer Salome (Renée Adorée), and "the Greek" (Lionel Barrymore). Browning incorporated a corking revenge death plot (the Greek uses both a sword and a venomous lizard to try to kill off his rival, with predictable results—Browning was to lift this subplot the following year for the deadly Lon Chaney–Joan Crawford–Norman Kerry circus love triangle in *The Unknown*).

Cock Robin is an enjoyably dastardly character and Jack obviously had great fun with him: he romances and robs innocent country girls, consorts with streetwalkers, even knocks Salome around when she interferes with his schemes. But that "reclamation" he complained about was indeed written in: Cock Robin is drawn into Salome's tragic family drama and falls to his knees before her, proclaiming, "God, you're a real dame—right straight through to the core."

Despite this, *The Show* is a hugely entertaining, fast-moving film, with plenty of Browning's dark, bizarre touches, some lewd humor, suspense, and a bit of melodramatic tear jerking. Credit must also be given to costume designer Lucia Coulter (who also had worked on *Bardelys*). Inspired by the striped sweater, neckerchief, and black pants worn by Joseph Schildkraut in the 1921 Broadway production of *Liliom,* she sexed it up and created what would become Billy Bigelow's iconic outfit for *Carousel:* skin-tight, closely striped sweater, scarf knotted at the neck, and tight, cinch-waisted black pants. John Raitt and Gordon MacRae wore it with great panache in the Broadway and film *Carousel*s, as did Charles Farrell and Charles Boyer in the 1930s version of *Liliom.* And the outfit made Jack—not Renée Adorée—the sex object in *The Show.* The camera lingers over his form, and when some female bit players gossip about Salome hiding Cock Robin in her room for weeks, one gives him the once-over and purrs, "Who *wouldn't?*"

Reviews were generally favorable: "Any one who is tired of drawing room dramas that are intensely unreal despite the fact that nothing particularly remarkable happens in them will have a wonderful time at *The Show,*" wrote the *New York Evening Post.* Richard Watts Jr. of the *New York Herald Tribune* compared Browning to Edgar Allan Poe,

Jack as Cock Robin in *The Show,* 1927 (Wisconsin Center for Film & Theater Research).

and another critic wrote that Jack "Takes his character and regenerates him . . . without a trace of implausibility—this is what marks Gilbert as one of the supreme actors of the screen." Jack himself bitterly called *The Show* "nothing whatever to be proud of. I wanted to do *Lilliom,* but was denied the privilege of making the fine story. *The Show* was its illegitimate spew. I was rotten in it." *The Show*—released in January 1927—cost $187,000, and made a profit of $178,000.

Over the weekend of February 12–13, 1927, Garbo and Gilbert vanished from Los Angeles. Gossip columnist Louella Parsons, hard up for scandal, broke the news that just *maybe* the two had rushed off to "a nearby village" and gotten married. Parsons was unable to find any licenses issued to John Gilbert or Greta Garbo—or John Pringle; Parsons, surprisingly, didn't know Garbo's real name was Gustafsson. "Repeated telephone calls at the Gilbert home in Beverly Hills failed to bring either a denial or affirmation," she wrote on February 14 (meaning, probably, no one answered or the maid hung up on her). "Two of Miss Garbo's close friends say she married Gilbert Friday and the entire story will be made public on Tuesday," she added. Of course, anyone who would make such a statement would not have remained "Garbo's close friend" for long—she was well known for cutting even her best friends dead if she thought they had so much as *smiled* at a reporter.

Rumors flew—as they continue to do—about that Valentine's Day weekend: perhaps the two had absconded not for an elopement but for a quick, quiet abortion? Irving Thalberg's biographer Mark A. Vieira even reports gossip that Jack had *shot* Garbo, or that she had shot him. A week later, a *Los Angeles Times* reporter tracked down Garbo at her Santa Monica home and got a statement from her—or so he claimed. Even as early as 1927, Garbo was unlikely to give a reporter the time of day. "An engagement to marry him?" Garbo (or her manager) said. "No, nothing like that. But we are as good friends as any two could possibly be and I hope we will always be the best of friends. I am one of Mr. Gilbert's most enthusiastic admirers [this is sounding less like Garbo—still learning English—and more like an MGM flack] and we have been much together . . . but I am not engaged to marry him. To be one of his admirers, yes, yes, yes!"

The bigger mystery is what happened to Jack, who turned up in the Monte Sano Sanatorium and Hospital in the Silver Lake neighborhood of Los Angeles after that "lost weekend." A lovely Spanish-style osteopathic hospital at Glendale Boulevard and Waverly Drive, Monte Sano was "envisioned as the perfect recuperation resort on its hill of health," according to its founders. Jack was claiming appendicitis: "They don't know yet, and may decide to operate in two or three days," he told a reporter, convincingly holding an ice pack to his abdomen. As for Garbo, "I concur in her denial of any engagement, and wish the same right back at her as to being one of her strongest admirers."

Appendicitis? Most friends and coworkers muttered about alcohol poisoning or drying out. King Vidor's story about the incident is "cute" enough to generate suspicion that it may be apocryphal: Vidor said Jack had come home from work to find a roast chicken dinner awaiting him, and happily wolfed it down. When the butler told him that he hadn't ordered or prepared it, Jack feared poisoning by a deranged stalker and rushed off to the hospital to have his stomach pumped. A concerned Vidor confirmed with a local market that the meal had been delivered by them, unpoisoned, and Jack "got the telephone number of the pretty red-haired nurse who attended him."

Well, *maybe*. But Jack was starting to have trouble with ulcers, which would get worse as the years went on—his "appendicitis" may very well have been bleeding ulcers, exacerbated by his drinking. (In May 1928 he was again hospitalized, "from lead poisoning on his face which, his physicians say, was caused from a poor makeup preparation." Quite possible; but again, eyebrows were raised and bootleg gin blamed.)

In March 1927, after the Los Angeles première of *Flesh and the Devil,* Garbo let down her guard enough to attend a party with Jack at the home of director Clarence Brown. The pair, wrote observant *Los Angeles Times* reporter Grace Kingsley, "seemed to eat little but dance together much! This was the first time they had been out together in quite a while, it having been reported that their engagement had been broken. Did you ever see such a handsome couple?" Clarence Brown wore his usual calm deadpan: "I'll bet if the end of the world were to come," wrote Kingsley, "and he had a commission to film it for the benefit of the inhabitants of Mars, he wouldn't show any excitement!"

Louise Brooks didn't believe for a moment that the romance was legitimate in the first place. The always contrarian and abrasive actress wrote to a friend in 1977, "Garbo was a lesbian, the Garbo-Gilbert romance a publicity comedy." No: "They were *really* two people utterly and totally in love," insisted the irrepressible romantic Adela Rogers St. Johns. "I have never seen two people so violently, excitedly in love. When she walked through the door if he was in the room, he went white

Garbo and Gilbert step out to the première of their first film together, *Flesh and the Devil,* January 1927 (Wisconsin Center for Film & Theater Research).

and took a great long breath and then walked toward her as if he was being yanked by a magnet." At least one of Garbo's friends, Frances Marion, felt that she was poison to Jack: "Only in legend does a man make incarnate a beautiful statue," she wrote years later.

Photoplay took some enjoyment in poking fun at them, snarkily writing,

> Off again, on again—Greta and John again—
> How they have stirred up the news for awhile!
> Making the critics sigh with them, die with them,
> Making the cynical smile!

Jack's demons became public on April 11, 1927. He was hosting what must have been a bang-up party at his home when some kind of disagreement broke out. Jack drove to the Beverly Hills police station at 3:00 a.m. and demanded that "someone" be arrested (that he was driving in his condition was never even remarked upon, which says much about road safety in the 1920s). He refused to say whom he wanted arrested, or why, and after a few minutes of drunk and disorderly conduct he was bundled off to the "tank" downstairs to sleep it off. Bail arrived at 8:00 the next morning, and Jack was surprisingly good humored about his dustup: "I must have been laboring under a hallucination and looking for trouble," he admitted. "I wasn't angry at any of my guests and I just went down to the station and the boys took care of me; very kind to me."

According to Colleen Moore, the night began with Garbo yet again standing Jack up: they were discussing marriage (again, according to Moore) when Garbo turned tail and ran. Jack drove to her apartment at the Miramar and tried (unsuccessfully) to scale an outside wall. He was pushed off, Mack Sennett comedy style, by Mauritz Stiller and somehow wound up in police custody. Another version had him arrested for speeding while on his way, gun in hand, to kill Stiller.

But the episode was not over: he reported to city recorder Seth Strelinger on April 18 and was sentenced to ten days in jail. "Do you think you can get away with such stunts in Beverly Hills?" asked Strelinger, and a chastened Jack admitted, "No, I didn't think so, and probably wouldn't do it again." "The actor took his sentence with a matter-of-fact grin," reported the *Los Angeles Times*. "Bang! Just like that, and here I am," Jack sighed. "Ought to be a nice quiet vacation, though."

But Jack was needed for work on *Twelve Miles Out* (ironically, a bootlegging story) and MGM did not want to wait ten days for him to vacation. On the morning of April 19, after twenty-four hours in jail, Jack was visited by Strelinger, Sydney Spaulding (president of the Beverly Hills Board of Trustees), and Douglas Fairbanks (a health nut and, at the time, nondrinker).

The good news: his sentence was reduced to one day in jail and he was free to go. "Mr. Fairbanks gave me a good talking-to," Jack recalled, adding, "They certainly treated me magnificently in that jail. I met a lot of swell guys around there. . . . I am not going around any more jails looking for trouble. Believe me, it sure feels good to get out, and I'm cured."

The bad news: waiting for him out on the sidewalk, with a posse

Jack looking unrepentant after his April 1927 disorderly conduct arrest (The Everett Collection).

of reporters, was a furious, self-righteous Louis B. Mayer. Jack was appalled and embarrassed but smart enough to control his temper and act the regretful little boy as Mayer all but hauled him by the ear into a studio car to report for work on *Twelve Miles Out*.

What was called Jack's "artistic temperament" began really hurting his social and professional life as he turned thirty. Considering what a tumultuous spring he'd had, he sounded surprisingly chipper about it. "It wasn't bad at all," he laughed to the *Los Angeles Times*. "I'd always been told I would feel old when I passed out of the twenties, but no, I feel just the same!"

It is tempting—and usually ill advised—to play armchair psychologist. But that "artistic temperament" might be diagnosed today as bipolar or manic-depressive disorder. He was, almost literally, a textbook case: the National Institute of Mental Health describes the condition as being characterized by "unusually intense emotional states" roller-coastering between "an overly joyful or overexcited state . . . and an extremely sad or hopeless state." The list of symptoms reads like a portrait of John Gilbert at his best and his worst: "Talking very fast, jumping from one idea to another, having racing thoughts. . . . Sleeping little. . . . Behaving impulsively and taking part in a lot of pleasurable, high-risk behaviors, such as spending sprees, impulsive sex. . . . Extremely irritable mood, agitation, feeling 'jumpy' or 'wired.' . . . A long period of feeling worried or empty."

Or on the other hand, he might simply have been a big drama queen. "Feverishly happy when he was happy, he sank to the deepest depths when ill fortune beset him," wrote the *Los Angeles Times*'s Edwin Schallert. "Liking companionship and the society of people when the gods smiled, he virtually shut himself off from the world when the clouds hovered. . . . There was nobody who could so retire into his shell, lead such a hermit-like existence, when events proved embittering and discouraging. Life was all extremes with Gilbert; it was his inner nature." "He was emotionally unstable," said Eleanor Boardman. "Gilbert was the type of man who would turn to the bottle at any disappointment. He used to come to our place on Sunday morning, presumably to play tennis or swim. If he had a bad review on one of his pictures, he was down in the dumps. Or if they said he was good, he was sky-high."

Jack also suffered from insomnia, deadly to anyone who has to be at work, bright and shining, early in the morning. He told Schallert that "there was nothing that afflicted him more during life. . . . Any worry would bring it on. He would lie awake until dawn night after night, get up and walk the floor endlessly; fear the least noise as if it were the booming of cannon."

But he did self-medicate with alcohol. Jack's form of alcoholism seems to have been binge drinking, trying—with increasingly disastrous results—to even out his moods. This, too, is a classic bipolar coping strategy. The Mayo Clinic notes, "Bipolar disorder and alcoholism often occur together. In fact, up to half the people who have bipolar disorder also struggle with alcoholism. Some people drink to ease depression, anxiety and other symptoms of bipolar disorder. Drinking may seem to help, but in the long run it generally makes symptoms worse. This can lead to more drinking—a vicious cycle that's difficult to overcome." Certainly as Jack's career problems worsened, so did his drinking—and, as a result, his marriages and friendships suffered. As did his physical health.

Alma Whitaker of the *Los Angeles Times* interviewed Jack in January 1927 and found him putting on his best adorable little boy act. "I am like that scared puppy who goes around wagging his tail, in the hopes that someone will notice him and pat him on the head," he claimed—with some justification. Approval was important to Jack and his feelings were very easily injured. But he went on to bite the hand that fed him, bad-mouthing his recent release *Bardelys:* "It wasn't honest," he said. "It is all impossible flap-doodle."

He was in no mood to make *Twelve Miles Out,* a surprisingly high-budgeted ($462,000) project based on a moderately successful Broadway play starring Warren William. Jack's costar was twenty-two-year-old Joan Crawford. She'd been at MGM for two years and had been working her way upward steadily, all big eyes and steely ambition. Crawford's childhood had been even harder than Jack's, but it affected her differently: she was almost pathetically grateful to MGM and Louis B. Mayer for making her a star. "At MGM we had a certain dignity," she later told interviewer Roy Newquist. "There were only so many good parts to be had in good films, so all of us had to take lousy parts in lousy films and count each good one as a special blessing."

Crawford was a Company Player to the tips of her fingernails. She recalled showing up for work once in slacks with a scarf over her head. Mayer "took one look at me, turned absolutely red, and told me to go back home and dress the way a star should be seen in public, and to never appear looking the way just 'any woman' would. . . . To this day, some little—or big—voice inside me says, 'Joan, go out there looking like a star.'" John Gilbert and Joan Crawford were cut from different cloth, so a fling between them was unlikely, even had Garbo not stood between them. Nonetheless, "*Twelve Miles Out* was the first time that magic man-woman chemistry happened in one of my films," Crawford recalled. "John Gilbert and I seemed to exude sex." It's true, they looked great onscreen together, all intense flashing eyes, and both were talented professionals, despite any deficiencies in the script or plot.

But it was not a happy set, Crawford later noted. She claimed Jack was still pursuing Garbo, with ever-decreasing success. "He'd stride onto the set in his stomping, military manner, rush to the phone to call her, only to find that her phone had been yanked out of the wall or her phone number changed—since last night! He fretted like thunder. He was impatient with the picture, the director. . . . The moment he finished

Jack as a dapper bootlegger and kidnapper in *Twelve Miles Out,* 1927 (The Everett Collection).

a scene, he'd rush to her set, to her dressing room, or he'd attempt again to call her. Thwarted, he was fury incarnate. He resented every minute on the set away from her." If the highly sexed Crawford had her heart set on an affair with her coworker, she quickly put that thought aside.

"Oh, I'm a bad lot," Jack said of his character in this film. "They wanted to make the heroine a prim New England maiden. Ugh! I can't

Two great profiles: Jack and Joan Crawford in *Twelve Miles Out,* 1927 (The Everett Collection).

make love to a prim New England maiden. I have to have an Adorée, a Garbo, a Pringle, a Mae Murray—someone that the audience knows right off the bat is a lip-to-lip, breast-to-breast subject, even if—er—if nothing like that ever happens." He must have been happy, then, with Crawford, who radiated modernity and sex, much in the way of a young Garbo or Aileen Pringle.

Twelve Miles Out still exists, in a chopped-up (sixty-two-minute), badly duped and retitled version (the titles were translated from English to French to English, resulting in such misspelled awkwardness as "What a drole type you have taken for a husband!"). Still, it is a fast-moving, tidy little gangster yarn starring Jack as bootlegger Jerry Fay, who kidnaps society girl Jane (Crawford) aboard his rum-running boat—when an even worse lot (the always terrifying Ernest Torrence) intrudes, Jerry finds himself playing Jane's protector.

It does not look like a $462,000 film, though, and one wonders where the money went. MGM supposedly refitted a yacht in San Pedro

Harbor to duplicate one captured by Prohibition agents, "equipped with special hatches and 'grab hooks' for handling liquor cargoes and unloading these into the sea quickly in case of the boat being overtaken." But the interiors appear to be shot on a small, dank MGM back-lot set. No one had any costume changes: Jack played nearly the whole film in a dark shirt and pants and a classic trench coat, while Crawford wore a sheer Rene Hubert party frock (she also sported a very severe Eton crop hairdo). Jack got to do some lively fight scenes with Torrence: looking just like Douglas Fairbanks in *The Black Pirate* (1926), with torn black shirt, he battled up and down the ship.

One critic felt that Jack was "glorious . . . he has all the dash and fire of *Bardelys* and all the romantic appeal of *The Merry Widow* all embodied in an ultra-modern young man." The film was released in July 1927 and brought in a respectable profit of $125,000.

Perhaps wanting to get far away from everyone—either with Garbo or without—Jack bought one of the classic perquisites of stardom: his own yacht. "I'm going to build myself a yawl and just vagabond around a bit, from port to port around through the South Seas and the Orient," he had said in 1925. "Somehow the continent has never had much fascination for me. But the Orient—I want to know every inch of its curious little islands and villages." His ninety-six-foot schooner the *Mabel Dell* (rechristened the *Temptress* after Garbo's second American film) was "probably the staunchest-built yacht in the local fleet," wrote a *Los Angeles Times* reporter. "Me, I don't know a thing about navigation, but I can learn, can't I?" said Jack. "I'm going down to Los Angeles harbor and take a course in handling a sailing boat and learn to shoot the sun and all those things. Won't it be glorious?" It was glorious—like John Barrymore and, later, Errol Flynn, Jack and guests bobbed amiably around the California coast—never getting anywhere near the Orient.

The maiden voyage was to be to Catalina, and Garbo agreed to accompany him and a handful of friends. Jack, proud and "resplendent in good-looking yachting attire," according to King Vidor, proudly welcomed his guests. Norma Shearer claimed to have spotted Garbo en route to the boat and asked after her: Jack's "expression seemed to say, 'Need you ask? You know Greta's eccentricities as well as I do.'" She was, it seemed, hiding—dodging and bobbing, actively avoiding having to say hello. "What was second nature for him was agony for her," said Carey Wilson.

Dinner that night was abruptly cancelled and the *Temptress* returned to port, the host looking glum and embarrassed. "I felt sorry for Jack," said Vidor. "I knew he would be dreadfully disappointed and would hate to return to his home. We could only conclude that Greta had been displeased and had given her famous pronouncement, 'I want to be alone—I think I go home.'" Shortly thereafter, the charm had worn off and the *Temptress* was soon put up for sale.

The always overwrought romantic Adela Rogers St. Johns claimed later that it was the loss of Garbo that ruined Jack's life, not the eventual ruin of his career. "I can only tell you that it was because if they married, he said, she wanted to retire from the screen, give up her career, buy a big ranch way away from everything, and have many children. And Jack still wanted the glamorous Garbo. . . . If he had known what it was like to lose her, perhaps no price would have been too high. But, you see, he didn't really believe he would lose her." St. Johns quoted Jack after he was dead and could no longer defend himself: "There has never been a day since Fleka [his supposed nickname for Garbo] and I parted that I haven't been lonely for her. And I think she has always been lonely for me. . . . I'd rather have one hour with Fleka than a lifetime with any other woman."

A more levelheaded version of their romantic breakup was voiced by Jack himself to Gladys Hall. "We were not suited to be together, Greta and I," he said. "She is a solitary person, very shy, fearful of intrusion, shrinking from people. I like people around me; life, good talk, excitement."

By the summer of 1927, open warfare raged between Jack and Louis B. Mayer, though the actor's assignments did not really warrant such rebellion. That year, he appeared in only one silly programmer (*Twelve Miles Out*); his other roles included a callow reporter (*Man, Woman and Sin,* opposite one of Broadway's great actresses), an outright cad (*The Show*), and Count Vronsky in a modern-dress version of *Anna Karenina,* with Garbo. Not at all a bad showing.

But "I don't like the stories and the management I've had lately, and I've told them so," Jack said to the *Los Angeles Times* on July 14. He and Mayer were not speaking—certainly not since his drunk and disorderly arrest, which might have gotten a lesser star fired. As for MGM producer Hunt Stromberg, "We go around glaring at each other like a lot of spoiled children." Joan Crawford may have recognized the need to take the occasional stinker at MGM, but not Jack, who said of *Twelve Miles Out,* "I haven't seen the picture and did not even go to the preview. It is not a good picture. We didn't have the proper story to work with. One thing that makes me furious is that there is a good story in the bootlegging industry. There is an epic tale there and someday someone is coming along to do it."

He went on to complain about how his character, and the plot, had been censored and softened: "Ten years ago, I would have been an out-and-out villain. A 'revenuer' would have come on board my rum-runner, given me the beating of my life, and left with the girl. Instead, I do the one 'big' thing of my life: I send her away from me, back to her own, voluntarily. I don't believe in being 'arty,'" he explained. "I do believe that a circle once begun should be completed and that, often, an arbitrarily 'happy' ending is more universally painful to the picturegoer than the sane and logical one, whatever that may happen to be."

Fistfights between Jack and Mayer were not needed—interviews like this were sufficient to breed hatred. Even today it is considered a betrayal to badmouth one's own movie or TV series—one "This series sucks" appearance on a talk show can get an actor fired. If this is what Jack was saying to reporters, one can imagine what he was saying in private to Mayer, Thalberg, and Stromberg. Biographer Scott Eyman quotes Mayer as saying, "We have no hate here, we have love. I love Irving [Thalberg]. I love everybody. Except John Gilbert, Sam Goldwyn, and Charlie Chaplin."

Jack's daughter Leatrice, years later, quoted Howard Strickling—a friend of both parties in question—as saying that "it was very strange, this thing between Mayer and Jack. Like he'd made up his mind to hate the guy from the first time he saw him. As far as I was concerned, Mayer was way off base in his feelings about Jack, but you couldn't tell him that." Strickling added, "Jack was one of the good guys. I was just getting started out there and he was very kind to me." Mayer's daughter Irene added that "just the sight of [John Gilbert] made him angry. Those two should never have been on the same planet, let alone the same studio." Star Colleen Moore told Jack's daughter that "Mayer was a great hater. . . . Jack would see him on the lot and give him this great big smile. It drove Mayer wild. . . . He let Mayer know what he thought of him in no uncertain terms."

To make matters worse, Mayer felt Jack was a bad influence on Greta Garbo even after their affair had ended: she turned down a project called *Diamond Handcuffs* in late 1926—on Jack's advice, Mayer believed. "That son of a bitch is inciting that damned Swede and it's going to cost us a fortune," Mayer reportedly fumed. She was suspended again in 1927, unhappy with her roles and her contract: not the yelling type, she famously said, "I t'ink I go home" and quietly walked out, seemingly perfectly content to return to Europe. Mae Murray had recently pulled the same stunt—walked out of her star contract to get married—and found her film career over.

Jack had certainly helped Garbo learn the ropes at MGM and had encouraged her to fight for better roles, but she was never anyone's pushover. Indeed, she could be rude to the point of unprofessionalism: "Greta has no idea of the conventional courtesies of the studio," said Jack, who was a fine one to talk (that quote must have made Mayer choke). "A certain director once wanted her to play in his picture . . . she turned to him coldly and said, 'but I do not wish to work for you.' Naturally, he was horribly insulted. After he walked off, I told her that she really ought not to speak so bluntly. 'But,' she insisted, 'I do *not* wish to work for him.'"

After the dust had settled a bit, Jack was able to admit his own culpability. "I became arrogant, of course," he said in 1933. "I admit it. I was John Gilbert, the supreme, the untouchable. . . . I forgot that I was just another actor earning his living. . . . I made the mistake of saying terrible things to my bosses. They said terrible things to me."

Still, when Mayer spoke in public of MGM's plans for the 1927–28 season, John Gilbert was right at the top of his list. The studio was aiming for 243 pictures—58 of them features—and bragged that Jack had "far outdistanced the field in a recent screen popularity contest, conducted by a New York newspaper." Among the John Gilbert films in planning stages were "a newspaper story written especially for him by Monta Bell" (*Man, Woman and Sin*), and a drama based on Ludwig Wolfe's *War in the Dark* (which went instead to Conrad Nagel—a lackluster choice; it turned into a Garbo vehicle, *The Mysterious Lady*). Yet another fey costume romance was slated for Jack, but Arthur Schnitzler's *Daybreak* was instead given to Ramon Novarro (who also couldn't save it). Speaking of Garbo, MGM was already touting her as Anna Karenina, but Jack was not yet attached to that project. Nipping at Jack's heels was William Haines, "elevated to the position of star since last year after his excellent work in *Brown of Harvard*."

Jack was also proposing story ideas to various MGM producers, with absolutely no success whatsoever. *The Hated,* he told the *Los Angeles Times,* he was working out with Edmund Goulding: the story of an idealistic German trying to do the right thing, till "the Kaiser's war machine, like a relentless juggernaut, mows him down at last" (it was basically *All Quiet on the Western Front,* two years before Erich Maria Remarque wrote the book). Likewise never filmed was *The Birth of the Blues,* a story Jack was working on with Monta Bell about a nightclub entertainer "and the subtle, corroding influence of the half-savage, jazz-mad universe in which he moves." Third on his list was a story that did, thank goodness, get filmed, though not for another five years: *Downstairs,* about "an insouciant, devil-may-care chauffeur—his domination and the havoc he wreaks." The *Los Angeles Times* called this last idea "a tale which would gladden the heart of Erich von Stroheim. . . . Jack greatly desires to play the chauffeur, but company officials, fearful of his prestige, say no."

John Gilbert was a naïve perfectionist who wanted to make Great Art, play Great Parts to the best of his ability. Mayer, Thalberg, Stromberg, Paul Bern, et al. were businessmen. Moviemakers, certainly, who wanted to put out good product (and occasionally a money-losing "prestige picture"). But paramount in their minds was making product people wanted to see: moneymaking entertainment. It couldn't all be *The Big Parade* and *The Snob;* sometimes it had to be *Twelve Miles Out* and *Bardelys the Magnificent.* "Gilbert may take a vacation of 'five, ten or fifteen years,'" said the *Los Angeles Times.* "And then again he may form his own company and have pictures to suit himself, he said."

A year after Valentino's death, another passing occurred that would impact Jack's career. On September 5, 1927, MGM's creator, Marcus Loew, died at the age of fifty-seven. This threw MGM into chaos: Mayer, of course, hoped that he would move up in the organization—he was not surprised but hugely hurt when it was announced that Loew had chosen Nicholas Schenck as his successor and left him controlling interest in Loew's Inc. Mayer still remained in virtual command at MGM's California headquarters, but he had Schenck in New York to deal with. So dismayed was he that Mayer put out stories that he might be leaving movies altogether, to go into politics or just retire to enjoy his family. No one who knew Mayer took this very seriously.

In June 1927 Jack began shooting his second project with Garbo, a modern-dress version of *Anna Karenina,* retitled *Love.* This gave the ad writers a chance to use the phrase "Greta Garbo and John Gilbert in *Love!*" (A trick that backfired in 1929 when a proposed film called *Heat* had to be retitled *Wild Orchids* to forestall "See Garbo in *Heat!*" jokes.)

Love had started with Ricardo Cortez in the male lead and the Russian import Dimitri Buchowetzki directing. But Garbo took ill—whether she was genuinely sick or merely unhappy with the production was widely argued—and *Love* began its new incarnation costarring Jack, with his friend Edmund Goulding directing. MGM had been anxious to reteam Garbo and Gilbert since their success in *Flesh and the Devil.* They had bought the novels *The Masks of Erwin Reiner* by Jacob Wasserman and *The Sun of St. Moritz* by Paul Oskar Höcker as possible costarring vehicles, but neither panned out (the Wasserman book was later filmed with Jack and Alma Rubens).

Novelist Vicki Baum (*Grand Hotel*) was bowled over by director Goulding: "One of the few truly original and interesting people I met in my brief film career," she wrote in her memoirs. "He had come up from the lowest depths of the London slums, and where, en route, he had acquired his sensitivity for the finest nuances in taste, speech, dress, behavior, I wouldn't know, unless it was by sheer talent." Goulding was the perfect combination of coarseness and sophistication, which Jack admired and enjoyed. He was also an excellent director who went on to helm *Grand Hotel, Dark Victory, The Razor's Edge,* and *Nightmare Alley.*

Goulding was also socially adept enough to stand back and let Jack coach Garbo. No matter what the state of their romantic affairs, Garbo trusted him as an actor: up till now, she had been seen in her American films as a great beauty and a fascinating "character," but not much of an actress. Her vamp roles really did not give her scope to do much. This changed with *Love,* Garbo's first real *performance* at MGM. It was her first full-blown "Garbo" role as a tragic victim of Great Love. She was vulnerable and human, not the vamp of her previous American movies—this was a template for many of her future roles.

"Garbo insisted that only Gilbert could direct her in the love scenes," wrote historian Kevin Brownlow. "Gilbert directed nearly half the picture, with the agreement of the credited director." "She followed his every word," claimed Jack's daughter Leatrice. "And she looked at him before any shot was made. If he didn't approve, it would be reshot." "He is so fine an artist that he lifts me up and carries me on with him," Garbo herself once said. "It is not just scenes I am doing—I am living."

The production went surprisingly quickly (it was shot in about a month) and with very little trauma. Jack and Garbo worked well together and whatever offscreen quarrels they had seemed to be cooling down. Indeed, *Love* is—arguably—the best film they made together, certainly a cut above the melodrama of *Flesh and the Devil.* They were certainly the most beautiful couple onscreen in 1927: he was handsome and dashing in his Russian military tunic, and she—well, she looked like Greta Garbo.

Love showed both performers displaying the height of silent-movie acting: subtle, human, their characters growing through the film. His Vronsky is vibrant, impulsive, and selfish; her Anna is wary and resigned—and their doomed love affair is more true to life than in any of their other movies ("You will destroy each other," Anna's husband rightly predicts).

Jack approved of this modern-dress scenario, believing it made the story more accessible to the audience. He'd told the *Los Angeles Times* back in July, "It's all very well to make pictures of these heroes and villains of the past, but are they honestly and truthfully any more romantic than the man who fills my gasoline tank? How do you know what emotions the man across the street from you is experiencing? How do you know what love has come into his life, what he feels?" He added that actors were getting the short end of the stick, less chance to express real emotions than their female costars: "The claim has been made that this is a woman's age, that men are stolid and dull, but it isn't so. Men are as romantic as they ever were."

Infuriatingly, MGM insisted on shooting an additional happy ending for those exhibitors who wanted it: Anna doesn't throw herself un-

Anna Karenina up-to-date: with Garbo in *Love,* 1927 (The Everett Collection).

der a train; instead, her husband dies and the lovers are reunited, leaving readers of Tolstoy to throw themselves under trains upon leaving the theater. (Jack was called from the set of *The Cossacks* for these retakes, and had already grown in his longer hair and fuller moustache).

Perhaps still smarting from this idiotic alternate ending, Jack was bitterly critical of *Love:* "A Russian *East Lynne,*" he scoffed in 1928, referencing a sturdy old melodrama. "A cheap interpretation of Tolstoi's story, which, though containing some memorable moments, is at best a sob sister's love tale." *Love,* which cost $488,000, was released in November 1927 and eventually brought in a profit of $571,000, doing better than any of Jack's other silents with Garbo. Though Garbo's rather sexless and stately 1935 remake of *Anna Karenina* is more often seen today, the silent *Love* is a much better film. Garbo's 1935 Anna is too much the Great Lady, and she has no chemistry with her Vronsky, Fredric March. *Love* remains the Garbo-Gilbert film to see.

His next leading lady was as talented and famous as Garbo, but more troubled. In mid-July 1926, Jack had thrown his house open to welcome Broadway star Jeanne Eagels, who had just arrived to appear with him in *Man, Woman and Sin.* He gave a party, which was attended by Mae Busch, Bea Lillie, Ethel Barrymore, Elinor Glyn, Edmund Goulding, and screenwriters Douglas Doty, Agnes Christine Johnston, Bess Meredyth, and Frank Dazey, among others. Jack's house, noted Grace Kingsley of the *Los Angeles Times,* "is away up on top of a Beverly Hills mountain, which you approach by a winding road. The large living-room is beamed and raftered after the fashion of Mexican and Spanish houses and churches. You feel as you are stepping right into the middle ages—until you sit down on the overstuffed davenports and happen to hear the tinkle of a telephone bell." Jeanne Eagels admitted, "I was awfully frightened driving up the road to this house. I told Mr. Gilbert he should never be able to get rid of me, because I shall simply never dare to drive down that road again." Eagels's timing was off: had it not been for Garbo, Jack would no doubt have taken her up on that.

And here we encounter the second "Mayer and Gilbert fistfight" rumor. Story editor Sam Marx—who, by the way, did not yet work at MGM in 1926—said in the 1970s that Gilbert tried to explain the poem "The Widow in the By Street" (which provided part of the film's plot) to Mayer. "It happened to be a story that didn't strike Louis B. Mayer very well," Marx told Kevin Brownlow. "At one point, he finally stopped and said, 'Are you telling me that this woman in this book is a whore?' And Gilbert said, 'What's wrong with that? My mother was a whore!' Whereupon Mayer's temper flashed, his fists went along with it, and he floored Gilbert with one blow."

Mayer was well known to have a mother fixation, and Jack used to poke him with a stick by telling stories like one about the time he was holding his mother's train during a stage performance as a child: "I lost my grip on the dress and she fell forward on her face. Her train flew up and she wasn't wearing any drawers. That was the last time I saw my mother's ass!" "No decent man would speak that way about his mother!" Mayer was fuming. "I hate the bastard."

There are several problems with Sam Marx's account (aside from the idea of John Gilbert and Louis B. Mayer beating each other up all over Hollywood like a couple of Rock 'em Sock 'em Robots). For one thing, the *Man, Woman and Sin* story idea was Monta Bell's, not Jack's. Bell, a former editor and publisher at the *Washington Herald,* had long wanted to direct a newspaper story. According to Irving Thalberg, Bell wrote the treatment and submitted it to him, not to Mayer. Also, the story as filmed is nothing out of the ordinary for 1920s-era MGM: a tidy little melodrama about a kept woman and a nice, naïve young man. There was one scene in which Jack enters what is obviously a whorehouse, but this had nothing to do with the plot and could easily have been cut (and wasn't). There might have been some objection to casting John Gilbert in the male lead; it wasn't a smoldering Great Lover part, but one that might have been played by Ramon Novarro, William Haines, or any other MGM boy-next-door.

MGM was taking a huge risk by hiring Jeanne Eagels. In fact, the only reason Eagels was available was because she had just been suspended from Actors Equity for failing to appear in *Her Cardboard Lover,* her current Broadway hit. Jeanne Eagels—lovely, high-strung, talented—had become Broadway's star of the decade as Sadie Thompson, the golden-hearted hooker browbeaten by an obsessed preacher in *Rain* (in which she starred from 1922 to 1926). She had made a handful of movies in the 1910s, but her career had never taken off. By 1927, when she was signed to play opposite Jack, she was in her late thirties, frightfully thin and frail, and notoriously battling the drug and alcohol use that would eventually kill her. She was also, famously, one of the most talented women of her generation, a great beauty, and—when she wanted to be—hugely charming.

That Monta Bell was directing was encouraging—he was calm, ingratiating, and could handle the most jittery of performers. Still, *Man,*

Woman and Sin proved to be a difficult shoot. Eagels's painful sinus infections, rumored drinking and drug binges, unexplained latenesses and absences, all dragged out the filming to the point where Bell threw in the towel and asked that she be fired and replaced. Eagels's biographer, Edward Doherty, reported in 1930 that "Jeanne repeated all she had said about stupidity in the movies. . . . She hated everyone on the lot, she said, except Monta Bell and John Gilbert." Greta Garbo, for all her emotional issues and quirks, must have seemed like a walk in the park by comparison.

Jeanne Eagels was bored, she was unprofessional—but she was so talented and so charming in her apologies that the cast and crew made allowances. It seemed Eagels's film career would end with *Man, Woman and Sin,* but talkies (and being kicked out of Actors Equity again for various hi-jinks in 1928) led her back to the movies, just as Jack was facing his own career crossroads. Eagels might have had some success; her first two talkies were well received—but in October 1929 she collapsed and died in her doctor's office, with a truly impressive amount of alcohol, chloral hydrate, and heroin in her bloodstream.

In *Man, Woman and Sin,* Jack played a poor, socially awkward slum kid who grows up to be a newspaper reporter and falls in love with the brittle, sophisticated society editor of a Washington, DC, newspaper—of course, it all winds up in disillusion, heartbreak, and tragedy. Even in the degraded print that survives, one can see that *Man, Woman and Sin* was a top-drawer production. The sets, costumes, camerawork, and lighting are all the height of silent moviemaking. Jack's mother was played by the great Gladys Brockwell (who was on her way to a brilliant career as a character actress in talkies when she died in a car accident in 1929). Both Jack and Jeanne Eagels give brilliant performances: he boyish and vulnerable, she jaded and world-weary—and both of them are among the most beautiful people onscreen in 1927.

Jack felt he had done a creditable job at playing "an unsophisticated newspaper reporter—provided that there is such an animal. I think I got over what I tried to. It meant, for me, unusual repression. To me it is the best work I have ever done. It is also Monta Bell's 'pet' picture." But nothing was ever perfect in Jack's world: "I only wish that we had been allowed to bring the story to its logical end," he complained, throwing in what today is known as a spoiler: "The boy should have been hanged; it would have pointed the whole thing. Instead he is released."

Director Monta Bell shows off his hunt-and-peck technique to Jack and Jeanne Eagels on the set of *Man, Woman and Sin,* 1927 (The Everett Collection).

Robert E. Sherwood in *Life* handed Jack a good review: "John Gilbert is the guileless, bewildered youth—a distinct departure from his usual style and an effective one." Broadway great Eagels, however, seemed "obviously ill at ease and inclined to blink in her quieter moments." Norbert Lusk in the *Los Angeles Times* likewise enjoyed Jack's performance: "It is comparatively simple to be effective in a showy military uniform, but a far more serious matter for a mature actor to present a believable figure as a 19-year-old youth in shabby clothes and a hired dress suit. This John Gilbert does with such skill and sympathy and sincerity as to efface almost all the other roles by which he has achieved his high position." Lusk, too, seemed unsure what to make of Jeanne Eagels: "The discerning will see in her a figure of amazing interest and a certain strangeness, quite unlike anyone else on the screen today."

Man, Woman and Sin ("My God, what a title!" laughed Jack) cost $236,000 and made a profit of $329,000 upon its November 1927 release. "It could have been great, but it wasn't," Jack said of this film a year after its release. "I have my own private reasons for its failure, which I am not permitted at this time to disclose."

Jack, by the way, loosened his "no visitors to the set" rule while filming *Man, Woman and Sin* when the year's hero, Charles Lindbergh, visited MGM, trailing Louis B. Mayer and William Randolph Hearst, and spent the day watching Jack, Marion Davies, Ramon Novarro, and William Haines at work on their sets.

In May 1928, just before the première of his next film, *The Cossacks, Vanity Fair* published one of the most jaw-dropping attack pieces ever written about a Hollywood celebrity, before or since. It was written by Jim Tully, novelist, newsman, and proudly pugnacious, self-described "hobo." A runaway, amateur boxer, and rail rider, Tully had his first hit with *Beggars of Life: A Hobo Autobiography* (1924) and went on to write such books as *Shanty Irish, Shadows of Men, Blood on the Moon*—and *Jarnegan* (1926), a diatribe about a Hollywood director that ran into censorship trouble and provided many a guessing game as to who the characters in the book were based on. "In hoarse whispers any one will tell who the villain of Jarnegan was, but no two hoarse whispers agree. Anyhow it made Mr. Tully about as popular in Hollywood as a Hopi Indian is at a Navajo ceremonial dance," wrote Harry Carr in *Smart Set* magazine.

Billed as "Hollywood's Severest Critic," Tully came out swinging in his two-page John Gilbert profile: "His emotion is on the surface," Tully wrote. "His nature is not deep. His enthusiasms are as transient as newspaper headlines. He has no sense of humor." What followed was both a professional and personal attack on Jack, shocking in its bitterness: "A man of neither education nor capacity, he is more opinionated than Elinor Glyn, and less profound."

He attacked Jack's talent ("Mr. Gilbert is not a gifted actor. . . . He plays every role the same") and even his bona fides as a sex symbol, comparing him with the late, sainted Rudolph Valentino: "Where Valentino had marched like a gallant Italian despoiler through the flower-bedecked portals of female hearts, Mr. Gilbert . . . was only able to enthrall the weaker subjects in his kingdom. Perhaps women are wiser than we know in such things. Valentino was very much a man" (ironically, Rudolph Valentino spent much of his offscreen time defending his masculinity and heterosexual credentials against just such attacks).

Tully accused Jack of ungraciously telling a female reporter that "women lose their charm after forty," then lost any points he'd gained by adding, "Save in a few cases, none of which I can now remember, Mr. Gilbert was right" (Tully himself was forty-two at the time and not exactly a matinee idol himself). For all of that, the article contained more than a few grains of truth, and had Tully cut the nasty personal attacks, it might have been an incisive character exposé of John Gilbert. Speaking of the actor's early years at Triangle and Fox, Tully wrote quite accurately, "There followed a long struggle in which was developed in the young player a persecution complex, which even now, at the height of transitory fame, he is not able to master. It appears insurmountable." Tully was also probably on target when he said, "He is blamed for much of the so-called temperament with which Miss Garbo punished the sensitive producers."

More troubling was the anonymous rat within the MGM ranks who was quoted liberally throughout the article. These stories, too, have the uncomfortable ring of truth about them: "His conceit and changeable moods make it uncertain just what he is going to be like from day to day," this inside source told Tully. "One day he will be affable and happy and work hard; another day, irritable, uncivil, and rebellious; another day lackadaisical and uninterested in his work." Jack would happily greet visitors or reporters during filming, it was said, "then nag an assistant director the rest of the day for letting the visitor on the set."

The question is not so much why *Vanity Fair* would print such a hatchet job (a controversial article by a famous writer about a big star? Of course the magazine printed it), but how much MGM knew about this article and why the studio let it go through. MGM did not, perhaps, have the power to dictate to *Vanity Fair* what pieces it could and could not publish. But if MGM executives got wind of it in time—and it's hard to believe they didn't, with reporters and studio insiders being quoted—they could have offered *Vanity Fair* something to make it worthwhile to drop the piece. The article was only a page and a half, not a cover story, and if MGM had offered *Vanity Fair*'s publisher, Condé Nast (a reasonable businessman), access to a star or director of his choice instead, he might well have been persuaded not to print the item. But the article took Jack down a peg or two—or three—and there were many people at MGM who would have seen this as a win-win situation.

Jack, understandably, was devastated and furious. He tried to make jokes in good humor, but he was thin-skinned and neurotic about his talent and his looks. "It crushed Jack," screenwriter Carey Wilson told the actor's daughter Leatrice of Tully's article. "For a while Jack acted as if he believed every rotten thing Tully said about him." But for all his self-dramatizing and mood swings, Jack knew himself and offered reporter Alma Whitaker a clear-eyed self-assessment. "I'm afraid I'm a dab at dramatizing myself," he admitted cheerfully. "But I do it more honestly now. I mean, you know, that when I was unhappy, I was in the last depths of despair. When I was happy I was on the top of the world. But now . . . well, I can laugh privately at myself, even when I am staging the despair."

The very next month—June 1928—*Photoplay* began running a four-part series of articles titled "Jack Gilbert Writes His Own Story." Magazines had too great a lead time for *Photoplay* to have tossed together a four-part series, complete with illustrations, after *Vanity Fair* hit the newsstands. So the magazine must have had warning—several months' worth, probably—to prepare a counterattack.

Celebrity journalism was nothing new in the 1920s, of course: for three hundred years, readers of news sheets and magazines had reveled in the scandals, fashions, and love lives of royalty, society leaders, artists, and stage stars. But the movies raised all this to a new height (or depth). *Photoplay* made its debut in 1912, and was followed by *Screenland, Modern Screen, Motion Picture,* and countless others, right down to today's minute-by-minute coverage on celebrity news websites.

The early fan magazines were surprisingly snarky and cynical, often giving bad reviews to big-studio films and taking stars to task for their on- and offscreen flaws. But Jack never really had a problem with them: he was friends with many of the regular writers and with *Photoplay* editor James Quirk; he was smart enough to use the press to his advantage. Indeed, Quirk published an editorial along with the first installment of Jack's *Photoplay* memoirs: "The Ingrate of Hollywood," he called Jim Tully. "The hobo who walked the ties into the studio city and was sheltered and petted by motion picture people to whom he appealed for help."

Quirk could be as personally insulting as Tully: "Utterly unlovable, he [Tully] wanted to be loved by everyone. Failing, he turned bitter and, under the guise of truth, has written more vicious stuff about motion picture people than any one man or woman has ever written." Tully's *Vanity Fair* piece, wrote Quirk, was "more vicious, more unfair, in worse taste, if possible, than anything else he has written about others." He gleefully twisted the knife: "I fear he hates handsome men and beautiful women. One thing I never read in his writings about Hollywood—he never accused a beautiful woman of annoying him with her attentions."

While billed as "Jack Gilbert Writes His Own Story," the article is an obvious pastiche, partially Jack's own off-the-cuff (and sometimes endearingly tactless) observations and partially classic *Photoplay* writing—the perfumed scent of Adela Rogers St. Johns's hand wafts over the article, as subtle as "a ton of coal clattering down the chute," to quote Dorothy Parker. But it serves as an excellent disclosure of what John Gilbert wanted us to know in late 1928; his view of his own life and personality. The facts may not be trusted, but what he says and what he leaves out tells us a lot, too. "Jim Quirk has asked me to write an outline of my career," wrote Jack (or his ghostwriter). His memoirs were put down, he said, "mostly as it happened, some of it censored, some of it omitted, none of it elaborated."

MGM went all out for Jack's next film, *The Cossacks;* it was his most expensive MGM silent, costing a stunning $694,000 (it eventually brought in a profit of $174,000). It looks expensive, too: the sets (both interior and exterior), costumes, extra-heavy scenes: all point to a top-notch production—a cliff collapse atop horseback riders is particularly impressive. Russian architect Alexander Toluhoff was hired to build a Cossack village in Laurel Canyon, which doubled as temporary home to the extras and stunt riders. MGM was bragging in press releases that it was shipping 112 Cossacks over from Russia, "a mixed contingent of Mohammedans and native Russian Cossacks, of the Tarek and Kouhan clans in the Caucasus Mountains." Most of *The Cossacks* was shot in this village, with only a few studio scenes; Jack noted that after a week or so, the scent of pork and potatoes on the location was overwhelming.

While many of Jack's complaints about his roles and scripts were on target and necessary, he bizarrely lashed out in the press about the cheapness of *The Cossacks* production. "We are making a Russian picture now built around the splendor and lavishness of the early days of the Russian Czar," he told the *Los Angeles Times* shortly before filming began. "The appropriation for this picture is $125,000. It can't be done on this sum. That's all there is to it. . . . It's really terrible." Either he was misinformed or he was deliberately being obtuse, but this sort of thing certainly aggravated his bosses even further.

Jack played Lukashka, the son of a Cossack leader (Ernest Torrence) who is rejected and taunted by his girl (Renée Adorée), his father, and just about everyone else in the village because he doesn't want to go out and massacre Turks. Lukashka finally snaps and pleases everyone (except the Turks) by becoming a killing machine, "slitting every unbelieving throat that gurgles in these mountains!" While he is off with a war party, his girl is betrothed to a visiting prince (Nils Asther, very good as the smarmy Other Man). It all ends with kidnapping, torture, and a good old-fashioned ride to the rescue.

When *The Cossacks* opened in the summer of 1928, it turned out to be exactly the sort of swashbuckling romance that would have suited Douglas Fairbanks or Rudolph Valentino—in fact, it had suited Valentino back in 1925, when he'd starred in a similar film, *The Eagle,* directed by Clarence Brown; *The Eagle* incorporated the kind of sly, self-mocking light comedy at which Valentino excelled. Brown was, in fact, brought in to heavily "assist" titular director George Hill, who was better known as a cinematographer. A copy of *The Cossacks* exists today along with its original orchestral soundtrack—already sound was intruding upon MGM silents.

Renée Adorée—in almost the exact same village girl outfit she wore in *The Big Parade*—looks adorable as the love interest. Jack, in a low-cut peasant shirt and big fur hat, is breathtaking. He got the chance to do some impressive horseback riding, though, of course, the most impressive moments were executed by a stunt rider. Frances Marion, who wrote the screenplay, recalled that during the Russian folk-dance scenes, Jack "leapt about like a goat with a bee in its ear (for close-up shots), while his double, a famed performer from the Russian ballet, leapt like a graceful antelope across mountain peaks. The contrast struck everyone's sense of humor and even Jack had to laugh at his own clumsiness. He could afford to laugh within the protective walls of the studio; it was still policy not to let audiences be disillusioned by

A Ruth Harriet Louise portrait from *The Cossacks,* 1928 (author's collection).

uncovering the fact that their heroes had other men break wild horses, fight, rush into burning buildings—and even dance the kazachok for them."

The Cossacks is an enjoyable, well-made film—basically a western with Russian hats. One problem is that there are no likeable characters: Lukashka and his father are bloodthirsty religious fanatics, Renée

Adorée's character is shallow and fickle, Nils Asther's is vain and dismissive. They all give terrific performances—Jack is lively, funny, sexy. But one doesn't really care what happens to these people. There was lots of entertaining trick riding (expensive imported Cossacks, or rodeo men brought in from Texas? Impossible to tell). One can see Jack's frustration: he did a lot of flashing of teeth, throwing his head back and laughing manfully, and passionate Renée Adorée–chasing; but it really wasn't *acting.*

The *Los Angeles Times* loved it: "It has all the sure-fire elements that compose a story of the red-blood sort," though Brown's taking over from Hill was not only an open secret, it was apparent on the screen: "There are evidences here and there of loose ends in the story possibly due to overfootage." As for Jack, "He dominates the action, despite the competition with so capable an actor as Ernest Torrence."

Jack's success in this romantic role points out one difference between silents and talkies that was to come back and bite him: intertitles like "The woods are full of lilies—and I know a brook where the wild turtle lives!" sound fine in the audience's mind. Said out loud, they would induce laughs and rude noises.

While shooting *The Cossacks,* Jack took part in an all-star cameo scene used in King Vidor's hilarious *Show People,* released in late 1928. Marion Davies—playing movie star Peggy Pepper—is seen in the MGM commissary, dining nonchalantly with fellow stars Jack (in full *Cossacks* gear), Renée Adorée, Douglas Fairbanks, William S. Hart, Aileen Pringle, Norma Talmadge—and Jack's ex-wife Leatrice Joy. It was one of several cameos he made over the years: Jack was also seen in the 1928 promotional short *Voices across the Sea,* which showed the opening of the Empire Theatre in London—Jack, Greta Garbo, Norma Shearer, Joan Crawford, and Marion Davies all spoke about the new theater—this was, technically, Jack's talkie debut, but it was little seen in the United States.

He was also reported to have been among the many famous stars viewing the great chariot race in *Ben-Hur,* filmed one Saturday in 1925 at a huge arena constructed at La Cienega and Venice boulevards. While Ramon Novarro, Francis X. Bushman, and their stunt riders raced around and around (coming close to tragedy more than once), nearly every star in Los Angeles donned biblical-era costumes and joined extras to cheer them on.

Two delightful home movies taken at William Randolph Hearst and Marion Davies's San Simeon estate in 1926 survive as well. That January Jack joined a Sunday excursion (Irving Thalberg, Elinor Glyn, King Vidor, Eleanor Boardman, Edmund Goulding, and British director Anthony Asquith were among those chauffeured in, many in fancy dress). Their bounding arrival was filmed—with funny titles—and later in the day Jack joined Thalberg and Asquith in making a parody western. The short clip—which, thank goodness, survives—shows cowboy Jack hopping up and down on a chair "horse," rescuing "my own little Irvina" (Thalberg in hugely unconvincing drag) from the clutches of Asquith. Jack's quivering-lip comic acting is over-the-top hilarious and makes one wish he had been given more comedy to do.

MGM's 1925 *Studio Tour*—happily, still viewable today—featured clips of Jack and numerous other MGM stars, writers, and directors (Joan Crawford, seen being fitted by Erté, was still called Lucille Le Sueur). The 1929 William Haines comedy *A Man's Man* incorporated 1927 newsreel footage of Jack and Garbo with director Fred Niblo at the Los Angeles première of *Flesh and the Devil;* more red-carpet footage of Jack showed up in the 1930 newsreel *Screen Snapshots.*

Four Walls reteamed Jack with Joan Crawford, who was rapidly climbing the ladder at MGM—her very next film, *Our Dancing Daughters,* would shoot her to stardom. Crawford was relieved to find that her temperamental costar from *Twelve Miles Out* had calmed down, and the two got along swimmingly. There was still no romance: Crawford was at the time engaged to Douglas Fairbanks Jr. Sadly, *Four Walls* was a run-of-the-mill programmer. Jack played an eager-to-reform gangster (interestingly, a Jewish one named Benny Horowitz) and Crawford his unhelpful moll—it was based on a 1927 Broadway play starring Paul Muni (still billed as "Muni Wisenfrend").

Four Walls opened in August 1928; the *New York Times* thought Jack gave "a capital performance," though finding the movie as a whole silly and tedious. One New York reviewer was not impressed by the film or its stars. Jack "never looks the part," the paper said. "One might say that he is one of the best dressed gangsters that ever came to the screen, for not only are his suits cut faultlessly, but his whole appearance is rather that of a banker or a broker than a killer living on the east side of Manhattan." As for Crawford, "she is beautiful, but hardly the type one would expect to see basking in the presence of burglars and murderers." *Four Walls*—sadly, a lost film—cost a rather modest $255,000 and made a profit of $289,000.

In the fall of 1928 Jack made his only film with the great Swedish director Victor Sjöström. *The Masks of the Devil* costarred Alma Rubens who, with her slumberous dark eyes and black hair, looked as though she might have been Jack's sister. In more ways than one: poor Rubens spent much of her life on the edge of disaster. A popular dramatic actress since the mid-1910s, she had been fighting heroin addiction for almost as long. It's interesting that even after years of multiple arrests and stints in rehab, Rubens was still able to get starring roles at major studios—MGM, Fox, and Universal gambled on her through the late 1920s. Also in *The Masks of the Devil* was German import Eva von Berne, "purchased" on one of Mayer's European shopping trips. Talkies put an end to her American career after this one film; she was shipped back to Germany and lived till 2010, dying at the age of one hundred.

Based on Jacob Wasserman's novel *Die Masken Erwin Reiners,* the film was "quite a good entertainment," wrote Mordaunt Hall in the *New York Times,* noting that Wasserman (and Sjöström) borrowed heavily from Oscar Wilde's *The Picture of Dorian Gray:* "Baron Reiner [the roué played by Jack] has only to look in a mirror and find that as time goes on he looks more and more like Satan. These double exposure effects are cleverly accomplished, and sometimes when Mr. Gilbert is not at his love-making he does some clever acting." Jack reveled in his charmingly evil character, and Hall approved: "Nobody else could have accomplished this except Mr. Gilbert."

The Masks of the Devil—sadly, also a lost film—was released as a silent with orchestral music and sound effects. The day Mordaunt Hall saw it, the early sound technology ground to a spectacular halt: "The music synchronization suddenly failed. So during these supposedly dramatic incidents three notes were repeated several times, until the audience was stirred to laughter. The disk arrangement could not be set to work before the end of the picture, and therefore the organist officiated for the final embrace." *The Masks of the Devil*—which was released in November 1928—cost a hefty $305,000 and made a profit of $248,000.

By the end of 1928 John Gilbert was the second-highest male earner for MGM. Number one was Lon Chaney (at $3,750 per week). Chaney, who had only two years to live, had played character roles in four non-horror films that year. Trailing close behind were the affable, boyish Ramon Novarro (with three romantic dramas that year) and the equally affable, boyish William Haines (whose five 1928 films included *Show People*).

Since the death of Marcus Loew, the vultures had been circling MGM, one of the biggest and most successful studios in the industry. The chief vulture was William Fox, who began talks with Nicholas Schenck to buy controlling interest in the company. Fox was a devious and little-trusted character, but he was riding high in 1928, as his studio was on the cutting edge of talkie technology.

At the same time—as if Mayer did not have enough worries—Jack was in New York, meeting with United Artists about signing with that studio. The deal was probably suggested by UA star Douglas Fairbanks, a friend of Jack's—certainly Fairbanks pushed Joseph Schenck to sign Jack. This was unusually generous of Doug, as Jack would be directly competing with him for roles at UA. The studio had a great string of releases in the late 1920s: Buster Keaton's *The General* and *Steamboat Bill, Jr.*, Gloria Swanson's *Love of Sunya* and *Sadie Thompson;* Mary Pickford's *My Best Girl,* Fairbanks's *The Gaucho,* Charlie Chaplin's *The Circus,* and the romances of Ronald Colman and Vilma Banky.

Adding John Gilbert to the roster would be a huge jewel in an already sparkling crown. To twist the knife even further, the president of UA was Joseph Schenck, brother of Louis B. Mayer's MGM nemesis, Nicholas Schenck. UA offered Jack a six-year deal, huge percentages of his films' grosses both in the United States and abroad, director and cast approval (with the possibility of directing himself), and *The Virginian* and *Cyrano de Bergerac* as his first two films, both talkies.

Panic ensued at MGM: Fox was not about to pay Nicholas Schenck's asking price for MGM if its top male star fled the nest. Nick Schenck needed John Gilbert, even if Louis B. Mayer would have been more than happy to let him go to brother Joseph at UA. Katherine Albert, writing in 1930, said that Nicholas Schenck asked Jack, "'What will make you stay?' His manager answered. He outlined a contract so absurd, so preposterous that he expected only loud guffaws. But the executive didn't laugh. He knew that if Gilbert didn't sign, the tremendous deal might fall through."

But meanwhile, Mayer and Thalberg were not about to sit back and let the Schencks and Fox ruin what they had been building up for the past four years. Mayer used what political contacts he had to file an antitrust suit with the Justice Department against Fox (and to be fair, Mayer really did have a good case). The deal stalled long enough for other circumstances to kill it: Fox was seriously injured in a 1929 car accident, and then the stock-market crash took whatever funds he had had to buy MGM.

By that time John Gilbert was firmly installed as the studio's biggest—and most highly paid—male star. In December 1928 newspapers reported that Jack had been re-signed by MGM "as its leading male star" for six pictures (two per year) at $250,000 per picture, and that "Gilbert is permitted a certain discretion in the matter of story, director and cast, although Gilbert is not granted full supervision in these matters." The same paper notes that Louis B. Mayer might be leaving MGM—and movies—altogether, "with a hint that he may have political aspirations." Jack was also given a $30,000 dressing room bungalow on the MGM lot, with a private garage "and a secret gateway . . . in the event some ardent young lady should slip past the cordon of armed guards at the entrance."

Jack still left no stone unturned in his efforts to plague Mayer: in the summer of 1928, his daughter later recalled, "You know, he gave $10,000 to the Al Smith campaign, while Louis B. Mayer was traveling all over the country campaigning for Herbert Hoover" (Smith was running for the Democratic nomination for president that year). It's not known if Jack was a devoted Democrat or Al Smith fan (though Smith was anti-Prohibition)—or if Jack would have donated to anyone Mayer hated.

As he saw Greta Garbo's popularity skyrocketing after only three years in the United States, Jack looked back at his own thirteen-year career and wondered how much longer he could last. He confessed to a *Los Angeles Times* reporter that his big fear was boring his audiences: "I will know I have my cue to retire with as much grace as I can muster from the screen—forever."

But Jack seemed unworried. He was interviewed at about this time regarding movie unions (Screen Actors Guild, or SAG—unfortunately called "Film Actors Guild" at first—was in its earliest birth throes, finally incorporating in 1933). "I [have always] solved all my problems by myself without the assistance of any group agency," said Jack, underestimating the problems he would soon be facing. His employers, he naïvely believed, with his shiny new contract in hand, "cannot touch me in any way. . . . The men for whom I work, despite our past differences in production values, have never heaped any injustices upon me. . . . My principal worry at the moment," he did recognize, "is to conquer a new technique, difficult and exacting, which has entered my business."

He was not the only performer to sign a huge new contract just as the silent era was ending; the *Los Angeles Times* noted, "The day of big salaries isn't over in the movies. Three prominent stars' stipends have just taken a jump." Jack, Corinne Griffith, and Richard Barthelmess (both at First National) all received huge increases—and all three careers would be crippled by talkies within two years. An interesting point is brought up by the *Times:* by the beginning of 1928 talkies were looming on the horizon, and already "demonstrated box-office value is a big factor in the salary advances of the present time, when added to the possession of excellent vocal qualities." Barthelmess and Griffith had serviceable enough voices, but *someone* at MGM must have realized that Jack's voice was a little light and strained. Just no one who was in on the panicked contract negotiations.

Mayer was stuck with Jack, but he determined to make the best of things and get his money's worth: the best way to do that was to reteam him with Garbo as soon as possible. In the summer of 1928 John Gilbert and Greta Garbo were MGM's biggest male and female stars. *Love* had been doing so well that a hot property was searched for and found in the 1924 Michael Arlen novel *The Green Hat.* Entirely too hot—it was the story of idealistic, fast-living flapper Iris March and her longtime beau Napier Harpenden, whose family feels Iris is "not quite their kind" (Iris has a hard-drinking scapegrace brother, who may or may not be bisexual). She marries the clean-cut Boy Fenwick, who—having a venereal disease—kills himself on their wedding night. Napier marries a nice young girl, gets the widowed Iris pregnant (she miscarries) and, in order to save him from herself, she crashes her car into a tree. (The book, by the way, has not aged well; it is eye-rollingly pretentious and full of hard-to-deal-with lines like "The great car stood like a bruise against the passage of eternity, dawn fought for it, night draped it, and the silver stork flew unseen.")

The book had been a scandalous, much-censored best seller; Tallulah Bankhead had played Iris March in a London stage production, which Katharine Cornell took over on Broadway. No movie studio would touch it, not even in those free and easy pre-Code days. MGM finally came up with a workable version: the title was changed to *A Woman of Affairs,* Boy's social disease became embezzlement, and the younger March's homosexual tendencies were excised.

Flesh and the Devil's Clarence Brown was brought in to direct; he would go on to helm another five Garbo films as well as some of the best work of Joan Crawford, Norma Shearer, and Jean Harlow. Jack's role was only a supporting one—his daughter claims he was fine with that and told Brown, "I'd rather you didn't touch my part a bit. My character is a weak character and he's got to be played that way." Iris and Napier were renamed Diana Merrick and Neville Holderness to further separate the film from its source.

They shot through August and September 1928, and by the end of that year Garbo and Gilbert finally seemed to have cooled down to a workable friendship. She didn't stay over at his house anymore; his yacht the *Temptress* had been sold. But they were occasionally seen together at parties or restaurants. They slowly, amicably drifted apart, and would not work together again for another four years.

Just shy of nineteen years old, Douglas Fairbanks Jr. had one of his first high-profile adult roles in the film. He later recalled the two stars acting like high-school lovers, and not in a good way. They passed notes to each other via Fairbanks, would quarrel, then "in a day or so . . . all would be well again." Clarence Brown told Kevin Brownlow that Jack demonstrated on set what he planned to do for his first talkie and "went completely ham in the middle of shooting . . . he began speaking titles with great flamboyance." One can only assume an actor as subtle as Jack was clowning around, but it did not bode well for the future. Indeed, a talking segment was planned for *A Woman of Affairs*—"part talkies" littered the theaters in 1928—and was dropped, probably because of the Swedish-accented Garbo's need for emergency vocal coaching (her talkie debut would not come till 1930).

The film itself turned out to be utterly humorless, much like its source material, and in love with its own melodrama—the very first title card ("The story of a gallant lady—a lady who was perhaps foolish and

Jack and Garbo in *A Woman of Affairs,* 1928 (The Everett Collection).

reckless beyond need—but withal a very gallant lady") tells us what we're in for. The plot turned on the ever-thwarted love of Diana and Neville (Garbo marries David Furness, played by big, athletic Johnny Mack Brown; he promptly gets arrested and kills himself; Jack marries sweet, understanding Dorothy Sebastian; everyone is frustrated and miserable).

The film *looks* gorgeous: the Adrian clothing, the William Daniels camerawork, Cedric Gibbons's art deco sets. The writing, though, is laughably awful ("David died for—decency"), and Jack got to do very little in the way of acting; his character mostly walks out, head bowed, on wives and lovers when they need him most. The best performance was given by young Douglas Fairbanks Jr. as Garbo's bitter, alcoholic kid brother.

A Woman of Affairs was released in December 1928; the film (which had cost $383,000) made a profit of $417,000 (one of the studio's most profitable projects that year). Reviews were mixed; everyone had read the novel and was morbidly curious to see how it had been bowdlerized for the screen. Pare Lorentz in *Judge* magazine wrote, "The most interesting feature of *A Woman of Affairs* is the treatment accorded it by the censors. . . . For some strange reason, instead of using the word 'purity' (the boy died for purity, according to Iris March) they substituted the oft-repeated word 'decency.' To anyone who can show me why 'purity' is a more immoral word than 'decency,' I'll gladly send an eighty-five cent Paramount ticket, to be used at your own risk. . . . The fact that [Garbo] rode down and practically eliminated John Gilbert's goggling is in itself grounds for recommendation." *Variety*'s critic found Jack's role "utterly blah . . . the idol of the flappers. . . . [He] just stands around, rather sheepishly, in fact, while others shape the events. At this performance (the second of the Saturday opening), whole groups of women customers audibly expressed their discontent with the proceedings."

Garbo went off on a vacation to her homeland in early 1929 and returned refreshed and smiling, to the amazement of the press. As soon as she set foot off her ship in New York and reached her hotel, she phoned Jack in Beverly Hills to catch up.

Jack's last silent movie, *Desert Nights,* was an unremarkable but tidy little adventure, shot in Movietone (Western Electric's sound-on-film system), with an effective orchestral score. Jack starred as a diamond-mining executive who is kidnapped by jewel thieves (played by Mary Nolan and—in his third and final film with Jack—Ernest Torrence). The kidnapping turns into a death march through "the burning wastes of the Kalahari Desert," which was portrayed by the burning wastes of the California desert.

It's a silly little film, but fairly enjoyable and with moments of sus-

Jack with Ernest Torrence and Mary Nolan in his last silent, *Desert Nights,* 1929 (The Everett Collection).

pense: director William Nigh and fabled cinematographer James Wong Howe allowed the stars to look realistically sweaty, disheveled, and filthy, Jack's beard growing heavier day by day.

Jack's leading lady, twenty-four-year-old blonde beauty Mary Nolan, already had a scandalous past behind her (and a tragic future awaiting her). As Imogene "Bubbles" Wilson, she had been a top model and a chorus girl, promoted to Glorified Ziegfeld Girl in the 1923 and '24 *Follies.* But she was drawn into an unhealthy, abusive relationship with blackface comic Frank Tinney, and the headlines (and her drinking problem) got her kicked off Broadway. She surfaced in Berlin, where—as Imogene Robertson—she starred in several films. Hollywood welcomed her, as long as she further buried her past by changing her name yet again: hence "Mary Nolan." Despite her looks and her talent (she is quite good in *Desert Nights,* and she appeared in a handful of other American movies), her demons and congenital hard luck won out. By the mid-1930s she was hooked on morphine and reduced to singing in cheap dives; she drank herself to death at the age of forty-three.

Desert Nights was released in March 1929; it had cost a modest $209,000 and brought in a profit of $292,000 at a time when silents were drawing fewer and fewer crowds. "Holds the interest," admitted Mordaunt Hall in the *New York Times*. "One gains a corking good conception of the heat and also the suffering through parched throats. Will Nigh has directed this silent picture with a good sense of drama during these sequences." Jack himself got a decidedly backhand compliment from Hall: "Mr. Gilbert gives an earnest showing as Rand, and only rarely does one perceive his wide, artificial smile."

A word about that "wide, artificial smile" and the "goggling" earlier mentioned by *Judge*. Jack's acting was—generally speaking and on good days—natural and unaffected. But like everyone—actor and civilian alike—he did have his own mannerisms and idiosyncrasies. Just as Rudolph Valentino's shorthand for passion was to narrow his eyes and flare his nostrils, Jack stared (or "goggled," as *Judge* would have it). Friends and lovers recalled that he did this offscreen as well: his flashing, dark, bedroom eyes latched onto one like a magnet. Onscreen, perhaps, it became his somewhat hackneyed signature. As for his smile, no one could argue with the *Times* that it was wide, but no one else seemed to find it artificial. Some fans found his distinctive goggling and smiling to be knee-weakening; some found it annoying and hammy—just as they differed on Mae Murray's pout, Garbo's furrowed brow, and, later, Marilyn Monroe's breathy whisper and Marlon Brando's mumbling and stammering.

Director Clarence Brown, for one, thought that Jack was "the best screen actor in the business and far and away the most serious-minded of them all. I prefer him to Jack Barrymore as a screen actor." Brown, who directed him in four films between 1920 and '28, added, "Gilbert wants to get at the heart of a character, and once you can convince him that the part he's playing is sincere and real, he'll work for you until the cows come home."

Part 3

The Decline

Chapter Ten

> The old-fashioned silent picture . . . is rapidly receding into the limbo of obsolescence.
>
> —*Charleston Gazette,* 1929

Everyone knows, of course, that talkies did not begin with *The Jazz Singer* in 1927—in fact, *The Jazz Singer* was not really a "talkie," it was a silent with recorded musical score and a handful of brief talking sequences thrown in (it was also a really terrible movie, which was noted in nearly every review at the time).

Sound had been experimented with back to the dawn of the movies, in the 1890s: the usual process was to simultaneously film a movie and make a record, then play them back in synchronization. In theory it was brilliant; in practice it rarely worked. From Thomas Edison's experiments in the 1890s (Kinetophone) through the Gaumonts' Chronophone, Orlando Kellum's Phonokinema in the early 1920s, and Warner Bros.' Vitaphone in the late '20s, various talking film systems were greeted with great enthusiasm before crashing and burning.

The two chief problems with sound on disc were synchronization and amplification. If the film and the recording did not start at the same instant and run at the same speed, the result was disastrous (and, of course, editing the movie was impossible without throwing the sound off). One projectionist recalled having to compensate for skips in the record: "We would count how many times it repeated until we could get to the machine and pick up the needle. . . . Then we'd look at the screen

Jack relaxing at home, 1927, in a photo taken by MGM's Ruth Harriet Louise (The Everett Collection).

to see if the sound was late or early; it was usually close, but not quite on." Making a record heard (and intelligible) throughout even a smallish theater was beyond the amplification systems of the early twentieth century. Also, records got lost or broken, which is why (frustratingly) we today have so many early sound films with no accompanying sound.

Given all these problems, inventors sought an alternative to sound on disc. Sound on film, in which sound is optically recorded on the filmstrip itself, was a logical solution, since it would solve the synchronization problem and eliminate those fragile records. Two fathers of sound-on-film technology (fathers who battled over paternity, too) were Lee De Forest and Theodore Case, both of whom had been experimenting—together and separately—with the technology since the 1910s. By the mid-1920s both De Forest and Case had released serviceable talkie shorts, though they were seen by very few. A fair number of early talkie shorts—both sound on disc and sound on film—have survived, and we can see and hear such 1920s delights as Eddie Cantor, Blossom Seeley, The Ingenues ("The Band Beautiful"), Burns and Allen, Witt and Berg, the deliciously bizarre comedy team Al Shaw and Sam Lee, and the unforgettable Gus Visser and His Singing Duck.

With experimental sound films of various kinds in circulation, audiences—at least the few with access to talkie-friendly theaters—were slowly getting accustomed to the idea of sound movies and were ready for a full-length sound feature when Warner Bros. decided to risk making use of Vitaphone, Western Electric's combination of a sound-on-disc system with new, effective amplification technology.

The night the talkies were really born was not the night of *The Jazz Singer*'s opening but August 6, 1926, with the première of Warner Bros.' *Don Juan,* along with eight sound shorts. *Don Juan*—a John Barrymore starrer—did not talk, but it had Vitaphone sound (orchestral accompaniment and sound effects). Will Hays introduced the film—onscreen, that is—and the shorts included such high-toned selections as classical artistes Giovanni Martinelli, Anna Case, and Efrem Zimbalist (though, frankly, most of the audience would have preferred Gus Visser and His Singing Duck).

The Jazz Singer was shot during the summer of 1927, with no little amount of bragging by the Warner brothers—so the film took no one by surprise when it premièred on October 6, 1927. What was surprising was the degree of audience enthusiasm. Critical reaction was mixed: no one felt *The Jazz Singer* was much good as a movie (its source author, Samson Raphaelson, called it "a dreadful picture . . . ill-felt, silly, maudlin," but he admitted, "I could see a whole new era had come into the theater").

The first real all-talking film, Warner Bros.' *Lights of New York,* premièred in July 1928. It was not nearly as bad as legend will have it, but it can be politely called "experimental." A gangster drama with some nightclub numbers tossed in, it did feature a great, searing turn by Gladys Brockwell (Jack's mother in *Man, Woman and Sin*) and did turn-away business, grossing well over $1 million.

Meanwhile, William Fox bought the rights to Theodore Case's sound-on-film process, renamed it Movietone, and began the regular release of newsreels in 1927; his Movietone News brought such celebrities as Charles Lindbergh, Mussolini, George Bernard Shaw, and Arthur Conan Doyle to audiences.

Both Vitaphone and Movietone needed theatrical amplification systems, of course, and these were under the exclusive control of Western Electric's subsidiary, Electrical Research Products Inc., or ERPI (thank goodness the phrase "Let's go to the Erpies" did not catch on). At first ERPI was legally tied to Vitaphone, but by 1928 it had broken free from its obligations and offered its services to all comers, and the talkie revolution really got under way: Paramount, MGM, and United Artists signed on in May—all of them opting for the use of Movietone, which was so much more reliable and convenient than Vitaphone.

For all its initial impact, Vitaphone would have a heyday of only three or four years—long enough for many theaters to be expensively converted for it, only to have to expensively reconvert when it was replaced by Movietone and its variants. Vitaphone was extinct by 1931, leaving behind it a trail of orphaned discless films and filmless discs, which archivists are today laboring to reunite. When they can, using modern advanced restoration techniques, these early sound-on-disc films are often a marvel and a delight.

Talkies were, in a way, much more traumatic for audiences than were such other entertainment innovations as record players, radio, television, the Internet: either you had one of those or you didn't, and one could go for a decade or more sullenly refusing to update to these modern inventions. But movie fans were dragged—sometimes kicking and screaming—into the talkie era. Silents simply did not exist anymore after 1930. No one even knew what to call these new movies: historian Scott Eyman lists such infelicitous late-1920s suggestions as Oralfilm, Actorphone, and Dictodrama. "Squawkies" and "Squeakies" were terms used too often and too accurately; eventually, "talkers" and then "talkies" were settled upon.

As traumatic as talkies were for audiences, they were of course life changing for those in the movie business. In July 1928 the *New York Times* was warning that "the 'doll-faced' and 'sheik' types of movie stars who lack ability and training to act speaking parts may disappear. It is even being debated whether the entire industry might not shift from Hollywood to New York. . . . Film stars, regardless of the present size of their 'fan mail,' might find themselves on the shelf." (The *Times* tantalizingly claimed there were "70 full-fledged stars" in Hollywood in 1928, though not naming any of them.)

There were other changes to the movie business, one of which Clara Bow complained made movies "no fun anymore." The director on a talkie set, noted the *Times,* "may toss no 'ad-lib' phrases now to help an actor suit an action to a word. He may call out no directions. . . . [Actors] must follow 'business' as rehearsed. They must repeat 'lines' as written." Reporter William Mountain quizzed stars about talkies in early 1929 and found opinion all over the map. Edward Everett Horton (a trained stage actor whose career flourished in talkies) enthused that talkies "are unlimited in scope and interest." Actor Russell Gleason felt that "they are a great idea and will become universally popular, . . . I like to work in them." But "they won't last a year," scoffed matinee idol Rod La Rocque. "The public will always seek the quiet of the silent film." United Artists producer Joseph Schenck agreed: "There will be silent pictures when talking pictures are forgotten."

Even lowly extras had to step up their act, as director Millard Webb noted: "Nowadays she is not just an extra, but a highly trained chorus girl, dancing and singing as well as acting." One fan magazine wondered if the old type of classic movie beauty—Garbo, Corinne Griffith, Clara Bow—would make way for the "ethnic" or downright dowdy looks of the invading Broadway army. But "beauty is a far greater attraction for fans than voice," maintained director George Fitzmaurice. "I would rank beauty, personality and acting ability all ahead of vocal talent. If I had my choice between an exquisitely beautiful girl with a poor voice or a less pretty girl with an excellent voice, I would choose the former without any hesitancy whatsoever."

Audiences used to seeing huge screen-high faces of stunning beauty were chagrined to see their stage favorites blown up to poster size. The *New York Times* noted that "there is no more touching sight in

Hollywood than the established stage favorite, accustomed to years of professional adulation, who for the first time beholds what he looks like on the screen."

One of the surprise successes was that of thirty-seven-year-old Ruth Chatterton, not a great beauty by anyone's standards. Yet from 1929 through the '30s, she was one of the unlikeliest sex symbols and character stars rolled into one. "A young girl is pretty to look at," Chatterton said confidently in 1929, "but she is mighty hard to listen to for very long. Now that the movies have grown up and have begun to talk, I think that the public will want to listen to something besides puppy-love patter." But even she had to deal with technological growing pains. "The microphone fascinates me. Sometimes I talk in my ordinary tones, and they tell me that I am talking too loud. Another time I scream and they tell me to talk louder."

Not only stars were affected by talkies: a look at *Variety*'s obituaries of the late 1920s and '30s shows a depressing increase of suicide among musicians. As of March 1929, eleven thousand members of the American Federation of Musicians had lost their jobs accompanying silent films in theaters. In New York alone, three thousand were thrown out of work.

In 1928, with talkies a growing certainty, MGM was signing and training a whole class of young leading men—all of them born after 1900. Lew Ayres, Joel McCrea, Johnny Mack Brown, William Bakewell, James Murray—all were being groomed as potential John Gilberts, Ramon Novarros, and William Haineses. Brown and Ayres were even cast opposite Greta Garbo in 1928 and '29 (as was rising young freelancer Douglas Fairbanks Jr.). Some of these young men would go on to long careers; others would vanish from the screen or (like James Murray) crash and burn. But MGM's highly salaried over-thirty leading men had to watch their backs.

James Spearing in the *New York Times* looked with some amusement at the panicking stars in the summer of 1928. He listed John Gilbert among the "true idols" of the day (along with Colleen Moore, Norma Shearer, Ronald Colman, Gloria Swanson, and Richard Barthelmess): "They are actors. The things they do mean something. They reveal thoughts and emotions by physical actions and attitudes. . . . That touches the core of it all. No matter what a man or a woman looks like . . . the photographic result is all that counts." But now "Hollywood is panicky. Nobody seems to know what is going to happen and everybody, it seems, is more or less perturbed." Very few movie actors, wrote Spearing—even the stage-trained ones—"are ready to step before the sound-recording machine without fear of unfavorable results. Their voices have never been trained, and many of them, exceptionally endowed with personality and appearance, are markedly deficient in voice."

MGM had a number of big-budget, high-profile silents (by now, with recorded orchestral accompaniment and an occasional distracting sound effect) in release in 1928, aside from Jack's films: *The Patsy* (Marion Davies), *The Cameraman* (Buster Keaton), *White Shadows in the South Seas, Show People* (Davies and William Haines), *West of Zanzibar* (Lon Chaney), *The Trail of '98, Our Dancing Daughters* (Joan Crawford and Anita Page), *Across to Singapore* (Crawford and Ramon Novarro), *The Flying Fleet* (Novarro and Page), *The Wind* (Lillian Gish and Lars Hanson), *The Viking,* and *Laugh, Clown, Laugh* (Chaney and Loretta Young). With so few theaters wired for sound, these late silents still brought in a healthy profit.

But panic was setting in: all bets were off in the early days of talkies. No one knew whose voice would record well or whose personality would "go over." Foreign accents were later rumored to have ended silent careers: Pola Negri, Karl Dane, Vilma Banky. But Greta Garbo, Lupe Velez, and Dolores Del Rio did quite well through the 1930s. Indeed, in 1929 and '30, studios signed up such new, heavily accented foreign talents (with varying degrees of success) as Marlene Dietrich, Maurice Chevalier, Bela Lugosi, Irene Bordoni, Lili Damita, Lyda Roberti, and Fifi D'Orsay. There were no rules—and common sense simply didn't apply. Changing public taste, new filming and directing styles, personal troubles: all ended careers.

This left openings for new stars: *Once in a Lifetime,* as the 1930 Kaufman and Hart show about those wild days had it. Some who had been slowly rising through the late 1920s as reliable bit players and second leads now burst into stardom: Joan Crawford, Myrna Loy, Carole Lombard, William Powell, Gary Cooper, Constance Bennett, Warner Baxter.

And then there were the Broadway and vaudeville stars. Musical-comedy and revue stars Sophie Tucker, Helen Kane, Fanny Brice, Bert Lahr, Ed Wynn, Jimmy Durante, and Marilyn Miller all tried their hands at movies, and all failed (though some, of course, had success much later in character parts). The people who really found success were the Broadway youngsters—up-and-coming, not really established players willing to toss aside iffy play prospects for a chance at a movie career. The list is breathtaking: in the late 1920s and early '30s, the westbound trains brought to the Hollywood studios James Cagney, Ruby Keeler, Joan Blondell, Claudette Colbert, the Marx Brothers, Barbara Stanwyck, Mae West, Edward G. Robinson, Sylvia Sidney, Fredric March, Clark Gable, Spencer Tracy, Bette Davis, Katharine Hepburn, Paul Muni, Ginger Rogers, Miriam Hopkins, Humphrey Bogart, Jeanette MacDonald. . . . Never before, and never since, has such a wealth of baby stars descended on Hollywood en masse.

But in the end there is no explaining the weird alchemy by which someone can be a star in one medium but not another. Many a Broadway great has flopped in the movies; some TV stars move to the big screen with great success and others don't—and vice versa. Who could have predicted that Fred Astaire would succeed in the talkies but not Marilyn Miller? That Ruth Chatterton would survive the end of silents but not Norma Talmadge? Garbo but not Gish? There is no logic to it, and one can go mad looking for reasons.

By April 1929 movie theaters were showing all kinds of hybrids. One newspaper of the day listed "the old-fashioned silent picture, which is rapidly receding into the limbo of obsolescence," the sound picture, "a quack product which has been produced first in silent form and then submitted to the mutilating process of . . . arbitrary addition of artificial sound effects," the part talkie, or sound and dialogue film, "a mongrel affair which is neither one nor the other. . . . In two or three episodes the words are spoken out loud," and finally the 100 percent talkie ("Before the year is out this type will have supplanted all the others"). One suggestion was roundly laughed out the door: "Talking pictures of the future will be in Esperanto," predicted Donald Parrish, an advocate of that language. "Nothing but a world language will ever make possible the production of talking films."

Still, as late as this, MGM was dragging its heels and hoping the talkie fad would pass. Norma Shearer's engineer brother Douglas, appointed head of MGM's sound department in 1927, proved to be a prodigy: over the next four decades, Shearer introduced numerous innovations and actually became more important to the studio than his glamorous sister. But he had quite a struggle in the late 1920s being midwife to MGM's talkies. He was not so much "hired" as "shanghaied," he later recalled. "Overnight I became the one-man sound department. They ordered me to do the job, they didn't just give it to me. And they probably wouldn't have given it to me except that they were desperate."

Irving Thalberg announced in 1929 that only half of that year's films would be in sound, "in the event of the failure of talking pictures to 'catch on' with the public." Thalberg said the studio would produce simultaneous talking and silent versions of many films. Fox had announced the month before that it was discontinuing silent picture production, but most other studios were hedging their bets, especially as so many theaters still were not equipped to show talkies (only 2,000 out of the country's 15,000 theaters—250 per month were changing over at no little expense). "Our aim is to protect all the motion-picture theaters who are playing our production," said MGM's Nicholas Schenck. "We will therefore supply them with the type of pictures they can use."

Chapter Eleven

> No one questioned my voice. I just had a voice, that's all, like anyone else's.
>
> —John Gilbert, 1933

At the beginning of 1929, the Russian drama *Redemption* and the costume romance *Olympia* were set as John Gilbert's first talkies, to be shot in that order. The choice of a depressing Russian play as his talkie debut is easy to second-guess in hindsight—but in their panic, studios scrambled to present their stars in any sound vehicle that looked viable in 1929 and '30. Jack was not the only one at MGM to be thrown into the deep end.

Lon Chaney fared best, with a remake of his silent crime drama *The Unholy Three* (released in July 1930, one month before Chaney's death from cancer). He looked to have a great future as a gravely voiced character actor, had he lived. Norma Shearer also did well with her feature debut, another crime drama, *The Trial of Mary Dugan* (April 1929). Greta Garbo's talking debut did not come till January 1930, with a film every bit as dreary as *Redemption:* Eugene O'Neill's *Anna Christie.* The role proved perfect for the Swedish-accented actress, and even two dreadful follow-ups (the melodramatic *Romance* and the silly *Inspiration*) didn't slow her ascent.

Screenwriter Frances Marion's memoirs are full of erroneous, easily disproved tales, so her version of MGM's sound tests must be viewed with some caution. She recalled reading slips of paper with Louis B.

Mayer's evaluations of stars' talkie prospects: Lionel Barrymore ("gilt edge"), Joan Crawford ("has some stage experience, good dancer, and can sing"), Aileen Pringle ("sounds too ladylike to the human ear"), Marion Davies ("stutters"), Ramon Novarro ("he can sing, play the guitar, but he talks with a south-of-the-border accent . . . can be cast in any picture where a guy speaks with a foreign accent"). Most interesting—if Marion can be trusted—is the report card on John Gilbert. "Arrogant cuss," wrote Mayer. "His voice sounds pretty anemic to me. But he's one of our biggest assets and I don't believe anything can threaten his future."

Jack's *Merry Widow,* Mae Murray, by the way, never got to make an MGM talkie. She walked out of her contract in the summer of 1926 to marry fake prince David Mdivani and was effectively blackballed from Hollywood (Mayer did not take kindly to contract breakers). By the time talkies hit, Murray was separated from her husband, broke, and emotionally fragile; after three talkies, she faded into a twilight of obscurity.

In March 1929 Jack's talkie debut—an adaptation of a Tolstoy play cheerfully titled *The Living Corpse*—was chosen (MGM went with the title *Redemption,* as had Broadway producers in 1918 and '28). Jack was surrounded by former costars and reliable MGM regulars Renée Adorée, Eleanor Boardman, and Conrad Nagel, and the crew was top-notch: sound wizard Douglas Shearer, art director Cedric Gibbons, costume designer Adrian. Fred Niblo (who had never worked with Jack before) was brought in to direct, but several important scenes were reshot by neophyte Lionel Barrymore, which was later seen either as a daring experiment or outright sabotage.

In April, just as Jack was preparing to start shooting *Redemption,* he attended a party where he met thirty-six-year-old Broadway star Ina Claire, in town to launch a talkie career with Pathé. Claire had started her career as plain song-and-dance girl Ina Fagan from Washington, DC, doing impersonations. But after becoming a Broadway star in 1911 with *The Quaker Girl,* she remodeled herself into a soigné comedienne. In such shows as *The Gold Diggers, Bluebeard's Eighth Wife, The Awful Truth,* and *The Last of Mrs. Cheyney,* Claire became Broadway's top light-comic star. Offstage, too, she had a reputation for being the smartest, bitchiest, and best-dressed actress in town. Pushing middle age when talkies came in, Claire decided to take the plunge (she had made a handful of silents, to no great effect).

The third Mrs. Gilbert: Broadway star Ina Claire, ca. 1929 (author's collection).

Fan magazine writer Leonard Hall claimed to have been at the party where Jack and Ina Claire met, and later described the pair as "two of the most vivid, arresting and colorful people in America. . . . He bubbled like a siphon of overcharged soda. . . . There isn't his equal for animal spirits when he feels good and his world is fair." Ina Claire, said Hall, was out of her element and nervous about her own talkie debut, having failed in silents. "Jack was enthralled by the discovery of a brilliant, sword-keen mind in a beautiful woman. Ina was fascinated by the spirit of a lad in a more or less mature man. . . . They caught fire like a drought hayfield."

Ina Claire and John Gilbert must have looked like an art deco fashion illustration by Paul Iribe when they met at that party: she was not a great beauty (lacking much in the way of a chin), but her style and glamour put most Hollywood stars in the shade. Jack "said something derogatory about himself," Claire recalled of their meeting. "Not exactly *derogatory,* but he sees himself as kind of a sex symbol. But it made me laugh, and I thought I wouldn't have expected that from him." He was impressed by her wit, self-assurance, and intelligence, and by the summer of 1929 the two were an item, seen about town at parties and nightclubs.

As Jack and his new love enjoyed each other's company and got to know and appreciate each other, shooting of *Redemption* continued, with anxiety growing day by day. Lionel Barrymore is best known today as an actor, of course (though his style has not aged well—he basically had two settings, "crotchety" and "twinkly"). He had directed a handful of silents and one short for MGM before the studio entrusted him with the Ruth Chatterton vehicle *Madame X* (the third of umpteen remakes of the reliable old mother-love melodrama).

Interviewed on the set of *Madame X* in April 1929, Barrymore sounded engaged and knowledgeable: "I stay up in the monitor room and hear every word, while my assistant stays on the floor and watches the action," he explained of his new method of direction. "I guess I'm the ear director and he's the eye director, so to speak. But that's the best way to get perfect speech recording, and I think, eventually, the two-director system will be the solution of our speech problems." Barrymore also said, "The voice is the thing in talkie pictures. It is what the actor has in his head that counts." Historian Scott Eyman reports that Barrymore even jerry-rigged a system whereby he would send actors an electric shock, as in a trained monkey act in vaudeville, to alert them to bump up their performance—one only hopes he did not try this with Jack.

Jack had never really acted onstage, but he was familiar with the technique; he certainly knew all there was to know about silent-movie acting. But this was a whole new art form: no one knew, really, how to act for the talkies yet. Musical-comedy star Irene Franklin wrote a

Jack in his first-completed talkie, *Redemption,* released in 1930 (author's collection).

jittery, panicked impression of making an early talkie short. "Keep the voice natural, expressive, vivid," was going through her head as she tried to act. "Keep the letter *S* clear, the letter *R* from hardening, and the pitch slightly nasal for distance. And at the same time, keep the overtaxed mind off the deadly mike-fright. . . . The quiet hurt my ears, the heat was frightful. I swallowed . . . good Lord, my throat began to tickle. I must clear it or I would cough." All that while trying to remember lines, hit marks, *and* give a good, thoughtful, casual-seeming performance.

Care was taken with, and money spent on, *Redemption:* Jack's courtroom meltdown was reshot because the down-and-out wig and beard he wore covered too much of his face and looked fake. In the released version, he simply has mussed-up hair and a three-days' beard.

Jack and Ina Claire continued to be seen around town together at parties, restaurants, and clubs; they attended Irving Thalberg's thirtieth birthday party at the Beverly Hills Hotel (awkwardly, Garbo was also there). Both were social and had many friends, so even the usually alert press did not make anything of this. Jack was in the midst of struggling through *Redemption* and Ina the film version of her stage hit *The Awful Truth* when they surprised all their friends by eloping to Las Vegas on May 9. They hired a private car on a train, accompanied by Pathé executive Benjamin Glazer and his wife, Jack's business manager Harry Eddington, and playwright Arthur Richman.

"It is our desire to avoid all fuss," Jack told the few tipped-off reporters before the train pulled out. "We are going to Las Vegas for a quiet wedding and will return to Los Angeles immediately, because both of us are engaged on motion-picture productions. For this reason we shall postpone our honeymoon for the present." The wedding was indeed small and quiet. In "a dingy little police courtroom" they were married by Justice of the Peace Roger Foley, as reporters and photographers as well as locals ("mostly cowboys, Indians and squatters of the desert") looked on from the hallway and outside.

They strolled through town, followed by avid fans, had lunch at the National Hotel, and phoned MGM to arrange for a plane back to L.A. At 4:00 p.m. the wedding party took off—and met with a two-hour delay due to head winds, leading to a minor panic back home, where a crash was feared. But they landed safely, took a limo back to Jack's home, and got dressed for a big congratulatory bash at King Vidor and Eleanor Boardman's home that night.

. . . Which, no one should have been surprised, led to Jack's calling in sick the next day. Ina Claire didn't have to be at work till the following Monday, but at 9:00 Jack called the studio to say he was at breakfast with his bride and "might" be back at work the following day "but that he wasn't sure."

A sad note was added to the marriage when eighteen-year-old extra Marie Stanley killed herself and was found clutching a photo of Jack and a note reading, "Without hope there is no use in life. Perhaps a cat can look at a king and forget. I can't forget—and I must. I wish them a long and happy married life. Fate is hard. It can't be helped."

At the end of May 1929 Jack was added to the cast of MGM's *Hollywood Revue of 1929.* In the early talkie years all of the major studios put out "revues," engagingly amateurish variety shows to introduce their players' voices to audiences. Most of these films, thank goodness, still exist, and they are a treasure trove of awfulness and brilliance. Warner Bros.' *The Show of Shows* (released in December 1929) was stolen by vaudevillian Winnie Lightner, who belted out two red-hot numbers; Beatrice Lillie was also seen in a very funny sketch, and there were several impressive production numbers. But John Barrymore came off as stagy and hammy in a scene from *Henry VI,* most of the comedy sketches fell flat (emcee Frank Fay is all but unwatchable today), and the "Meet My Sister" number highlighted the flat-footed hoofing and quavery voices of several under-rehearsed siblings (Dolores and Helene Costello, Viola Dana and Shirley Mason, and Loretta Young and Sally Blane among them).

Paramount on Parade (released in the spring of 1930) was a bit more polished, featuring some terrific musical numbers with Maurice Chevalier, Helen Kane, Jack Oakie and Zelma O'Neal, and Lillian Roth, and surprisingly good turns by Clara Bow and Nancy Carroll. Still, most of the comedy seemed labored even in 1930, a love ballad by Ruth Chatterton sent audiences running, and little Mitzi Green's routines are pretty hard to take. Fox's *Happy Days* (released early in 1929) had a showboat plot, with "guest appearances" by such contract players as Janet Gaynor and Charles Farrell, Victor McLaglen and Edmund Lowe, George Jessel, Will Rogers, Warner Baxter, and Ann Pennington. Fox also put out two *Movietone Follies* in 1929 (now lost) and 1930, but both were weighed down by "Let's put on a show!" plots and neither featured big stars (Stepin Fetchit, Warren Hymer, Sue Carol, the unbearable El Brendel, and the wonderful Marjorie White).

England got into the act, too, with 1930's *Elstree Calling* revue, a typical mixture of the wonderful (Lily Morris, Cicely Courtneidge), the horrible (most of the comedy sketches), and the jaw-dropping (Anna May Wong and Donald Calthrop's take on the Pickford/Fairbanks *Taming of the Shrew,* incorporating a motorcycle and a pie fight).

Through the spring of 1929, MGM's players were put through their paces for *The Hollywood Revue of 1929* (it was released nationwide in late November after a few big-city previews that summer). Everyone at MGM was called upon to make an appearance—except for Lon Chaney and Greta Garbo, who pointed to their contracts and stood on their dignity (Chaney was ill, and Garbo still working on her English, so they were excused). Those who were currently working on other projects had to shoot their segments at night, and the twenty-four-hour workdays did not make for peppy performances. Jack was struggling through his second talkie when called upon to do a comedy sketch with pal Norma Shearer and Lionel Barrymore—filmed in two-strip Technicolor.

Like the other studio revues, *Hollywood Revue* is a bizarre mixture of deliciousness and astonishing missteps. It opens with a minstrel show, then Joan Crawford does a very game song and dance routine (introduced by Conrad Nagel as "the personification of youth and beauty and joy and happiness," which really does describe Joan in 1929). Forgettable numbers and comedy routines by Charles King, Anita Page, Jack Benny (who had not yet found his trademark character and comes off as smug and unpleasant), Cliff "Ukelele Ike" Edwards, and William Haines follow. King sang the weepy ballad "Your Mother and Mine," which Warner Bros. poked fun at in their *Show of Shows*—a joke lost on today's viewers. Then some really dispiriting musical and comedy routines by the ill-used Bessie Love, Marie Dressler, and Laurel and Hardy, and a military toe-tap number by the always-enthusiastic Marion Davies (done up in a cadet uniform—William Randolph Hearst's particular kink).

After an intermission, what audience remained was treated to a slightly more bizarre second act: an "underwater" ballet and its painful parody by poor Buster Keaton (whose career and life in general, much like Jack's, would soon be destroyed by MGM, talkies, and alcohol). Gus Edwards then did a completely insane musical number about the missing-in-action Lon Chaney, surrounded by monster-masked chorines. After an adagio dance came Jack's turn, a six-minute sketch with Norma Shearer, beginning with the balcony scene from *Romeo and Juliet.*

This was audiences' first (and last) look at the stars in Technicolor,

"I'm uts-nay about ou-yay!" *Hollywood Revue of 1929,* with Norma Shearer (The Everett Collection).

and it is impressive. The Shakespeare, less so—Jack and Shearer declaim with all the earnestness and passion of fairly talented high-school drama students. (This was a dry run for Shearer, who would play Juliet in 1936 opposite Leslie Howard.) In the background we hear Tchaikovsky's *Romeo and Juliet* overture—admirably accurate but laughably overused for romantic effect to the ears of modern audiences. After their last "Parting is such sweet sorrow," we hear "Cut!" and we break—the stars stroll offset to chat with "director" Lionel Barrymore, who tells them the studio wants to update the play with modern dialogue, "pep it up," and retitle it *The Neckers*.

The result is what always happens when middle-aged writers try to ape "how the kids talk." It's ten years out of date and not very funny: "Julie, baby, I'm gaga about you," Jack tells Shearer, who replies, "You're just about the cookies to me, boyfriend." Most memorably, Jack exits with the pig Latin farewell, "I'm uts-nay about ou-yay!" It's cute, and fun to see Jack and Shearer kid themselves and do comedy, but it's not as witty as it should have been.

Jack looks great in color, and his voice—while a bit nasal—is perfectly fine (his Shakespeare, again, not terrific). The real magic of this spot, what makes it so precious, is that moment between the straight and spoof balcony scenes. It was not improvised on set, of course—or at least the improvisations were written down and rehearsed. Jack, Shearer, and Barrymore banter in a friendly way; Jack puts an arm around Shearer affectionately and says, "Auntie, it was swell to work with you." "I don't like that 'Auntie' stuff," Shearer laughs, and he replies, "Well, I call Irving 'Uncle.'" It's as close to a home movie of the two as we will ever get.

The hit of *Hollywood Revue* came after Jack and Norma: the classic "Singin' in the Rain" number, with Cliff Edwards, the Brox Sisters, and a wonderful art deco backdrop. A handful of indifferent music and comedy bits followed, ending with a Technicolor reprise of "Singin' in the Rain" featuring the whole cast in rain slickers—the whole cast minus John Gilbert and Norma Shearer, that is. *Hollywood Revue* cost $426,000 to make and—probably just on its novelty value alone—brought in an impressive $1.125 million.

At the beginning of June 1929, Jack was rushed right from the still-unreleased *Redemption* into *Olympia,* adapted from Ferenc Molnár's recent (unsuccessful) Broadway play. The *New York Times*'s Brooks Atkinson had called *Olympia* "high comedy beaten thin," and the show closed in just a little over a month. MGM bought the rights, retitled it *His Glorious Night,* and had successful playwright Willard Mack (*Kick In, The Noose, A Free Soul*) adapt it for the screen. *His Glorious Night* was an arch bedroom comedy about millionaires, military officers, and minor royalty mingling at a European spa—just the kind of thing that Ernst Lubitsch was spinning into sexy, hilarious gold with Maurice Chevalier over at Paramount. But *His Glorious Night* did not have an ounce of humor, except of the unintentional kind. Catherine Dale Owen—a Broadway ingénue making her talkie debut—starred as the young, widowed Princess Orsolini, who is carrying on a secret affair with the dashing Hungarian officer Captain Kovacs (Jack)—who may or may not really be an "international swindler and gentleman criminal."

Shooting this project was an exercise in anxiety. Lionel Barrymore was not a calming influence and knew just as little about talkie technique

His Terrible Movie: Jack with Catherine Dale Owen in *His Glorious Night,* 1929 (The Everett Collection).

as Jack did. They shot through June and July, taking about a month to complete the project. Ina Claire had just wrapped her first talkie, *The Awful Truth,* and was full of helpful advice, which Jack did not want to hear. Producer Irving Thalberg had his hands full with panicked actors and could not be bothered (his wife, Norma Shearer, had three talkies in production in 1929, and his attention was naturally geared more toward her). Sound engineer Douglas Shearer could not be on set at all times, as he was supervising every new talkie at MGM.

A rare pleasant reminder of Jack's childhood came with Willard Mack, who was having his dreadful way with *His Glorious Night*'s script. When Mack had acted in Marjorie Rambeau's touring company of *Madame X,* Ida Gilbert had been in the show, dragging her son along. Jack would steal Willard Mack's greasepaint to draw pictures in the wings, and Mack had to chase him down to recover it. "Guess he's entitled to greasepaint if he wants it now," Mack said, handing Jack a stick for the MGM press people.

By the time *His Glorious Night* wrapped, no one knew if they had a passable film or a flop. Neither it nor *Redemption* was going to make Jack the king of the talkies, but there was no indication that disaster was in store, either. But *His Glorious Night* is jaw-droppingly bad. Jack's voice was the least of the film's problems—it was a perfectly acceptable, mid-tone voice, a tad affected or strained in a few scenes, but the rest of the cast members were obviously feeling their way, too. The main torpedoes were the antiquated, flowery script and the stodgy, tin-eared direction. Jack's repeated "I love you—I love you!" is frequently brought up as a laugh getter. According to Adela Rogers St. Johns, Jack said, "I was the first man to ever say 'I love you' out loud on the screen. It ruined me. They laughed . . . and you know you can survive anything but ridicule." But there were many worse lines he had to read: "Oh, darling, dearest one, what have I ever done but wait, wait, ever since I've known you? What is a man to do, darling, when he loves so helplessly as I?" And, even worse, read with a straight face: "It was your jewels that attracted me—oh, I don't mean the pearls in your necklace, but the diamonds in your eyes!" Any audience who *didn't* laugh at that had a deficient sense of humor.

The cherry on top was Lionel Barrymore's direction, or lack of it. In scene after scene, Jack and Catherine Dale Owen were filmed in medium two-shots, standing stock-still, too close together, and declaiming at each other. There was no movement, no change of camera angles, no close-ups. And the characters had no chemistry; they did not even appear to like each other. Princess Orsolini rejects Captain Kovacs, and he pleads and rebukes—again and again and again. When they finally clinch in the last scene, one cannot imagine why.

Jack had no chance to break out and show any charm in *His Glori-*

ous Night; he rarely even smiled. He was still vocally uncomfortable ("jewels" became "*jew*-ells") and he did indeed seem stiff and unhappy. If this was the first glimpse audiences had of him in a talkie, they might legitimately feel that he was not much of an actor, after all. It was a shocking drop in artistic quality since *Desert Nights,* shot just a few months earlier, and not an isolated case; the advent of talkies looked like the end of a wonderful movie-making era.

The $250,000 question is, why did MGM opt to hold back on *Redemption,* not releasing it till April 1930, and set *His Glorious Night* loose on theaters first, in September 1929? This still has conspiracy theorists buzzing: was *Redemption* so obviously awful that it was held back for fear of hurting Jack's career? Or was *His Glorious Night* so obviously awful that it was rushed out in the hopes of hurting Jack's career? Both theories have their champions, and no one will ever know. It was not unusual for films to be released out of order, due to post-editing, too many similar films in theaters, a star's career needing (or not needing) a particular kind of change. Jack's first MGM project, *His Hour,* was not released till after his second, *He Who Gets Slapped.* The rescheduling of *Redemption* and *His Glorious Night* may have been a completely innocent bit of corporate paperwork—or it may have had darker implications!

It must be remembered that MGM released several really dreadful talkies in 1929 and '30, featuring their biggest stars. Ramon Novarro and William Haines had rocky talking debuts: Novarro in the Napoleonic musical romance *Devil-May-Care* (December 1929) and Haines in the part talkie *Alias Jimmy Valentine* (November 1928). Haines's film had been shot silent, but the cast had been called back to add two final reels of sound. Joan Crawford's first sound feature was the abysmal *Untamed* (November 1929, costarring MGM newcomer Robert Montgomery). Crawford played a feral jungle girl brought to the big city, and it's a wonder her career survived this fiasco. Marion Davies, too, had tough sledding with *Marianne* (1929) and *Not So Dumb* (1930), though she brought her customary charm to hopeless scripts. Even Mrs. Irving Thalberg herself had to cope with such stagy teacup dramas as *Their Own Desire* (1929) and *Let Us Be Gay* (1930).

On July 21, 1929, Mr. and Mrs. John Gilbert took off for what they hoped would be three carefree months in Paris, the Riviera, Italy, Spain,

Jack and Ina Claire on their honeymoon cruise, 1929 (The Everett Collection).

and England. It was Jack's first trip abroad—that hoped-for honeymoon with Leatrice Joy never took place—and the worldly Ina Claire was eager to show him around. Jack worked on *His Glorious Night* retakes till the very last moment. They took the train to New York, were cornered by a horde of photographers and reporters at Pennsylvania Station, and were chased all the way to their Ritz apartment "at a sixty-mile-an-hour clip." Their respective PR flacks booked them in loudly at the front desk as "Ina Claire and husband" and "John Gilbert and wife," to the strained amusement of the couple. Jack good-naturedly "flashed his smile at his wife, and the cameraman. . . . He turned his profile that way and that. He mopped his brow with a small ball of white handkerchief." He even agreed to go up to the hotel roof to oblige two photographers whose flashbulbs were not working.

While Jack enjoyed Europe, there came news that his father, John Pringle, had died on August 12, 1929, at the age of sixty-four. They'd had no contact in years; his widow, Florence, had him buried in an unmarked grave in what is now Hollywood Forever Cemetery.

While John Pringle's career had faltered, Jack's stepfather Walter Gilbert settled into a respectable niche as a character actor. In local stock companies, touring plays, and on Broadway, Gilbert worked steadily through the 1920s and '30s, never once capitalizing on his famous stepson. He played opposite Tallulah Bankhead in her 1935 revival of *Rain,* also appearing on Broadway in *Lost Horizons, Farewell Summer, Lightnin',* and *Skylark;* in 1941 he was voted onto the Actors' Equity Council (he turned down the post during an argument over whether the board had been taken over by Communists). In 1947—having outlived his wife and stepson—Walter Gilbert keeled over dead on a Brooklyn subway (the Smith and Ninth Street station, for those who might want to make a pilgrimage).

In October 1929 Jack returned from what one hopes was a delightful and relaxing honeymoon to find that the reviews had hit the fan when *His Glorious Night* opened in late September. Ina Claire later told Jack's daughter Leatrice that he never saw the disaster coming: "He had no idea what it looked like." He never saw the film till his return to the States, and Claire guessed that he may have sneaked into a New York showing upon his return from Europe. "He would have been perfectly horrified at Lionel's butchery and the overall quality of the picture," Claire assumed. "He would have looked at the picture through a director's eye and what he saw would have made him sick."

When asked by reporters in his Ambassador Hotel room upon his return if he would go back to silent movies, he scoffed, "Of course not." Perhaps take a stage role for experience? "No, why should I? I shall master the talking films." He later added, "No one questioned my voice. I just had a voice, that's all, like anyone else's. . . . They never previewed that picture except in the studio. The employees who saw (and heard) it were all wildly enthusiastic. I was magnificent, they said. I had nothing to worry about. I was waiting to go to Europe on my honeymoon trip with Ina. They wished me Godspeed, with pats on the back and upturned, admiring faces. When I got back, the face of the world had changed. There were no pats on the back. There were nothing but averted faces. I couldn't even get Nick Schenck and other executives on the phone—men who had once offered to fix me up with theatre tickets, bootleggers, anything I wanted because I wanted it."

"I wasn't overly surprised," Jack later sighed. "I'd been in the theatre, on the screen, for too long. I'd seen these things happen before to others. I figured that they hadn't taken into consideration that no one, as yet, was expert in mixing, in regulating the voice and so on. I knew that no one could have anticipated the fact that a spoken love scene on the screen would seem that most damnable of things—funny."

Actress Louise Brooks—who, you'll recall, also felt the whole Garbo-Gilbert romance was invented by MGM to cover Garbo's lesbianism—saw conspiracies in Jack's downfall. Jack, she accurately said, "had a good middle range voice," adding, "It was simple for the sound man to mix it higher." She told editor Tom Dardis that Lionel Barrymore had "sold himself to Mayer as the MGM rat. . . . It is rather comical that Mayer's rat Fred Niblo made quite a good picture of Gilbert's first 'bad' talkie, *Redemption,* shelved, then released after *His Glorious Night* was made by Mayer's super-rat Lionel Barrymore (and Howard Dietz did a super job on vicious publicity)."

Hedda Hopper agreed that Lionel Barrymore had been a disastrous choice for *His Glorious Night* ("I watched Jack Gilbert being destroyed on the sound stage by one man, Lionel Barrymore") but never made the leap from incompetence to an outright plot by Mayer to destroy Jack's career. Eleanor Boardman was of the opinion that "Jack's voice was perfectly normal," as she told writer Michael Ankerich. Boardman then went on to claim that "Mayer gave out bad publicity that his voice was no good, which was ridiculous. They even tried to fiddle with the film to make it worse." Actress Blanche Sweet's oddball theory—everyone, it seems, had one—was that "they put the wrong people to contrast with his voice, a lot of heavy-voiced people. Therefore, John sounded as if he had a falsetto voice, which he didn't."

For all the bad press and its reputation of having been a career-destroying torpedo, *His Glorious Night,* which cost only $210,000, amazingly made a profit of $202,000. Audiences were either desperate to see talkies, especially to hear John Gilbert talk, or theaters were full of masochists and people who had lost bets. As was often the case in the early talkie era, MGM filmed a foreign-language version at the same time—*Olimpia* was released in Spanish, starring José Crespo in Jack's role, with Chester Franklin and Juan de Homs directing (one hopes, better than Lionel Barrymore had done). When Paramount shot the story again in 1960—starring John Gavin and Sophia Loren—it wisely changed the title to *A Breath of Scandal,* to avoid bad memories. But even director Michael Curtiz could not bring this vehicle to life.

By November 1929 there were indications that all was not going well with Mr. and Mrs. Gilbert. They shared his Tower Grove Drive house with a Dutch gardener, two British chauffeurs, a Filipino butler, and all of Ina Claire's twenty trunks of clothes and accessories (she did not take her reputation as Broadway's Best-Dressed Woman lightly). "My home, as you know, was built for a bachelor and consequently the arrangements for the sleeping quarters are not what they should be," Jack explained when it was learned that Ina Claire had moved, bag and baggage, into a hotel suite. "Carpenters are busy now remodeling the house and building an addition and we thought it best to take another home temporarily. We are still very much in love, aren't we, dear?" "Why certainly, there is no question about that," Ina replied. But insiders knew the brief marriage was all but over.

Mollie Merrick of the *Los Angeles Times* wrote what Hollywood was whispering: the marriage's breakup "dates to an evening when Ina Claire told Jack Gilbert just what was wrong with his talking pictures. She told him frankly as one workman to another—as an actress of superb ability with years of work with the human voice. . . . He resented it actively, it seems." "She is always telling me to speak in pear-shaped tones!" he complained to King Vidor. "My voice is what it is, and I have no desire to change it."

As early as February 1930—with only one talkie in release—

Photoplay jumped the gun with an article headlined "Is Jack Gilbert Through?" Writer Katherine Albert stated that "Hollywood says that the great Gilbert, the amazing lover of the screen, is through—has failed at the very height of his career." No one, of course, was saying anything like that yet—except for *Photoplay.* Albert said of *His Glorious Night,* "Gilbert's voice! You heard it . . . it is high-pitched, tense, almost piping at times. . . . While other stars were trotting to voice specialists, Gilbert was flying to an obscure town in Nevada to be married to Ina Claire." Albert said of *Redemption,* as yet unseen by the public, "It was a great mistake. He tried too hard. . . . *Redemption* was a sorry affair . . . he *must* learn to talk. But how?" Albert added, "Hollywood said that Corinne Griffith couldn't talk, but she learned. Hollywood said that Gloria Swanson was through, but she isn't. Some folks in Hollywood persist that Jack Gilbert is finished."

Speaking of Corinne Griffith, her contract was bought out by her studio, First National, by the end of 1930: $250,000 to get rid of her (her last film there, amusingly, was titled *Back Pay*). Monte Blue was paid $50,000 by Warner Bros. to say good-bye, and the same studio found itself saddled with Broadway singer Vivienne Segal, who had signed a long-term contract and then flopped in several 1930 films. Studios learned their lesson: "They're not signing stage stars for any one-year or half-year terms any more," wrote *Photoplay.* "They're signing them for one picture, with an option to renew if they click."

Katherine Albert ended her *Photoplay* story "hopefully" with, "Gilbert is not through! He'll learn. He'll equip himself. He'll show them. And more power to him!" But raising the very question "Is Jack Gilbert Through?" after one not-badly-received talkie was an answer to its own question. It can't be a coincidence that just one month earlier Albert had written a *Photoplay* piece called "The Girl Who Just Missed Stardom," crying crocodile tears over Renée Adorée: "She should have been, after *The Big Parade,* the greatest, most glamorous star of the screen. Instead, she has no assignment from MGM . . . and her first talking picture, *Redemption,* with Jack Gilbert, has been temporarily shelved." Both stars of *Redemption:* Jack (expensive and ill tempered) and Renée Adorée (French-accented and dying) stabbed in the back shortly before *Redemption* was set to open.

Photoplay got plenty of hate mail for the Gilbert article, and to its credit the magazine printed some of it: "The most unfair and irresponsible thing you've ever printed," wrote a reader from Maine. Another, from Rhode Island, added, "Our Jack, our hero of the screen! A man who has made hearts beat as he has ours—no, he can not be through!" From Arkansas: "If anyone has ever talked any better, show him to the world!" And a Tennessee reader got to the heart of the matter: "Who is trying to ruin this man? This genius? It surely can't be anything but politics!"

Jack did not have the kind of worshipful give-and-take with his fans that Joan Crawford had with hers; there is no evidence that he ever answered—or even read—his fan mail. "Letters published in magazines, characterizing me as being hateful, cowardly, egotistical, selfish, inartistic, ungrateful, ugly, colorless and insipid do not contribute greatly to my happiness," he once admitted. "Neither do such misguided epistles disturb me to any great extent. The best way to get back at my bad acting is by not going to see my pictures."

In April 1930 MGM finally released *Redemption,* to nearly unanimous howls of dismay. *Variety* called it "dull, sluggish, agonizing. Hardly a redeeming aspect. Even the photography, editing and other taken-for-granted items are under standard." *Redemption,* which had cost $561,000, was Jack's first film to lose money: $215,000.

Seen today, *Redemption* is not terrible, and could safely have been released before *His Glorious Night.* The main problem was the script, not the acting. Screenwriter Edwin Justus Mayer had been a silent-movie title writer and had not yet learned to create realistic, flowing dialogue (he did learn: his later films included Jack's *The Phantom of Paris* and the excellent *Desire* and *To Be or Not to Be*). No one could mouth the stilted, awkward lines in *Redemption.*

Given the awful script, the melodramatic plot, and a character who is a self-pitying dishrag, Jack actually did quite well for himself. He portrayed a Russian playboy who marries his best friend's fiancée and makes her so miserable he skulks off with the Gypsies and fakes his own death; it all ends in a bigamy trial, poverty, and suicide.

Jack's voice was perfectly fine in *Redemption:* not at all high or strained or affected—the same voice that was later praised in *Queen Christina* and *Downstairs.* Indeed, he had one emotional meltdown scene during a trial that was one of the finest pieces of acting before

1929 cameras. Costars Eleanor Boardman and Conrad Nagel did not fare as well: both played dull, one-dimensional characters, and neither ever really come to life in the film. The real scene stealer (apart from character actor Sidney Bracey in a wonderful bit as a "genius" waiter) was Renée Adorée. Playing a Gypsy girl infatuated with Jack, she is funny and sympathetic and more alive than anyone else in the film—her accent is strong, but she is completely intelligible. (She is also stuck back into what seems to be her exact same peasant costume from *The Big Parade* and *The Cossacks*.)

The problem with Jack's voice was not its timbre but his need to relax. As stage and screen director Robert Milton wisely noted in 1929, "Talking pictures and elocution simply do not go together. The players are not speaking 'pieces' before the cameras. They are telling a story, first by their action, second with their words. Stilted, exaggerated styles of speaking and overemphasis on precise enunciation is [to be] shunned." Faced with awkward dialogue, lackluster direction, and a terror of looking silly, Jack was doomed unless he could relax and visibly enjoy himself onscreen.

Adela Rogers St. Johns was pretty much on target when she claimed that Ina Claire was the worst possible match for Jack, especially at this time. "Ina Claire, in my opinion, is the best actress on the American stage," St. Johns wrote. "She is also, with the exception of Dorothy Parker, the most brilliant woman conversationalist. . . . Ina probably knows more about speaking lines, more about how to get shades of feeling and emotion into the voice . . . than any other woman in America. . . . But she didn't know how to get over to Jack what she knew without reducing him to a pulp. Without forcing him to defend his masculine pride. I saw it with my own eyes when I was with them. Everyone saw it. . . . It robbed Jack of his last remnants of belief in himself—and he never got it back."

"I made more bad mistakes," Jack later admitted about this perilous time in his career. "I wouldn't talk to anyone. I refused all interviews. . . . While Ina and I were married, she would fall into a fury over the whole damnable situation. She would cry out, 'Why don't you tear the contract up? Or why don't you tell the so-and-so—' I said, 'No. You know your theatre. I know my movies. I'm staying.'"

"Mr. Gilbert's popularity waned," the *New York Times* said in retrospect, three years later. "All attempts to get him to readjust his contract to meet the times and his new valuation met with failure. He continued to collect his quarter of a million, although the studio declared the returns on his films justified but a fraction of that pay."

In 1933 Jack told Gladys Hall of some of the fights he had with MGM, "holding on to that contract with my teeth though they had every lawyer in the country, scrupulous and unscrupulous, examine it in the hopes of breaking it—then the executives used to call me into their offices almost daily and say to me, '*will* you get out?' Of course I wouldn't get out. Not when a million and a half dollars were in the bag for me." MGM could be just as obstreperous, refusing to loan Jack out to First National, where Howard Hawks wanted him for a 1930 version of *The Dawn Patrol.*

Jack was spoiling for a fight in February 1930 when he found himself across the room from Jim Tully at a Los Angeles restaurant. Someone shouted something—whether it was Jack or Tully depends on whose friends one believes—and Jack came rushing at the short but burly ex-boxer. Tully decked Jack with one punch and his friends rushed him out. "It is true Tully knocked me down, but I was never out," Jack told a reporter several days later. "I did only what any man would have done under the circumstances." Tully proved as pugnacious as ever: "Gilbert had better attend to his motion picture career and let rough ex-tramps and pugilists alone," he said. "I learned to fight where brickbats were daisies; in a school that, had Gilbert attended, he would not have survived to become a motion picture actor."

Immediately jokes ricocheted around the film world: *Photoplay* printed a no doubt apocryphal tale of a messenger boy coming into the fight and asking, "Is Mr. Gilbert in?" Ina Claire cast her eyes over her unconscious husband and coolly replied, "No, he's out." And "some smart guy in Baltimore" was said to have posted $10,000 for an official rematch between Jack and Tully.

In July 1930 Ina Claire returned to Broadway, her own talkie career hitting a rough patch. *The Awful Truth* and *The Royal Family of Broadway* (though the latter is a delight) did not make her a movie star, and she accepted an offer to take over Hope Williams's role in the arch comedy *Rebound* at the Plymouth Theater in New York. Claire was as shaken by her experience as Jack was by his. "Hollywood had given me an inferiority complex," the usually unflappable actress admitted. "They used to say in New York that I was the biggest box office name on the stage. Six months ago, I perhaps wouldn't point out that fact. Now I shout it if necessary." She denied any break with Jack: "Because of his contract, Jack cannot leave Hollywood now; I want to be with him." Besides, the Park Avenue swan added unconvincingly, "I like Hollywood. I love the outdoor life, the swimming, riding, the tennis, the informality."

Hollywood wasn't so sure about her, though, and *Photoplay*'s "Cal York" (for California/New York) needled her about trying to look like Garbo: "Ina's Johnny was Garbo's Yonny, we mustn't forget, and Mr. Gilbert is being blamed for the best-dressed woman in New York's [Claire] apparent effort to look like the worst-dressed woman in Hollywood [Garbo]."

Writer Gladys Hall found Ina Claire amusingly brittle in an interview she did around this time. "She wishes she had a baby but knows that said infant would cost her $100,000 what with loss of time and other incidentals," Hall wrote. "She wears French imports, considers hats the most important item in any wardrobe, is very sure of herself, talks a lot, is a good mixer, fond of the table, the wine cellar and the library. She has had the same maid for ten years, if you are looking for a certificate of character." "It isn't so hard to see fame go," Claire said, touching on a subject she and Jack must have been discussing at length. "One can live on the memory of fame. It is harder to see money go—and friends. If one can learn to . . . have wisdom and philosophy. To read books one has never had time to read. To gain security. Then we're safe when the public turns its back."

In October 1929 Jack lost heavily in the stock market, but thanks to an honest and clever business manager, Charles Greene, he had diversified investments and savings that could not be touched. It was worrying nonetheless, at a time when he had so many other worries. Claire told Edwin Schallert that she and Jack had been attending a party with good friends when he just turned and walked out for a long solitary stroll. "He isn't well, he hasn't been sleeping," Claire explained to the other guests; "he gets so frightfully depressed."

King Vidor recalled some dicey moments between the two. They were returning from a party—Jack in no condition to drive and doing so at sixty miles per hour down Wilshire Boulevard. Vidor was in the front passenger seat; Claire was trying to nap (or was cowering in fear for her life) in the back seat. Vidor warned Jack about an oncoming dip in the road, and Jack petulantly sped up: "The car flung itself violently in the air. . . . Turning rearward, I saw Ina's body still in its reclining position but it was now several feet in the air. . . . I hoped the car would still be under her when she returned."

Chapter Twelve

With each picture I made I knew I was sinking lower and lower.
—John Gilbert, 1933

MGM's other silent-era male leads were not doing much better. Chipper, brash William Haines was still in his late twenties when talkies hit, but he was already becoming slightly pudgy, and his hair was thinning. What really killed his career was the type of parts he played: the wise-ass frat boy who charms and wheedles his way into a girl's heart. In silent films this could indeed be cute and charming—in talkies it was obnoxious. In such light romantic comedies as *The Girl Said No, Way Out West,* and *Just a Gigolo,* he harasses and stalks and prods his leading ladies to the point where any sane woman would take out an order of protection—instead, of course, they lose their hearts to him.

Like Jack, Haines was put into cheaper and cheaper vehicles, none of which showed him off to good effect (except for the terrific but little-seen *Are You Listening?*). He was out of MGM by 1932, and out of films by 1934. Haines had a happy afterlife as one of the nation's leading interior designers, and he enjoyed one of Hollywood's longest, happiest marriages, with his partner Jimmie Shields (who committed suicide shortly after Haines's 1973 death). Haines's open and unabashed homosexuality had nothing to do with the end of his career: neither Mayer nor anyone else in charge at MGM cared about their stars' sexual orientation as long as it was kept out of the press.

Ramon Novarro, too, was gay, but he was neither open nor unabashed about it. From a very religious family (several siblings became priests and nuns), poor Novarro was tormented by his situation. He drank heavily and never had a steady partner to give him ballast. Novarro's problem at MGM was his accent, though his excellent singing voice was utilized in a film or two. He, like Haines, was getting rather paunchy in his early thirties (the drinking did not help matters—it made Jack lose weight, but Novarro became doughy). And his MGM talkies were easily as dreadful as anything Jack was assigned—even worse, many of them. He had Ruritarian romances and musicals (*Daybreak, Devil-May-Care, The Cat and the Fiddle, The Night Is Young*), he played a cringe-making Indian (from India, in *Son of India*) and Indian (as in Navaho, in *Laughing Boy*). He was even Chinese (as was Helen Hayes!) in the truly awful *The Son-Daughter.*

Ramon Novarro was dropped by MGM in 1935, but after a rough middle age he had a comeback as a very busy and dapper character actor in films and on TV. He was still acting in 1968 when he was murdered in his home by two male prostitutes (his killers got life sentences, but both were paroled in the 1970s).

John Barrymore was lucky—things might not have gone well for him: as the talkies hit he was pushing fifty and his lifestyle was catching up to him. Within just a couple of years he had become flabby and debauched looking. But his talent and his wonderful voice were untouched, and he managed to segue into character roles. Barrymore was never again effective as a lover in talkies—and we shall discuss *Grand Hotel* shortly—but as a dramatic actor (*A Bill of Divorcement, Dinner at Eight, Counsellor at Law*) and an over-the-top comic actor (*Twentieth Century, Midnight*), he was matchless.

Jack's longtime pal Richard Barthelmess, too, seemed to become middle-aged overnight. Only thirty-four in 1929, he looked easily fifty. His voice was serviceable, though, and First National kept him working in leads for several years (most notably in *The Dawn Patrol* and *The Cabin in the Cotton,* opposite a vampy young Bette Davis). He was amazing in William Wellman's dark, pre-Code *Heroes for Sale* as a drug-addicted, out of work World War I veteran. But age, competition, and increased weight had him down to supporting and character roles by the time he retired (very wealthy, through real-estate investments) in 1942.

Of all Jack's friends and contemporaries, it was Ronald Colman who hit the jackpot. No one else had a voice like that: dark velvet, with a dreamy, posh British accent. Colman was nearing forty when talkies hit, but unlike Novarro, Haines, and Barthelmess, he only got handsomer with middle age. Goldwyn knew it had a winner with him, and Colman's first talkie, the 1929 detective caper *Bulldog Drummond,* was indeed a smash. Yet Colman had shied away from talkies at first: "Except as a scientific achievement, I am not sympathetic to this 'sound business,'" he said. "It does not properly belong to my particular work." But he caved in and signed a talkie contract against his better judgment. The early-1930s *Raffles* and *Arrowsmith* cemented Colman's new standing as a talkie star, and even the silly, dull *Condemned* and *The Unholy Garden* didn't slow him down. Colman's career ascended through success after success (including a 1947 Oscar for *A Double Life*).

Meanwhile, everyone piled on to find fault with John Gilbert's perfectly serviceable and agreeable voice. The voices of Douglas Fairbanks Sr., Charles Farrell, and even newcomer Clark Gable were an octave higher than Jack's, but he was branded with the "high and squeaky" reputation. The *Los Angeles Times*'s Edwin Schallert provided one of the more sympathetic and incisive comments. It "had a tense, nervous and excited note . . . essentially an expression of his personality." If the studio had the time, the money, and the inclination, it could have channeled this quality into the proper roles—but there were schedules to be met and other stars to be coddled, and why should the prickly, always complaining John Gilbert get special treatment?

In September 1930 Louis B. Mayer gave an extraordinary interview to Marie Hicks Davidson of the *San Francisco Bulletin* as he was stopping at the Palace Hotel. "Jack Gilbert is one of the stars who has benefited by sound pictures," he said—a statement that even at the time raised many eyebrows. "When he found that his voice did not reproduce satisfactorily, he took a course of voice culture, training as vigorously as an opera student," an ostensibly encouraging and friendly Mayer went on. "The result is a picture which we shall shortly release, *The Way of a Sailor* [*sic*], which we believe will be a stupendous hit."

Mayer added, perhaps a bit ominously, "The talkies have created a new aristocracy in filmdom and a genre different from anything we dreamed. By the same token it has retired many favorites." He may have been sending a coded message to Jack—but to the public at large, his fans, it seemed that MGM still had great hopes and plans for him. There was certainly no public bad-mouthing or undermining. Mayer's daughter Irene had a different take: she recalled her father smugly reading the bad reviews for Jack's early talkies and saying, "That should take care of *Mr.* Gilbert."

Jack's third talkie was a tough little buddy comedy, *Way for a Sailor,* which had a surprisingly large budget of $889,000—costing nearly as much as *Redemption* and *His Glorious Night* combined. It doesn't look like $889,000 on the screen; no newly built sets, and the rear-projection scenes are laughably cheesy. Besides Jack's salary, the main expense seems to have been a bang-up storm at sea with a lifeboat rescue.

Way for a Sailor was light on plot: the adventures of three rowdy merchant marines and Jack's pursuit of leading lady Leila Hyams (in a particularly nasty plot twist, he tricks her into marriage by lying about giving up the sea). Wallace Beery (who had not yet found top stardom in *Min and Bill* and *The Champ*) played one of the pals—the other, in what was a huge slap in the face to Jack, was played by his *Vanity Fair* nemesis, writer Jim Tully. It's beyond belief that John Gilbert and Jim Tully—both pig-headed grudge holders with thin skins—resolved to become pals and put all that real nastiness behind them. It's equally hard to believe, though, that either of them would agree to a PR-inspired forgive-and-forget fake story: but MGM released a publicity photo of the two good-naturedly sparring with boxing gloves.

Indeed, if Mayer was looking for a way to make Jack completely lose his composure, casting Tully in this film was a master stroke. Amazingly, Jack displayed enviable self-control and gave no indication of annoyance (true, he may have been so depressed by this time that he just didn't care anymore). *Photoplay* joined in the fun by teasing Tully (editor James Quirk, remember, hated the man): "Jim Tully . . . is no great shakes as an actor," ran a September 1930 piece. "It is being whispered about that Mr. Tully is not an unqualified success in the talking cinema. In fact, there is more than a possibility that *Way for a Sailor* may be remade with the pugilistic Mr. Tully conspicuous by his absence. John Gilbert, so the yarn goes, is laughing up his sleeves. Rushes have revealed that

Jack taking no chances with Jim Tully while shooting *Way for a Sailor,* 1930 (Wisconsin Center for Film & Theater Research).

Jim Tully has a voice at least as high-pitched as his!" To be fair, Tully wound up giving quite a good performance, though *Way for a Sailor* marked his only acting role.

Way for a Sailor wasn't a bad film, but it never seemed to take off, just meandered from scene to scene. It was definitely pre-Code in its bawdiness: Tully encountering look-alike illegitimate sons in every port, Beery emerging from what is obviously a Singapore whorehouse, a chamber pot being emptied over some sailors, a man leering at passing women, "*That's* what I call seafood!" and Wallace Beery's character being nicknamed "Tripod" (which *really* does not bear thinking about).

Jack—who is also named "Jack" in this film—looks the part: clean-shaven, with tousled hair and decked out in rumpled work clothes. But he never really seems at home as a tough, devil-may-care roustabout. His best scene comes on a beach, explaining to Hyams why he loves the sea—he's heartfelt and unaffected.

Jack's role was obviously the starring part—he was in nearly every frame—and his contract stated that he must have star billing in the credits. But in advertising, Wallace Beery got top billing. When *Way for a Sailor* opened in November 1930, the *Los Angeles Times* was undeservedly vicious in its appraisal. "The idea was that Jack was to make an impression as a rough swearing, cud-chewing roughneck," wrote Harry Carr. "But with his little pipe-stem arms and his slender form lost in a baggy sailor suit, his fate was completed. . . . The adoring fans expected Mr. Gilbert to rumble like a pipe organ. He squeaked." But the film could not have been made with an eye to undoing the damage inflicted by *Redemption* and *His Glorious Night*—MGM files show that all three had been scheduled for Jack as of May 1929, while *Redemption* was still in mid-production (the same files show that Lon Chaney was slated for *Chéri-Bibi,* but after his death it was retitled *The Phantom of Paris* and given to Jack).

One critic cut the venom a bit: "This can't be considered complete ruination for Gilbert. . . . His voice isn't bad at all. His diction merely doesn't suit a hard-boiled sailor." British humorist P. G. Wodehouse, working at MGM as a screenwriter at the time, repeated the common gossip to a friend: "The thought of having to pay those smackers [Jack's $250,000 per film salary] gashes them like a knife. The rumor goes that in order to avoid this, they are straining every nerve to ensure that his next picture will be such a flop that he will consent to a broken-hearted settlement." If that was indeed the plan, "they" (Mayer, no doubt) did not take into account Jack's stubbornness and vengefulness when crossed.

Way for a Sailor lost $606,000, and MGM began making louder and louder noises about adjusting Jack's contract downward—or canceling it altogether. But Jack was nothing if not determined. "They offered to buy me off," he said. "After each picture the offer was renewed—and raised. I refused to quit. It would have been easier to go. I stuck it through and with each picture I made I knew I was sinking lower and lower." Mayer's biographer Scott Eyman writes that Jack almost was fired; Mayer was eagerly looking for ways to legally boot him out as his films lost more and more money. But entertainment lawyer Fanny Holtzmann talked him out of it: "You still own thousands of feet of Gilbert footage usable in many parts of the world," she told him. "Why throw away the assets in your vault?" Besides, she coolly noted, "There's the public relations aspect. How do you think movie fans would feel about Louis Mayer throwing out the former idol who did so much for him?" She suggested Mayer just sit back, eat the $250,000 per picture, and "leave him alone and maybe he'll drink himself to death. Or let him take a swing at somebody in public, and you'll have legal cause."

Newspapers and fan magazines had always found Jack to be chatty, charming, and cooperative, so the gathering of vultures was both sympathetic and yet deadly in its very sympathy. "They wrote things about me in the papers and magazines," Jack said in 1933. "They meant to be kind, perhaps. I was too raw to know. But it was the kindness that kills a man already half dead. One story was titled, 'Is John Gilbert Through?' The question was its own answer. Another editor wrote that, after seeing and hearing me in *His Glorious Night,* he felt as though he had just had news that his dearest friend had been stricken with a malignant and incurable disease."

In February 1931 Jack's marriage to Ina Claire finally ground to a halt. She returned to Los Angeles with two contracts in her pocket: one from RKO to shoot *Rebound* (an all but unwatchable teacup comedy) and one from Goldwyn to film her 1919 hit *The Gold Diggers.* The result was *The Greeks Had a Word for Them* (retitled *Three Broadway Girls* at the censors' demand), a funny, nasty, bawdy comedy about three hard-boiled tarts (Claire, Joan Blondell, and Madge Evans) on the make.

Leonard Hall wrote in *Photoplay,* viciously but accurately, that "Ina found herself, once the moonlight had worn off, hitched to an impetuous, dizzy schoolboy who laughed, pouted and raved by turns. And Jack, to his dismay, discovered that in the palace of Ina Claire, queen of New York's uptown wits, there was room for only one throne—and that was hers. The stormy Gilbert just hasn't any answers for the mental machine-gunning of a girl like Claire. I dare say there's hardly a man alive who could go up against Ina at her rapier-like best and finish better than second!"

Ina Claire was back on top, and Jack was struggling through his next film, *Gentleman's Fate*. He never came to meet her at the train station—he first claimed he was in bed with a cold, then admitted that he was playing tennis with Ronald Colman in Malibu. Ina Claire moved into the Beverly-Wilshire Hotel—not her husband's home—and told the *Los Angeles Times* that she and Jack had indeed separated. "Any difficulty or misunderstanding we have had probably is at least as much my fault as his," she said. Then she went on to complain about the constant press scrutiny: "Continually we read where we had parted, or that there was some difficulty between us. I was not accustomed to the ways of Hollywood, and naturally this caused a great deal of disturbance. I had become accustomed to living a life like anyone else, and I guess this cannot be done here."

As Ina Claire's star rose again, Jack seemed stuck in the mud. The *Los Angeles Times* wrote of her Goldwyn contract, then twisted the knife: Jack was "fast slipping into the discard. The full power of the largest studio group in the country doesn't seem to be able to cover certain talking deficiencies which the movie audience finds in Jack Gilbert. All the money involved in the Gilbert contract—and it runs into millions—can't be sacrificed, so one type of story after another has been tried to salvage this one-time matinee hero supreme of the silver screen."

In March 1931 Ina Claire took up the clichéd but required residency in Reno, and in August she and her lawyer—the same Fanny Holtzmann who had advised Mayer on how to handle Jack—appeared in Judge Joseph P. Sproul's courtroom. All the polite talk about careers and "it was my fault as much as his" fell to one side. "He said he wanted to be left alone," said Ina Claire, too clever not to know she was paraphrasing Greta Garbo. "He was very irritable and moody. I attempted, then and there, to pacify [him], to restore peace and harmony, in our lives, but . . . he said I was a woman with too much intellect—whatever he meant by *that.*" Jack's old friend Paul Bern testified that "Jack was very much distressed with his stock-market losses, and dissatisfied with his own pictures." In the middle of a conversation, said Bern, "he would suddenly turn away and leave the room."

Jack spoke on his own behalf only through two letters, which were read in court. To his wife, he wrote, "I try and try to make a go of this, but it seems hopeless. . . . I'm going to miss you terribly but I am not fit company now, nor do I want anyone about me." Through his attorney, Peyton Moore, he stated, "Everyone naturally regrets a failure and I regret that this marriage is ending in a divorce. . . . Whatever the reasons . . . one thing has been established, and that is the dignity of the lady who was Mrs. Gilbert. . . . She has been more than fair in every way and refused all offers of a financial settlement from me."

The divorce was granted, and would become final at the beginning of 1932. There was a flurry of unpleasantness and hurt feelings when Jack requested—in writing—assurances that Claire would not try to claim half of his assets under California's community property laws (remember, Jack had ably held on to much of his fortune through the stock-market crash, and his earning future was obviously shaky). Ina Claire was miffed. "Imagine that!" she exclaimed to his daughter decades later, still annoyed. "I didn't marry him for his money." She tearfully told Jack's lawyer, "I know money means a great deal to him. He thinks I'm after his money. I don't want a penny of it."

But by late 1931 Jack and Ina Claire were the best of friends again—indeed, his ex-wives and girlfriends had nothing but kind words for him. There were even rumors of a remarriage, but Jack told the *Los Angeles Times,* "We do desire to be the best of friends. There will not be, decidedly not, reconciliation between Miss Claire and myself." She remained sympathetic—from a distance—and viewed with sorrow the continuing downfall of Jack's career. He would go to MGM, she told his daughter Leatrice years later, and "sit there all day and do nothing. . . . They practically spit on him from up above as he walked down the street."

Jack's fourth MGM talkie was a tidy little gangster film called *Gentleman's Fate,* by novelist Ursula Parrott (whose *Ex-Wife* became a huge hit for Norma Shearer as *The Divorcée*). Jack portrayed a society playboy who discovers that his family is in the bootlegging business—he is unwillingly drawn in and finds, to his chagrin, that he is actually rather good at it. Jack does a very good job at taking his character from lighthearted man-about-town to bitter, resigned gangster. The supporting cast was inexpensive but talented: reliable contract player Leila Hyams as his appalled society fiancée and Anita Page as a broken-blossom moll who takes a shine to Jack. Stealing every scene was plug-ugly Louis Wolheim as Jack's brother (several jokes are tossed in about their lack of family resemblance, which was rather tough on poor Wolheim) and the always-wonderful Marie Prevost as a wise-cracking hotel clerk ("You ever hear from that wife o' yours in Philadelphia, PA?" she asks her boyfriend. "She just won't die, will she?").

Gentleman's Fate is not a bad little film, though it cannot compare to other 1931 gangster classics (*Public Enemy, Dance, Fools, Dance, A Free Soul*). Director Mervyn LeRoy (*Little Caesar, I Am a Fugitive from a Chain Gang, Gold Diggers of 1933*) brought some wonderful touches to it—but it is a bit slow moving and very sloppily edited (William Gray is credited as editor, but he must have phoned it in). And, ominously, the cast was a veritable stock company of the walking dead. Anita Page—a talented, once-promising starlet of the late 1920s—was on the outs at MGM; depending on what story you believe, either her agent demanded top billing for her, or she said "no" to either Mayer or executive Eddie Mannix. Louis Wolheim—who had made such a hit in *All Quiet on the Western Front*—died of cancer before *Gentleman's Fate* was even released. And poor Marie Prevost—such a brilliant comic and dramatic actress—found that ten or twenty extra pounds of weight made her unemployable, and was well on the way to drinking herself to death.

Costar Leila Hyams told Jack's daughter Leatrice that his desperate career problems never found their way to the set: "He never mentioned them to me," Hyams said. "He was always anxious to keep the atmosphere happy on the set. He didn't fuss." She added that he lent a charming continental touch to the atmosphere. "He used to serve a beautiful lunch in his dressing room. A lot of the cast would go there for lunch instead of the commissary."

Costar Anita Page told this writer in 1993, "I loved John Gilbert. He was a great actor. Once he was lying on a couch playing a death scene, and he cried like a baby [actually, it was Page who cried in this scene, and very nicely, too]—and I thought, gosh, how can you do this? Little girls are allowed to cry, but little boys aren't supposed to! He said, 'If the scene plays true, I can do it every time. If there's one false moment and I don't believe it, I can't.'" Page backs up accounts of Jack's sociability and cheerfulness on the set: "He used to invite me to his bungalow to have lunch." The rather sheltered and virginal Page added, "I trusted him, he was a gentleman. I knew the people I could trust."

Ramon Novarro's biographer, André Soares, brings up the excellent point that Jack's salary was such a huge part of each film's budget that it "made it nearly impossible for the studio to pair him with a costly leading lady or director. . . . Without the backup of an important female lead or expensive productions, Gilbert's movies did not perform as well at home or, especially, abroad." Which is true: from 1930 to 1933, Jack might have appeared opposite MGM contract stars like Garbo, Norma Shearer, Helen Hayes, Joan Crawford, Jean Harlow, Marion Davies—their fans alone would have boosted the box office. Instead he was paired with Hyams, Page, Provost and, later, Natalie Moorhead, Lois Moran, Madge Evans, Virginia Bruce, Mae Clarke—charming actresses, but inexpensive contract players who brought few loyal fans to the theaters.

Costing an impressive $500,000 and released in March 1931, *Gentleman's Fate* lost $216,000.

By mid-1931 John Gilbert might as well have been *Sunset Boulevard*'s Norma Desmond or one of the Edies from *Grey Gardens,* as far as Hollywood was concerned. "Hollywood's Unhappiest Man," a *Los Angeles Times* story dubbed him. "He is so miserable that he never comes to the studio if he can possibly avoid it. When he has to come, he walks in with his hat pulled down over his eyes; avoiding everyone, speaking to no one—a picture of abject misery. Whatever he has come for, he finishes in the shortest possible time and skulks away again."

Finally Jack got a really good vehicle—even if it was secondhand. Lon Chaney had been slated for *The Phantom of Paris.* Jack starred as Chéri-Bibi, the antihero of a series of novels by Gaston Leroux (creator of *The Phantom of the Opera*). The film was directed by John Robertson, a longtime veteran who had piloted some workmanlike successes (Mary Pickford's *Tess of the Storm Country,* Lillian Gish's *Annie Laurie,* Garbo's *The Single Standard*), but had never really had an artistic or financial hit.

The Phantom of Paris is an enjoyable but oddly flawed film. Jack portrays Chéri-Bibi, a French Houdini-like escape artist. His romantic rival, the marquis du Touchais (Ian Keith), murders their love object's rich father, frames Chéri-Bibi, and marries the girl (played rather wanly by Leila Hyams). Tracked by a relentless Inspector Javert–like detective, Chéri-Bibi goes slightly mad, hiding in a sunless cellar for four years and finally taking over the identity of du Touchais, who has conveniently died of the flu. All this has been fast moving and diverting (and Natalie Moorhead gave a great performance as an ice-cold villainess). But the plot hits a brick wall when Chéri-Bibi disguises himself as du Touchais and moves into his mansion: Jack looked nothing like Ian Keith, who was a good head taller and a bit stouter. Jack looked very fetching in his goatee and monocle, but he looked like John Gilbert in a goatee and monocle, not like Ian Keith. The fact that MGM did not simply cast an actor who looked like Jack—or even have Jack play both roles, in a split screen—makes one almost suspect that maybe some sabotage was going on. Or, at least, no one cared enough to make the effort.

Nonetheless, Jack shouldered through the improbable plot and had some very good moments: hiding in a friend's toy-shop cellar, he is spring-coiled mad, his hands obsessively grasping at a chair back. Peering at the detective through a fireplace grate, he looks downright satanic. And a scene with du Touchais' young son, played by six-year-old Douglas Scott, is charming.

The Phantom of Paris wrapped in mid-June 1931 and was released in September. *Photoplay* noted happily that "when anyone can stir a Baltimore audience to applause, he must be great. . . . They forgot *The Phantom of Paris* was just a picture and applauded with such vigor as has not been shown here since *The Big Parade*." Mordaunt Hall in the *New York Times* called *The Phantom of Paris* "a highly improbable but none the less interesting tale," adding that Jack "gives quite a good performance, although the microphone is not especially kind to his voice." The film, which cost $533,000, nonetheless lost $243,000.

In the fall of 1931 Jack embarked on a brief but vivid affair with gorgeous twenty-three-year-old Lupe Velez, who was herself on the rebound from a failed romance with Gary Cooper. Velez was talented, funny, and *exhausting*. Later nicknamed "the Mexican Spitfire," she followed the same career path as Jean Harlow: starting out as a heavy-lidded vamp

Jack and Natalie Moorhead in one of his better talkies, *The Phantom of Paris,* 1931 (The Everett Collection).

then bursting forth in the early 1930s as a brilliant comedienne. That was yet to come; when she and Jack met she was still appearing in such dramas as *The Squaw Man* and *The Cuban Love Song.* That October Velez accompanied Jack on a trip to Paris. An engagement was immediately rumored: "I admire him very much," Velez told Louella Parsons.

Jack had a brief fling with Lupe Velez in late 1931 (author's collection).

"I won't say whether I am going to marry him or not. Why should I put Mr. Gilbert in an embarrassing position by saying we are going to get married and then the next day we decide not to marry? I change my mind often! So does he. So I won't say we are engaged—but maybe later—who knows?"

Jack had little patience with or love for Louella Parsons, but he told her, "I am not legally free from Ina Claire. I think it would be in very bad taste for me to say anything about marriage to Miss Velez while I am still legally the husband of another woman. When I am free, maybe later, we might both have something to say." He added, "I am going to Europe for a rest, I am tired. It means a lot to me to come back and make a good picture. . . . I am not even going to think about work until I have had a long rest."

For a short term, at a bad time in his life, Lupe Velez was just the pick-me-up Jack needed. She was effervescent, sexy, and had more energy than a roomful of squirrels. "Lupe is splendid, isn't she?" Jack said in October 1931. "She has such a great sense of humor. She is the best companion in the world. We have lots of fun together." In November the last of their affair was noted limply in the press, as poor Lupe threw up all the way from Paris to Cherbourg on a storm-tossed plane. Velez was still so queasy after landing "that the captain's cabin on the tender which took her out to the liner was turned over to her." Lupe never did anything quietly. It's doubtful that air- and seasickness actually ended their romance, but by the beginning of 1932 Jack was back on the market (and Lupe on her way to marriage with Johnny "Tarzan" Weissmuller).

At the same time Jack was romancing Lupe Velez, his wife Ina Claire was in a relationship with forty-two-year-old Robert Ames, who was costarring with her in the film *Rebound*. On November 27 Ames died in his New York hotel room, done in by too much alcohol. *Rebound* seems to have been cursed: another leading player, Robert Williams, was on his way to a James Stewart–type career but was felled by appendicitis and died shortly after the film opened.

By late 1931 the Depression was deepening, with no end in sight. We look back on the early 1930s as a brilliant age of motion-picture genius and experimentation, of new stars being born—but it was a time of panic and desperation in Hollywood. Film receipts were off 65 percent by November 1931, and after a meeting of the Motion Pictures Producers and Distributors Association, it was decided that studios would have to cut costs by 20–50 percent to survive the next year. "The 'in-betweens' whose names mean little or nothing at the box office will be most seriously affected," wrote an Associated Press reporter. "They will be warned that if they refuse to accept cuts the axe is very likely to fall when option time comes around. Most stars earned weekly salaries *while working*—of course, under the current system, their unpaid leave could stretch indefinitely, and they were barred from seeking work elsewhere."

Some stars though, were paid per film: Jack, most famously, earned $250,000 per movie. Others in that same situation were Richard Barthelmess (also on a career downslide, at $187,000 a picture), character stars George Bancroft ($100,000) and Walter Huston ($50,000), and up-and-coming starlets Lupe Velez ($35,000), Joan Bennett, and Barbara Stanwyck (both at $25,000 a picture).

Jack's final 1931 release, the romantic drama *West of Broadway,* cost a surprisingly high $585,000 to make—much of that being Jack's salary, of course—and wound up losing $322,000. For all its bad reviews and worse box office, *West of Broadway* is a charming, unpretentious little movie. Jack starred as a returning World War vet (though the film was obviously set in 1931, Prohibition and all) who is dumped by his fiancée, goes on a binge, and marries a gold digger with a heart of gold. He goes to his Arizona ranch to escape his new wife (and looks much more at home in his Broadway tux than he does in cowboy togs); she follows him and tries to win him over—it's obvious from the get-go how the plot will wind up, but Jack and baby-faced Lois Moran are terrific together, circling each other warily, sparring and fighting their attraction. (Mention must also be made of Gwen Lee, who was terrific as Lois Moran's wise-cracking roommate.)

Moran recalled Jack as "the handsomest of men and a good fellow," and confirmed that his voice was perfectly fine: "I would have noticed it, being extremely voice-conscious." Her opinion was that "the early sound tracks are what did him in." Ralph Bellamy, who played a small role in *West of Broadway,* recalled, "Jack told me that the studio put him in this picture hoping he'd refuse it and break his contract." But Jack banked his paycheck, stuck to his guns, right or wrong, and stubbornly told Bellamy, "I'll do anything. I'll clean spittoons if those bastards tell me to, until this contract is up."

There were many echoes of Jack's own life in *West of Broadway,* and a few premonitions of the future. His Jerry Seevers drinks too much and doesn't eat enough; his doctors give him "six months to live" unless he shapes up. Lois Moran's attempts to buck him up and dry him out are a foreshadowing of Marlene Dietrich's reclamation program four years in the future. And watching him nastily snap at and insult his new wife uncomfortably brings to mind his own wives' divorce papers.

The film runs a little over an hour and the only real bump in the road is costar (billed second) El Brendel, playing the same annoying character that Karl Dane had played in *The Big Parade*. A "Swedish" dialect comic (actually from Philadelphia), Brendel enjoyed a brief and inexplicable popularity in the early 1930s that has not worn well: "Obviously one person Will Rogers never met, he forever embossed his clod of a footprint on that era justifiably known as The Great Depression," says historian and critic Mel Neuhaus. "Gilbert's voice they carped about, but *this* idiot they couldn't get enough of."

One critic wrote, "If it was the purpose of MGM to lead John Gilbert to the guillotine and end the waning popularity of one of the most popular stars the silver screen has ever known, then *West of Broadway* is a great success." The script doctor, Gene Markey, himself had nothing good to say about *West of Broadway*. "It was written by a couple of actors who decided they were screenwriters too," he told Jack's daughter Leatrice. "It was a flimsy story. I never believed in it, but I did the best I could. . . . It was poorly directed, and I must confess that my script was no great shakes." Markey did not buy into any great studio plots to ruin Jack, instead attributing the missteps to incompetence. "It was not the vehicle Jack should have had, but the studio chief cockroaches thought it would be good to give Jack a change of pace."

James Quirk of *Photoplay* pondered Jack's future—and recent past—as his MGM contract ground on. "He has had a pretty miserable two years of it," Quirk wrote, "with an unsuccessful marriage and a collection of weak pictures to struggle through [not to mention several coffin-nailing pieces from *Photoplay*]. His company has tried all types of stories for him, but nothing has clicked. I am afraid bidding will not be too hectic for Jack's time and manly beauty when the Metro contract expires. He's in a tough spot, and we must all pull hard for him, for he's a fine actor and a swell guy, too." "At that," Quirk finished, writing at the depth of the Depression, "you can wipe away a lot of tears with a ten-thousand-dollar pay check every week!"

Chapter Thirteen

Virginia's sweetness, her sympathy and understanding, are beyond belief.

—John Gilbert, 1935

In early 1932 Jack met the woman—still a girl, really—who would become the fourth and final Mrs. John Gilbert. Virginia Bruce was twenty-one when they met, a delicate-looking Dresden-doll blonde. But her looks were deceiving: Bruce was smart, tough, and strong minded enough to assure that this marriage was doomed from the start.

A talented singer and pianist, Bruce was expelled from her North Dakota high school for mouthing off to her teachers; she moved to Los Angeles in 1928 not to break into the movies but to attend UCLA as a piano student. But her blonde good looks guaranteed money in the movies: "I had never given motion pictures a thought," Bruce said in 1928, "but it is the chance of a lifetime. I had planned to continue my vocal and piano lessons . . . but I think I shall like the screen." The sensible young lady did not become a star right away, but she earned a respectable living doing extra and bit parts for the next three years (she can be spotted in the background of such hits as *The Love Parade, Raffles,* and *Whoopee!*).

As talkies took off, so did Bruce's career, with slightly larger roles in *Safety in Numbers, The Miracle Man, Sky Bride* (all at Paramount), and *Winner Take All* (Warner Bros.). In early 1932 she and fellow blonde Jean Harlow were signed by Irving Thalberg as MGM contract players (both were tested for *Red-Headed Woman,* which helped make Harlow a star). Bruce had been on the MGM lot for several months and of course had noticed the great John Gilbert. Sometimes while lunching in the commissary, "I'd happen to look up and I'd catch his eye, you know what flashing black eyes he has. And every time I met his eyes, a shock would go through me. I couldn't look at him. I'd never felt anything like it before."

According to Bruce, the two met formally after she had tested for his first 1932 film, *Downstairs;* he sent for her to come to his dressing-room bungalow so he could tell her how much he liked her test footage. He invited her to his house to play tennis—when she declined, he asked about the next day. Bruce said yes. "That first night, too, I found a big box of red roses waiting for me when I got home." Frankly, she was a little scared by Jack, and probably rightly so. "When he looked at me, I felt all funny inside," she recalled. "I've never seen eyes so intense and penetrating. I couldn't imagine anyone feeling easy and natural with Mr. Gilbert, and I was sure I wouldn't like him."

Desperate after the failure of his three 1931 releases, Jack had convinced Irving Thalberg to okay his story *Downstairs,* which he had been shopping around since 1927. Budgeted at a respectable $494,000, *Downstairs* was directed by Monta Bell and had an impressive A-list crew: screenwriter Lenore Coffee, cinematographer Hal Rosson, art direction by Jack's friend Cedric Gibbons (who came up with some looming, atmospheric Old Country House sets). The cast, though, was cut rate: inexpensive nonstellar contract players such as Bruce, Paul Lukas, Hedda Hopper, and Karen Morley.

Downstairs was the lurid story of chauffeur Karl Schneider, who happily sleeps, thieves, and blackmails his way through life (he smiles insinuatingly at previous employer Hedda Hopper, "I thought I had given Madam complete *satisfaction*"). Obtaining a position with the Baron and Baroness von Burgen, he proceeds to seduce and steal from their cook (Bodil Rosing, in a heartrending performance), blackmail the adulterous baroness (Olga Baclanova), and bed Anna, the innocent young maid (Virginia Bruce), who has just married the older, stuffy butler (Paul Lukas). Karl is coarse and oversexed and remorseless—and he commits all his sins with a wide-eyed shrug and childlike glee. After being found out by Anna's husband, Karl is run out of town with a beating—but

Jack in his best talkie, *Downstairs*, 1932 (author's collection).

lands happily in the final scene with a sexy new boss (a cameo appearance by rising star Karen Morley).

"I am happier than I've been in years," Jack enthused during filming. "It's a psychological study, a cross-section view of two strata in life. . . . The chauffeur is a swaggering Don Juan who makes up in audacity what he lacks in conscience. He is an outright villain, but nevertheless, a fascinating chap. He will be hated for his villainy, but he's bound to be interesting."

Story editor Sam Marx suggested to the writers' and readers' department during shooting that the working title *Downstairs* had to go: "We do not want a title that is particularly indicative of the servant's quarters, but rather one with an implication of sex. The usual award of fifty dollars will be given the winning title. We will appreciate your sending your suggestions to this office soon." Penciled in at the top of his notes are a few suggestions: *The Servant and His Mistress, Indiscretion, Ladies Man, Servants Secrets*. In the end, *Downstairs* it remained.

On July 2, 1932, in the midst of filming *Downstairs,* Jack and Virginia Bruce attended the wedding of his old friend Paul Bern to rising MGM star Jean Harlow. The romance was a shocker to fans—gorgeous sexpot Harlow marrying the balding, middle-aged producer—but to his friends it was an old story. Bern had previously fallen madly in love with actresses Barbara La Marr, Mabel Normand, and Joan Crawford; the naïve, unsure-of-herself Harlow was charmed and flattered that this intellectual older man took her seriously. What Harlow didn't know (and it's unclear whether Jack and his other friends knew) was that Paul Bern had a common-law wife, Dorothy Millette. A former actress, Millette had emotional problems, made worse after reading that her husband had just married the nation's leading new sex symbol. It all came to a head on the night of September 4—just two months after the wedding—when Paul Bern was found dead in his Benedict Canyon home, a bullet in his head and a gun in his hand. He left a very vague suicide note, which was addressed to "Dearest Dear"—Harlow? Millette? No one knows.

MGM went into face-saving overdrive, with their top new star's career in danger and one of their biggest producers dead. District attorney Buron Fitts handled the investigation, and Fitts was widely known to be

Among the guests at Jean Harlow and Paul Bern's 1932 wedding were Jack (behind the groom's shoulder), Irving Thalberg and Norma Shearer (left), Virginia Bruce (third from right), and David O. Selznick (right) (The Everett Collection).

the most corrupt official in L.A. (no mean feat, considering the competition). Poor Harlow was cross-examined and cleared, and poor Dorothy Millette jumped off a boat in Sacramento and drowned. Harlow handled herself like a champ—in the midst of shooting *Red Dust,* she reported back to work a week later and refused to play the victim. Luckily for her, MGM banked on her future and stood behind her.

Jack attended Bern's funeral on September 9, as did Mayer and Thalberg and a nearly collapsing with grief Harlow, heavily veiled. Bern's death was ruled a suicide, brought on by the embarrassing reappearance of his common-law wife, but the scandal followed Jean Harlow for the rest of her life and beyond, with dubious biographies and lurid rumors concerning her marriage and Bern's death. One recent, unverifiable claim is that at Bern's funeral, "a mechanical pulley that was attached to the coffin brought the coffin to a nearly vertical position and the lid slid open to show Bern, as though he was standing in front of everyone in the chapel. Thalberg burst into tears. John Gilbert, another close friend of Bern, vomited."

There were other scares in the summer of 1932: on Friday, June 3, the First National Bank of Beverly Hills shut its doors after panicked clients rushed for $300,000 in deposits. The bank's president insisted that there was no irregularity, that more than $5 million was safely on deposit—but that $300,000 was just not available on hand. While federal examiners took over, Jack (along with Greta Garbo, Wallace Beery, Jean Harlow, Robert Montgomery, and other clients) found their ready cash momentarily dried up, and the panic of the Depression affected them a bit more forcefully. Jack was certainly less inclined than ever to forfeit his MGM contract.

Jack had a great time filming *Downstairs:* director Monta Bell let him write some of his own dialogue, his character was dark and roguish, he was even able to throw in some vulgar touches (belching; nonchalantly digging his finger in his ear and his nose, then wiping it on his shirt) that he knew would infuriate Mayer—nonetheless, they were left in (though we don't know what else might have been cut). Besides having a good script and accommodating director, Jack also had a beautiful, unmarried leading lady to fall in love with, which always cheered him: Jack was on her like a lion on a wildebeest. His campaign was one that even a strong-minded young woman could not withstand: flowers, jewelry, flirtation, burning glances, every weapon in his impressive armory.

Jack asked Virginia Bruce to the première of *Grand Hotel* at Grauman's Chinese Theater on April 12; not having a nice enough gown, she said no, and Jack petulantly said that he wouldn't go either, then. He relented to an extent: they skipped the première but attended the *Vanities* with friends Cedric Gibbons and Barney Glaezer: "I can't remember ever having so much fun before," Bruce recalled. Every time Jack would whisper words of love to her, his friends would butt in with, "Don't believe him, Virginia, that's the way he gets with all his women."

After *Downstairs* wrapped, Jack continued showering his leading lady with gifts: a blue Packard roadster, "one of the biggest diamond rings in Hollywood," and a diamond and platinum wristwatch. "Our courtship has been one of whirlwind nature," Bruce understated to wire service reporter Wallace Rawles in May. They had only known each other a week, she said, when Jack first proposed. They were sitting by his pool one Saturday afternoon when he said, seemingly out of the blue, "I want you to marry me, Virginia. I want you to be my wife." "You could have knocked me over with a ping pong ball," said Bruce, who up till then was not sure whether or not to take Jack's professions of love (and wildly expensive gifts) seriously. "I became so confused I stammered, 'ye-es, Mr. Gilbert'—I was still calling him that."

At which point Virginia's parents made themselves known to their prospective son-in-law. Her father insisted on Jack's writing a new will, leaving all his assets to her and her family—and he guaranteed in writing to his son-in-law that the bride was a virgin. "Jack thought it was hilarious," said Bruce, "but I think he was also excited about it. I don't think he'd known many virgins in his life. I know this sounds crazy, but my father allowed me to spend one night with Jack before we married so that he could see for himself that I was a virgin. But he had to promise to return me to my father in the same condition."

They took out a marriage license on August 4 at the county clerk's office, posing happily for the gathered press—just moments earlier, Jack had gotten his final divorce decree from Ina Claire (he was taking no chances this time). Still, the John Gilbert/Virginia Bruce wedding on August 10 felt like a rushed affair, conducted in Jack's dressing-room bungalow on the MGM lot. Bruce was currently working on *Kongo,* a jungle adventure starring Walter Huston and Jack's recent girlfriend Lupe Velez. "We're going to be married at 6:00 in my bungalow," came the call—Bruce was still in costume and makeup and had not so much as a bouquet ready. But with a fresh-scrubbed face and wearing a black and white day frock, she showed up on time, greeted by her father and best man Irving Thalberg. Norma Shearer, Dolores del Rio, and a few less glamorous friends attended as well.

The *Syracuse Herald* called *Downstairs* a "flimsy yarn" and added a bit of etymology: "there are far too many of those things which popular wit periodicals have named 'burps,'" complained the prim reviewer. The *New York Times* didn't get around to reviewing *Downstairs* till October, and then Mordaunt Hall was lukewarm: "The chief points of interest in it are Mr. Gilbert's somewhat ingenuous attempt to impersonate a rascally automobile driver and Virginia Bruce's charming presence. Anyone might sit through this production without suspecting that Monta Bell

Jack with Virginia Bruce in *Downstairs,* 1932 (The Everett Collection).

directed it; but Mr. Bell was evidently hampered by the strange tale." *Time* magazine, anyway, approved, and felt this was a promising turning point for Jack: "When John Gilbert found that he had ceased to be a hero, he resolved to turn villain. The brilliance of his strategy is plain in this picture."

It's hard today to understand the lukewarm reception *Downstairs* received; it is by far Jack's best talkie and a hugely enjoyable pre-Code film. Jack is gleefully evil, grinning and skulking and seducing right and left; he even throws some autobiographical touches in, with the help of screenwriters Lenore Coffee and Melville Baker ("I never had much of a chance," he insincerely tells Bruce's character. "I never had anyone tell me the right thing to do. I had to fight my way alone"). His Karl is also the most hateful character he ever played, and Jack makes a delightful villain, dismissing the poor cook and pushing her away after stealing her life savings: "With a face like that, you oughta pay plenty—goodbye, grandma!"

Virginia Bruce acquits herself well, too; indeed, the most searing scene belongs to her, and she runs with it. Her husband finds out that Karl has seduced her, and Bruce does not deny it—instead, she lets him know that now she's had John Gilbert, Paul Lukas will no longer do: "There's a kind of way of making love that drives you mad and crazy, so that you don't know what you're doing," she tells him. "You think you can make love in the same frozen way you do everything else—and you think that's all I should have any wish for . . . I thank heaven I found there *is* something else—something that makes you so dizzy you don't know what's happened and you don't care!" It's a stunning scene, and Bruce shows a talent that would never be rewarded with stardom.

Downstairs is a funny, sexy, morally dubious little film, typical of the best of the pre-Code lot. It had sharp dialogue, a good cast, strong production values. The only misstep was placing it in a *mittel*-European setting—American audiences in 1932 (and today) would have found it much more accessible had it taken place in a medium-sized American town. But *Downstairs* lost $286,000.

It had a lot of impressive competition; it was made and released in what may have been the most delicious year in movie history. While 1939 is often called Hollywood's Golden Year, it barely holds a candle to the racy, exciting pre-Code fare of 1932. Talkies were still new enough to have a fresh excitement to them, but the kinks of the earliest experiments had been worked out. The censorship that clamped down in mid-1934 and sucked much of the sex and off-the-cuff freshness out of scripts had not yet arrived. MGM released a number of remarkable films that year in addition to *Downstairs:* the all-star *Grand Hotel,* the raunchy

Red Dust and *Red-Headed Woman*, the still-shocking *Freaks*. Even the studio's low-budget fare that year was impressive: the B films *Skyscraper Souls, Night Court,* and *Are You Listening?* feature some terrific acting and screenwriting.

But all studios, large and small, were hitting it out of the ballpark in 1932. Mae West made her film debut in *Night After Night*, and Katharine Hepburn in *A Bill of Divorcement*. That last movie almost starred Broadway's Peg Entwistle, who instead appeared in RKO's bizarre *Thirteen Women* and, that same year, leaped to her death from the HOLLYWOOD sign. Audiences had the choice in 1932 of top gangster films (*Scarface, I Am a Fugitive from a Chain Gang, Three on a Match, 20,000 Years in Sing Sing*), horror and suspense (*Freaks, The Mummy, Island of Lost Souls, The Mask of Fu Manchu, The Old Dark House, Murders in the Rue Morgue*), delirious screwball comedies (*Horse Feathers, Million Dollar Legs, Red-Headed Woman, If I Had a Million, The Greeks Had a Word for Them, Blessed Event, The Half-Naked Truth*), musicals (Maurice Chevalier in *Love Me Tonight* and *One Hour with You; The Big Broadcast*), and other such treats as Marlene Dietrich's ultra-glam *Shanghai Express* and *Blonde Venus; The Sign of the Cross;* Clara Bow's wonderfully insane *Call Her Savage;* the *A Star Is Born* precursor *What Price Hollywood?; Taxi!* the tearjerker *One Way Passage; Two Seconds; The Dark Horse; Flesh; Ladies of the Jury; The Heart of New York*—hardly a week passed that year without some classic hitting the theaters.

The year 1932 was also the breaking-point year when it came to bringing down the wrath of censors, and films like *Downstairs* were one important reason. In March 1930 studios and theater owners agreed to abide by the first talkie-era censorship code, issued by the Association of Motion Picture Producers and the Motion Picture Producers and Distributors of America. This resulted in what we know as the golden age of pre-Code films—which weren't pre-Code at all, of course. The 1930 Code was simply ignored and "gotten around." "No picture shall be produced that will lower the moral standards of those who see it. Hence the sympathy of the audience should never be thrown to the side of crime, wrongdoing, evil or sin," stated this Code. Murder and other crime, "scenes of passion . . . suggestive postures and gestures. . . . Sex perversion or any inference of it. . . . Vulgarity, profanity" were all proscribed.

From 1930 till mid-1934—by which time Jack was out of the business anyway—directors and producers winked at this Code and got away with an amazing amount of delicious shenanigans. But by 1932 religious and other moralizing groups complained loud and long about this increasingly bold nose thumbing. Paramount hired Mae West—already scandalous from her Broadway shows—to appear in films. At Warner Bros., Barbara Stanwyck played, in *Baby Face* (1933), a gold digger "so hard-boiled you could roll her on the White House lawn," to borrow Dorothy Parker's description of Dashiell Hammett. *Baby Face* was reshot with a cop-out ending, wherein she Learns Her Lesson, but the preceding hour was burned into audiences' brains.

At MGM, Jean Harlow appeared in the star-making *Red-Headed Woman* (based on a delightful Katherine Brush novel), playing an oversexed social climber who cheats on, then shoots, her husband—and is seen at the film's end, happy and unrepentant, having hooked another sugar daddy and a hot chauffeur. *Downstairs*'s Karl Schneider provided a male counterpart to *Red-Headed Woman*'s Lil Andrews: like Harlow, Jack was seen at the end of the movie about to land butter side up with another lovely mark, set to happily continue his thieving and fornicating.

Moralizers also had issues with Jean Harlow's cheerful whore in *Red Dust,* Clara Bow's masochistic gay-bar habitué in *Call Her Savage,* Myrna Loy's nympho countess in *Love Me Tonight,* Joyzelle Joyner's lesbian vamp in *The Sign of the Cross.* And of course, well, *Freaks* was in a class by itself.

With the failure of his beloved *Downstairs* to make a splash and no decent projects in the offing, Jack was having a hard time keeping up his spirits. He wanted to work, and work was what he was not getting. Jack may have been falling apart on the inside, but one couldn't tell by looking at the outside. While his fellow silent stars Ramon Novarro, William Haines, and Richard Barthelmess grew increasingly pudgy, John Gilbert remained trim and handsome. Some of the trimness may have been due to his ulcers, but he also kept active: Jack was an enthusiastic and competitive swimmer, golfer, and tennis player. *Motion Picture Classic* noted in 1930 that "our tennis world revolves around two factions: Marion Davies's and Jack Gilbert's. The Gilbert group consists of himself, King Vidor, and . . . [screenwriter and producer] Benjamin Glazer, [screenwriter] Chandler Sprague, and [producer] Arthur Hornblow."

Jack enjoying his tennis court, early 1930s (The Everett Collection).

As well as the lack of good films being given willingly to Jack, it is heartbreaking to see the roles that he lost. Many projects were dangled in front of him like bright shiny toys, then yanked cruelly away. He was name-dropped at MGM for the "other man" role opposite Joan Crawford and Robert Montgomery in *Sacred and Profane Love,* an adaptation of Arnold Bennett's *The Book of Carlotta,* which never got made. The 1929 P. G. Wodehouse play *Candle Light* (which had starred Leslie Howard) was talked of as a vehicle for him, as was the novel *Susan Lenox (Her Fall and Rise)* (which went to Clark Gable, opposite Garbo). Most tantalizingly, in late 1931 the romantic scoundrel Baron von Gaigern in *Grand Hotel* was announced as a John Gilbert role: he would play opposite Garbo and Joan Crawford in what turned out to be one of the biggest films of 1932. But the role went to the much older, and just as troublesome, John Barrymore. Other early casting suggestions for *Grand Hotel* are equally fascinating: Buster Keaton as Kringelein (he would have been superb) and Clark Gable as Preysing (for which he was much too young).

In the early summer of 1932 Irving Thalberg took the 1928 Wilson Collison play *Red Dust* out of mothballs and put it into production as a Garbo/Gilbert vehicle. It was a "tramp in the tropics" story in the Sadie Thompson line—and soon MGM newcomer Jean Harlow was thought a better fit for the role of hooker-with-a-heart-of-gold Vantine, marooned on an Indochina rubber plantation with a lusty overseer. Thalberg saw that the role of the rough, cynical plantation manager Dennis Carson might be a good fit for Jack—and he thought being paired with platinum sexpot Harlow might jump-start his career. Jacques Feyder—who had guided Garbo through her talkie debut, *Anna Christie*—was chosen to direct (he was eventually replaced by Victor Fleming). Jack was excited—not only about the promising film, but because Irving Thalberg still had his back, had confidence that the last two years had just been a temporary setback.

Red Dust's screenwriter, John Lee Mahin, recalled, "Harlow was supposed to help Gilbert's fading image. He was too thin from drinking . . . and nervous because he was unsure of himself." The young, socially active Mahin was assigned to babysit Jack through pre-production and keep him happy and cheerful and off the bottle. Then Mahin caught *Hell Divers,* a late 1931 release starring Clark Gable. "You're crazy if you use Gilbert with Harlow," Jack's supposed new friend told producer Hunt Stromberg. "I just saw this new boy. . . . I told him Gable and Harlow would be a natural." Jack was out; Clark Gable was in. Sam Marx said the disappointment of losing *Red Dust* and *Grand Hotel* finally evaporated whatever trust Jack had in Irving Thalberg. "They would continue to communicate thereafter—it was necessary in order to do business—but their friendship was finished." Leatrice Fountain, decades later, stood up for Thalberg: "He tried to intervene in Mayer's destruction of my father's career. Mr. Thalberg was respected by the entire film industry, unlike Louis B. Mayer." Norma Shearer herself—the loyal Mrs. Thalberg—agonized over her old friend Jack Gilbert's fate at MGM and her husband's part in it. "I wonder now why Irving could not help him," she wrote years later. "Irving was known for salvaging careers. The renaissance of personalities was his specialty. He held out his frail hand to many, and many found strength in it, but not Jack Gilbert."

As big a blow as the loss of *Red Dust* was for Jack, one cannot fault Thalberg or Stromberg, or even the turncoat Mahin—Clark Gable *was* perfect for the role, and his sexy, playful chemistry with Harlow led to another four successful teamings. Jack would have made a capable enough leading man in *Red Dust,* but this casting change was spot-on. Still, it was painful. It had already been announced in the press that Jack would be starring in the film, and being replaced by this up-and-coming MGM star—only four years younger than Jack—reinforced the notion of his being finished. The nastiest crack came from the *Los Angeles Times,* which in May 1932 made a passing reference about Jack having been "once regarded as the 'great lover' of the screen—that is to say, in the year B.G. (Before Gable)."

In August 1932 Louis B. Mayer sent a form letter to all MGM employees begging them to take pay cuts. Mayer himself had taken a 35 percent pay cut, though he was hardly financially disadvantaged. Mayer put "the tragic economic condition existing in our country" before his actors, adding that "members of the other departments in our organization, almost without exception, have taken reduction in salaries." Mayer pleaded for "the same loyalty and devotion to this organization," but what he got was an almost unanimous slap in the face. MGM files show that nearly every star, character actor, and bit player contacted said no, either by letter or in person. Only Hollywood team player (and kiss-up) Hedda Hopper, bit player David Newell, and character actresses Ruth Rennick and Claire Du Brey agreed to pay cuts. Jack, of course, said no (orally, not by letter, and no doubt with some force). Greta Garbo, oddly, was not even on the list—perhaps even Louis B. Mayer feared to tread there.

Over at Paramount, Clara Bow was suffering much the same fate as

The other great victim of the talkies, Clara Bow (author's collection).

Jack at MGM. The two stars had a lot in common: both were only children from poor households, with bitter parent issues (Bow's mother has been painted as a murderous schizophrenic and her father a child abuser, though none of this can be verified). Both stars were great talents—Bow at home in both comedy and drama. She entered films as a teenager in 1922, and by 1925 was one of Paramount's top stars—she was not the screen's first flapper or jazz baby (that honor goes to Olive Thomas and Clarine Seymour), but she was the pinnacle of the type.

With her heart-shaped face, perfect features, and bright smile, Bow did not need to be a good actress, but she was. Through the silent era, in *Dancing Mothers, Mantrap, It, Children of Divorce, Wings,* she could do no wrong. Then—as with Jack—everything went straight to hell at the end of the 1920s. Bow was sued for alienation of affection; accused of not paying a gambling debt; her blackmailing secretary dragged her name through the mud. Sexually enthusiastic, Bow had a long list of famous lovers—while that sort of thing made Jack a Don Juan, it branded a woman as a slut. Then came talkies: again, like Jack's, Bow's voice was not terrific, though it was serviceable. Hollywood lore has it that her "Brooklyn honk" (like Jack's "high, squeaky voice") finished her off. But Bow's voice was no more "New Yawky" than those of Barbara Stanwyck or Mae West, both of whom flourished in talkies.

Her main career trouble was that her early films just weren't very good: none of them were *His Glorious Night*–caliber disasters, but Paramount was taking no better care of her than MGM was of Jack. She was expensive, she was embarrassing with all her personal problems—and run-of-the-mill fluff like *The Saturday Night Kid, True to the Navy,* and *Her Wedding Night* was all she was given. Not till the gangster drama *Kick In* (1931) and the over-the-top *Call Her Savage* (1932) did she get vehicles worthy of her. But by then it was too late.

Like Jack, Clara Bow was an emotional mess by 1932. Thin-skinned and easily hurt, she was tired of her career, and she hated making talkies. She missed the ability to improvise that silents had provided; learning lines and hitting marks was *work,* not fun. She married cowboy actor Rex Bell and retired, emotionally broken.

Nineteen thirty-two seems to have been the dividing line between silent and talkie careers. By the end of the year it was clear that a number of fresh newcomers (Gable, Harlow, Cagney, West, Hepburn, Colbert, Tracy, Muni, Robinson, Stanwyck) were indeed the coming thing. And the careers of many of the greatest stars of only five years ago were—it could no longer be denied—obviously on the skids. John Gilbert and Clara Bow were publicly and unironically referred to as has-beens, as were the great Mary Pickford and Douglas Fairbanks, Gloria Swanson, Harold Lloyd, Buster Keaton, the Gish and Talmadge sisters, Pola Negri,

Ramon Novarro, and William Haines. Some of them made comebacks, some returned triumphantly to the stage—but the early 1930s saw them dumped unceremoniously from the heights by unsympathetic studios, fickle fans, and changing times.

And the saddest stories, the *What Price Hollywood?* and *Sunset Boulevard*–caliber tragedies, began to emerge in the 1930s. As the combination of the worldwide economic downturn and the end of silent films coincided, the deaths mounted: Marie Prevost (broke, she drank herself to death in 1937); the great early silent star Florence Lawrence (out of work and dying of a painful bone disease, she drank insecticide in 1938); Jack's *Big Parade* costar Karl Dane (he shot himself in 1934); *The Crowd*'s James Murray (he drowned in 1936). Silent serial queen Pearl White died in 1938, the victim of the pain medications she needed for her work-related injuries. Silent star John Bowers, widely (though probably not accurately) thought of as the inspiration for *A Star Is Born*'s Norman Maine, drowned himself in 1936. Both comic great Mabel Normand (1930) and Jack's frequent costar Renée Adorée (1933) succumbed to tuberculosis. Jack's *Masks of the Devil* costar, Alma Rubens, died in 1931 after a ten-year battle with drugs.

By the fall of 1932—with *Downstairs* released and forgotten about and no promising projects on the horizon—Jack was talking again about writing and directing. He and Virginia Bruce honeymooned in Europe and he took his typewriter along, hoping to hammer out a saleable script or story proposal (she took along her parents). On his way home from the voyage he noted that he had seen several "very good" English talkies, and that they were well attended. Yes, he was still filming for MGM but no, he did not know what his next assignment would be.

As for Bruce, just at the dawn of her promising career she was talking about giving it up. "Jack has had two actress wives who kept on with their careers after marriage and I'm going to make a go of our marriage even at the cost of my career," she told a reporter. And, indeed, Virginia Bruce would not make another film till her marriage was over.

Jack was bucked up by his wife's faith in him and their marriage, and happily told reporter Harrison Carroll, "Virginia thinks, as I do, that one career in the family is enough. Last week she explained her ideas to the studio and," Jack noted with understandable amazement,

Jack and the fourth Mrs. Gilbert, Virginia Bruce, 1932 (Wisconsin Center for Film & Theater Research).

"they were very nice about it. It makes me proud to think she is willing to give up a chance of stardom for my sake." Virginia Bruce was just what he needed at this desperate point in his career—his MGM contract (to which he clung with ferocity) was running out, and even the film he believed in so strongly, *Downstairs,* had not made any impact. Having a bright-eyed girl of twenty-two gazing up at him starry-eyed brought him out of his depression, at least in the short term.

Jack's former costar Anita Page reminisced, "I felt so sad for him, but I think he was happy with Virginia Bruce; he loved to tell me about how happy John Barrymore was with Dolores Costello." "Virginia personifies peace and tranquility," Jack told reporter Juliette Laine. "I feel like a shipwrecked man who has been clinging to a spar, and then suddenly finds himself washed ashore in a beautiful, sheltered haven. Virginia's sweetness, her sympathy and understanding, are beyond belief."

The honeymoon didn't last long—they never did. By December 1932 there was already gossip that a stay at the El Mirador Hotel in Palm Springs had ended in "tantrums." Neighboring vacationers were eager to tell reporters that they heard an ongoing argument from the Gilberts' bungalow, and that Jack had finally stormed off in his car, saying to someone—the resort's management? A nosy neighbor?—"Tell my wife I will send the chauffeur back for her" before departing "in a cloud of sand and indignation." The next day Virginia Bruce was reported to be hosting a small party of friends in her rooms, smiling calmly and appearing quite unruffled.

Decades later Bruce told Jack's daughter Leatrice Fountain how far downhill he had already slid by 1932: "Sometimes he'd be awake drinking all night," she said, "then in the morning he'd get me to throw him into the swimming pool so he could clear his head. . . . He had bleeding ulcers. He used to throw up blood in the morning until he fainted." A doctor would come by the house at night to inject him with sodium amytal—a barbiturate derivative—to help him sleep, à la Michael Jackson. "He was not very pretty to look at, he had all kinds of infections," said Bruce.

Bruce realized very quickly what a mistake she had made: "I knew it couldn't last. I just couldn't go on like that for the rest of my days!" She wanted to go out and enjoy life: parties, dances, nightclubs. He wanted to stay home and brood. "He hated being dragged around," said Bruce. "He'd done all the partying he'd wanted to, years ago, and it no longer held any thrill for him."

Chapter Fourteen

> I told him [Louis B. Mayer] that it would make it easier for me . . . if he could have, and show, just a little faith in me. I needed faith.
>
> —John Gilbert, 1933

In January 1933 production on Jack's last assignment under his MGM contract, *Rivets* (eventually retitled *Fast Workers*), was announced. It was produced and directed by Tod Browning—late of *The Show*—and had dialogue by Lawrence Stallings, all of which should have been a great sign.

But Browning was perhaps the only man at MGM farther in the doghouse than Jack. After his success at Universal with *Dracula* (1931), Browning had been hired by Thalberg to come up with another box-office horror hit for MGM. Instead Browning came up with *Freaks*. Now considered a classic of the horror genre, it was a disaster at the time of its release, and the fact that Thalberg oversaw it proved a thorny issue with the prissy Mayer. *Freaks* was yanked from whatever theaters hadn't banned it outright, and it lost $164,000 for MGM. Assigning Browning to a John Gilbert film was actually considered a punishment for both men.

Surprisingly for these pre-Code days, *Fast Workers* still ran into censorship issues. Will Hays ordered Nicholas Schenck to cut a bit where Jack spots two lesbians cuddling at a bar and cracks, "They're making it tougher for us every day." "A definite inference of sex perversion, and as such in violation of the Code," wrote one censor. Even more surprisingly, the line wasn't touched on first release. An offended Hays wrote Schenck, "The failure of the studio to eliminate this line . . . was very unfortunate." MGM finally caved and cut the line for national release, and it is no longer to be heard in the film.

Fast Workers is a cheap, nasty film about cheap, nasty people—but for all that, it is fun and fast moving (at little more than an hour). Though purportedly based on a play by John McDermott, it used the exact same plot as the 1928 silent *A Girl in Every Port,* which had recently (1931) been remade as *Goldie*. Indeed, Robert Armstrong reprised his *Girl in Every Port* role for *Fast Workers*. The movie concerns two backstabbing, brawling pals—sailors in the earlier films, now New York construction workers—who take great pains to prove that the other's latest lady love is just a two-bit whore.

Jack was surrounded by an inexpensive but talented cast: Armstrong as his trusting, ape-like pal (he has a terrific moment of homicidal menace toward the end of the film); tough, wise-cracking broads Mae Clarke and Muriel Kirkland; and fellow riveters Sterling Holloway and Vince Barnett. Only Jack was fatally miscast: the role called for a tough mug like Spencer Tracy (who had played the equivalent role in *Goldie*) or James Cagney. Jack came off as more of a lounge lizard, the kind of smoking-jacketed smoothie played so effectively by Ralf Harolde and Monroe Owsley in the early '30s. He was also starting to show his age. In *Fast Workers* Jack looked every day of his thirty-four years, and one could see the handsome, weathered middle-aged man he might have become.

The *New York Times* did not think much of *Fast Workers,* and downright hated Jack's character: "The suspicion grows, watching Gunner Smith at his increasingly moronic tricks, that in real life Gunner would be pitched from a convenient skyscraper by his outraged fellow-workers for one-tenth the things he does in this picture." *Fast Workers* cost $525,000—still quite a high-budgeted film, especially in the price-cutting year of 1933—and lost $360,000 when it was released in March 1933.

When Jean Arthur left Columbia in 1944, she reportedly ran through the lot screaming, "I'm free! I'm free!" Jack did not go to those lengths, but he professed himself to be glad to be out of MGM and took some vicious pleasure in noting that "the Depression has finally caught up with

Butching it up in *Fast Workers*, 1933 (The Everett Collection).

them." He told the *New York Herald Tribune*, "It looks as if the days of the big studios are over and that a chance for individual expression may come out of the general reorganization now being undertaken."

"The day I left MGM for the last time, after fourteen years, I felt like a man must feel who is leaving the walls of a prison where the faces of his keeper have been mocking and unkind," he told *Modern Screen*. "I felt, at the same time, like a man must feel who is leaving the home of his birth, where he had lived for many years and where he has known both great happiness and bitter defeat." Though off the lot for good—so he hoped—Jack stayed friends with his fellow MGM leading man Ramon Novarro—a talented singer, Novarro had his own theater built into his house, and throughout the early 1930s he invited such friends as Jack and Virginia Bruce, Myrna Loy, Cary Grant, Gloria Swanson, Norma Shearer, and Jeanette MacDonald to "at-homes," including concerts and amateur productions.

In April 1933 Jack and a pregnant Virginia took off for New York via a long, leisurely southern cruise on the liner *Santa Paula*. He claimed he wanted two weeks of "seeing shows," but immediately it was known about town that producer Dwight Deere Wiman wanted him for a play called *Gaily I Sin,* opposite Helen Mencken. Wiman's thirty-year Broadway career included such hits as *The Little Show, Gay Divorce, On Your Toes, Babes in Arms, Old Acquaintance, On Borrowed Time,* and *The Country Girl.* The very fact that he was interested in Jack showed that his was still a name of importance. But *Gaily I Sin* never made it to Broadway, and neither did Jack.

Jack and Virginia's daughter Susan Ann Gilbert was born on August 2, 1933, at Cedars of Lebanon Hospital in Los Angeles, Jack pacing the waiting room like a sitcom dad ("Both father and baby are doing nicely," the maternity doctor, Norman Williams, told the *Los Angeles Times*). But Jack rarely saw or took much interest in either of his daughters; "I don't feel a bit paternal," he told writer Alma Whitaker in 1934.

The same month his daughter was born, the new father was talking with Sol Wurtzel at Fox about directing: Wurtzel, "bless his soul, gave me the opportunity of sitting by while Ken MacKenna did a picture," Jack later said. MacKenna, another actor who was dipping his toes into directing, was directing *Walls of Gold,* a Sally Eilers drama, and it was in the press that Jack would work "passively" with MacKenna: "Mr. Gilbert is described as a 'looker-on,' without salary and without responsibility," said the *New York Sun.* "Universal had called me about a couple of scripts they were keen about," said Jack hopefully. "If I liked them, too, Junior [Laemmle] would be interested in talking to me about directing them."

Kenneth MacKenna mentioned to Jack in an offhand way that he was being talked up for the male lead in a new Garbo picture at MGM, but Jack laughed: "I didn't believe a word of it." Then, in the summer of 1933, Jack got a call at home from MGM producer Walter Wanger. "He told me to come right over. . . . I laughed. I said I was sorry I couldn't, but I was working. He said over the phone, very low, 'Better come, Jack, they want you for the Garbo picture.'"

The Garbo picture was to be a biography of Sweden's eccentric Queen Christina, who had abdicated in 1654. This was a very personal film for Garbo, not only because of her Swedish heritage but because she and Christina had so much in common. Both were reclusive eccentrics; neither ever married; both preferred men's clothing and were rumored to be lesbians; both walked away from their life's work. Garbo's friend Salka Viertel made her screenwriting debut with this film, and she wrote in many personal quirks of its star.

Garbo had just signed a new MGM contract—$400,000 a picture—and this one wound up costing $1.144 million. According to Garbo's biographer Karen Swenson, every conceivable leading man was considered, and a few inconceivable ones, too (Leslie Howard, Clark Gable, Franchot Tone, Ronald Colman, Nelson Eddy, Fredric March, John Barrymore). "Everyone but Ben Turpin," wrote the *Hollywood Reporter* (Garbo and Ben Turpin in *Queen Christina* would have been an act of genius). Finally, twenty-six-year-old Laurence Olivier was signed. Olivier already had quite a stage reputation but so far had been flailing about in films. From the start, he was not a good fit. Prettier than Garbo, he was too lightweight and the pair threw off no sparks. After a few days of worsening takes, Olivier was let go.

Indeed, Garbo hadn't had much luck with leading men since talkies came in: most of them (Ramon Novarro, Robert Montgomery, Gavin Gordon) had been hired just to gaze adoringly at her and not get in the way. She and Clark Gable—in *Susan Lenox (Her Fall and Rise)*—had been from different universes and had no chemistry; John Barrymore (*Grand Hotel*) seemed more like her affectionate father than her lover. Only Erich von Stroheim—as her evil Svengali in *As You Desire Me*—really provided any spark. She never did find another John Gilbert, though Melvyn Douglas, in three films, turned out to be her best talkie partner, as his wry detachment took her down a peg or two.

When Laurence Olivier was bounced and Jack hired, MGM found that freelance costar Ian Keith's contract called for second billing: obviously, the Garbo/Gilbert reunion had to be given precedence. "It was our intention when we signed John Gilbert for this part," Eddie Mannix wrote to Keith's agent, "to bill the picture Greta Garbo in '*Queen Christina* with John Gilbert.'" They got their way: posters and ads trumpeted GARBO in *Queen Christina,* and under a small "with," in order, came John Gilbert, Ian Keith, Lewis Stone, and Elizabeth Young.

Even more terrifying and exhilarating than costarring with his ex-lover was facing down Louis B. Mayer in his office again. The office that Jack knew was not yet the famous chamber of intimidation that Mayer had designed in the late 1930s, with its white leather walls and huge, raised scary desk; it was still dark paneled wood. But Mayer's presence itself was enough to daunt most employees. Jack strode in—announced and scheduled this time, not one of his 1920s "burst in unexpectedly" meetings—and said, "Here I am. What are you going to do about me?" Mayer, he clearly could see, was "still a little skeptical," and that was putting it politely. "I was there under duress—Garbo's duress. He was wary about believing in me, in my sincerity. I tried to tell him. I said that I had made many mistakes, mistakes that I would make no longer. I knew, now, that I couldn't criticize my bosses. . . . I also knew, I said, that I was an actor working under orders."

Jack agreeably accepted a salary "so nominal that it would have seemed insulting to the old John Gilbert" and made no claim to his luxurious old dressing-room bungalow ("Actors have always dressed in plain dressing-rooms, haven't they?"). But one thing he asked for he never got, at least not from Louis B. Mayer: "I told him that it would make it easier for me if he could manage to feel just a little bit glad to have me there; it would make it easier for me if he could have, and show, just a little faith in me. I needed faith."

And at first Jack was naïvely happy with his new MGM deal: "a seven-year contract subject to my performance in *Queen Christina,*" he bragged to *Modern Screen.* "It is the kind of a contract I have always wanted, short of one for producing on my own. I am paid only for the pictures I direct or act in. I am to have three stories a year submitted to me. If I do not choose any one of the three stories, I receive no money. If I choose one story I am paid accordingly." What could go wrong? His contract, he told Gladys Hall, "sounded swell to me at the time. . . . You must remember that I was sore to the bone over the rotten bad stories they had been giving me. You and I knew what they were doing to me, those stories. Here, then, it appeared, was my chance, more vital to me than anything else in the world—to have the right to reject stories that would continue to ruin me."

He was, he later admitted, living in a dream world. "It never occurred to me, then, that the old enmity might still persist, that they might, deliberately, submit to me stories I *couldn't* do—Little Lord Fauntleroy or something—and that as a consequence, I couldn't work, I could do nothing."

His first meeting with Garbo was awkward enough, but was made worse by the presence of a photographer. Jack, noticeably underweight, joshed and laughed with his ex-lover; they smiled for the camera and shook hands. "We met again for the first time in two and a half years," he recalled. "Of course, things were different between us. . . . We were self-conscious, mute, I didn't know what to say. Neither did she. I knew what she had done and why she had done it. She felt that I had helped her a little once. She wanted, now, to help me. She was making a gracious gesture toward someone of whom she had been a little fond."

"When they started to make publicity stills of us we stood stiffly apart," Jack recalled. "The cameraman said, 'Stand a little closer to Mr. Gilbert, please, Miss Garbo.' And Greta said to me, very low, very shy, 'Not too much of this, you know. You have a lovely wife, a darling baby at home.' And I said, 'Greta, what of you? Where are you living now?' She said, 'In Santa Monica—if you can call it living.'"

For all her kindness—and it was kind, and brave, of her to take this risk for Jack—Garbo was the only ex-wife or lover to speak slightingly of him. Salka Viertel told actor Jack Larson that she and Garbo had seen John Gilbert one day out driving on Sunset Boulevard. "Heavens, what did I ever see in him?" Garbo sighed. And playwright S. N. Behrman once asked her, "How could you ever get mixed up with a fellow like that?" Far from standing up for Jack, Garbo replied, "I was lonely—and I couldn't speak English."

They stopped work early their first day of shooting. "We were both self-conscious and both felt awkward," said Jack. "We have to have a little time to become accustomed again. . . . I have made of [director

Jack and Garbo's first awkward day on the set of *Queen Christina,* 1933 (Wisconsin Center for Film & Theater Research).

Rouben] Mamoulian . . . only one request. It is this: to leave me alone as much as possible. Let me have the scope and swing and freedom that were mine in the old days of silent pictures [those "old days" were, remember, five years ago]. Let me give my own performance in my own way. I don't mean that I resent direction or suggestion. I am just raw and sensitive from the last years. . . . I may be kicked off the set. Nothing could surprise me any longer. They tell me I am no good, am not getting it. Well, I have nothing more to lose."

There is much that is remarkable about *Queen Christina:* chief among them is Garbo showing herself to be a soft-hearted, loyal pal ready to put her foot down for an old friend—perhaps the only time in her life that this happened. Equally remarkable is the contract that Jack and MGM signed. Not just a one-film deal, it gave the studio an option for his services over the next seven years—through 1940—claiming that if he got work anywhere else, MGM would be due a portion of his salary. Just what could Jack—and MGM—have been thinking? He had just gotten out of a torturous contract with the studio, and it in turn had been delighted to see the back of him. It's unlikely Garbo would have gotten involved in the intricacies of his contract—and even if she had insisted on a multi-picture deal, why would he have agreed to it?

There was no way Garbo was going to ever talk to anyone about her decision to cast Jack. But he—certainly against her wishes—did talk. "Oh, it is so damn beautiful—this thing that Garbo has done for me," he told *Modern Screen*'s Gladys Hall. "I have had my head on the guillotine for years. She has taken the block from under my head and with one simple, magnificent gesture removed the falling knife. . . . And she had done all this without one public gesture, without one word to me, with no wish for credit. The shyest woman in the world—and I know—she would shrink from credit."

In October, as work on *Queen Christina* was past the halfway point and dailies were being seen and discussed, "reports on his work in the picture indicate a real comeback," according to the *Los Angeles Times.* "The outlook seems highly optimistic," the reporter wrote, as if discussing a patient recovering from a bout of deadly pneumonia, not a thirty-six-year-old who had been a major star four years ago. "[Gilbert] is said to give a portrayal very much like the old-time Gilbert."

The love scenes were not half as hot as they had been in the 1920s, however. One studio source reported that Garbo herself ordered them cooled off: "Mr. Gilbert is a married man now, with a wife and a baby—and I think it will be better that we tone that scene down," she was heard to have told Rouben Mamoulian.

Things were not going well on the set, as Jack confessed angrily to Gladys Hall during production. "I was nervous, shy, raw, almost sick with excitement and the thrill of the thing." Garbo was "gracious and friendly . . . never once did she fail in her consideration of me, in tact, in saying and doing the right thing at the right moment." But production was slow and tense: "The executives were looking at me with the old-time, all-too-familiar suspicion and hostility. . . . I felt that only Garbo really wanted me there." One crew member recalled that Jack "seemed like a man who had been floored by life, and was too tired to make the effort to get up from the canvas and continue the fight."

The press noticed—probably alerted by some unfriendly person on set. The *Hollywood Reporter* nastily noted that Jack "certainly makes it tough to determine whether he's ridiculously temperamental or whether the strain of how much this picture means to him is enough to keep the highly-strung Gilbert in a perpetual state of hysteria!" Both Jack and Garbo called in sick through the late fall and early winter of 1933: she with nebulous ailments and he with nose and throat problems.

Things came to a head during Christina's reunion scene with Jack's character, the Spanish ambassador. The two had spent five days of anonymous love-making at an inn, and now he discovers that she is the queen of Sweden. "It should be a terrific scene," Jack reasoned. "I should revile her roundly for the unspeakable thing she has done to me. These Spaniards are queer hombres, but they have their own honor." Instead, the shock of revelation was played down in the shooting script, and Jack insisted on a rewrite: "Every executive on the lot came down to the set. They yelled at me. They pinned me against the wall. They wanted to know what the hell I wanted, what I was after, what I thought I was doing, having an idea!"

Jack yelled right back: told them he had been a director, a screenwriter, and an actor for nearly twenty years and "I knew my job and, damn it, I cared about my job! They advised me to mind my own business. They knew what was good for me, they said. . . . Is that the way to treat an actor who is nervous? I've lost ten pounds since I started to work on the picture," he told Hall. The scene stayed as written: when the Spanish ambassador discovers his new love is really the queen of Sweden—seemingly toying with him—he simply says, "I'm not angry"—though Jack makes clear that he is—"I appreciate a royal jest."

Jack and Garbo in *Queen Christina,* 1933 (The Everett Collection).

By the time *Queen Christina* wrapped in December 1933, Jack's prospects at MGM—no matter how good his performance had been—were dire. He told Gladys Hall that he was still on top of the world after shooting ended, grateful to be working again and optimistic. Then he called an MGM executive to touch base and all hell broke loose. Jack never names the executive in question—or Gladys Hall was too prudent to repeat the name—but "I started in to say thank you to him," he told Hall. "I was just trying to say thanks—THANKS—T-H-A-N-K-S. I didn't want any more dough. I just tried to get through to him, that I wasn't asking for *anything.* I was *trying* to say thanks to him—so what the hell? It wasn't any use. He wanted to tell me that he didn't have any use for any part of me. He wanted to tell me that I'd work again when *Christina* had been, not only previewed at the studio and for the press, but it had run for four to five months throughout the country at large in order to get the full public reaction to me. Then and only then would they have anything to say to me about anything."

One may pretty safely assume Jack was talking about Louis B. Mayer, the only top MGM executive known to hate his insides. But there were other executives at MGM in the early 1930s who may conceivably have been the unnamed villain: producers Walter Wanger or Hunt Stromberg or the famously combative Eddie Mannix, who always sided with Mayer.

"They told me I'd been sitting around for months before I made *Christina* and I could sit around on my so-and-so [one gets the feeling Hall is paraphrasing him here] for thirty-six months more and it wouldn't hurt me any. I knew then that the old days were back again, never having gone." Now Jack wanted out of his new contract, but found himself forced into both servitude and inactivity. "I *want* to get out," he told Hall. "And they say they won't let me go. They want me here. They *don't* want me here. What is it for? To torture me? Good God, what am I? I tell them that I am an actor and I want to go back to work and do my job like any other man. . . . They sit back and regard me with suspicion in their eyes."

"I want to work," he pleaded. "I don't understand it. I know that they hate me. Even that isn't a sufficient explanation. Why don't they let me go? . . . Why do they treat me in such a manner as to destroy the only value I have to them? Why ruin the stock on their own shelves?"

MGM should have been pleased with both the movie and with Jack: *Queen Christina* opened in New York in December 1933 and throughout the country in early 1934, and eventually made a profit of $632,000. But no more viable offers were made to Jack. For all his self-doubts, Jack did give a good performance in *Queen Christina;* he looks dashing in his seventeenth-century costumes, though silly in an unflattering hairpiece and what is now known as a "soul patch."

The film itself is enjoyable, though too full of politics and agonized soul-searching. The costumes and sets show every cent of the $1.14 million budget (none of which seems to have been wasted on the rear-projection scenes, which are shockingly cheesy). Jack makes the most of his little screen time, though nearly every frame focuses on Garbo, often in idolizing close-up. The script—Salka Viertel was assisted by several others, including S. N. Behrman and Ben Hecht—worked in a few bawdy pre-Code gay references. The only unintentionally hilarious moments come when Garbo—in men's riding togs but full lipstick and inch-thick eyeliner—is at first mistaken for a young man by Jack's character.

By October 1933 Jack had reached a frightening low, according to Gene Fowler, biographer of his neighbor John Barrymore. Fowler, in his entertaining but factually questionable book *Good Night, Sweet Prince,* claimed that Noll Gurney—an agent and friend of Jack's—knocked on Barrymore's door that Halloween and asked him to go next door to see the suicidally depressed Jack. Perhaps a case of the pot being asked to counsel the kettle, but the thought that one hopeless alcoholic might emotionally support another had its logic, too.

So John Barrymore played a trick-or-treat call on Jack: "I had a grandmother who went broke for the tenth time when she was seventy-two," Fowler has Barrymore lecture his neighbor. "Did she bump herself off? No, she had guts, God bless her! She went out and got a job. It makes me sick when these lollipop Hollywood bastards go around with their heads in the clouds after a taste of notoriety, but at the smallest setback to their egos they put their taffy-coated skulls in their precious hands and begin to wail. . . . You can dig ditches, can't you? Or get a job with Western Union?"

In a scene right out of a bad movie, Barrymore had (the hugely nonpaternal) Jack go into the nursery and pick up little Susan Ann. "Then Barrymore put his hand on Gilbert's shoulder. He now spoke slowly and with great tenderness. 'Doesn't that make you feel something? Isn't she more important than a bit of newspaper gossip?' Gilbert was crying as he held the sleeping child." One can practically hear the Max Steiner music swelling in the background.

By January 1934 Jack's fourth and final marriage appeared to be winding down: Bruce had "gone home to Mother's" in Toluca Lake, California, and "Mother" was telling reporters, "It is certain there will never be reconciliation." Bruce had resumed her career and was working on *Jane Eyre* (the good news: it was a starring role; the bad news: it was being filmed by Monogram). In May Bruce was granted a divorce on grounds of cruelty—her secretary, Jean Bray, testified that Jack "drank heavily and abused Mrs. Gilbert . . . frequently called his wife vile names and humiliated her in public. . . . Mrs. Bray said she heard the actor order his wife out of the house."

As this fourth marriage disintegrated, reporters asked, "Why can't the screen's greatest lover be a success with love in real life?" Virginia Bruce was chatty and forgiving, telling the Associated Press, "If there is anything wrong with him, it is because he is a victim of his own driving ambition. His work is his mistress." But in court she was not so demure. All during their April 1933 trip from Los Angeles to New York by way of the Panama Canal, he had been drunk and abusive, she claimed; he had "used profane language toward her . . . and subjected her to great unhappiness and humiliation." He wanted her at home, his dinner and slippers figuratively waiting for him, and "abused her if she slipped away to a matinee or for any afternoon."

"Our conversations became dramatic episodes," Bruce told reporter Virginia Maxwell during this separation. "And we were together continually. Perhaps too much so. I was very much in love with him when I married him, and all the while we were married. But living together is something else. . . . His state of mind makes mountains out of mole hills. He is always quite sure that no one likes him, that the world is down on him, when everyone, including myself, thinks the world of him." She sighed hopelessly but realistically, "I don't believe any woman can ever really and truly make Jack happy."

"It was my own fault, of course. I was bad," Jack told Gladys Hall in the summer of 1934. "I was arrogant, nervous, over-strung. I said things I didn't mean to say, did things I didn't mean to do." The trauma of *Queen Christina* was playing havoc with his self-esteem: "I knew that I was giving a bad performance, I was under terrific pressure. The whole thing kept twisting and turning in me like a knife, where I was most vulnerable."

No woman had yet been able to cope with John Gilbert as a husband—or even a lover—for long. As for Virginia Bruce, "I forgot how young she is." But he had the insight to admit, "Who am I to suppose that I can go through life being arrogant and overstrung and expecting people to 'understand?'"

Decades later, Virginia Bruce told Jack's daughter Leatrice Gilbert, "It was living a tragedy to be with him. . . . He was so depressed, he was destroyed really by Mayer and what the studio had done to him, and he felt helpless to go against them. . . . Jack still had his looks. He was young, highly intelligent and bent on self-destruction."

She was awarded the divorce on May 25, 1934, along with custody of their daughter, $42,500 in community property, alimony of $92.31 a week, and $150 a month in child support—all of which was problematic, as Jack was unemployed and Virginia Bruce had a long-term contract with MGM. By February Jack had boarded a steamer and was bound for a quiet trip to Honolulu, alone with his thoughts, his typewriter, and a lot of booze.

The former couple did not speak for several months thereafter—even with a baby in the picture. In September 1934 they spoke on the phone, though Bruce admitted, "I don't expect to see him again, anyway for a long time. I'm afraid some of the old arguments might start again." Still, Jack had a hold on her: Bruce saw a reissue of *The Big Parade* that same month and sounded schoolgirlish over young Jack: "I think he and Ronald Colman are the handsomest men on the screen. . . . I hope never to see another smile like that!"

By early 1934 that *Queen Christina* contract was weighing on Jack. MGM still had an option on him—those endless studio options would not be successfully contested till the late 1930s. Jack's lawyer, Peyton Moore, filed suit in Los Angeles Superior Court against the studio in early February, demanding it void his contract and free him. On March 21 Jack took out a full-page ad in a trade paper reading, "Metro-Goldwyn-Mayer will neither offer me work nor release me from my contract." Just what he thought he would accomplish by that—other than further infuriating Louis B. Mayer—can only be imagined.

He called Gladys Hall the day after he'd taken out that ad and vented to her: "I have been on the screen for twenty years and all I have managed to squeeze out of it is *complete unhappiness*." He told her, "I can't get a job. I mean exactly that—I. Can't. Get. A. *Job*." Four years ago he had been making a notoriously publicized $250,000 per picture, but "today I can't get a job for twenty-five dollars a week, or nothing at all. It doesn't make sense. But there it is."

Jack never had to go to court—MGM thought better of having a replay of 1930–33, with Jack lingering resentfully around the studio and giving belligerent interviews to the press. His new *Queen Christina*–inspired contract was allowed to quietly lapse.

His drinking increased—as did his bleeding ulcers—and Jack

spent most of his days and sleepless nights holed up in his beautiful hilltop man-cave. Some Hollywood biographers—of Irving Thalberg, Greta Garbo, and others—also claim that Jack was brandishing a gun or sleeping with one by his pillow; but they cite no sources or firsthand witnesses. Certainly he showed no signs of paranoia or suicidal tendencies (other than perhaps drinking himself to an early grave). King Vidor wrote that Jack's bedside gun—"one of the largest automatic pistols I have ever seen"—was bought for a perfectly logical and nonsuicidal reason. "He said that the screen door was secured only by a small hook. Anyone could reach in with a piece of wire, a hairpin would do, and the hook could be flipped out of the eyelet. He had heard noises in the night recently and he wanted to be ready to shoot before an intruder could enter the room."

Opera singer Grace Moore—who had a brief film career in the 1930s—told a friend of a particularly startling encounter with Jack at his lowest ebb. He had invited her to hear his enviable collection of opera records, and while Moore sat in his cavernous living room enjoying the concert, Jack distractedly wandered off for a midnight swim in his pool. "Suddenly he reappeared," she wrote. "My eyes popped in amazement. Mr. Gilbert was virtually naked." Whatever "virtually naked" may have meant, Moore was aghast at a situation many fans might have thought the answer to their prayers. Jack "leaned his head back on the couch and fell fast asleep. I tiptoed out for fear I should disturb him, such was his power to wake concern in a woman's heart. . . . Next day in my dressing room appeared twelve dozen American Beauty roses with a card inscribed, 'Why didn't you nudge me?'"

Shortly after his death, a reporter noted that Jack shut himself off from his friends in this last year, was "morose—he had a temperament like Edgar Allan Poe's, said one—and that the reason was due to his conviction that he was a failure. Nothing they could say would alter his viewpoint."

He wasn't broke—Jack's salary had been wisely banked and invested, and he could live comfortably for the rest of his life without working another day. But, he complained, "What am I to *do?* Sit up here on this hill-top and listen to the music of the silences? People advise me to 'go to Europe.' What for? I don't want to *go* anywhere. I want to *work*. I want the simple right of every creature that walks the

The trim, dapper John Gilbert of the early 1930s (The Everett Collection).

earth, the right to earn my own living. I want to work for the sake of it and because I love it."

He had been offered a personal appearance tour, the thought of which—exhibiting himself like a zoo animal—horrified him. A possible offer from a British film studio was talked of, but accepting such an offer was well known in the 1930s to be an admission of unemployability and failure, career-wise. Early in 1933 he was offered the lead in a Broadway show by a newcomer, Sidney Kingsley. "I read the script and turned it down," he told Gladys Hall. "I said that it was morbid, depressing and that I didn't believe audiences, sufficiently depressed already, wanted to be further dragged down in the theaters. I said that it wouldn't go." The play, *Men in White,* went on to win the 1934 Pulitzer Prize for Drama (and, ironically, Clark Gable was to star in the screen version).

"Everyone knew Jack could direct but the offers didn't come," recalled actress Colleen Moore. "Not because of drinking or Louis Mayer but because word had gotten around that his health was so precarious. When you hire a director, you have to know that he's going to be there every day." Moore emphasized that Jack, she felt, was not actively suicidal. "He could never understand people giving up like that. He was too full of life."

A potential savior came in the unlikely form of Harry Cohn, the wild man of Columbia Pictures. Abrasive, autocratic, and opinionated, he was feared and hated by many of his stars (a beloved Hollywood legend has it that—at Cohn's well-attended funeral—Red Skelton quipped, "Give the people what they want, and they'll turn out for it!"). Harry and his brother Jack headed Columbia Pictures, which by the early 1930s was known for comedy shorts and low-budget fare, some of which succeeded admirably (most notably Frank Capra's superb and critically acclaimed *The Miracle Woman, Platinum Blonde, American Madness, Lady for a Day,* and *It Happened One Night*). Columbia built up such baby stars as Jean Harlow, Barbara Stanwyck, and Carole Lombard, and propped up the waning careers of Jack Holt, Monte Blue, Laura La Plante, and Lew Cody.

So it is not surprising that Harry Cohn made it his mission to revive John Gilbert's career. It helped matters that he hated Louis B. Mayer like poison and envied MGM's huge budgets and stable of stars—if he could succeed with Jack where Mayer had failed, so much the better. Cohn was Mayer's evil twin: coarse and vulgar, he would delight in Jack's filthy "mother" stories and nose-picking characters.

Director Lewis Milestone brought Jack's dilemma to Cohn's attention. Milestone had never worked with Jack but was eager to try: he had recently helmed such great films as *All Quiet on the Western Front* and *The Front Page* and had coaxed out what was probably Joan Crawford's greatest performance, in *Rain.* "I know Jack very well," Cohn's biographer Bob Thomas has Milestone saying. "I'm convinced he can come through with a performance. . . . It's a gamble, but a good gamble. Everybody in town is kicking Jack, now that he's down. Here's a chance to prove them wrong." Cohn agreed to screen test Jack, which in itself might be seen as a slap in the face to such a huge star. But Milestone urged him to swallow what was left of his pride and do it: "I'll do everything I can to make it easier for you in this test. If you want, I'll shoot it at six in the morning. We'll be finished by eight o'clock, and you can be out of the studio before anybody knows about it." Jack aced the test, and a delighted Cohn signed him in June 1934 to a five-year contract—with options, of course, for Columbia to drop him at any time.

His debut with Columbia was a comedy-drama called *The Captain Hates the Sea;* kind of a floating *Grand Hotel* aboard a California to New York cruise ship. The titular sea-hating captain was played by gruff character actor Walter Connolly; his motley passengers included a detective (Victor McLaglen) and his prey (con artists Fred Keating and Helen Vinson), a roguish dowager (the delightfully vulgar Alison Skipworth), a South American revolutionary (Akim Tamiroff), an unhappily married ex-hooker (Wynne Gibson, in a particularly moving turn), and assorted passengers and crew played by the reliably entertaining Donald Meek, Leon Errol, Walter Catlett, Claude Gillingwater, and Arthur Treacher. Jack—billed fourth—played an alcoholic Hollywood screenwriter working on a novel, seen off on his trip by his sadly hopeful society girlfriend (Tala Birell).

Harry Cohn told Jack that "if you keep your nose clean on this picture, I'll see that you get work. I'll go to bat for you with every producer in town." Jack's nose was not kept clean. Much of the film was shot aboard a ship in Los Angeles Harbor, which became a floating bar. Fellow cast members Connolly, McLaglen, Errol, and Catlett were, if not full-fledged alcoholics, heavy drinkers, and Jack kept his vow to stay dry for exactly one week—longer than the character he played, who started belting them back as soon as he got on board ship. As if that weren't enough, the Three Stooges were in the film, too, playing cameos as orchestra musicians. According to the *Los Angeles Times,* Larry, Moe, and Curly provided "good, clean fun" on the set by pushing each other off the steamship and pretending they couldn't swim, further holding up production.

Some scenes were shot in the studio, but many sequences had to be filmed at sea, aboard ship: weather interfered, and so did the casts' drinking (Jack was so ill by this time that a day of imbibing led to at least a day at home with bleeding ulcers). "He was a quiet, strange man," recalled sound engineer Irving Libbott, "and he drank *all* the time." As *The Captain Hates the Sea* fell further behind schedule through the summer of 1934, Cohn cabled Milestone—according to Hollywood legend, anyway—"Hurry up. The cost is staggering." Milestone supposedly replied, "So is the cast." Milestone told Jack's daughter Leatrice, "When he wasn't drunk, he was being sick at home. He had bleeding ulcers and sometimes fever and hallucinations—raving out of his mind."

The Captain Hates the Sea is a brisk, entertaining B movie, a nice mixture of wise-cracking comedy and dark drama, with some terrific performances. Jack is noticeably wobbly on his feet, but he is playing a drunk, so it is hard to tell where real life and acting intersect. He does make his Steve a sad, charming loser, a sort of late-career F. Scott Fitzgerald type. For a post-Code movie (the Hays Office began a major censorship crackdown in mid-1934), it also got away with an eyebrow-raising number of lewd lines and shocking situations.

And it was a bittersweet last glimpse at John Gilbert for audiences. The year before John Barrymore had played an exaggerated version of himself in MGM's *Dinner at Eight:* Larry Renault, a washed-up, alcoholic ex-matinee idol. And here was John Gilbert as a Hollywood refugee, unapologetically drinking himself into cheerful oblivion. In the last few moments of the film, his girlfriend greets him at the dock: "Did you stop drinking?" "No," he smiles. "Did you start your book?" "No."

Despite its charm, this ship sank upon release in October 1934. "Something went agley with *The Captain Hates the Sea,*" wrote the *New York Times.* "It had a workable story, a good cast, a fine director. . . . Yet the final result, as set before its audience last night, is an indefinite, round-about and generally meaningless production. . . . Some of the things that happen are funny," the reviewer admitted, "and some are tragic." But, he felt, "some are just dull, as trying to understand what Mr. Gilbert is supposed to be doing."

Jack's last movie, *The Captain Hates the Sea,* with Victor McLaglen, 1934 (The Everett Collection).

Jack's Columbia contract was quietly allowed to lapse. "It's too goddam bad," said Cohn. "But if a man wants to go to hell, I can't stop him." And by 1934, most friends agreed that Jack did indeed want to go to hell. "I'd like to be sixty-seven instead of thirty-seven," he told Gladys Hall. "It's horrible to think that life has ended before it should have got into midstream." He spent his days, he sighed, "sitting here on this hill watching the panorama of the sky in which I take no part."

Chapter Fifteen

> Nothing could surprise me any longer. . . . Well, I have nothing more to lose.
>
> —John Gilbert, 1933

Virginia Bruce was making some tentative overtures of friendship by early 1935, trying to get Jack to come over and see their daughter more often. "I think we failed to make a go of it because Jack was so unhappy in his work," she said. "He is more encouraged now, so maybe . . ." She trailed off. She added, "I would rather have had Jack for the father of my baby than any other man in the world."

Jack made the news in April 1935, but not because of a new film role or a new romance—a housebreaker cut his (or perhaps her) way through Jack's French door window screen late one night. Jack, stepping out of his bath, heard someone bumping about in his bedroom and emerged in a towel, chasing the shadowy figure outside and then calling the police. Only his .38 caliber gun was missing.

Back in the summer of 1934, with Virginia Bruce in the rear-view mirror, Jack had told Gladys Hall, "I am probably through with marriage. I don't care to become the [six-times-married actor] Nat Goodwin of my time. I would feel ridiculous if I should start to court a girl again. I can't imagine any girl taking me seriously."

But someone did take him seriously, and courted him: and she was no "girl," she was a thirty-three-year-old steamroller named Marlene Dietrich. The glamorous blonde had been a minor film and revue presence in her native Germany, till *The Blue Angel* had made her a star—in 1930 Paramount snapped her up as their very own Greta Garbo. By mid-1935 she had starred in six increasingly bizarre and outré films directed by her mentor, Josef von Sternberg. By the time the last of these—*The Devil Is a Woman*—was released in May 1935, everyone knew a change was needed. The previous Dietrich/von Sternberg projects (*Morocco, Dishonored, Shanghai Express, Blonde Venus, The Scarlett Empress*) had been odd but hugely entertaining—*The Devil Is a Woman* was a mess. Incoherent script, bad acting, and Dietrich's makeup was beginning to make her look like a Halloween drag version of herself.

Dietrich had a husband and little daughter, neither of whom overly concerned her. But what she lacked in wifely and maternal devotion she made up for in being a loyal and supportive friend. She genuinely loved and admired Jack, but she also saw him as a reclamation project: Dietrich loved nothing so much as taking sad puppies home. In later years she attempted to slap into shape Ernest Hemingway, Edith Piaf, and Judy Garland, among others (either Dietrich tended to pick hopeless cases, or she was the world's least successful life coach).

Like Jack, Marlene was a social animal: she loved parties, premières, shows. Through late 1935, the impossibly gorgeous couple was seen at nightclubs, restaurants, and Hollywood get-togethers. Jack could afford the best clothes, and he reveled in them; he was seen on Dietrich's arm in cashmere overcoats and neatly tailored suits, always looking natty and elegant. Dietrich was a renowned fashion plate, decked out in furs, gems, and the delightfully insane little hats of the mid-1930s.

The *Los Angeles Times*'s Edwin Schallert recalled seeing Jack and Dietrich at a party given by screenwriter Frances Marion. Jack "was the gayest sort in his periods of real enjoyment of life," wrote Schallert, and that night "he was in just that exuberant state." After his death, friends noted that they were happy to see Jack about town with Dietrich, at tennis matches, the races, playing golf, "outwardly cheerful. . . . He escorted Marlene Dietrich to the opening of a play recently and none in the audience appeared to enjoy the jests and antics of the stage comedians more than he."

Even ex-wife Virginia Bruce declared herself happy to see Jack out on the town with the glamorous Marlene: "I wasn't with him," she said months later. "I couldn't be, and I am glad that Marlene was. Marlene spoiled Jack in just the way spoiling should be done."

Out on the town with Marlene Dietrich, 1935 (Wisconsin Center for Film & Theater Research).

Dietrich saved Jack's brief notes—most of them accompanying bouquets of flowers—and they are heartbreaking in their affection and happiness. "Love Face," he addresses her, "I'm so happy today and it's such a nice feeling. Let's try and remain this way always. I love you." Another read: "Just because you are so sweet and beautiful and generous and fine. How nice a world if all people were like you." That he and Marlene Dietrich shared a lewd sense of humor can be seen in his sign-off nickname, "G.D.F.S.O.B.," for "God Damn Fucking Son of a Bitch."

In the fall of 1935 Dietrich's next project was a crime comedy for Paramount, based on a German play, to be directed by Frank Borzage (*7th Heaven, Secrets*) and scripted by a team of writers (some of whom had been responsible for such delights as *Love Me Tonight, Island of Lost Souls, The Gay Divorcee, Waterloo Bridge,* and Jack's own *Phantom of Paris*). The film—titled *Desire*—was a funny, sexy caper about

Jack in a publicity still for *Desire,* with Marlene Dietrich, before a heart attack sidelined him, autumn 1935 (author's collection).

a jewel thief (Dietrich) who uses a vacationing rube to act as her unwitting fence—that role was to be played by Gary Cooper, Dietrich's previous love interest (on- and offscreen) in *Morocco.* The third point in the triangle was the thief's business and romantic partner, an older, suave, charming rogue. That role, she told Paramount producer Henry Herzbrun, could *only* be played by John Gilbert.

Gary Cooper, John Halliday (in the role meant for John Gilbert), and Marlene Dietrich in *Desire,* released in 1936 (author's collection).

She was right: this was just the kind of supporting character role that Jack could have made his forte well through middle age. Herzbrun okayed him, and Jack was once again back in the game. Publicity photos taken on set show Jack looking happy and healthy, and a brief, silent test gives us a precious glimpse of him in glorious Technicolor (*Desire* was, in the end, a black-and-white film).

But in December 1935, while swimming in his pool, Jack suffered what was diagnosed as a heart attack. "He just laughed and said it was indigestion," Dietrich recalled later. But Paramount did not laugh: Henry Herzbrun invoked the medical conditions of Jack's contract and had him fired. Marlene Dietrich was a hard-headed professional, and as much as it pained her, she did not break stride. John Halliday—nearly twenty years Jack's senior—was hired to replace him as Carlos Margoli. Halliday was a smooth, accomplished actor and gave a perfectly good performance—but it is distressing today to watch *Desire* and imagine Jack in the role.

At least once a week, sometimes more, Jack visited the set. He tortured himself (and poor John Halliday) by watching the making of a movie that might have been his comeback as a character actor. Seeing Dietrich with her ex (and possibly current) lover Gary Cooper cannot have been good for Jack, either. "He never gave the slightest hint that he might be secretly wishing to be her, or some other star's, leading man," wrote a reporter shortly after Jack's death. "A photographer who saw Gilbert on the Dietrich set says, instead, he appeared to be happy to be on the sidelines, content with once having been one of Hollywood's highest paid stars, pleased now with his security."

What Jack probably knew, subconsciously at least, was that he was dying, and he was relieved to go. He holed up in his hilltop home, rarely calling or visiting friends: Cedric Gibbons and Dolores del Rio, King Vidor, Carey Wilson, and a few others saw him during these last weeks. He went for long solitary drives, and spoke with no enthusiasm about that offer to make a film in England.

In that last year, Jack had reconnected with his elder daughter, Leatrice Gilbert—the eleven-year-old had written him a fan letter ("A fan letter, for God's sake!" she marveled decades later) and the two had tentatively made contact. "All I knew were bits and pieces of him," she wrote in her biography of her father, "private lunches and quiet walks along the beach. . . . He listened carefully when I talked with him and . . . answered my questions thoughtfully. . . . He'd turn those fantastic brown eyes and that smile toward me and the whole room would light up. I'd feel that I was the only person in the world who mattered to him. Later, when I learned that he made almost everyone he liked even a little feel that way, I didn't really mind."

Colleen Moore had a different version of how father and daughter reconnected: she told historian William Drew in the 1980s that Jack had told her that "Leatrice would never let him see their little girl. . . . I called Leatrice up and she said, 'That's utterly ridiculous. It isn't true at all. We'll set it right up and he can see her.'" Moore recalled, "He was never as nervous calling on a young lady as he was when he called to pick up his daughter to take her to a movie. He didn't know what to bring her, so he had a little bouquet of flowers that he gave her. He was so nervous that the little girl took charge of the conversation. . . . He was proud of her and adored her."

In her book, Leatrice quoted some poignant letters he wrote to her in that last year: "I have been very ill, angel," he wrote. "So ill, in fact, that I cannot write this letter myself, but I am slowly recovering." He added an interesting, hopeful career note, if he was not just spinning tales: "If all goes well I leave in about three weeks for New York to do a play. It is an entirely new adventure for me and to be truthful I am scared to death." On New Year's Day 1936, he wrote to Leatrice that he was still quite ill, but "just as soon as I am strong enough I'll call you and hope you will come up and see me soon."

Jack's doctor, Leo Madsen, assigned a home nurse, a rather attractive blonde named May Jordan, to stay with him. He suffered another attack on January 2, "but he appeared to get better and was able to get up and walk around the house," said Jordan. "Two weeks ago, he felt well enough to attend a luncheon." His huge canopied bed was not suitable for a convalescent, so he moved into his guest room and a smaller bed, with a tufted satin headboard (the "girlfriend room").

At about 2:00 a.m. on January 9, Jack awoke and went into the kitchen for a glass of water, Jordan by his side. He fell asleep around 4:00 a.m. and woke up just after dawn. He "tried to lift his hands as though to ask for something," the *Los Angeles Times* relayed. "Gee, but I'm awfully sleepy" seem to have been his last words. Jordan administered whatever "stimulant" Dr. Madsen had prescribed and called the doctor, who arrived sometime before 7:30 (she also called his business manager, Charles Greene, so Jack's condition must have been alarming). Dr. Madsen summoned the West Los Angeles fire department for their Pulmotor (a device for pumping oxygen into the lungs, in common use in the 1930s). Dr. Madsen later estimated that Jack died at 7:44 a.m., but firemen Alex Peterson and Jerry Tramutto kept working over him for nearly another hour.

Marlene Dietrich's daughter, Maria Riva, who was eleven at the time, claimed decades later that her mother had been with Jack when his attack came, and that she had selfishly fled to avoid publicity: Dietrich called "one of her string of unsavory doctors, who could be counted on to keep their mouths shut. . . . The proclaimed epitome of pure motherhood could not be discovered in her lover's bed!" But Riva was either unaware of or chose not to mention the live-in nurse or Dr. Madsen;

even had Dietrich been with Jack when he died (and one really hopes she was), her presence or absence would not have affected the outcome in any way.

Dr. Madsen listed acute myocarditis (an inflammation of the heart muscle) as the immediate cause of death—no autopsy was performed. Robert Pinals, MD, clinical professor of medicine, UMDNJ–Robert Wood Johnson Medical School, says today that the description of Jack's death "is certainly compatible with a heart attack. Pain is frequently in the upper abdomen rather than the chest, and death may occur a week or two later from various complications, like bleeding into the pericardium, rupture of dead heart muscle, abnormal rapid heart rhythm and several others." But Pinals adds that due to Jack's drinking, his ulcers and stomach upsets may have mimicked a heart attack: "He might have had sudden massive hemorrhage from a gastric ulcer or perforation of an ulcer, leading to rapid fall in blood pressure and loss of consciousness."

Pinals does not second-guess Dr. Madsen and does not find it odd that Jack was not hospitalized. "Treating a heart attack at home was not unusual in 1936," he says. "He might have had an electrocardiogram to confirm his diagnosis; portable ECG machines were introduced in 1935, so it might possibly have been done at home."

Calls went out and friends gathered at Jack's home: former MGM coworkers Cedric Gibbons, Edmund Goulding, Howard Strickling, and Willis Goldbeck; Jack's lawyer, Peyton Moore.

John Gilbert's death made the front pages, with a flattering headshot and "star" in the headline: "He was beloved by all who knew him," the *Los Angeles Times* kindly exaggerated, and his recent failure was all but ignored in what had become his hometown paper. His career was "obstructed," wrote the memorialist, "with the advent of the talking pictures to which his voice was not entirely suited." The *Los Angeles Times* also, rather cutely and primly, noted that his recent relationship with Marlene Dietrich was platonic, as "Miss Dietrich has a husband." The *New York Times* was nastier: "A high-pitched voice, difficult to control, spoiled the otherwise fine performances. . . . Gilbert remained a memory, and a fast-fading memory, to a more or less fickle public."

Jack's ex-wives and lovers were hunted down for quotes. Garbo, vacationing in Sweden, was waylaid during the intermission of a show.

Not surprisingly, she had no comment—she returned to the theater, then dashed out unescorted and vanished into the night. Dietrich was more forthcoming, calling Jack a beloved character "whose passing will be felt not only in the film world, but by his millions of admirers who had come to feel they knew him personally." She added that he had recently been offered a British movie and had received several American offers as well—a nice coda to his story, but of course he was uninsurable (otherwise he'd have been in *Desire*).

The wives, too, had their say. Olivia Burwell, tracked down in Phoenix—good work by the *Los Angeles Times* on short notice—said, "Of course I am sorry he died, just as I am sorry that anyone has to die. But I have never regretted divorcing him. Life has turned out fine for me. . . . I hadn't seen nor heard from him since our divorce." Leatrice Joy either could not be reached or would not offer comment. Ina Claire was "terribly shocked and very sorry to hear of it. We were still good friends. I heard from him at Christmas, he wired me greetings." The feelings got stronger the closer the wife was chronologically. Virginia Bruce wrote to journalist Gladys Hall—still on her "Virginia Bruce Gilbert" letterhead—on January 23, "I still cannot think of his being gone—he was just too beautiful to ever go away as far as that we couldn't touch him and feel his fire and intensity."

Jack was in very good financial shape for someone who'd not worked steadily in years and had lost in the stock market—thanks mostly to his business manager, Charles Greene. He had $186,306 deposited in various banks, two life insurance policies and six annuities, $78,775 in stocks and $2,000 in government bonds, $10,000 in Los Angeles real estate, a home appraised at $40,000, and cars and furniture valued at $6,527.

His will—made in 1932 during his last marriage and not updated since then—left the bulk of his estate to Virginia Bruce and his youngest daughter. Six life annuities of $25,000 each went to Bruce as well as whatever was left over from the estate after other gifts were distributed. If Virginia Bruce, her daughter, and her parents all died while there was money in the bequest fund, it was to go to the Los Angeles Orthopedic Foundation to help "children of parents working in the motion picture industry." His daughter by Leatrice Joy got $10,000 (whereas the son of his friend Adela Rogers St. Johns was left $25,000). His stepfather,

Walter Gilbert, was bequeathed $5,000, as were various friends (including Howard Strickling and his doctor). Jack named lawyer Moore and business manager Greene executors (and left each $10,000). His servants—chauffeur, valet, cook, secretary—got between $1,000 and $2,500 each.

Less than a month before Jack's death, comic star Thelma Todd had died at the age of thirty. Found in her garage, full of booze and carbon monoxide, Todd was genuinely well liked in Hollywood, and her funeral became a public holiday of over-the-top mourning. She was laid out at Pierce Brothers mortuary in an open casket, banked in flowers. Photos of her dead body—both in her car and, more horrible, at the morgue—were passed around by the morbid (and are now easily seen online).

Cedric Gibbons said that he and Jack had found all this horrifying. "I talked with Jack three weeks ago. He said to me, 'Gibbie, if you are anywhere around when I am gone, don't let them bury me like they did Thelma. Don't let anyone see me after I am dead.'" So, happily for him, no postmortem photos of John Gilbert are to be found online. His gray coffin was blanketed in pink roses and sweet peas, with floral displays from his three most recent wives and Marlene Dietrich as well as bouquets from friends, both famous and obscure.

Leatrice Joy and Virginia Bruce wept through the service (Bruce "hysterically," according to one reporter). Marlene Dietrich, dressed in black, shockingly sans makeup, was led in by Dolores Del Rio and Cedric Gibbons.

Attendance was by invitation only at Beverly Hills's B. F. Dayton mortuary chapel, though crowds stood outside in a chilly rain, perhaps to see the stars enter (Myrna Loy, Gary Cooper, John Barrymore, and Dolores Del Rio, in addition to the expected wives and lovers). The Reverend Neal Dodd of the Church of St. Mary of the Angels read the service, after which Jack was taken to the Hollywood Crematory. His remains were cremated, and a bronze urn was quietly interred at Forest Lawn Memorial Park, with only Charles Greene attending as witness. Today John Gilbert rests on a sloping hill at the famed cemetery in Glendale under a small, flat plaque bearing his signature and the words "In Memoriam." Among other Forest Lawn residents are his former friends and coworkers Clarence Brown, Edmund Goulding, Mary Pickford, Norma Shearer and Irving Thalberg, Lon Chaney, Enid Bennett, Frank

Borzage, Rouben Mamoulian, Victor McLaglen, Marian Nixon, Ernest Torrence—and his old foe Jim Tully.

Tully had the gall to hold forth to the press about his "friend," sounding much more on target and sympathetic than he had when Jack was alive to hear him. "The screen was his life," he told a reporter. "But the screen turned him down. . . . He was a person whose energy burned him up. His natural outlet for this energy was the motion picture, in some creative form, but this, for reasons he nor any other man could fathom, was denied him."

Irving Thalberg—who would be dead of heart disease before the year was out—told Leatrice Joy, "Jack was on the verge of a real comeback. He had a contract waiting to be signed, but I honestly don't believe he wanted it any more." This story struck Joy—and later her daughter—as a pathetic attempt by Thalberg to ease his own conscience. "Thalberg was tormented by his failure to stand up against Mayer for the man who had been his close friend," said Leatrice Fountain.

Almost immediately the fight over Jack's money began—with two ex-wives, two minor daughters, and such an unfair division of bequests, that was not unexpected. On January 18, 1936, Leatrice Joy demanded a larger slice of the pie for their daughter, claiming Jack wanted to leave half his estate to her.

By 1936 Virginia Bruce was still living with her parents and toddler daughter, but her career was going great guns: leading roles in *The Mighty Barnum, Jane Eyre,* and *Times Square Lady,* and two of her biggest hits—*The Great Ziegfeld* and *Born to Dance*—ready for release later that year. Leatrice Joy, married to well-to-do businessman William Hook, had not made a movie since 1930. She was not hurting for money, but rightfully felt that her eleven-year-old daughter by Jack had as much right to his inheritance as did Susan Ann.

Marlene Dietrich's daughter claimed that her mother raged to Leatrice Joy, "That gold-digger Virginia Bruce, she has stolen his last will! . . . I told him he could not leave everything to that awful woman. . . . But now, no one can find that will . . . and that Bruce woman is shaking in her shoes!" (Dietrich's daughter, Maria, it must be noted, was twelve years old at the time, but claimed in her memoirs to recall these rants verbatim.)

A celebrity estate auction is always a crowd-pleaser. In August 1936

Jack's executors gave over to a Wilshire Boulevard auctioneer everything that had not been previously gifted. The house arranged for a four-day sale, and on August 25 eager bidders crowded in. A few days earlier Marlene Dietrich had spent $600 to buy all of Jack's bedsheets and pillowcases, in what was either a really sweet or a monumentally creepy gesture. (Speaking of creepy, child star Jackie Coogan's mother bought Jack's guest-room deathbed, along with some chairs and lamps—his huge canopied bed went to the Summit Hotel's John Gilbert Honeymoon Suite for $1,250.) Clarence Brown bought a leaf of Jack's Guttenberg Bible ($165), and Jack's guitar went to an unnamed bidder for a mere $18.

"Articles of clothing which presumably had personal contact with the Gilbert torso aroused the most spirited bidding among women," noted one attendee. "Each time they went on the block, ladies would haul their chairs forward, set their lips grimly and bid until they reached the bottom of their pocketbooks." Of course, not only female fans wanted to get into Jack's underwear: "A slender white-haired woman who must have been 60 groaned audibly when a pair of the great Gilbert's BVDs went to a prosy little man with spats for 60 cents a pair. She had bid 50 cents. A moment later she got four bars of Gilbert's toilet soap for 15 cents a bar."

Leatrice Gilbert was brought to the sale by her aunt, as her mother was in Europe. Having just met and lost her father in the space of a year, she was desperate for some keepsake. Screenwriter Chandler Sprague battled with Leatrice over a chess set, but the girl finally won out, for $47. She bid on a set of rare Bibles and an early edition of Shelley, but two rather cold-blooded men outspent her. Actress Florence Roberts helped Leatrice buy Jack's makeup box (which she got for $14.50), and she bought a bracelet he'd worn in *Cameo Kirby* (for $16)—and that's about all she took home with her (except for some very sad memories).

Afterword

> He was always an enigma. Jack Gilbert was mercury—you'd touch him, and he'd vanish.
>
> —Leatrice Joy, 1979

In 1984 glamour photographer Horst and interviewer James Watters put out a fascinating "Where are they now?" coffee-table book titled *Return Engagement.* Seventy-four actresses were profiled, from early silent stars to 1940s and '50s glamour queens. Coincidentally, three of the featured stars were John Gilbert's ex-wives: Leatrice Joy, Ina Claire, and Virginia Bruce (Olivia Burwell was still alive when these interviews were being conducted in the early 1980s—contrasting with his own early death, Jack's wives were tenacious). Leatrice Joy was ninety-one when *Return Engagement* hit the bookstores: robust and cheerful, she posed on her front porch, laughing and white-haired, trading quips with her daughter. Leatrice Joy's stardom had skidded to a halt with the coming of sound—her southern lilt was lovely, but after a handful of lukewarm talkies at MGM, Fox, First National, and the poverty-row Tiffany, she fled the screen. "I retired at my height," she said to Watters. "I could never see myself getting old on the screen." Joy did some character work later, and worked in TV; she remarried twice, but always called John Gilbert the love of her life. She told Watters he was the only man "I truly, truly loved, and I'm just grateful to be the mother of his daughter." Leatrice Joy died the following year.

Jack and Leatrice's daughter inherited her parents' good looks, most noticeably her father's dark flashing eyes. Louis B. Mayer—perhaps for the publicity, certainly not out of guilt—gave the girl a small role in the 1938 film *Of Human Hearts* and dangled the lead in *National Velvet* before her, only—in an echo of her father's experience with *Red Dust* and *Grand Hotel*—to give it to Elizabeth Taylor. Leatrice Gilbert had bit parts in such 1940s films as *Random Harvest, Reunion in France,* and *Thirty Seconds over Tokyo,* but her acting career was over by her twenties. She married and had children, and she enjoyed a close relationship with her mother, who told her many tales of Hollywood and John Gilbert.

"She never played the star when she talked about Father," Leatrice wrote, "just a woman who loved a man and who cried at what might have been." Inspired and curious, Leatrice Gilbert Fountain became a film historian, tracking down and interviewing her parents' friends and costars through the 1960s and '70s when several were still alive. "I was just in time," she rightly said, as so many of those people were gone by the time her affectionate book, *Dark Star,* was published in 1985.

Some of her many children—Jack's grandchildren by Leatrice Joy—also went into show business. Jack's granddaughter Lorin Hart is a singer and songwriter, and his grandson John Fountain also went into acting, appearing in a handful of movies and TV shows, including *Dr. Quinn, Medicine Woman* and *Gosford Park*—and in the 1988 Hollywood-based western *Sunset,* Fountain played his grandfather. Leatrice's other sons are Christopher, Anthony, and Gideon, and some of these children have children: "My mom is a matriarch," says Lorin Hart.

Ina Claire, also ninety-one in 1984, was ensconced in her elegant San Francisco apartment when Watters interviewed her. Still chic and witty, she was attended by loyal friends but was too frail to socialize, and the death of longtime husband William Wallace in 1976 had hit her hard. After her initial lack of success in films, Claire returned to Broadway, where she enjoyed success after success: *Biography, End of Summer, Barchester Towers, The Talley Method, The Confidential Clerk.* She even made a few more movies—notably *Ninotchka,* in which she played the deliciously bitchy rival of Greta Garbo. Gossip writers ached for a feud between the two, but disappointingly Ina Claire and Greta Garbo were friendly and professional on set. The two remained distant friends, and decorator Billy Baldwin recalled it was Claire, not Garbo, who drew the line at bitchy reminiscences. "Shut up, you damned fool. I married him," she snapped at Garbo after hearing one too many unflattering

John Gilbert stories. Ina Claire retired in the 1950s; like Leatrice Joy, Ina Claire died in 1985.

Virginia Bruce, sadly, was dying when interviewed by Watters. Looking frail and exhausted in her photo, she put on her best pearls and posed bravely in her room at the Motion Picture Country House Hospital. She was philosophical about her life—"Maybe I haven't had it so tough"—and was still visited by fans, friends, and former costars. Bruce's talent and looks were never rewarded by stardom, but she worked steadily through the 1950s, both in movies (*The Invisible Woman, Pardon My Sarong, Brazil, Night Has a Thousand Eyes, Strangers When We Meet*) and on TV (some good showcases on the anthologies of the 1950s). She married screenwriter, producer, and director J. Walter Ruben and had a son by him, but Ruben—like Jack—died young of a heart attack. Her third marriage was complicated by military and immigration woes (her husband was Turkish). She told Jack and Leatrice Joy's daughter in 1973, "All the money I am living on today is from the two annuities your father gave me in our divorce agreement. Everything else is gone." Lending a wistful touch to her final interview, Bruce asked Watters, "Do you think when I'm gone, anyone will remember that I had awfully dreamy eyes?" She died in 1982, at the age of seventy-one.

Jack and Virginia's daughter, Susan Ann, grew up to be a great beauty—how could she not? She married several times—an advertising executive, a Realtor, a gardener and horse trainer—and had a son and a daughter. She moved to Oregon and never told her children of the Hollywood royalty in their background. After Susan Ann died in 2004, her son David was shocked when he went through her memorabilia. "My mother kept us away from the Hollywood scene," he told Virginia Bruce's biographer, Scott O'Brien. "I didn't even know. . . . I just realized all this stuff since my mother passed away."

Two of Jack's chief loves were not, of course, seen in *Return Engagement*—both Greta Garbo and Marlene Dietrich were alive in the 1980s, but neither was the chatty, reminiscing type. Garbo retired from films in 1941 and became the world's most famous "Flying Dutchman," traveling alone, filthy rich (she still had the first dollar she earned), and making a great show of avoiding the press. Her "I vant to be alone" persona seems to have been a combination of genuine pathological shyness and a savvy protection of her mystique. The faster she ran, the more she intrigued

Jack in his backyard with some friends, 1924 (The Everett Collection).

the press and fans, and to the end of her days a blurry snapshot of her walking down the street was newsworthy. Garbo, of course, never spoke of John Gilbert—but he may have been the chief romantic relationship in her life. Greta Garbo died in New York in 1990, aged eighty-four.

Marlene Dietrich had retired to her Paris apartment by the early 1980s, unwilling to destroy her legend by letting her fans see her frail and aging. Unlike Garbo, she went from career success to success, giving brilliant performances (*Destry Rides Again, A Foreign Affair, Witness for the Prosecution, Judgment at Nuremberg*) well into middle age. She made a great splash as a chanteuse, touring in sold-out concerts worldwide, till her retirement in the mid-1970s. She also did yeoman service in World War II, not only entertaining the troops in North Africa, Italy, France, and Germany, but donating money and jewels to the Allied cause (and, some reports state, acting as a secret courier for the military). After Dietrich's death in 1992, aged ninety, her estate was found to be a treasure trove of memorabilia. Among her keepsakes were John Gilbert's love letters and an ankle bracelet engraved in his handwriting: "Angel—keep on loving me, rush home to me, I love you so. Jack."

Acknowledgments

First, my thanks to Leatrice Gilbert Fountain for giving me her blessings for this book about her father (and about her mother) and for not asking to peruse and approve it before publication. I nervously hope she likes it.

This book certainly could not have been written without the help of James Zeruk Jr., the best researcher I have ever known. James is a historian and writer himself—his biography of Peg Entwistle promises to be amazing—so he knew just what would be useful to me and what would not. He is enthusiastic, tireless, good-humored, and altogether a dream of a researcher.

As usual, my thanks to Richard Kukan for editing, fact checking, spell checking, and generally de-stupiding my manuscript. I would be lost without him.

My appreciation as well to Michael Ankerich, Kate Anthony, Charles Cisneros, Willam M. Drew, Scott Eyman, Lorin Hart, Dorinda Hartman (the Library of Congress), Richard Lamparski, Donna Lethal, Joan Myers, Mel Neuhaus, Scott O'Brien, Stephen "Tad" O'Brien, the late Anita Page, James Robert Parish, Robert Pinals, Charles Silver (the Museum of Modern Art), Zoran Sinobad (the Library of Congress), Sheryl Stinchcum, and Ashley Swinnerton (the Museum of Modern Art) for their specific contributions.

Thanks to everyone who supplied me with copies of John Gilbert films via DVD and VHS: Mel Neuhaus, James Robert Parish, Scott Eyman, Dennis Payne, Eric Monder. Thanks too to the good folks who arranged screenings for me at the Museum of Modern Art (*Cameo Kirby, His Hour*) and the Library of Congress (*Golden Rule Kate, Happiness, The Hater of Men, His Glorious Night*).

Filmography

The Triangle Years (1915–1918)

The Coward (1915)

Directed by Reginald Barker and Thomas H. Ince. Story and screenplay by Thomas H. Ince. Produced by Thomas H. Ince. Cinematography by Joseph H. August and Robert Newhard.
Cast: Frank Keenan (Colonel Jefferson Beverly Winslow), Charles Ray (Frank Winslow), Gertrude Claire (Mrs. Elizabeth Winslow), Patricia Palmer (Amy), Nick Cogley (a Negro servant), Charles K. French (a Confederate commander), Leo Willis (Union soldier). With John Gilbert, Bob Kortman.

Matrimony (1915)

Directed by Scott Sidney (assistant director, Eliot Howe). Scenario by C. Gardner Sullivan. Produced by Thomas H. Ince. Cinematography by Devereaux Jennings.
Cast: Louise Glaum (Thelma Iverson), Julia Dean (Diana Rossmore), Howard C. Hickman (Weston Rossmore), Betty Burbridge (Antoinette), Lou Salter (Nurse), Thelma Salter (Viola). [John Gilbert (extra).]

The Corner (1916)

Directed by Walter Edwards (assistant director, F. Harmon Weight). Story and screenplay by C. Gardner Sullivan. Cinematography by Otis M. Gove and Devereaux Jennings.

Cast: George Fawcett (David Waltham), Willard Mack (John Adams), Clara Williams (Mrs. Adams), Louise Brownell (Mrs. Waltham), Charles Miller (rent collector). [John Gilbert (extra).]

Bullets and Brown Eyes (1916)

Directed by Scott Sidney. Scenario by J. G. Hawks and Thomas H. Ince. Produced by Thomas H. Ince. Cinematography by Devereaux Jennings.
Cast: William Desmond (Prince Carl), Bessie Barriscale (Countess Olga), Wyndham Standing (Count Michael), Joseph J. Dowling (Count Ivan), J. Barney Sherry (the king), Roy Laidlaw (the grand duke), Louise Brownell (Prince Carl's mother), Leonard Smith (Lieutenant Alexis of the Hussars). With Jack Gilbert, Jean Hersholt.

The Last Act (1916)

Directed by Walter Edwards. Scenario by C. Gardner Sullivan and Thomas H. Ince. Produced by Thomas H. Ince.
Cast: Bessie Barriscale (Ethel Duprey), Clara Williams (Mrs. Cora Hale), Miss Allen (Suzette), Harry Keenan (Ernest Hale), Robert McKim (Lewis Bressler). [John Gilbert (extra).]

Hell's Hinges (1916)

Directed by Charles Swickard. Story and screenplay by C. Gardner Sullivan. Titles by Mon Randall. Produced by Thomas H. Ince. Cinematography by Joseph H. August. Original music by Victor Schertzinger. Stunts by Buddy Roosevelt.
Cast: William S. Hart (Blaze Tracy), Clara Williams (Faith Henley), Louise Glaum (Dolly), Jack Standing (Rev. Robert Henley), Alfred Hollingsworth (silk miller), Robert McKim (clergyman), J. Frank Burke (Zeb Taylor). With John Gilbert, Jean Hersholt, Bob Kortman, Wheeler Oakman, Leo Willis (extras).

The Aryan (1916)

Directed by Reginald Barker, William S. Hart, and Clifford Smith. Story and screenplay by C. Gardner Sullivan. Produced by Thomas H. Ince. Cinematography by Joseph H. August. Original music by Hugo Riesenfeld.
Cast: William S. Hart (Steve Denton), Gertrude Claire (Mrs. Denton),

Charles K. French ("Ivory" Wells), Louise Glaum (Trixie, "the Firefly"), Herschel Mayall (Chip Emmett), Ernest Swallow (Mexican Pete), Bessie Love (Mary Jane Garth). With Enid Bennett, Jean Hersholt, John Gilbert.

Civilization (1916)

Directed by Reginald Barker, Thomas H. Ince, and Raymond B. West. Scenario by C. Gardner Sullivan. Produced by Thomas H. Ince and Al Woods. Cinematography by Joseph H. August, Dal Clawson, Clyde De Vinna, Otis M. Gove, Devereaux Jennings, Charles E. Kaufman, Robert Newhard, and Irvin Willat. Original music by Victor Schertzinger. Art direction by Joseph H. August.
Cast: Howard C. Hickman (Count Ferdinand), Enid Markey (Katheryn Haldemann), Lola May (Queen Engenie), George Fisher (the Christ), Herschel Mayall (the king of Wredpryd), Kate Bruce (a mother), J. Frank Burke (Luther Rolf, the peace advocate), Charles K. French (the prime minister), J. Barney Sherry (blacksmith), Jerome Storm (the blacksmith's son), Lillian Reade (young child). With Claire Du Brey, Fanny Midgley, John Gilbert.

The Apostle of Vengeance (1916)

Directed by William S. Hart and Clifford Smith (assistant director, Clifford Smith). Story and screenplay by Monte M. Katterjohn. Produced by Thomas H. Ince. Cinematography by Joseph H. August.
Cast: William S. Hart (David Hudson), Nona Thomas (Mary McCoy), Joseph J. Dowling (Tom McCoy), Fanny Midgley ("Marm" Hudson), Jack Gilbert (Willie Hudson), Marvel Stafford (Elsie Hudson). With Gertrude Claire, Jean Hersholt.

The Phantom (1916)

Directed by Charles Giblyn. Scenario by J. G. Hawks. Cinematography by Dal Clawson.
Cast: Frank Keenan ("Phantom" Farrell), Enid Markey (Avice Bereton), Robert McKim (Crabbe), P. Dempsey Tabler (James Blaisdell), Charles K. French (Dr. Ratcliffe), J. Barney Sherry (James Bereton), Jack Gilbert (Bertie Bereton).

Eye of the Night (1916)

Directed by Walter Edwards. Scenario by C. Gardner Sullivan. Cinematography by Devereaux Jennings. Art direction by Robert Brunton.
Cast: William H. Thompson (David Holden), Margery Wilson (Jane), Thornton Edwards (Rob Benson), J. P. Lockney (Denby), Aggie Herring (Mrs. Denby). [John Gilbert (extra).]

Shell 43 (1916)

Kay-Bee Pictures, New York Motion Picture (distributed by Triangle). Directed by Reginald Barker. Scenario by C. Gardner Sullivan. Produced by Thomas H. Ince. Cinematography by Charles E. Kaufman. Art direction by Robert Brunton.
Cast: H. B. Warner (William Berner), Enid Markey (Adrienne von Altman), Jack Gilbert (English spy), George Fisher (Lieutenant Franz Hollen), Margaret Thompson (Helen von Altman), Louise Brownell (Baroness von Altman), J. P. Lockney (German Secret Service agent), Charles K. French (German commander).

The Sin Ye Do (1916)

Kay-Bee Pictures, New York Motion Picture (distributed by Triangle). Directed by Walter Edwards (assistant director, David Hartford). Scenario by J. G. Hawks. Story by John Lynch. Cinematography by Devereaux Jennings.
Cast: Frank Keenan (Barret Steele), Margery Wilson (Alice Ward), David Hartford (Dace Whitlock), Margaret Thompson (Rose Darrow), Louise Brownell (Mary Ward), Jack Gilbert (Jimmy), Howard C. Hickman (Robert Darrow), Cleo Morrow (maid), Walt Whitman (Thompson).

The Weaker Sex (1917)

Directed by Raymond B. West. Scenario by Monte M. Katterjohn. Story by Alice C. Brown. Produced by Thomas H. Ince. Cinematography by Dal Clawson. Art direction by Robert Brunton.
Cast: Dorothy Dalton (Ruth Tilden), Louise Glaum (Annette Loti), Charles Ray (Jack Harding), Robert McKim (Raoul Bozen), Charles K. French (John Harding), Margaret Thompson (Marjory Lawton), J. Barney Sherry (Edward Tilden), Nona Thomas (Mary Wheeler). [John Gilbert (extra).]

The Bride of Hate (1917)

Directed by Walter Edwards. Story by John Lynch. Adaptation by J. G. Hawks. Produced by Thomas H. Ince. Cinematography by Charles E. Kaufman. Art direction by Robert Brunton.

Cast: Frank Keenan (Dr. Dudley Duprez), Margery Wilson (Mercedes Mendoza), Jerome Storm (Paul Crenshaw), David Hartford (Judge Shone), Elvira Weil (Rose Duprez), Florence Hale (Mammy Lou), J. P. Lockney (Don Ramon Alvarez), Nona Thomas (Don Ramon's daughter), Jack Gilbert (Dr. Duprez' son).

Princess of the Dark (1917)

Directed by Charles Miller. Story by Lanier Bartlett and Monte M. Katterjohn. Produced by Thomas H. Ince. Cinematography by Clyde De Vinna.

Cast: Enid Bennett (Fay Herron), Jack Gilbert ("Crip" Halloran), Alfred Vosburgh (Jack Rockwell), Walt Whitman (James Herron), J. Frank Burke (Crip's father).

The Dark Road (1917)

Directed by Charles Miller. Story by J. G. Hawks and John Lynch. Produced by Thomas H. Ince. Cinematography by Clyde De Vinna. Art direction by Robert Brunton.

Cast: Dorothy Dalton (Cleo Morrison), Robert McKim (Carlos Costa), Jack Livingston (Captain James Morrison), Jack Gilbert (Cedric Constable), Walt Whitman (Sir John Constable), Lydia Knott (Lady Mary Constable).

Happiness (1917)

Directed by Reginald Barker. Scenario by C. Gardner Sullivan. Produced by Thomas H. Ince. Cinematography by Robert Newhard. Art direction by Robert Brunton.

Cast: Enid Bennett (Doris Wingate), Charles Gunn (Robert Lee Hollister), Thelma Salter (Dolly Temple), Andrew Arbuckle (Nicodemus), Gertrude Claire (Miss Pratt), Adele Belgrade (Priscilla Wingate), Jack Gilbert (Richard Forrester).

The Millionaire Vagrant (1917)

Directed by Victor Schertzinger. Scenario by J. G. Hawks. Produced by Thomas H. Ince. Cinematography by Paul Eagler.
Cast: Charles Ray (Steven Du Peyster), Sylvia Breamer (Ruth Vail), J. Barney Sherry (Malcolm Blackridge), Jack Gilbert (James Cricket), Elvira Weil (Peggy O'Connor), Dorcas Matthews (Betty Vanderfleet), Aggie Herring (Mrs. Flannery), Josephine Headley (Squidge), Carolyn Wagner (Rose), Walt Whitman (old bookkeeper).

The Hater of Men (1917)

Directed by Charles Miller. Scenario by C. Gardner Sullivan. Produced by Thomas H. Ince. Cinematography by Clyde De Vinna. Art direction by Robert Brunton.
Cast: Bessie Barriscale (Janice Salsbury), Charles K. French (Phillips Hartley), Jack Gilbert (Billy Williams).

The Mother Instinct (1917)

Directed by Lambert Hillyer and Roy William Neill. Scenario by Lambert Hillyer and Maude Pettus.
Cast: Enid Bennett (Eleanor Coutierre), Rowland V. Lee (Jacques), Margery Wilson (Marie Coutierre), Tod Burns (Pierre Bondel), Jack Gilbert (Jean Coutierre), Gertrude Claire (Mother Coutierre), William Fairbanks (Raoul Bergere).

Golden Rule Kate (1917)

Directed by Reginald Barker. Scenario by Monte M. Katterjohn. Cinematography by Joseph H. August and Robert Newhard.
Cast: Louise Glaum (Golden Rule Kate), William Conklin (Rev. Gavin McGregor), Jack Richardson ("Slick" Barney), Mildred Harris (Olive), John Gilbert (the Heller), Gertrude Claire (Mrs. McGregor), Josephine Headley (Vegas Kate), J. P. Lockney ("Nose Paint"), Milton Ross (Jim Preston).

The Devil Dodger (1917)

Directed by Clifford Smith. Scenario by J. G. Hawks.
Cast: Roy Stewart (Silent Scott), Jack Gilbert (Roger Ingraham), Carolyn Wagner (Fluffy), John Lince (Ricketts), Anna Dodge (Mrs. Ricketts), George Willis (Bowie). With Belle Bennett, Josie Sedgwick.

Up or Down? (1917)

Directed by Lynn Reynolds. Scenario by Lynn Reynolds. Cinematography by Clyde Cook.
Cast: George Hernandez (Mike), Fritzi Ridgeway (Esther Hollister), Jack Gilbert (Allan Corey), Elwood Bredell (boy), Jack Curtis ("Texas" Jack), Graham Pettie (sheriff), Edward Burns (ranch foreman).

Nancy Comes Home (1918)

Directed by John Francis Dillon. Scenario by Robert F. Hill. Story by B. D. Carber. Cinematography by Stephen S. Norton.
Cast: Myrtle Lind (Nancy Worthing), George C. Pearce (Mortimer Worthing), Myrtle Rishell (Mrs. Mortimer Worthing), Eugene Burr (Clavering Hayes), Anna Dodge (Mrs. Jerry Ballou), Percy Challenger (Jerry Ballou), Jack Gilbert (Phil Ballou), J. P. Wild (Stillson).

The Mask (1918)

Directed by Thomas N. Heffron. Screenplay by E. Magnus Ingleton. Cinematography by C. H. Wales.
Cast: Claire Anderson (Sally Taylor), Ray Godfrey (Babe Taylor), Grace Marvin (Marybelle Judson), Bliss Chevalier (Mrs. Massington), Jack Gilbert (Billy Taylor), Edward Hearn (Sam Joplin), Harry Holden (Silas Taylor), Marie Van Tassell (Miss Prim), Lillian West (Miss Beech).

The Freelance Years (1918–1921)

Shackled (1918)

Paralta Plays Inc. (distributed by W. W. Hodkinson). Directed by Reginald Barker. Story by J. Grubb Alexander, Lawrence McCloskey, and Fred Myton. Cinematography by L. Guy Wilky.
Cast: Louise Glaum (Lola Dexter), Charles West (Walter Cosgrove), Jack Gilbert (James Ashley), Roberta Wilson (Edith Danfield), Lawson Butt (Thomas Danfield), Herschel Mayall (Henry Hartman), Roy Laidlaw (Major Duval).

More Trouble (1918)

Anderson-Brunton Company (distributed by Pathé Exchange). Directed by Ernest C. Warde. Screenplay by Ouida Bergère and Edgar Franklin. Cinematography by Charles E. Kaufman.

Cast: Frank Keenan (Lemuel Deering), Jack Gilbert (Harvey Deering), Ida Lewis (Mrs. Deering), Roberta Wilson (Miriam Deering), Joseph J. Dowling (Cecil Morrowton), Jack Rollens (Harold Morrowton), Helen Dunbar (Mrs. Morton Wells), Albert Ray (Jack Wells), Clyde Benson (Barnabas Bandwig), Aggie Herring (Mary), Lule Warrenton (housekeeper).

One Dollar Bid (1918)

Paralta Plays Inc. (distributed by W. W. Hodkinson). Directed by Ernest C. Warde. Screenplay by Thomas J. Geraghty, from the novel *Toby* by Credo Fitch Harris. Cinematography by Charles J. Stumar.
Cast: J. Warren Kerrigan (Toby), Lois Wilson (Virginia Dare), Joseph J. Dowling (Colonel Poindexter Dare), Leatrice Joy (Emily Dare), Arthur Allardt (Ralph Patterson), Jess Herring (Dink Wallerby), Elvira Weil (Nell Wallerby), Clifford Alexander (Bob Clark). With Jack Gilbert.

Wedlock (1918)

Paralta Plays Inc. (distributed by W. W. Hodkinson). Directed by Wallace Worsley. Story and screenplay by Denison Clift. Produced by Robert Brunton. Cinematography by L. Guy Wilky.
Cast: Louise Glaum (Margery Harding), Jack Gilbert (Granger Hollister), Herschel Mayall (George Osborne), Charles Gunn (Rev. Grover King), Joseph J. Dowling (Philip Merrill), Beverly Randolph (Catherine Merrill), Leatrice Joy (Jane Hollister), Harry Archer (Lord Cecil Graydon), Ida Lewis (Mrs. Merrill), Clifford Alexander (Jason Strong), Aggie Herring (Mrs. Martin). With Helen Dunbar.

Doing Their Bit (1918)

Fox Film Corporation. Directed by Kenean Buel. Screenplay by Kenean Buel. Cinematography by Joseph Ruttenberg.
Cast: Jane Lee (Janie O'Dowd), Katherine Lee (Kate O'Dowd), Franklyn Hanna (Michael O'Dowd), Gertrude Le Brandt (Bridget McCann O'Dowd), Alexander Hall (Miles O'Dowd), Beth Ivins (Patricia O'Dowd), Kate Lester (Mrs. Velma Vanderspent), William Pollard (Alfred Caesar Vanderspent), Jay Strong (Jerry Flynn), Aimee Abbott (Mrs. Mary Flynn), Eddie Sturgis, R. R. Neill (German spies). With Jack Gilbert.

Three X Gordon (1918)

Jesse D. Hampton Productions (distributed by W. W. Hodkinson). Directed by Ernest C. Warde. Screenplay by Kenneth B. Clarke. Produced by Jesse D. Hampton. Cinematography by Charles J. Stumar.
Cast: J. Warren Kerrigan (Harold Chester Winthrop Gordon), Lois Wilson (Dorrie Webster), Charles K. French (Jim Gordon), Gordon Sackville (Mr. Webster), John Gilbert (Archie), Jay Belasco (Walter), Leatrice Joy (farmer's daughter), Walter Perry (Farmer Muldoon), Don Bailey (Josiah Higgins), Stanhope Wheatcroft (Thomas Jefferson Higgins).

The Dawn of Understanding (1918)

Vitagraph Company of America. Directed by Charles R. Seeling and David Smith. Screenplay by Edward J. Montagne, from the Bret Harte story "The Judgment of Bolinas Plain." Produced by Albert E. Smith. Cinematography by Charles R. Seeling.
Cast: Bessie Love (Sue Prescott), George A. Williams (Silas Prescott), Jack Gilbert (Ira Beasley), J. Frank Glendon (Jim Wynd), George Kunkel (Sheriff Jack Scott), Jacob Abrams (Parson Davies).

The White Heather (1919)

Maurice Tourneur Productions (distributed by Paramount Pictures). Directed by Maurice Tourneur. Screenplay by Cecil Raleigh, based on the play by Henry Hamilton. Produced by Maurice Tourneur. Cinematography by René Guissart and Harold S. Sintzenich. Art direction by Ben Carré.
Cast: Holmes Herbert (Lord Angus Cameron), Ben Alexander (Donald Cameron), Ralph Graves (Alec McClintock), Mabel Ballin (Marion Hume), Jack Gilbert (Dick Beach), Spottiswoode Aitken (James Hume). With Gibson Gowland.

The Busher (1919)

Thomas H. Ince Corporation (distributed by Paramount Pictures). Directed by Jerome Storm. Scenario by R. Cecil Smith, based on the story "South Paw" by Earle Snell. Produced by Thomas H. Ince. Cinematography by Chester A. Lyons.
Cast: Charles Ray (Ben Harding), Colleen Moore (Mazie Palmer), Jack Gilbert (Jim Blair), Jay Morley (Billy Palmer), Otto Hoffman (Deacon

Nasby), Margaret Livingston (the city vamp). With Louis Durham, Jack Nelson.

The Man Beneath (1919)

Haworth Pictures Corporation (distributed by Robertson-Cole Distributing Corporation). Directed by William Worthington. Screenplay by L. V. Jefferson, from the novel *Only a Nigger* by Edmund Mitchell. Produced by Sessue Hayakawa. Cinematography by Frank D. Williams. Technical director, Frank Ormston.
Cast: Sessue Hayakawa (Dr. Chindi Ashutor), Helen Jerome Eddy (Kate Erskine), Pauline Curley (Mary Erskine), Jack Gilbert (James Bassett), Fontaine La Rue (Countess Petite Florence), Wedgwood Nowell (François). With Fanny Midgley.

A Little Brother of the Rich (1919)

Universal Film Manufacturing Company. Directed by Lynn Reynolds. From the novel by Joseph Medill Patterson. Cinematography by Phil Rosen.
Cast: J. Barney Sherry (Henry Leamington), Kathryn Adams (Sylvia Castle), Frank Mayo (Paul Potter), Lila Leslie (Muriel Evers), John Gilbert (Carl Wilmerding). With Ruth Royce.

The Red Viper (1919)

Tyrad Pictures Inc. Directed by Jacques Tyrol. Screenplay by Winifred Dunn. Produced by Jacques Tyrol. Cinematography by Edward Wynard.
Cast: Gareth Hughes (David Belkov), Ruth Stonehouse (Mary Hogan), Jack Gilbert (Dick Grant), Irma Harrison (Yolanda Kosloff), R. H. Fitzsimmons (Charles Smith), Alberta Lee (Mrs. Hogan), Alfred Hollingsworth (Pat Hogan).

For a Woman's Honor (1919)

Jesse D. Hampton Productions (distributed by Robertson-Cole Distributing Corporation). Directed by Park Frame. Scenario by George Elwood Jenks, from a story by Clifford Howard. Produced by Jesse D. Hampton.
Cast: H. B. Warner (Captain Clyde Mannering), Marguerite De La Motte (Helen Rutherford), John Gilbert (Dick Rutherford), Carmen Phillips (Valeska De Marsay), Hector Sarno (Rajput Nath). With Olive Ann Alcorn, Roy Coulson, Carl Stockdale.

Widow by Proxy (1919)

Paramount/Famous Players–Lasky Corporation. Directed by Walter Edwards (assistant director, Fred J. Robinson). Scenario by Julia Crawford Ivers, from a play by Catherine Chisholm Cushing. Produced by Adolph Zukor. Cinematography by James Van Trees and Hal Young.
Cast: Marguerite Clark (Gloria Grey), Agnes Vernon (Dolores Pennington), Gertrude Norman (Sophronia Pennington), Gertrude Claire (Angelica Pennington), Nigel Barrie (Lieutenant Steven Pennington), Jack Gilbert (Jack Pennington), Al W. Filson (Alexander P. Galloway), Rosita Marstini (Mme. Gilligan).

Heart o' the Hills (1919)

Mary Pickford Company (distributed by First National Exhibitors' Circuit). Directed by Joseph De Grasse and Sidney Franklin. Produced by Mary Pickford. Cinematography by Charles Rosher. Edited by Edward M. McDermott. Art direction by Max Parker.
Cast: Mary Pickford (Mavis Hawn), Harold Goodwin (young Jason Honeycutt), Allan Sears (adult Jason Honeycutt), Fred Huntley (Granpap Jason Hawn), Claire McDowell (Martha Hawn), Sam De Grasse (Steve Honeycutt), W. H. Bainbridge (Colonel Pendleton), Jack Gilbert (Gray Pendleton), Betty Bouton (Marjorie Lee), Fred Warren (John Burnham).

Should a Woman Tell? (1919)

Screen Classics Inc. (distributed by Metro Pictures Corporation). Directed by John Ince. Scenario by Finis Fox. Produced by Maxwell Karger. Cinematography by Sol Polito (assistant cinematographer, Earl Rolfe). Edited by Edward M. McDermott. Art direction by Amos Myers.
Cast: Alice Lake (Meta Maxon), Frank Currier (Mr. Maxon), Jack Mulhall (Albert Tuley), Nellie Anderson (Mrs. Maxon), Lydia Knott (Clarissa Sedgwick), Don Bailey (doctor), Jack Gilbert (villain), Richard Headrick (Maxon boy), Carol Jackson (Maxon girl).

The White Circle (1920)

Maurice Tourneur Productions (distributed by Paramount Pictures). Directed by Maurice Tourneur. Scenario by John Gilbert and Jules Furthman, from the story "The Pavilion on the Links" by Robert Louis

Stevenson. Produced by Maurice Tourneur. Cinematography by Alfred Ortlieb and Charles Rosher. Art direction by Floyd Mueller.
Cast: Spottiswoode Aitken (Bernard Huddlestone), Janice Wilson (Clara Huddlestone), Harry Northrup (Northmour), Jack Gilbert (Frank Cassilis), Wesley Barry (Ferd), Jack McDonald (Gregorio).

The Great Redeemer (1920)

Maurice Tourneur Productions (distributed by Metro Pictures Corporation). Directed by Clarence Brown and Maurice Tourneur (assistant director, Charles Dorian). Produced by Maurice Tourneur. Cinematography by Charles Van Enger. Art direction by Floyd Mueller.
Cast: House Peters (Dan Malloy), Marjorie Daw (the girl), Jack McDonald (the sheriff), Joseph Singleton (the murderer). With John Gilbert.

Deep Waters (1920)

Maurice Tourneur Productions (distributed by Paramount Pictures). Directed by Maurice Tourneur. Scenario by Jack Gilbert, from the novel *Caleb West, Master Diver* by F. Hopkinson Smith and the play *Caleb West* by Michael Morton. Produced by Maurice Tourneur. Cinematography by Alfred Ortlieb and Homer Scott. Art direction by Floyd Mueller.
Cast: Broerken Christians (Caleb West), Barbara Bedford (Betty West), Jack Gilbert (Bill Lacey), Florence Deshon (Kate Leroy), Jack McDonald (Morgan Leroy), Henry Woodward (Henry Sanford), George Nichols (Captain Joe Bell), Lydia Yeamans Titus (Aunty Bell), Marie Van Tassell (Barzella Busteed), James Gibson (Squealer Vixley), Ruth Wing (Zuby Higgins), B. Edgar Stockwell (Seth Wingate), Charles Millsfield (Professor Page), Siggrid McDonald (Page's niece).

While Paris Sleeps (made ca. 1920, released 1923)

Maurice Tourneur Productions (distributed by W. W. Hodkinson). Directed by Maurice Tourneur. Screenplay by Wyndham Gittens, from the story "The Glory of Love" by Leslie Beresford. Produced by Maurice Tourneur. Cinematography by René Guissart. Scenic effects by Floyd Mueller.
Cast: Lon Chaney (Henri Santodos), Mildred Manning (Bebe Larvache), John Gilbert (Dennis O'Keefe), Hardee Kirkland (Dennis's father), Jack McDonald (Father Marionette), J. Farrell MacDonald (George Morier).

The Servant in the House (1921)

H. O. Davis (distributed by Federated Film Exchanges of America). Directed by Jack Conway. Screenplay by Lanier Bartlett, from the play by Charles Rann Kennedy. Cinematography by Elgin Lessley.
Cast: Jean Hersholt (Manson, the servant in the house), Jack Curtis (Robert Smith, the drain man), Edward Peil Sr. (William Smythe, the vicar), Harvey Clark (the bishop of Lancashire), Clara Horton (Mary, the drain man's daughter), Zenaide Williams (Martha, the vicar's wife), Claire Anderson (Mary Smith, the drain man's wife), Jack Gilbert (Percival), Anna Dodge (janitress).

Ladies Must Live (1921)

Mayflower Photoplay Company (distributed by Paramount/Famous Players–Lasky Corporation). Directed by George Loane Tucker. Screenplay by George Loane Tucker, from the novel by Alice Duer Miller.
Cast: Robert Ellis (Anthony Mulvain), Mahlon Hamilton (Ralph Lincourt), Betty Compson (Christine Bleeker), Leatrice Joy (Barbara), Hardee Kirkland (William Hollins), Gibson Gowland (Michael Le Prim), Jack Gilbert (the gardener), Cleo Madison (Mrs. Lincourt), Snitz Edwards (Edward Barron), Lucille Hutton (Nell Martin), Lule Warrenton (Nora Flanagan), William V. Mong (Max Bleeker), Jack McDonald (the butler), Marcia Manon (Nancy), Arnold Gray (Ned Klegg). With Dorothy Cumming, Richard Arlen.

The Fox Film Corporation Years (1921–1924)

Shame (1921)

Directed by Emmett J. Flynn. Screenplay by Emmett J. Flynn and Bernard McConville, from the story "Clung" by Max Brand. Produced by William Fox. Cinematography by Lucien N. Andriot.
Cast: John Gilbert (William Fielding/David Field), Michael D. Moore (David, at five), Frankie Lee (David, at ten), George Siegmann (Foo Chang), William V. Mong (Li Clung), George Nichols (Jonathan Fielding), Anna May Wong (Lotus Blossom), Rosemary Theby (the Weaver of Dreams), Doris Pawn (Winifred Wellington), David Kirby ("Once-Over" Jake).

Gleam O'Dawn (1922)

Directed by John Francis Dillon. Screenplay by Jules Furthman. Produced by William Fox. Cinematography by Don Short.
Cast: John Gilbert (Gleam O'Dawn), Barbara Bedford (Nini), Jim Farley (Caleb Thomas), John Gough (Gordon Thomas), Clarence Wilson (Pierre), Edwin B. Tilton (Silas Huntworth).

Arabian Love (1922)

Directed by Jerome Storm. Screenplay by Jules Furthman. Produced by William Fox. Cinematography by Joseph H. August.
Cast: John Gilbert (Norman Stone), Barbara Bedford (Nadine Fortier), Barbara La Marr (Themar), Herschel Mayall (the sheik), Bob Kortman (Ahmed Bey), William Orlamond (Dr. Lagorio), Adolphe Menjou (Captain Fortine).

The Yellow Stain (1922)

Directed by John Francis Dillon. Screenplay by Jules Furthman. Produced by William Fox. Cinematography by Don Short.
Cast: John Gilbert (Donald Keith), Claire Anderson (Thora Erickson), J. P. Lockney (Quartus Hembly), Mark Fenton (Olaf Erickson), Herschel Mayall (Dr. Brown), William Robert Daly (Daniel Kersten), Mace Robinson (Lyman Rochester), James McElhern (clerk), Frank Hemphill (Pete Borg), May Alexander (Mrs. Borg).

Honor First (1922)

Directed by Jerome Storm. Screenplay by Joseph F. Poland, from the novel *The Splendid Outcast* by George Gibbs. Produced by William Fox. Cinematography by Joseph H. August.
Cast: John Gilbert (Jacques Dubois/Honoré Dubois), Renée Adorée (Moira Serern), Hardee Kirkland (Barry Serern), Shannon Day (Piquette), Clarence Wilson (Tricot).

Monte Cristo (1922)

Directed by Emmett J. Flynn. Screenplay by Charles Fechter, Bernard McConville, and Sandro Salvini, from the novel *Le comte de Monte Cristo* by Alexandre Dumas. Produced by William Fox. Cinematography by Lucien N. Andriot.

Cast: John Gilbert (Edmond Dantes, Count of Monte Cristo), Estelle Taylor (Mercedes, Countess de Morcerf), Robert McKim (De Villefort, the king's attorney), William V. Mong (Caderousse, the innkeeper), Virginia Brown Faire (Haidee, an Arabian princess), George Siegmann (Luigi Vampa, ex-pirate), Spottiswoode Aitken (Abbé Faria), Ralph Cloninger (Fernand, Count de Morcert), Albert Prisco (Baron Danglars), Al W. Filson (Morrel, ship owner), Harry Lonsdale (Dantes, father of Edmond), Francis McDonald (Benedetto), Jack Cosgrave (governor of Chateau d'If), Maude George (Baroness Danglars), Renée Adorée (Eugénie Danglars, her daughter), George Campbell (Napoleon), Willard Koch (tailor at Cheateau d'If), Howard Kendall (surgeon). With Gaston Glass.

Calvert's Valley (1922)

Directed by John Francis Dillon. Produced by William Fox. Cinematography by Don Short.
Cast: Jack Gilbert (Page Emlyn), Sylvia Breamer (Hester Ryma), Philo McCullough (James Calvert/Eugene Calv), Herschel Mayall (Judge Rymal), Lule Warrenton (the widow Crowcroft).

The Love Gambler (1922)

Directed by Joseph Franz. Screenplay by Jules Furthman. Produced by William Fox. Cinematography by Joseph H. August.
Cast: John Gilbert (Dick Manners), Carmel Myers (Jean McClelland), Bruce Gordon (Joe McClelland), C. E. Anderson (Curt Evans), W. E. Lawrence (Tom Gould), James Gordon (Colonel Angus McClelland), Mrs. Cohen (Mrs. McClelland), Barbara Tennant (Kate), Edward Cecil (Cameo Colby), Doreen Turner (Ricardo).

A California Romance (1922)

Directed by Jerome Storm. Screenplay by Charles E. Banks and Jules Furthman. Produced by William Fox. Cinematography by Joseph H. August.
Cast: John Gilbert (Don Patricio Fernando), Estelle Taylor (Donna Dolores), George Siegmann (Don Juan Diego), Jack McDonald (Don Manuel Casca), C. E. Anderson (Steve).

Truxton King (1923)

Directed by Jerome Storm. Screenplay by Paul Schofield, from the novel *Truxton King: A Story of Graustark* by George Barr McCutcheon. Produced by William Fox. Cinematography by Joseph H. August.
Cast: John Gilbert (Truxton King), Ruth Clifford (Lorraine), Frank Leigh (Count Marlaux), Michael D. Moore (Prince Robin), Otis Harlan (Hobbs), Henry Miller Jr. (Count Carlos Von Enge), Richard Wayne (John Tullis), Willis Marks (William Spanz), Winifred Bryson (Olga Platanova), Mark Fenton (Baron Dangloss).

Madness of Youth (1923)

Directed by Jerome Storm. Screenplay by Joseph F. Poland, from the story "Red Darkness" by George F. Worts. Produced by William Fox. Cinematography by Joseph H. August.
Cast: John Gilbert (Jaca Javalie), Billie Dove (Nanette Banning), D.R.O. Hatswell (Peter Reynolds), George K. Arthur (Ted Banning), Wilton Taylor (Theodore P. Banning), Ruth Boyd (Madame Jeanne Banning), Luke Lucas (Mason), Julanne Johnston (dancer).

St. Elmo (1923)

Directed by Jerome Storm. Screenplay by Jules Furthman, from the novel by Augusta Jane Evans Wilson. Produced by William Fox. Cinematography by Joseph H. August.
Cast: John Gilbert (St. Elmo Thornton), Barbara La Marr (Agnes Hunt), Bessie Love (Edna Earle), Warner Baxter (Murray Hammond), Nigel De Brulier (Rev. Alan Hammond), Lydia Knott (Mrs. Thornton).

Cameo Kirby (1923)

Directed by John Ford. Screenplay by Robert N. Lee, from the play by Booth Tarkington and Harry Leon Wilson. Produced by William Fox. Cinematography by George Schneiderman.
Cast: John Gilbert (John "Cameo" Kirby), Gertrude Olmstead (Adele Randall), Alan Hale (Colonel Moreau), Eric Mayne (Colonel Randall), W. E. Lawrence (Tom Randall), Richard Tucker (cousin Aaron Randall), Phillips Smalley (Judge Playdell), Jack McDonald (Larkin Bunce), Jean Arthur (Ann Playdell), Eugenie Forde (Madame Davezac). With Frank Baker, Ken Maynard, Ynez Seabury.

The Exiles (1923)

Directed by Edmund Mortimer. Screenplay by Frederick J. Jackson, from a story by Richard Harding Davis. Produced by William Fox.
Cast: John Gilbert (Henry Holcombe), Betty Bouton (Alice Carroll), John Webb Dillon (Wilhelm von Linke), Margaret Fielding (Rose Ainsmith), Fred Warren (Dr. Randolph).

Just Off Broadway (1924)

Directed by Edmund Mortimer. Screenplay by Fanny Hatton, Frederic Hatton, and Jack Wagner. Produced by William Fox. Cinematography by G. O. Post.
Cast: John Gilbert (Stephen Moore), Marian Nixon (Jean Lawrence), Trilby Clark (Nan Norton), Pierre Gendron (Florelle), Ben Hendricks Jr. (Comfort).

The Wolf Man (1924)

Directed by Edmund Mortimer. Screenplay by Fanny Hatton, Frederic Hatton, and Reed Heustis. Produced by William Fox. Cinematography by Michael Farley and Don Short.
Cast: John Gilbert (Gerald Stanley), Norma Shearer (Elizabeth Gordon), Alma Francis (Beatrice Joyce), George Barraud (Lord Rothstein), Eugene Pallette (Pierre), Edgar Norton (Sir Reginald Stackpoole), Thomas R. Mills (Caulkins), Max Montisole (Phil Joyce), Charles Wellesley (Sam Gordon), Richard Blaydon (Lieutenant Esmond), Richard Blaydon (Lieutenant Esmond), Mary Warren (English barmaid), Ebba Mona (ballet girl).

A Man's Mate (1924)

Directed by Edmund Mortimer. Screenplay by Charles Kenyon. Produced by William Fox. Cinematography by G. O. Post.
Cast: John Gilbert (Paul), Renée Adorée (Wildcat), Noble Johnson (Lion), Wilfrid North (Monsieur Bonard), Thomas R. Mills (Father Pierre), James Neill (Veraign), Jack Giddings (Lynx), Patterson Dial (Sybil), Dorothy Seay (child).

The Lone Chance (1924)

Directed by Howard M. Mitchell. Screenplay by Frederick J. Jackson and Charles Kenyon. Produced by William Fox. Cinematography by Bert Baldridge.

Cast: John Gilbert (Jack Saunders), Evelyn Brent (Margaret West), John Miljan (Lew Brody), Edwin B. Tilton (governor), Harry Todd (Burke), Frank Beal (warden).

Romance Ranch (1924)

Directed by Howard M. Mitchell. Screenplay by Jessie Maude Wybro and Dorothy Yost. Produced by William Fox. Cinematography by Bert Baldridge.

Cast: John Gilbert (Carlos Bren), Virginia Brown Faire (Carmen Hendley), John Miljan (Clifton Venable), Bernard Siegel (Felipe Varillo), Evelyn Selbie (Tessa).

The Metro-Goldwyn-Mayer Silent Years (1924–1929)

His Hour (1924)

Directed by King Vidor (assistant director, David Howard). Screenplay by Maude Fulton, Elinor Glyn, and King Vidor, from the novel by Elinor Glyn. Produced by Irving Thalberg and Louis B. Mayer. Cinematography by John J. Mescall. Art direction by Cedric Gibbons. Costume design by Sophie Wachner. Technical advisor, Mike Mitchell.

Cast: Aileen Pringle (Tamara Loraine), John Gilbert (Prince Gritzko), Emily Fitzroy (Princess Ardacheff), Lawrence Grant (Stephen Strong), Dale Fuller (Olga Gleboff), Mario Carillo (Count Valonne), Jacqueline Gadsden (Tatiane Shebanoff), George Waggner (Sasha Basmanoff), Carrie Clark Ward (Princess Murieska), Bertram Grassby (Boris Varishkine), Jill Reties (Sonia Zaieskine), Wilfred Gough (Lord Courtney), Frederick Vroom (English minister), Mathilde Comont (fat harem lady), E. Eliazaroff (Khedive), David Mir (Serge Greskoff), Bert Sprotte (Ivan). With George Beranger, Mike Mitchell, Jack Parker, Thais Valdemar.

He Who Gets Slapped (1924)

Directed by Victor Sjöström. Screenplay by Victor Sjöström and Carey Wilson, from the play by Leonid Andreyev, translated by Gregory Zillboorg. Produced by Irving Thalberg and Victor Sjöström. Cinematography by Milton Moore. Edited by Hugh Wynn. Sets by Cedric Gibbons. Costume design by Sophie Wachner.

Cast: Lon Chaney (Paul Beaumont), Norma Shearer (Consuelo), John Gilbert (Bezano), Ruth King (Maria Beaumont), Marc McDermott (Baron Regnard), Ford Sterling (Tricaud), Tully Marshall (Count Mancini), Erik Stocklassa (ringmaster), Paulette Duval (Zinida), Harvey Clark (Briquet), Bartine Burkett (bareback rider), Clyde Cook, George Davis, Brandon Hurst (clowns). With Edward Arnold, Holly Bane, Carrie Daumery.

The Snob (1924)

Directed by Monta Bell. Screenplay by Monta Bell, from a novel by Helen Reimensnyder Martin. Cinematography by André Barlatier. Edited by Ralph Lawson. Sets by Cedric Gibbons. Costume design by Sophie Wachner.

Cast: John Gilbert (Eugene Curry), Norma Shearer (Nancy Claxton), Conrad Nagel (Herrick Appleton), Phyllis Haver (Dorothy Rensheimer), Hedda Hopper (Mrs. Leiter), Margaret Seddon (Mrs. Curry), Aileen Manning (Lottie), Hazel Kennedy (Florence), Gordon Sackville (Sherwood Claxton), Roy Laidlaw (doctor), Nellie Bly Baker (maid).

The Wife of the Centaur (1924)

Directed by King Vidor (assistant director, David Howard). Screenplay by Douglas Z. Doty, from a novel by Cyril Hume. Cinematography by John Arnold. Edited by Hugh Wynn. Art direction by Cedric Gibbons. Costume design by Sophie Wachner.

Cast: Eleanor Boardman (Joan Converse), John Gilbert (Jeffrey Dwyer), Aileen Pringle (Inez Martin), Kate Lester (Mrs. Converse), William Haines (Edward Converse), Kate Price (Mattie), Jacqueline Gadsden (Hope Larrimore), Bruce Covington (Mr. Larrimore), Philo McCullough (Harry Todd), Lincoln Stedman (Chuck), William Orlamond (Uncle Roger). With Betty Francisco.

The Merry Widow (1925)

Directed by Erich von Stroheim (assistant directors, Louis Germonprez and Edward Sowders). Screenplay by Erich von Stroheim and Benjamin

Glazer, from the play by Viktor Léon and Leo Stein, and the operetta by Franz Lehár. Titles by Marian Ainslee. Produced by Irving Thalberg. Cinematography by Oliver T. Marsh, William H. Daniels, Ray Rennahan, Ben F. Reynolds, and Cliff Shirpser. Edited by Frank E. Hull and Margaret Booth. Sets by Richard Day and Cedric Gibbons. Costume design by Richard Day. Choreography by Ernest Belcher.

Cast: Mae Murray (Sally O'Hara), John Gilbert (Prince Danilo), Roy D'Arcy (Crown Prince Mirko), Josephine Crowell (Queen Milena), George Fawcett (King Nikita), Tully Marshall (Baron Sadoja), Edward Connelly (ambassador), Gertrude Bennett (Hard-Boiled Virginia), Sidney Bracey (Danilo's footman), Estelle Clark (French barber), Albert Conti (Danilo's adjutant), D'Arcy Corrigan (Horatio), Xavier Cugat (orchestra leader), Anielka Elter (blindfolded musician), Dale Fuller (Sadoja's chambermaid), Jacqueline Gadsden (Madonna), Harvey Karels (Jimmy Watson), Hughie Mack (innkeeper), Ida Moore (innkeeper's wife), Lucille Van Lent (innkeeper's daughter), Charles Margolis (Flo Epstein), George Nichols (doorkeeper), Lon Poff (Sadoja's lackey), Eugene Pouyet (Francois), Frances Primm, Clara Wallacks (Hansen sisters), Don Ryan (Mirko's adjutant), Rolfe Sedan (waiter at Maxim's), Carolynne Snowden (black dancer), Merewyn Thayer (Baroness Popoff), Edna Tichenor (Dopey Marie), Wilhelm von Brincken (Danilo's aide-de-camp), Zack Williams (George Washington White), Zalla Zarana (Frenchie Christine), Beatrice O'Brien, Anna Maynard, Louise Hughes, Helen Howard Beaumont (chorus girls). With Ellinor Vanderveer, Clark Gable, Irene Lentz, Walter Plunkett, Bernard Berger, Oscar Rudolph.

The Big Parade (1925)

Directed by King Vidor and George W. Hill (assistant director, David Howard). Screenplay by Harry Behn and Laurence Stallings, from the story "Plumes" by Laurence Stallings. Titles by Joseph Farnham. Produced by Irving Thalberg. Cinematography by John Arnold and Charles Van Enger. Edited by Hugh Wynn. Sets by James Basevi, Robert Florey, and Cedric Gibbons. Visual effects by Max Fabian. Costume design by Ethel P. Chaffin and Robert Florey. Casting by Robert McIntyre. Unit production manager, Dave Friedman. Electrician, Carl Barlow. Military advisor, Carl Voss.

Cast: John Gilbert (James Apperson), Renée Adorée (Melisande), Hobart

Bosworth (Mr. Apperson), Claire McDowell (Mrs. Apperson), Claire Adams (Justyn Reed), Robert Ober (Harry Apperson), Tom O'Brien (Bull), Karl Dane (Slim), Rosita Marstini (Melisande's mother), Julanne Johnston (Justine Devereux), Kathleen Key (Miss Apperson), Carl Voss (officer). With George Beranger, Harry Crocker, Dan Mason, Carl "Major" Roup.

Flesh and the Devil (1926)

Directed by Clarence Brown (assistant director, Charles Dorian). Screenplay by Benjamin Glazer, Hanns Kräly, and Frederica Sagor, from the novel *The Undying Past* by Hermann Sudermann. Titles by Marian Ainslee. Produced by Irving Thalberg. Cinematography by William H. Daniels. Edited by Lloyd Nosler. Sets by Cedric Gibbons and Fredric Hope. Costume design by André-ani.
Cast: John Gilbert (Leo von Harden), Greta Garbo (Felicitas von Rhaden), Lars Hanson (Ulrich von Eltz), Barbara Kent (Hertha), William Orlamond (Uncle Kutowski), George Fawcett (Pastor Voss), Eugenie Besserer (Leo's mother), Marc McDermott (Count von Rhaden), Marcelle Corday (Minna), Philippe De Lacy (Leo as a boy), Virginia Marshall (Hertha as a girl), Maurice Murphy (Ulrich as a boy), Polly Moran (family retainer with bouquet), Russ Powell (family retainer with flag), Glen Walters (family retainer), Carl "Major" Roup (train station vendor), Rolfe Sedan (women's hat salesman), Max Barwyn, Frankie Darro, Cecilia Parker, Linda Parker, Ellinor Vanderveer (guests at ball).

La Bohème (1926)

Directed by King Vidor. Screenplay by Fred De Gresac, Ray Doyle, and Harry Behn, from the novel *Scènes de la vie de Bohème* by Henri Murger. Titles by Ruth Cummings and William M. Conselman. Produced by Irving Thalberg (production assistant, Robert Florey). Cinematography by Hendrik Sartov. Edited by Hugh Wynn. Costume design by Erté.
Cast: Lillian Gish (Mimi), John Gilbert (Rodolphe), Renée Adorée (Musette), George Hassell (Schaunard), Roy D'Arcy (Vicomte Paul), Edward Everett Horton (Colline), Karl Dane (Benoit), Mathilde Comont (Madame Benoit), Gino Corrado (Marcel), Eugene Pouyet (Bernard), Frank Currier (theater manager), David Mir (Alexis), Catherine Vidor (Louise), Valentina Zimina (Phemie), Agostino Borgato (editor), Blanche Payson (factory supervisor). With Harry Crocker.

Bardelys the Magnificent (1926)

Directed by King Vidor. Screenplay by Dorothy Farnum, from the novel by Rafael Sabatini. Cinematography by William H. Daniels. Sets by James Basevi, Richard Day, and Cedric Gibbons. Costume design by André-ani and Lucia Coulter.

Cast: John Gilbert (Bardelys), Eleanor Boardman (Roxalanne de Lavedan), Roy D'Arcy (Chatellerault), Lionel Belmore (vicomte de Lavedan), Emily Fitzroy (vicomtesse de Lavedan), George K. Arthur (St. Eustache), Arthur Lubin (King Louis XIII), Theodore von Eltz (Lesperon), Karl Dane (Rodenard), Edward Connelly (Cardinal Richelieu), Fred Malatesta (Castelrous), John T. Murray (Lafosse), Joe Smith Marba (innkeeper), Daniel G. Tomlinson (sergeant of dragoons), Emile Chautard (Anatol), Max Barwyn (Cozelatt), Gino Corrado (dueling husband), Lon Poff (prison friar), Rolfe Sedan (fop), Carl Stockdale (judge of the Tribunal).

The Show (1927)

Directed by Tod Browning. Screenplay by Waldemar Young, from the novel *The Day of Souls* by Charles Tenney Jackson. Produced by Tod Browning. Titles by Joseph Farnham. Cinematography by John Arnold. Edited by Errol Taggart. Sets by Richard Day and Cedric Gibbons. Costume design by Lucia Coulter.

Cast: John Gilbert (Cock Robin), Renée Adorée (Salome), Lionel Barrymore (the Greek), Edward Connelly (the soldier), Gertrude Short (Lena), Russ Powell (Konrad Driskai), Andy MacLennan (the Ferret), Agostino Borgato (snake-oil salesman), Betty Boyd (Neptuna), Edna Tichenor (Arachnida), Zalla Zarana (Zela, the Half-Lady), Jules Cowles (Robin's dressing aide), Jacqueline Gadsden (blonde barmaid), Polly Moran, Bobby Mack (sideshow spectators), Dorothy Sebastian (Salvation Army worker). With Barbara Bozoky, Cecil Holland, Ida May, Francis Powers, Billy Seay, Dorothy Seay, Kit Wain.

Twelve Miles Out (1927)

Directed by Jack Conway. Screenplay by A. P. Younger, from the play by William Anthony McGuire. Titles by Joseph Farnham. Produced by Irving Thalberg. Cinematography by Ira H. Morgan. Edited by Basil Wrangell. Sets by Cedric Gibbons and Eugene Hornboestel. Costume design by René Hubert.

Cast: John Gilbert (Jerry Fay), Ernest Torrence (Red McCue), Joan Crawford (Jane), Edward Earle (John Burton), Eileen Percy (Maizie), Paulette Duval (Trini), Dorothy Sebastian (Chiquita), Gwen Lee (Hulda), Bert Roach (Luke), Tom O'Brien (Irish). With Frederick Peters.

Man, Woman and Sin (1927)

Directed by Monta Bell (assistant director, Nick Grinde). Screenplay by Monta Bell and Alice D. G. Miller. Titles by John Colton. Cinematography by Percy Hilburn. Edited by Blanche Sewell. Art direction by Cedric Gibbons and Merrill Pye. Costume design by Gilbert Clark.
Cast: John Gilbert (Albert Whitcomb), Jeanne Eagels (Vera Worth), Gladys Brockwell (Mrs. Whitcomb), Marc McDermott (Bancroft), Philip Anderson (Al Whitcomb as a child), Hayden Stevenson (reporter), Charles K. French (city editor), Nanci Price (child). With Aileen Manning, Margaret Lee, Robert Livingston, Robert Cain.

Love (1927)

Directed by Edmund Goulding. Screenplay by Frances Marion and Lorna Moon, from the novel *Anna Karenina* by Leo Tolstoy. Titles by Marian Ainslee and Ruth Cummings. Produced by Edmund Goulding. Cinematography by William H. Daniels. Edited by Hugh Wynn. Sets by Cedric Gibbons and Alexander Toluboff. Costume design by Gilbert Clark.
Cast: John Gilbert (Vronsky), Greta Garbo (Anna Karenina), Brandon Hurst (Karenin), Philippe De Lacy (Serezha), George Fawcett (grand duke), Emily Fitzroy (grand duchess), Mathilde Comont (Marfa), Edward Connelly (priest), Carrie Daumery (dowager), Nicholai Konovaloff (cavalryman), Margaret Lee (blonde flirt). With Dorothy Sebastian, Jacques Tourneur.

The Cossacks (1928)

Directed by George W. Hill and Clarence Brown. Screenplay by Frances Marion, from the novel by Leo Tolstoy. Titles by John Colton. Cinematography by Percy Hilburn. Edited by Blanche Sewell. Art direction by Cedric Gibbons. Sets by Alexander Toluboff. Costume design by David Cox. Technical advisor, Theodore Lodi.
Cast: John Gilbert (Lukashka), Renée Adorée (Maryana), Ernest Tor-

rence (Ivan), Nils Asther (Prince Olenin Stieshneff), Paul Hurst (Sitchi), Dale Fuller (Maryana's mother), Mary Alden (Lukashka's mother), Josephine Borio (Stepka), Yorke Sherwood (Uncle Eroshka), Joseph Mari (Turkish spy), Sidney Bracey (Prince Olenin's orderly). With Neil Neely, Russ Powell.

Four Walls (1928)

Directed by William Nigh. Screenplay by Alice D. G. Miller, from the play by George Abbott and Dana Burnet. Titles by Joseph Farnham. Cinematography by James Wong Howe. Edited by Harry Reynolds. Costume design by David Cox.
Cast: John Gilbert (Benny), Joan Crawford (Frieda), Vera Gordon (Benny's mother), Carmel Myers (Bertha), Robert Emmett O'Connor (Sullivan), Louis Natheaux (Monk), Jack Byron (Duke Roma).

The Masks of the Devil (1928)

Directed by Victor Sjöström (assistant director, Harold S. Bucquet). Screenplay by Frances Marion and Svend Gade, from the novel *Die Masken Erwin Reiners* by Jakob Wassermann. Titles by Marian Ainslee and Ruth Cummings. Cinematography by Oliver T. Marsh. Edited by Conrad A. Nervig. Art direction by Cedric Gibbons. Costume design by Adrian.
Cast: John Gilbert (Baron Reiner), Alma Rubens (Countess Zellner), Theodore Roberts (Count Palester), Frank Reicher (Count Zellner), Eva von Berne (Virginia), Ralph Forbes (Manfred), Ethel Wales (Virginia's aunt), Polly Ann Young (dancer).

A Woman of Affairs (1928)

Directed by Clarence Brown (assistant director, Charles Dorian). Screenplay by Bess Meredyth, from the novel *The Green Hat* by Michael Arlen. Titles by Marian Ainslee and Ruth Cummings. Cinematography by William H. Daniels. Edited by Hugh Wynn. Art direction by Cedric Gibbons. Costume design by Adrian. Miss Garbo's stand-in, Geraldine Dvorak.
Cast: Greta Garbo (Diana Merrick Furness), John Gilbert (Neville Holderness), Lewis Stone (Dr. Hugh Trevelyan), Johnny Mack Brown (David Furness), Douglas Fairbanks Jr. (Jeffry Merrick), Hobart Bos-

worth (Sir Morton Holderness), Dorothy Sebastian (Constance), Anita Louise (Diana as a child), Agostino Borgato (French police inspector), Alphonse Martell (French hotel concierge), Frank Finch Smiles (butler). With Gertrude Astor, William H. O'Brien.

Desert Nights (1929)

Directed by William Nigh. Screenplay by Endre Bohem, Lenore J. Coffee, Willis Goldbeck, John T. Neville, and Dale Van Every. Titles by Marian Ainslee and Ruth Cummings. Produced by William Nigh. Cinematography by James Wong Howe. Music by William Axt. Edited by Harry Reynolds. Art direction by Cedric Gibbons. Costume design by Henrietta Frazer.
Cast: John Gilbert (Hugh Rand), Ernest Torrence (Lord Stonehill), Mary Nolan (Lady Diana Stonehill), Claude King (the real Lord Stonehill).

The Talkie Years (1929–1934)

His Glorious Night (1929)

Directed by Lionel Barrymore. Screenplay by Willard Mack, from the play *Olympia* by Ferenc Molnár. Produced by Irving Thalberg. Cinematography by Percy Hilburn. Original music by Lionel Barrymore. Edited by William LeVanway. Art direction by Cedric Gibbons. Costume design by David Cox. Sound engineer, Douglas Shearer.
Cast: John Gilbert (Captain Kovacs), Catherine Dale Owen (Princess Orsolini), Nance O'Neil (Eugenie), Gustav von Seyffertitz (Krehl), Hedda Hopper (Mrs. Collingswood Stratton), Doris Hill (Priscilla Stratton), Tyrell Davis (Prince Luigi Caprilli), Gerald Barry (Lord York), Madeline Seymour (Lady York), Richard Carle (Count Albert), Eva Dennison (Countess Lina), Youcca Troubetzkov (Von Bergman), Peter Gawthorne (General Ettingen).

The Hollywood Revue of 1929 (1929)

Directed by Charles Reisner (assistant directors, Lionel Barrymore, Jack Cummings, Sandy Roth, and Al Shenberg). Screenplay by Al Boasberg, Robert E. Hopkins, and Joseph Farnham. Produced by Joseph Farnham and Irving Thalberg. Cinematography by John Arnold, Max Fabian, Irving Reis, Irving G. Ries, and John M. Nickolaus. Original music

by Arthur Lange. Edited by William S. Gray and Cameron K. Wood. Art direction by Erté. Art department, Richard Day, Cedric Gibbons. Costume design by David Cox, Erté, Henrietta Frazer, and Joe Rapf. Choreography by George Cunningham, Sammy Lee, and Joyce Murray. Production manager, J. J. Cohn. Sound engineers, Douglas Shearer, William E. Clark, Russell Franks, Wesley C. Miller, and A. T. Taylor.
Cast: Conrad Nagel, Jack Benny, John Gilbert, Norma Shearer, Lionel Barrymore, Joan Crawford, Marion Davies, William Haines, Buster Keaton, Bessie Love, Marie Dressler, Polly Moran, Cliff Edwards, Stan Laurel, Oliver Hardy, Anita Page, Charles King, Nils Asther, Gus Edwards, Karl Dane, George K. Arthur, Gwen Lee, Renée Adorée, the Brox Sisters, Natova and Company, the Albertina Rasch Ballet, the Rounders, Nacio Herb Brown, Ray Cooke, Ann Dvorak, Ernest Belcher's Dancing Tots, the Biltmore Quartet, Nora Gregor, Carla Laemmle, Angella Mawby, Claudette Mawby, Claudia Mawby, Myrtle McLaughlin, Natova and Company, June Purcell.

Redemption (1930)

Directed by Fred Niblo and Lionel Barrymore. Screenplay by Edwin Justus Mayer, from the novel *The Living Corpse* by Leo Tolstoy and the play *Redemption* by Dorothy Farnum and Arthur Hopkins. Produced by Arthur Hopkins and Irving Thalberg. Cinematography by Percy Hilburn. Original music by William Axt. Edited by Margaret Booth. Art direction by Cedric Gibbons. Costume design by Adrian. Sound engineer, Douglas Shearer.
Cast: John Gilbert (Fedya Protasoff), Renée Adorée (Masha), Conrad Nagel (Victor Karenin), Eleanor Boardman (Lisa Protasoff), Claire McDowell (Anna Pavlovna), Nigel De Brulier (Petushkov), Tully Marshall (Artimiev), Mack Swain (magistrate), Erville Alderson (bearded mariner in café), George Spelvin (magistrate), Sidney Bracey (waiter), Richard Alexander (policeman), Charles Quatermaine (Artimiev), Agostino Borgato (Petushkov), Geraldine Dvorak (Anna Pavlovna's maid), Lena Malena (gypsy), Kit Wain (boy). With Stanley Blystone.

Way for a Sailor (1930)

Directed by Sam Wood. Screenplay by Laurence Stallings, W. L. River, Charles MacArthur, and Al Boasberg. Produced by Sam Wood and

Irving Thalberg. Cinematography by Percy Hilburn. Edited by Frank Sullivan. Art direction by Cedric Gibbons. Costume design by Vivian Baer. Sound engineers, Douglas Shearer and Robert Shirley.
Cast: John Gilbert (Jack), Wallace Beery (Tripod McMasters), Jim Tully (Ginger), Leila Hyams (Joan), Polly Moran (Polly), Doris Lloyd (Flossy), Alice Belcher (London wharf floozie), Daisy Belmore (*Canadian Queen* passenger), Herbert Evans (ship's officer), John George (dwarf), Tiny Jones (pub customer), Lena Malena, Toshia Mori (Singapore party girls), Ray Milland (ship's officer), Desmond Roberts (*Canadian Queen* captain), Sôjin (Singapore brothel proprietor), Robert Adair, Pat Moriarity, Leo White, Harry Wilson (sailors).

Gentleman's Fate (1931)

Directed by Mervyn LeRoy. Screenplay by Ursula Parrott and Leonard Praskins. Cinematography by Merritt B. Gerstad. Music by Domenico Savino. Edited by William S. Gray. Art direction by Cedric Gibbons. Costume design by René Hubert. Jewelry by Eugene Joseff. Sound engineer, Douglas Shearer.
Cast: John Gilbert (Giacomo Tomasulo/Jack Thomas), Louis Wolheim (Frank Tomasulo), Leila Hyams (Marjorie Channing), Anita Page (Ruth Corrigan), Marie Prevost (Mabel), John Miljan (Florio), George Cooper (Mike), Ferike Boros (Angela), Ralph Ince (Dante), Frank Reicher (Papa Francesco Tomasulo), Paul Porcasi (Papa Mario Giovanni), Tenen Holtz (Tony), Leila Bennett (lunch counter attendant), Edward LeSaint (Detective Meyers).

The Phantom of Paris (1931)

Directed by John S. Robertson (assistant director, Errol Taggart). Screenplay by Bess Meredyth, Edwin Justus Mayer, and John Meehan, from the novel *Chéri-Bibi* by Gaston Leroux. Cinematography by Oliver T. Marsh. Edited by Jack Ogilvie. Art direction by Cedric Gibbons. Costume design by René Hubert. Jewelry by Eugene Joseff. Sound engineer, Douglas Shearer.
Cast: John Gilbert (Chéri-Bibi), Leila Hyams (Cecile), Lewis Stone (Costaud), Jean Hersholt (Herman), C. Aubrey Smith (Bourrelier), Natalie Moorhead (Vera), Ian Keith (marquis Du Touchais), Alfred Hickman (Dr. Gorin), Sidney Bracey (volunteer from audience), Tyrell Davis

(annoying party guest), Lloyd Ingraham (prison warden), Claude King (attorney), Louise Mackintosh (Madame Frontenac), Fletcher Norton (Raoul), William H. O'Brien (Chéri-Bibi's valet), Rose Plumer (nurse), Angelo Rossitto (prisoner), Douglas Scott (Jacques), Philip Sleeman (prisoner), Ellinor Vanderveer (party guest).

West of Broadway (1931)

Directed by Harry Beaumont (assistant director, Sandy Roth). Screenplay by Ralph Graves, Bess Meredyth, Gene Markey, and James Kevin McGuinness. Cinematography by Merritt B. Gerstad. Edited by George Hively. Art direction by Cedric Gibbons. Costume design by Vivian Baer. Sound engineer, Douglas Shearer.
Cast: John Gilbert (Jerry Seevers), El Brendel (Axel Axelson), Lois Moran (Dot), Madge Evans (Anne), Ralph Bellamy (Mac, the ranch foreman), Frank Conroy (Judge Barham), Gwen Lee (Maizie), Hedda Hopper (Mrs. Edith Trent), Ruth Renick (Barbara Main), Willie Fung (Wing, the cook), William Bailey (Herbert, the maître d'), Jack Baxley (policeman in court), Everett Brown (Joe Williams), Richard Carlyle (butler), Bill Elliott (nightclub patron), Sherry Hall (court clerk), William Le Maire (Tex), Margaret Mann (justice of peace's wife), John Miljan (Norm), William H. O'Brien (waiter), Dennis O'Keefe (nightclub patron), Jack Raymond (soldier on ship), Kane Richmond (Reggie), Larry Steers (army officer on ship), Charles Sullivan (cab driver), Theodore von Eltz (Tony), Tom London, Kermit Maynard, Bob Reeves, Buddy Roosevelt (cowboys).

Downstairs (1932)

Directed by Monta Bell (assistant director, Harry Sharrock). Screenplay by Lenore J. Coffee, Melville Baker, and John Gilbert. Produced by Monta Bell. Cinematography by Harold Rosson. Edited by Conrad A. Nervig. Art direction by Cedric Gibbons. Sound engineer, Douglas Shearer.
Cast: John Gilbert (Karl Schneider), Paul Lukas (Albert), Virginia Bruce (Anna), Hedda Hopper (Countess De Marnac), Reginald Owen (Baron "Nicky" von Burgen), Olga Baclanova (Baroness Eloise von Burgen), Bodil Rosing (Sophie), Otto Hoffman (Otto), Lucien Littlefield (Françoise), Marion Lessing (Antoinette), Torben Meyer (café waiter), Karen

Morley (Karl's new employer), Russ Powell (café proprietor), Nicholas Soussanin (wedding guest), Ellinor Vanderveer (party guest), Michael Visaroff (servant).

Fast Workers (1933)

Directed by Tod Browning (assistant director, Errol Taggart). Screenplay by Laurence Stallings, Ralph Wheelwright, and Karl Brown, from the play *Rivets* by John McDermott. Produced by Tod Browning. Cinematography by J. Peverell Marley. Music by William Axt and David Broekman. Edited by Ben Lewis. Art direction by Cedric Gibbons. Recording director, Douglas Shearer. Sound mixer, Fred Morgan.
Cast: John Gilbert (Gunner Smith), Robert Armstrong (Bucker Reilly), Mae Clarke (Mary), Muriel Kirkland (Millie), Vince Barnett (Spike), Virginia Cherrill (Virginia), Muriel Evans (nurse), Sterling Holloway (Pinky Magoo), Guy Usher (Scudder), Warner Richmond (Feets Wilson), Bob Burns (Alabam'), Reginald Barlow (judge), Herman Bing (Schultz), Stanley Blystone (policeman in alley), Nora Cecil, Florence Roberts (matronly window shoppers), Irene Franklin (Lily White), Otto Hoffman (peddler), Hans Joby (waiter at Schultz's), Charles R. Moore (liar fined in court), Ben Taggart (Millie's dance partner), Fred "Snowflake" Toones (Mike). With Frank Austin, Pat Moriarity.

Queen Christina (1933)

Directed by Rouben Mamoulian (assistant director, Charles Dorian). Screenplay by H. M. Harwood, Salka Viertel, S. N. Behrman, and Ben Hecht, from a story by Salka Viertel and Margaret P. Levino. Produced by Walter Wanger. Cinematography by William H. Daniels. Original music by Herbert Stothart. Orchestration by Maurice De Packh and Herbert Stothart. Edited by Blanche Sewell. Production design by Edgar G. Ulmer. Art direction by Alexander Toluboff. Sets by Edwin B. Willis. Costume design by Adrian. Jewelry by Eugene Joseff. Sound engineers, Douglas Shearer and Art Wilson. Stunts by Harry Froboess, Audrey Scott, and Fred Cavens.
Cast: Greta Garbo (Christina), John Gilbert (Antonio), Ian Keith (Magnus), Lewis Stone (Oxenstierna), Elizabeth Young (Ebba), C. Aubrey Smith (Aage), Reginald Owen (Charles), Georges Renavent (French ambassador), David Torrence (archbishop), Gustav von Seyffertitz (general),

Ferdinand Munier (innkeeper), Bodil Rosing (innkeeper's wife), Hooper Atchley (Antonio's companion in coach), Barbara Barondess (Elsa), James Burke (blacksmith), Cora Sue Collins (Christina as a child), Muriel Evans (barmaid at inn), Edward Gargan (drinker betting on "nine"), Paul Hurst (drinker betting on "six"), Edward Norris (Count Jacob), Tiny Sandford (cook at the inn), C. Montague Shaw (King Gustavus Adolphus), Akim Tamiroff (Pedro). With Richard Alexander, Carrie Daumery, Lawrence Grant, Sam Harris, Wade Boteler, Gladden James, Fred Kohler, Frank McGlynn Jr.

The Captain Hates the Sea (1934)

Columbia Pictures Corporation. Directed and produced by Lewis Milestone. Cinematography by Joseph H. August. Music by Louis Silvers. Edited by Gene Milford. Costume design by Robert Kalloch. Continuity, Arnold Belgard.

Cast: Victor McLaglen (Junius P. Schulte), Wynne Gibson (Mrs. Jeddock), Alison Skipworth (Mrs. Yolanda Magruder), John Gilbert (Steve Bramley), Helen Vinson (Janet Grayson), Fred Keating (Danny Checkett), Leon Errol (Layton), Walter Connolly (Captain Helquist), Tala Birell (Gerta Klangi), Walter Catlett (Joe Silvers), John Wray (Mr. Jeddock), Claude Gillingwater (Judge Griswold), Emily Fitzroy (Mrs. Victoria Griswold), Donald Meek (Josephus Bushmills), Luis Alberni (Juan Gilboa), Akim Tamiroff (General Salazaro), Arthur Treacher (Major Warringforth), Inez Courtney (Flo), Moe Howard, Curly Howard, Larry Fine (ship's orchestra), G. Pat Collins (Donlin), Tony Casten (Mong), B. B. Creary (quartermaster), George Villasenor (Andrecito), Fred Watt (deck steward), Abdullah Abbas (Felix), George Beranger (jeweler), Matthew Betz (Gus), James Blakeley (Pinky), Monte Carter (barber), Heinie Conklin (assistant bartender), Frank Conroy (state's attorney), A. R. Haysel (detective), Dell Henderson (Mr. Holman), Charles H. Hickman (pilot). With Doris Campbell, Jean Castle, Bluma Crockin, Lucille De Nevers, Ciel Duncan, Otto Gervice, LaGreta, Gladys Meyers, Marian Montgomery, Sharon O'Farrell, Betty Oreck, Frank Walsh, Fred J. Williams, Lowden Adams, Ernie Alexander, Robert Allen, Eddie Baker, Marion Bardell, Art Berry Sr., Ethel Bryant, Edmund Burns, James Carlisle, Robert Cauterio, Franco Corsaro, Sidney D'Albrook, Diane Dahl, Lew Davis, Joan Dix, Joe Dominguez, Harry Dunkinson, Jay

Eaton, Jim Farley, Budd Fine, Sammy Finn, J. C. Fowler, Jean Fowler, Gladys Gale, Fernando García, Harris Gordon, Margaret Gray, Roger Gray, Harrison Greene, Carlton Griffin, Harry Holman, Fred Howard, George Humbert, Gladden James, Charles King, Isabel La Mal, Mimi Lawler, Carl M. Leviness, J. L. Lindsey, Tom London, Leota Lorraine, Buddy Mason, Charles R. Moore, Bert Moorhouse, Clive Morgan, Miki Morita, Edmund Mortimer, Bea Nigro, Sam Rice Jr., Beatrice Roberts, Patricia Royale, Fred Santley, Elmer Serrano, Tamara Shayne, Pietro Sosso, Ray Spiker, Vera Steadman, Charles Sullivan, John Sylvester, Serge Temoff, Harry Tenbrook, Sammee Tong, Maude Truax, Ray Turner, Emmett Vogan, Max Wagner, Blackie Whiteford, Harry Wilson.

Notes

Introduction

3 "Both Mr. Gilbert and Catherine Dale Owen contribute competent performances" (*New York Times,* October 6, 1929).
3 "A few more talker productions like this" (*Variety,* October 9, 1929).
3 "John makes the grade with ease" (Fountain, *Dark Star,* 180).
3 "He'd told me about his trouble" (ibid., 178).
4 "like a slap in the face" (Gladys Hall Papers, Academy of Motion Picture Arts and Sciences, Beverly Hills).

Chapter One

7 "the great comedy success" (*Spirit Lake (Iowa) Beacon,* January 24, 1900).
8 "especially engaged for the role of Anne of Austria" (Clara H. Blaney, *The Albee Alumni: A History of the Eleven Years of the Edward F. Albee Stock Company* [Providence: EF Albee, 1912]).
8 "It has enjoyed a run of nearly two years" (*Theatre,* December 1906).
8 "wide experience and unusual talents" (*Billboard* clipping, 1907).
9 "greeted by an enthusiastic and appreciative audience" (*Seattle Republican,* 1906 clipping).
9 "Chicago, New York and other eastern cities" (*Salt Lake Tribune,* August 14, 1929).
9 "Human bones were strewn about" (Lewis, *Trouping,* 115).
9 "Actors, like soldiers, can bed down anywhere" (Gish, *The Movies,* 15).
10 "we were often very poor" (*Los Angeles Times,* January 16, 1927).
10 "Even in the one-night towns" (Lewis, *Trouping,* 7).
11 "could not *afford* to get sick (ibid., 116).
12 "Lovely Ida, as profligate as a Winter wind, as vivid as a sunset" (*Photoplay,* February 1930).
12 "Jack loved her" (*Photoplay,* February 1936).
12 "a good trouper . . . but she had a blind spot about that boy" (Fountain, *Dark Star,* 9).

12 "I was only seven but I knew more about the world than many people ever discover" (ibid., 10).
13 "The players were briefly the best-known people in town" (Lewis, *Trouping,* 117).
14 "His mother had not wanted him" (Brownlow, *Hollywood*).
14 "He hardly ever went to school" (ibid.).
16 "Ringing the curtain up and down" (*Photoplay,* June 1928).

Chapter Two

17 "Mr. Ince says he can give the boy fifteen dollars a week" (*Photoplay,* June 1928).
18 "It is not the great stars that can give advice" (*Motion Picture,* April 1917).
18 "Can't see you today, Miss Booth" (ibid.).
18 "In 1914, the American studios start batting out one terrific feature film after another" (Richard Kukan to author, October 12, 2011).
18 "An actor can now count on being visible" (ibid.).
20 "Ince demanded and received absolute obedience" (Lahue, *Dreams for Sale,* 45).
20 "most of it foothill country and beach" (*Los Angeles Times,* November 25, 1914).
20 "There have been some great changes" (ibid.).
20 "Go and get the scenario department" (*Los Angeles Times,* September 24, 1916).
22 "Men who had never been inside a studio were given directing assignments on pure bluff" (Vidor, *A Tree Is a Tree,* 70).
22 "Heavy tarpaulins were used to cover the sets" (ibid., 64).
22 "How do I get out there?" (*Photoplay,* June 1928).
22 "God knows how" (ibid.).
23 "and drank Coca-Cola" (*Photoplay,* July 1928).
23 "I opened my eyes and discovered that my shoes were burning briskly" (ibid.).
23 "that is, the actors who played parts" (ibid.).
24 "people in various costumes [running] about the place like ants" (ibid.).
25 "a step forward in the moving picture art" (*Variety,* October 8, 1915).
25 "Not only is the picture photographically excellent" (*New York Times,* October 4, 1915).
25 "a corking story of capital vs. labor" (*Variety,* December 11, 1915).
25 "There is a wallop, a punch, and a heap of suspense" (*Variety,* December 29, 1916).
25 "reopens a thoroughly thrashed-out subject for those who are interested" (*Variety,* October 29, 1915).
25 "a big dramatic western play of the Bill Hart type" (*Los Angeles Times,* August 12, 1917).
26 "dashing romantic love and action story" (*Variety,* February 25, 1916).

26 "It's safe to say every Film Fannie will take a peep at beautiful Bill Desmond" (*Los Angeles Times,* March 16, 1916).
27 "I shall never forget the thrill of having successfully played my first part in pictures" (*Photoplay,* August 1928).
27 "A photoplay thriller that will live long and prosper" (*Variety,* June 16, 1916).
27 "sulked through the Hawaiian picture" (*Photoplay,* July 1928).
27 "smacks strongly of Catholicism" (*Variety,* June 9, 1916).
27 "I have learned that there is a certain type of play" (Taves, *Thomas Ince,* 97).
28 "small and fresh and feminine" (*Photoplay,* July 1928).
28 "Agonized shrieks, rearing horses, dust, curses, shouts, bedlam, hell!" (ibid.).
30 "All the elements that go toward making a successful picture production" (*Variety,* June 23, 1916).
30 "the sort of 'sob stuff' that rings true" (*Variety,* July 7, 1916).
30 "One of the strongest stories of modern times yet screened" (*Variety,* December 1, 1916).
30 "sure to offend some of the people of the South" (*Variety,* December 29, 1916).
30 "I believe that our capacity" (Lahue, *Dreams for Sale,* 112).
30 "The general impression audiences will carry away after seeing the feature" (*Variety,* February 9, 1917).
32 "I had found my place at last!" (*Photoplay,* August 1928).
32 "exceedingly slow" (*Variety,* May 4, 1917).
33 "nothing thrilling about it in any manner" (*Variety,* July 27, 1917).
33 "are welcome at all times to come eat or drink" (*Variety,* June 22, 1917).
33 "was a very lonely kid" (Fountain, *Dark Star,* 29).
34 "It has been rumored out here that Triangle is about to disband" (Lahue, *Dreams for Sale,* 115).
35 "As businessmen and persons they were efficient and charming" (*Photoplay,* August 1928).
35 "John Gilbert adds the comedy touches" (*Variety,* September 6, 1918).
35 "thumbed my nose at their contract" (*Photoplay,* August 1928).

Chapter Three

37 "Goody-goodies like Harvey may exist" (*Variety,* May 31, 1918).
38 "but they would have none of my five feet eleven" (*Photoplay,* August 1928).
38 "was to pray and believe" (ibid.).
38 "bore no resemblance to my scenario" (*Photoplay,* September 1928).
40 "The parts of Cosgrove [Jack's rival] and Ashley are excellently taken by Charles West and John Gilbert" (*Variety,* October 18, 1918).
40 "a primitive sort who has two Chinese servants" (*Variety,* September 20, 1918).

40 "I came out from New Orleans" (*Los Angeles Times*, February 12, 1922).
40 "I actually went hungry" (ibid.).
40 "I almost stumbled over a figure huddled in a chair" (*Photoplay*, August 1928).
42 "He was more on the ball photographically" (Brownlow, *Parade's Gone By*, 140–41).
42 "my god. I owe him everything" (ibid., 153).
42 "The time has come when we can no longer merely photograph" (*Motion Picture*, September 1918).
42 "The star system of today is proving its fallacy" (*Motion Picture World*, April 13, 1918).
43 "The sublime but forbidden love" (undated newspaper clipping, Academy of Motion Picture Arts and Sciences, Beverly Hills).
43 "Jack Gilbert did a corking fall" (*Variety*, May 9, 1919).
43 "Day after day after day the rounds of the studios" (*Photoplay*, September 1928).
43 "That night I stared at a woman sitting opposite me in my apartment" (*Photoplay*, August 1928).
43 "She would not complain" (*Photoplay*, September 1928).
43 "I corresponded with Olivia" (ibid.).
44 "a Hindoo who has been educated in England" (*Variety*, June 27, 1919).
44 "When Jack Gilbert arrived, my mother was horrified" (Ankerich, *Sound of Silence*, 66)
44 "fit only for second grade houses" (*Variety*, July 11, 1919).
45 "Loose ends are such at the finish" (*Variety*, October 3, 1919).
46 "The gymnasium and swimming pool would put on much-needed weight" (*Photoplay*, August 1928).
46 "I have never been so happy" (*Photoplay*, September 1928).
47 "My God! He's ruined my story!" (*Photoplay*, September 1928).
47 "I think I lost my cookies" (Brownlow, *Parade's Gone By*, 142).
47 "I should like to make pictures that dealt simply in humanity" (Fujiwara, *Tourneur*, 16).
48 "self-conscious and had no knowledge of timing" (*Photoplay*, July 1928).
48 "Jack Gilbert has left for New York" (*Los Angeles Times*, July 30, 1920).
48 "It's so bad it's funny" (*Los Angeles Times*, January 2, 1922).
49 "What a picture I made!" (*Photoplay*, July 1928).
49 "wasn't bad" (Fountain, *Dark Star*, 63).
50 "I had no more right at that time to undertake the making of a motion picture" (*Photoplay*, September 1928).
50 "Jack, gregarious by nature" (Marion, *Off with Their Heads*, 131).
50 "It was awful" (Brownlow, *Parade's Gone By*, 144).
51 "I would not act" (*Photoplay*, September 1928).
52 "Sadly, the site is now an empty lot in a mostly industrial area" (http://allanellenberger.com/book-flm-news/selig-polyscope-studios/).

52 "I was unhappy most of the time" (*Photoplay,* September 1928).
52 "Stardom is to be conferred" (*Los Angeles Times,* June 1, 1921).
52 "We'd love to see a story in which the hero or heroine really was half-caste" (*Los Angeles Times,* January 23, 1922).
54 "My mother really loved being a star" (*Classic Images,* May 1996).
54 "Mr. Gilbert is one of the most talented and promising of the younger male stars" (*Los Angeles Times,* February 25, 1921).
54 "Modesty should prevent my saying it" (Brownlow, *Hollywood*).
54 "Jack and I had a little game we used to play" (Drew, *Speaking of Silents,* 74–75).
56 "Both are numbered among the most promising film stars of the day" (*Los Angeles Times,* January 31, 1922).
56 "my mother didn't particularly care for him" (Drew, *Speaking of Silents,* 66).
56 "All our lives long" (*Los Angeles Times,* February 12, 1922).
56 "and Jack hold long conversations about the war" (ibid.).
57 "torrid affair" (*Classic Images,* May 1996).
57 "The phone rang at about two in the morning" (Fountain, *Dark Star,* 80).
57 "certainly handles the role" (*Variety,* May 5, 1922).
57 "You may notice, if you are very keen" (*Los Angeles Times,* June 25, 1922).
58 "interesting actor in the person of John Gilbert" (*Variety,* May 19, 1922).
58 "Seldom do you feel any vital regard" (*Motion Picture,* September 1922).
58 "John Gilbert . . . might well be proud of his work" (*Los Angeles Times,* undated clipping, Academy of Motion Picture Arts and Sciences, Beverly Hills).
59 "He believes in giving the hero character" (*Los Angeles Times,* May 21, 1922).
59 "working out your play without the aid of scenario" (ibid.).
60 "just a western" (*Variety,* March 22, 1923).
60 "It's hoak pure and simple" (*Variety,* May 17, 1923).
61 "Gilbert gives an interesting performance that will please the fans" (*Variety,* April 15, 1923).
61 "In those days the shaggy-haired Twain would sit with Gilbert" (*Los Angeles Times,* November 25, 1923).
62 "the only fine thing I was associated with at the studio" (*Photoplay,* September 1928).
63 "terribly earnest" (*Variety,* December 6, 1923).
63 "Gilbert, who heretofore has been seen usually in heavy roles" (*Variety,* May 7, 1924).
63 "gets rough when in liquor" (*Variety,* April 16, 1924).
64 "displays real talent as one of the Parisian gamines" (*Variety,* May 21, 1924).
64 "casual western of the well-known type" (*Variety,* July 16, 1924).
65 "know what they've got" (*Photoplay,* September 1928).

65 "I greatly appreciate everything which the Fox people have done for me" (*Los Angeles Times,* March 7, 1924).
65 "Despite his resolution to sign no more contracts" (*Los Angeles Times,* May 1, 1924).
65 "I consider my present engagement a very excellent one" (ibid.).

Chapter Four

67 "A noted actress who tried the cure" (*Chicago American,* February 9, 1922, via Taylorology 71 [November 1998], www.silent-movies.com/Taylorology/).
68 "'orgies,' narcotics, alcohol, vice, extravagant living" (*New York Herald,* 1922, via Taylorology13 [January 1994], www.silent-movies.com/Taylorology/).
68 "in parts of Los Angeles it is sold openly" (ibid.).
68 "My impression" (ibid.).
69 "Nero . . . would have turned his head in shame" (*New York American,* September 16, 1921, via Taylorology 71 [November 1998], www.silent-movies.com/Taylorology/).
69 "innumerable . . . chorus girls who have come to Hollywood" (*Movie Weekly,* June 24, 1922, via Taylorology 71 [November 1998], www.silent-movies.com/Taylorology/).
70 "What Arbuckle's defense maintained is that Virginia's bladder ruptured" (Joan Myers to author, September 29, 2011).
70 "I wouldn't call her a *tramp*" (Brownlow, *Hollywood*).
70 "Since [then], the Hollywood film colony has 'gone to bed' at 11 o'clock" (*New York Evening World,* September 17, 1921, via Taylorology 71 [November 1998], www.silent-movies.com/Taylorology/).
71 "There should be some effective way to remove the garbage element" (*Omaha Bee,* February 26, 1922, via Taylorology 9 [September 1993], www.silent-movies.com/Taylorology/).
71 "When I walk down the street nowadays and someone recognizes me" (*Movie Weekly,* April 1, 1922, via Taylorology 9 [September 1993], www.silent-movies.com/Taylorology/).
71 "Dope is expensive and how could they afford to stay hopped-up" (*Austin American,* March 19, 1922, via Taylorology 9 [September 1993], www.silent-movies.com/Taylorology/).
72 "attempted to attack the girl" (*LA Examiner,* February 16, 1924).
72 "when corroboration of her story could not be obtained" (undated newspaper clipping).
72 "irrespective of the manner in which they are treated" (*Motion Picture Production Code 1927, 1930*).

Chapter Five

78 "Any one of fifty men could have played the part" (*Photoplay,* September 1928).

79 "This part, as small as it is, will do you more good" (ibid.).
79 "Chaney was disgusted" (*Vanity Fair,* May 1928).
80 "small, shabby and jury-rigged" (Eyman, *Lion of Hollywood,* 91).
80 "Ah—behold the black stallion" (Vieira, *Hollywood Dreams,* 38).
80 "This is trash!" (ibid.).
81 "a wild young man" (Museum of Modern Art, New York; titles translated by Lenka Pichlikova Burke).
81 "not displeasing" (*New York Times,* October 27, 1924).
82 "we have seen Mr. Gilbert, but never has he made our heart beat" (newspaper clipping, 1924).
83 "Mr. Bell drums home his ideas" (*New York Times,* December 15, 1924).
83 "All the more credit, then, to John Gilbert" (Academy of Motion Picture Arts and Sciences files, Beverly Hills).
83 "Jack Gilbert carries off the acting honors in the title role" (Academy of Motion Picture Arts and Sciences files, Beverly Hills).
84 "a rare opportunity to demonstrate" (*Los Angeles Times,* November 16, 1924).
84 "The stage doesn't have the same hard and fast rules" (*Los Angeles Times,* December 14, 1924).
84 "The presence of Jack Gilbert in a picture is evidently good insurance" (*Los Angeles Times,* November 17, 1924).
84 "A good many of my friends criticized my judgment" (*Los Angeles Times,* December 14, 1924).
85 "Do '*Hollywood*'" (Eyman, *Speed of Sound,* 254).
85 "habitual intemperance" (*Los Angeles Times,* August 13, 1924).
85 "The fault was ninety-nine and nine-tenths mine" (*Photoplay,* September 1928).
85 "When Leatrice and I were married" (Gladys Hall Papers, June 10, 1927, Academy of Motion Picture Arts and Sciences, Beverly Hills).
85 "was the straw that broke the camel's back" (Drew, *Speaking of Silents,* 79).
86 "with most divorces it's an aggressive woman" (ibid.).
86 "What are you doing here?" (Vieira, *Hollywood Dreams,* 39).
86 "It's so great to be a part of anything like this" (ibid.).
86 "When we all began at MGM" (*Modern Screen,* November 1933).
87 "I had retained my own ideas as to how certain emotions should be expressed" (undated newspaper clipping).
87 "the kid himself" (undated newspaper clipping).
87 "It is a keen character study of a charming pagan" (undated newspaper clipping).

Chapter Six

88 "queens and ladies" (*Classic Images,* May 1996).
89 "they played records all night" (Vieira, *Hollywood Dreams,* 25).
89 "He has a Magdelene complex" (ibid.).

90 "Paul had put his head in the toilet to drown himself" (ibid.).
90 "He scarcely ever missed the opera" (*Los Angeles Times,* 1936 clipping).
90 "Jack would put a glass of Scotch-and-soda on the mantelpiece" (Fountain, *Dark Star,* 172).
92 "It has at times been quite a close race" (*Los Angeles Times,* October 26, 1924).
92 "I'd rather play the part" (*Los Angeles Times,* July 13, 1924).
93 "I am forced to use you in my picture" (*American Film,* July–August 1981).
93 "that disagreement cemented a relationship" (*Photoplay,* September 1928).
93 "I will have no trouble giving my best" (Murray, *The Self Enchanted,* 144–46).
94 "He had a spark toward me in the beginning" (1960 interview CD).
94 "Von Stroheim yelled at Jack" (*Photoplay,* April 1934).
94 "left for South America" (Murray, *The Self Enchanted,* 153).
94 "And another time, when everything seemed to go wrong" (*Photoplay,* April 1934).
95 "Jack is terribly sensitive" (ibid.).
95 "Each day's work was a duel of wills" (Murray, *The Self Enchanted,* 146–48).
97 "Louse-y, just as I knew it would be" (ibid., 153).
97 "This is not a Mae Murray Production" (*American Film,* July–August 1981).
97 "They were taking their jobs in their hands" (ibid.).
97 "They applauded" (ibid.).
98 "I am unspeakably pained to see myself travestied by a cheap cinema star" (letter from MGM files, Margaret Herrick Library, Los Angeles).
99 "John Gilbert has never before done anything to compare" (*New York Herald Tribune,* undated clipping).
99 "the most promising star since Valentino" (undated newspaper clipping).
99 "There is just one bright spot in Broadway's film world this week" (*Los Angeles Times,* September 6, 1925).
100 "I've a lovely place way up high, oh, miles high" (*Los Angeles Times,* June 7, 1925).
102 "and other tributes" (*Architectural Digest,* April 1996).
102 "I may have to paint my face for a living" (*Architectural Digest,* April 1994).
102 "a drunken debauch asserted to have been staged by her husband" (*Los Angeles Times,* May 29, 1925).
103 "about any one of three subjects: steel, wheat, or war" (Vidor, *A Tree Is a Tree,* 111).
103 "wanted it to be the story of a young American" (ibid.).
103 "This is all too fantastic and unreal" (ibid., 113).
104 "He wanted to be ready to do the scene" (ibid., 115).
104 "Sequence after sequence was good" (*Photoplay,* September 1928).
104 "Renee Adoree . . . never knew that she was even going to chew gum" (*Los Angeles Times,* July 31, 1927).
106 "I didn't have a big voice" (Brownlow, *Parade's Gone By,* 74).

107 "He was real and honest" (*Los Angeles Times,* July 17, 1927).
107 "it proved successful not because it was a war drama" (newspaper clipping, 1926).
107 "I would rather direct than eat, write, paint or compose" (*Los Angeles Times,* August 16, 1925).
108 "No love has ever enthralled me as did the making of this picture" (*Photoplay,* September 1928).
108 "We never made it" (*Los Angeles Times,* December 11, 1927).
108 "I don't want to be labeled 'star'" (*Los Angeles Times,* June 7, 1925).
108 "If the story is good and the cast is good" (ibid.).
109 "If I do make an awful flop" (ibid.).
109 "During this last picture, *The Big Parade*" (ibid.).
109 "Married men can't do those things" (ibid.).
109 "'Lucky Break' has become John Gilbert's middle name" (*Los Angeles Times,* February 14, 1926).
111 "I asked Irving for its director and entire cast" (Gish, *The Movies,* 278).
111 "I could not impose my kind of rehearsal on the others" (ibid., 279).
111 "I found that all the costumes looked like brand-new dresses" (ibid., 278).
112 "'These are poor Bohemians'" (ibid., 279).
112 "both King Vidor and John Gilbert fell in love with Lillian" (ibid., 280).
112 "It seemed to me that, if we avoided showing the lovers in a physical embrace" (Vidor, *Tree Is a Tree,* 130).
112 "Oh, dear, I've got to go through another day of kissing John Gilbert" (Gish, *The Movies,* 280).
113 "When I would take her hand when talking about the part" (Vidor, *A Tree Is a Tree,* 131).
114 "the mistress of one of [Rodolphe's] friends" (Henri Murger, *The Bohemians of the Latin Quarter* [London: Vizetelly, 1888], 156).
114 "I went to a hospital to observe the progress of tuberculosis" (Affron, *Lillian Gish,* 210).
114 "appearance to a group of flappers caused such palpitation" (*Los Angeles Times,* May 16, 1926).
115 "It is not a great production" (*Los Angeles Times,* May 15, 1926).
115 "artistic and delicate, but never believable" (*Photoplay,* August 1927).
115 "I never go to bed" (Gladys Hall Papers, June 10, 1927, Academy of Motion Picture Arts and Sciences, Beverly Hills).
116 "took to each other immediately" (Fountain, *Dark Star,* 134).
116 "Peter Pan" (*Los Angeles Times,* August 15, 1926).

Chapter Seven

117 "Greta Garbo will play the leading role" (*Los Angeles Times,* June 27, 1926).
119 "Hello, Greta!" (Swenson, *Garbo,* 119).
119 "you just didn't go up to Garbo and say hello!" (Anita Page to author, 1993).

119 "Pardon me, madam, I thought you were a guy I knew in Pittsburgh" (David Niven, *Bring on the Empty Horses* [New York: G. P. Putnam's Sons, 1975], 165).

119 "love at first sight" (Swenson, *Garbo,* 119).

119 "At first Gilbert didn't know if he wanted to work with her" (quoted in Vieira, *Hollywood Dreams,* 69).

120 "Neither Gilbert nor Miss Garbo would deny the report" (*Los Angeles Times,* summer 1926).

120 "had a style that allowed us to rehearse and to find our own characters" (Ankerich, *Sound of Silence,* 157).

121 "It has broken all records for audience attendance" (*Los Angeles Times,* undated clipping).

122 "the first German picture made in America" (*Santa Monica Outlook,* July 24, 1927).

122 "Mildly exciting because of its brazen display of sex lure" (*Photoplay,* September 1928).

122 According to Hedda Hopper (Hopper letter, July 30, 1942, Academy of Motion Picture Arts and Sciences, Beverly Hills).

122 "Jack lived like a prince of the realm" (Vieira, *Hollywood Dreams,* 70).

122 "Tennis and other games would scarcely be under way" (Vidor, *A Tree Is a Tree,* 135).

123 "around Jack Gilbert's garden perfectly nude" (Brownlow, *Hollywood*).

123 "Grasping the racket well up toward the throat" (Swenson, *Garbo,* 129).

123 "When I said, 'I'm going out'" (Dietz, *Dancing in the Dark,* 53).

124 "much to everyone's surprise" (Ankerich, *Broken Silence,* 65).

125 "Gilbert kept getting drunker and drunker" (ibid., 65–68).

125 "I was upstairs" (Brownlow, *Hollywood*).

125 "If Gilbert would have hit Mayer" (Eyman, *Lion of Hollywood,* 134).

125 "I think Mayer was a bastard" (Drew, *Speaking of Silents,* 47).

126 "she always kept him at arm's length (Swenson, *Garbo,* 125–26).

127 "A great many stories have been broadcast concerning the romance" (*Photoplay,* February 1927).

127 "Jack Gilbert was in love" (*Photoplay,* January 1927).

127 "Gustafsson's youngest boy" (Swenson, *Garbo,* 31).

127 "and lies, and lies . . ." (Paris, *Garbo,* 264).

127 "She is like a statue" (*Photoplay,* February 1927).

128 "I jumped in my car and motored for miles" (ibid.).

128 "I hadn't much time to sample the local joie de vivre" (Lillie, *Every Other Inch,* 173).

128 "Jack opened the door" (ibid., 175).

128 "Jack really believed the studio press releases" (ibid., 172).

Chapter Eight

129 "Valentino won't have his clothes torn off his back anymore" (*Los Angeles Times,* December 27, 1925).

129 "the Metro-Goldwyn lion had them all [other studios] terrified" (ibid.).
130 "The death of Valentino is a terrific loss to the screen" (undated newspaper clipping).
130 "Jack Gilbert is a flashing, daring, swashbuckling cavalier" (*Los Angeles Times*, September 5, 1926).
133 "How come you're not putting Colman in a picture" (Marion, *Off with Their Heads*, 122).
135 "the price of fame" (Gladys Hall Papers, June 10, 1927, Academy of Motion Picture Arts and Sciences, Beverly Hills).
135 "After living at top speed" (ibid.).
136 "absolutely wrapped up in it" (ibid.).
136 "If a new assignment were a dashing Cossack officer" (Vidor, *A Tree Is a Tree*, 134).
137 "a composite of d'Artagnan, Don Juan and that millionaire cowboy" (*New York Times*, November 1, 1926).
137 "Jack Gilbert's most elaborate starring feature during his career" (*Los Angeles Times*, October 1, 1926).
137 "masterly Doug Fairbanks stunts of acrobatic miracles" (*Los Angeles Times*, September 26, 1926).
138 "John Gilbert's attempt to duplicate a feat" (*Los Angeles Times*, November 28, 1926).
138 "I don't want to be portraying this incredible 'magnificent' stuff" (*Los Angeles Times*, January 16, 1927).
138 "Gilbert's acting is of the smooth, restrained sort" (undated newspaper clipping).
138 "Applesauce" (*Photoplay*, September 1928).

Chapter Nine

139 "is more than keen to annex Gilbert at the expiration" (*Los Angeles Times*, January 2, 1927).
139 "I am a low-down bum of a sideshow barker" (*Los Angeles Times*, January 16, 1927).
139 "We had to get some reclamation in the end" (*Photoplay*, August 1928).
140 "He was very difficult to work with" (Skal, *Dark Carnival*, 172).
141 "Any one who is tired of drawing room dramas" (ibid., 109).
142 "Takes his character and regenerates him" (undated newspaper clipping).
142 "nothing whatever to be proud of." (*Photoplay*, September 1928).
143 "a nearby village" (newspaper clipping, 1927).
143 "An engagement to marry him?" (*Los Angeles Times*, February 24, 1927).
143 "They don't know yet, and may decide to operate" (ibid.).
144 "got the telephone number of the pretty red-haired nurse who attended him" (Vidor, *A Tree Is a Tree*, 140).
144 "from lead poisoning on his face" (*Los Angeles Times*, May 24, 1928).
144 "seemed to eat little but dance together much!" (*Los Angeles Times*, March 6, 1927).

144 "Garbo was a lesbian" (Louise Brooks to Tom Dardis, April 4, 1977, Academy of Motion Picture Arts and Sciences, Beverly Hills).

144 "They were *really* two people utterly and totally in love" (Brownlow, *Hollywood*).

145 "Only in legend does a man make incarnate a beautiful statue" (Marion, *Off with Their Heads*, 153).

145 "Off again, on again" (*Photoplay*, February 1928).

146 "I must have been laboring under a hallucination" (*Los Angeles Times*, April 16, 1927).

146 "Do you think you can get away with such stunts in Beverly Hills?" (*Los Angeles Times*, April 19, 1927).

146 "Mr. Fairbanks gave me a good talking-to" (*Los Angeles Times*, April 20, 1927).

147 "It wasn't bad at all" (*Los Angeles Times*, July 17, 1927).

147 "unusually intense emotional states" (www.nimh.nih.gov/).

148 "Feverishly happy when he was happy" (*Los Angeles Times*, January 12, 1936).

148 "He was emotionally unstable" (Ankerich, *Broken Silence*, 65–68).

148 "there was nothing that afflicted him more during life" (*Los Angeles Times*, January 12, 1936).

148 "Bipolar disorder and alcoholism often occur together" (www.mayoclinic.com/).

148 "I am like that scared puppy" (*Los Angeles Times*, January 16, 1927).

149 "At MGM we had a certain dignity" (Newquist, *Conversations with Joan Crawford*, 47).

149 "took one look at me, turned absolutely red" (ibid., 54).

149 "*Twelve Miles Out* was the first time that magic man-woman chemistry" (ibid., 69).

149 "He'd stride onto the set" (Crawford, *Portrait of Joan*, 31).

150 "Oh, I'm a bad lot" (*Los Angeles Times*, January 16, 1927).

150 "equipped with special hatches and 'grab hooks'" (undated newspaper clipping).

152 "glorious . . . he has all the dash and fire of *Bardelys*" (ibid.).

152 "I'm going to build myself a yawl" (*Los Angeles Times*, June 7, 1925).

152 "resplendent in good-looking yachting attire" (Swenson, *Garbo*, 156).

153 "I felt sorry for Jack" (Vidor, *A Tree Is a Tree*, 136–37).

153 "I can only tell you that it was because if they married" (*Photoplay*, March 1936).

153 "We were not suited to be together" (*Modern Screen*, November 1933).

153 "I don't like the stories and the management I've had lately" (*Los Angeles Times*, July 14, 1927).

154 "Ten years ago, I would have been an out-and-out villain" (*Los Angeles Times*, December 11, 1927).

154 "We have no hate here" (Eyman, *Lion of Hollywood*, 164).

154 "it was very strange" (Fountain, *Dark Star,* 102).
154 "just the sight of [John Gilbert] made him angry" (Eyman, *Lion of Hollywood,* 133).
154 "Mayer was a great hater" (Fountain, *Dark Star,* 205).
155 "That son of a bitch is inciting that damned Swede" (Swenson, *Garbo,* 137).
155 "Greta has no idea of the conventional courtesies of the studio" (*Photoplay,* February 1927).
155 "I became arrogant, of course" (*Modern Screen,* November 1933).
155 "far outdistanced the field in a recent screen popularity contest" (undated newspaper clipping).
156 "elevated to the position of star since last year" (ibid.).
156 "the Kaiser's war machine" (*Los Angeles Times,* December 11, 1927).
156 "Gilbert may take a vacation of 'five, ten or fifteen years'" (*Los Angeles Times,* July 14, 1927).
157 "One of the few truly original and interesting people I met" (Baum, *It Was All Quite Different,* 340).
158 "Garbo insisted that only Gilbert could direct her in the love scenes" (Brownlow, *Hollywood*).
158 "It's all very well to make pictures of these heroes and villains" (*Los Angeles Times,* July 17, 1927).
159 "A Russian *East Lynne*" (*Photoplay,* September 1928).
159 "is away up on top of a Beverly Hills mountain" (*Los Angeles Times,* July 11, 1926).
160 "It happened to be a story that didn't strike Louis B. Mayer very well" (Brownlow, *Hollywood*).
161 "I lost my grip on the dress and she fell forward on her face" (Marx, *Mayer and Thalberg,* 59).
162 "Jeanne repeated all she had said about stupidity in the movies" (Doherty, *The Rain Girl,* 261).
162 "an unsophisticated newspaper reporter" (*Los Angeles Times,* December 11, 1927).
163 "John Gilbert is the guileless, bewildered youth" (*Life,* January 5, 1928).
163 "It is comparatively simple to be effective in a showy military uniform" (*Los Angeles Times,* December 11, 1927).
163 "My God, what a title!" (*Photoplay,* September 1928).
163 "It could have been great, but it wasn't" (ibid.).
164 "In hoarse whispers any one will tell who the villain of Jarnegan was" (*Smart Set,* undated clipping).
164 "His emotion is on the surface" (*Vanity Fair,* May 1928).
164 "Mr. Gilbert is not a gifted actor" (ibid.).
165 "women lose their charm after forty" (ibid.).
165 "His conceit and changeable moods make it uncertain" (ibid.).
166 "It crushed Jack" (Fountain, *Dark Star,* 152).

166 "I'm afraid I'm a dab at dramatizing myself" (*Los Angeles Times,* January 16, 1927).

166 "The Ingrate of Hollywood" (*Photoplay,* June 1927).

166 "Utterly unlovable, he [Tully] wanted to be loved by everyone" (ibid.).

167 "Jim Quirk has asked me to write an outline of my career" (ibid.).

167 "a mixed contingent of Mohammedans and native Russian Cossacks" (MGM press release, 1927, Academy of Motion Picture Arts and Sciences, Beverly Hills).

167 "We are making a Russian picture" (*Los Angeles Times,* July 14, 1927).

168 "leapt about like a goat with a bee in its ear" (Marion, *Off with Their Heads,* 168).

170 "It has all the sure-fire elements that compose a story" (*Los Angeles Times,* June 24, 1928).

171 "a capital performance" (*New York Times,* August 20, 1928).

171 "never looks the part (newspaper clipping, August 26, 1928).

172 "quite a good entertainment" (*New York Times,* November 25, 1928).

172 "the music synchronization suddenly failed" (ibid.).

173 "'What will make you stay?'" (*Photoplay,* February 1930).

174 "as its leading male star" (newspaper clipping, December 1928).

174 "and a secret gateway" (undated newspaper clipping).

174 "You know, he gave $10,000 to the Al Smith campaign" (*San Francisco Chronicle,* July 6, 2005).

174 "I will know I have my cue to retire" (*Los Angeles Times,* December 11, 1927).

174 "I [have always] solved all my problems by myself" (*Los Angeles Times,* June 13, 1929).

175 "The day of big salaries isn't over in the movies." (*Los Angeles Times,* January 13, 1928).

175 "The great car stood like a bruise against the passage of eternity" (Michael Arlen, *The Green Hat* [New York: George H. Doran, 1924], 51).

176 "I'd rather you didn't touch my part a bit" (Fountain, *Dark Star,* 160).

176 "in a day or so . . . all would be well again." (Swenson, *Garbo,* 172).

176 "went completely ham in the middle of shooting" (Brownlow, *Parade's Gone By,* 152).

178 "The most interesting feature of *A Woman of Affairs* is the treatment" (*Judge,* January 1929).

178 "utterly blah . . . the idol of the flappers" (*Variety,* January 23, 1929).

180 "Holds the interest" (*New York Times,* May 6, 1929).

180 "the best screen actor in the business" (Fountain, *Dark Star,* 160).

Chapter Ten

183 "We would count how many times it repeated" (Eyman, *Speed of Sound,* 268).

185 "a dreadful picture" (ibid. 140).

187 "the 'doll-faced' and 'sheik' types of movie stars" (*New York Times*, July 15, 1928).
187 "no fun anymore" (*Charleston Gazette*, April 14, 1929).
187 "may toss no 'ad-lib' phrases now" (*New York Times*, July 15, 1928).
187 "are unlimited in scope and interest" (International News Service release, February 4, 1929).
187 "Nowadays she is not just an extra" (*Charleston Gazette*, September 1, 1929).
187 "beauty is a far greater attraction for fans than voice" (undated newspaper clipping).
187 "there is no more touching sight in Hollywood than the established stage favorite" (*New York Times*, August 19, 1928).
188 "A young girl is pretty to look at" (*New York Times*, May 5, 1929).
188 In New York alone, three thousand were thrown out of work (*New York Times*, March 21, 1929).
188 the "true idols" (*New York Times*, August 19, 1928).
190 "the old-fashioned silent picture" (*Charleston Gazette*, April 14, 1929).
190 "Talking pictures of the future will be in Esperanto" (*New York Times*, July 12, 1929).
191 "Overnight I became the one-man sound department" (Eyman, *Speed of Sound*, 245).
191 "in the event of the failure of talking pictures to 'catch on' with the public" (*New York Times*, April 18, 1929).
191 "Our aim is to protect all the motion-picture theaters" (*New York Times*, March 26, 1929).

Chapter Eleven

193 "gilt edge . . . has some stage experience" (Marion, *Off with Their Heads*, 182).
194 "two of the most vivid, arresting and colorful people in America" (*Photoplay*, October 1931).
195 "said something derogatory about himself" (undated newspaper clipping, New York Public Library, Lincoln Center files).
195 "I stay up in the monitor room and hear every word" (*New York Times*, April 7, 1929).
195 "The voice is the thing in talkies pictures" (*New York Times*, September 30, 1928).
195 he would send actors an electric shock (Eyman, *Speed of Sound*, 282).
196 "Keep the voice natural, expressive, vivid" (ibid., 218).
197 "It is our desire to avoid all fuss" (*Los Angeles Times*, May 9, 1929).
197 "a dingy little police courtroom" (*Los Angeles Times*, May 10, 1929).
197 "might" (*Los Angeles Times*, May 11, 1929).
198 "Without hope there is no use in life" (ibid.).
201 "high comedy beaten thin" (*New York Times*, October 17, 1928).

203 "Guess he's entitled to greasepaint if he wants it now" (*Los Angeles Times,* June 9, 1929).
203 "I was the first man to ever say 'I love you' out loud on the screen" (*Photoplay,* March 1936).
206 "at a sixty-mile-an-hour clip" (*New York Times,* July 28, 1929).
206 "He had no idea what it looked like" (Fountain, *Dark Star,* 188).
206 "Of course not" (*New York Times,* October 20, 1929).
207 "No one questioned my voice" (*Modern Screen,* November 1933).
207 "I wasn't overly surprised" (ibid.).
207 "had a good middle range voice" (Louise Brooks to Tom Dardis, April 4, 1977, Academy of Motion Picture Arts and Sciences, Beverly Hills).
207 "I watched Jack Gilbert being destroyed on the sound stage" (Hopper, *From under My Hat,* 164).
207 "Jack's voice was perfectly normal" (Ankerich, *Broken Silence,* 65–68).
207 "they put the wrong people to contrast with his voice" (Drew, *Speaking of Silents,* 238).
208 "My home, as you know, was built for a bachelor" (*Los Angeles Times,* November 20, 1929).
208 "dates to an evening when Ina Claire told Jack Gilbert" (*Los Angeles Times,* February 15, 1930).
208 "She is always telling me to speak in pear-shaped tones!" (Vidor, *A Tree Is a Tree,* 138).
209 "Hollywood says that the great Gilbert" (*Photoplay,* February 1930).
209 "They're not signing stage stars for any one-year or half-year terms" (*Photoplay,* December 1930).
209 "hopefully"! (*Photoplay,* February 1930).
209 "She should have been, after *The Big Parade,* the greatest, most glamorous star" (*Photoplay,* January 1930).
210 "The most unfair and irresponsible thing you've ever printed" (*Photoplay,* June 1930).
210 "Letters published in magazines" (*Photoplay,* September 1928).
210 "dull, sluggish, agonizing" (Vieira, *Hollywood Dreams,* 121).
211 "Talking pictures and elocution simply do not go together" (*New York Times,* February 3, 1929).
211 "Ina Claire, in my opinion, is the best actress on the American stage" (*Photoplay,* March 1936).
211 "I made more bad mistakes" (*Modern Screen,* November 1933).
211 "Mr. Gilbert's popularity waned" (*New York Times,* January 29, 1933).
212 "holding on to that contract with my teeth" (Gladys Hall Papers, 1933, Academy of Motion Picture Arts and Sciences, Beverly Hills).
212 "It is true Tully knocked me down" (undated newspaper clipping).
212 "Is Mr. Gilbert in?" (*Photoplay,* May 1930).
212 "Hollywood had given me an inferiority complex" (*Los Angeles Times,* July 27, 1930).

213 "Ina's Johnny was Garbo's Yonny" (*Photoplay,* November 1930).
213 "She wishes she had a baby but knows that said infant would cost her $100,000" (Gladys Hall Papers, Academy of Motion Picture Arts and Sciences, Beverly Hills).
213 "He isn't well, he hasn't been sleeping" (*Los Angeles Times,* January 12, 1936).
214 "The car flung itself violently in the air" (Vidor, *A Tree Is a Tree,* 139).

Chapter Twelve

217 "Except as a scientific achievement, I am not sympathetic" (Eyman, *Speed of Sound,* 264).
217 "had a tense, nervous and excited note" (*Los Angeles Times,* January 12, 1936).
217 "Jack Gilbert is one of the stars who has benefited by sound pictures" (*San Francisco Bulletin,* September 9, 1930).
217 "The talkies have created a new aristocracy in filmdom" (ibid.).
218 "That should take care of *Mr.* Gilbert" (Fountain, *Dark Star,* 186).
218 "Jim Tully . . . is no great shakes as an actor" (*Photoplay,* September 1930).
220 "The idea was that Jack was to make an impression" (*Los Angeles Times,* August 3, 1931).
220 "This can't be considered complete ruination for Gilbert" (Vieira, *Hollywood Dreams,* 122).
220 "The thought of having to pay those smackers" (ibid.).
221 "They offered to buy me off" (Gladys Hall Papers, December 4, 1933, Academy of Motion Picture Arts and Sciences, Beverly Hills).
221 "You still own thousands of feet of Gilbert footage" (Eyman, *Lion of Hollywood,* 186).
221 "They wrote things about me in the papers and magazine" (*Modern Screen,* November 1933).
221 "Ina found herself, once the moonlight had worn off" (*Photoplay,* October 1931).
222 "Any difficulty or misunderstanding we have had" (*Los Angeles Times,* February 14, 1931).
222 "fast slipping into the discard" (*Los Angeles Times,* February 15, 1931).
222 "He said he wanted to be left alone" (*Los Angeles Times,* August 5, 1931).
223 "I try and try to make a go of this" (ibid.).
223 "Imagine that!" (Fountain, *Dark Star,* 202).
223 "We do desire to be the best of friends" *Los Angeles Times,* September 1, 1931).
223 "sit there all day and do nothing" (Fountain, *Dark Star,* 193).
224 "He never mentioned them to me" (ibid., 212).
224 "I loved John Gilbert" (Anita Page to author, 1993).
225 "made it nearly impossible for the studio to pair him" (Soares, *Beyond Paradise,* 189).

225 "He is so miserable that he never comes to the studio" (*Los Angeles Times,* August 9, 1931).

226 "when anyone can stir a Baltimore audience to applause" (Vieira, *Hollywood Dreams,* 139).

226 "a highly improbable but none the less interesting tale" (*New York Times,* November 14, 1931).

227 "I admire him very much" (*New York American,* October 15, 1931).

228 "I am not legally free from Ina Claire" (ibid.).

229 "Lupe is splendid, isn't she?" (ibid.).

229 "that the captain's cabin on the tender which took her out to the liner was turned over to her" (*New York American,* October 15, 1931).

229 "The 'in-betweens' whose names mean little or nothing" (newspaper clipping, 1931).

230 "the handsomest of men and a good fellow" (Ankerich, *Broken Silence,* 218).

230 "Jack told me that the studio put him in this picture" (Vieira, *Hollywood Dreams,* 139).

231 "Obviously one person Will Rogers never met" (Mel Neuhaus to author, December 9, 2011).

231 "If it was the purpose of MGM to lead John Gilbert to the guillotine" (Vieira, *Hollywood Dreams,* 139).

231 "It was written by a couple of actors" (Fountain, *Dark Star,* 219).

231 "He has had a pretty miserable two years of it" (*Photoplay,* August 1931).

Chapter Thirteen

232 "I had never given motion pictures a thought" (*Los Angeles Times,* November 27, 1928).

233 "I'd happen to look up and I'd catch his eye" (*Movie Classic,* August 1932).

233 "That first night, too, I found a big box of red roses" (ibid.).

233 "When he looked at me, I felt all funny inside" (O'Brien, *Virginia Bruce,* 62).

235 "I am happier than I've been in years" (Fountain, *Dark Star,* 224).

235 "We do not want a title that is particularly indicative" (MGM files, July 8, 1932, Academy of Motion Picture Arts and Sciences, Beverly Hills).

236 "a mechanical pulley that was attached to the coffin" (http://thoughtfulthinkingthoughts.wordpress.com/).

237 "I can't remember ever having so much fun before" (O'Brien, *Virginia Bruce,* 67).

237 "one of the biggest diamond rings in Hollywood" (*Los Angeles Times,* July 24, 1932).

237 "Our courtship has been one of whirlwind nature" (*Fresno Bee,* May 28, 1932).

238 "I want you to marry me, Virginia" (*Movie Classic,* August 1932).

238 "You could have knocked me over with a ping pong ball" (*Screen Life,* July 1940).

238 "Jack thought it was hilarious" (Fountain, *Dark Star,* 226–27).
238 "We're going to be married at 6:00 in my bungalow" (*Los Angeles Times,* August 11, 1932).
238 "flimsy yarn" (*Syracuse Herald,* August 13, 1932).
238 "The chief points of interest in it" (*New York Times,* October 8, 1932).
239 "When John Gilbert found that he had ceased to be a hero" (*Time,* August 8, 1932).
241 "No picture shall be produced that will lower the moral standards" (Balio, *American Film Industry,* 381).
242 "our tennis world revolves around two factions" (Eyman, *Lion of Hollywood,* 95).
244 "Harlow was supposed to help Gilbert's fading image" (Lyn Tornabene, *Long Live the King,* 150).
244 "You're crazy if you use Gilbert with Harlow" (Charles Samuels, *The King,* 170).
244 "They would continue to communicate thereafter" (Marx, *Mayer and Thalberg,* 188).
245 "He tried to intervene in Mayer's destruction of my father's career" (*Classic Images,* May 1996).
245 "I wonder now why Irving could not help him" (Vieira, *Hollywood Dreams,* 140).
245 "once regarded as the 'great lover' of the screen" (*Los Angeles Times,* May 26, 1932).
245 "the tragic economic condition existing in our country" (MGM memo, August 6, 1932, Academy of Motion Picture Arts and Sciences, Beverly Hills).
248 "Jack has had two actress wives" (*Oakland Tribune,* September 13, 1932).
248 "Virginia thinks, as I do" (*San Mateo Times,* September 23, 1932).
250 "I felt so sad for him" (Anita Page to author, 1993).
250 "Virginia personifies peace and tranquility" (*Modern Screen,* January 1935).
250 "Tell my wife I will send the chauffeur back for her" (*Daily Oklahoman,* December 6, 1932).
250 "Sometimes he'd be awake drinking all night" (Fountain, *Dark Star,* 228).
250 "I knew it couldn't last" (*Modern Screen,* January 1935).

Chapter Fourteen

251 "A definite inference of sex perversion" (Skal, *Dark Carnival,* 187).
252 "The suspicion grows" (*New York Times,* March 20, 1933).
252 "the Depression has finally caught up with them" (*New York Herald Tribune,* April 13, 1933).
253 "The day I left MGM for the last time" (*Modern Screen,* November 1933).
254 "seeing shows" (*Los Angeles Times,* May 3, 1933).
254 "Both father and baby are doing nicely" (*Los Angeles Times,* August 3, 1933).

254 "I don't feel a bit paternal" (*Los Angeles Times,* April 15, 1934).

254 "bless his soul" (Gladys Hall Papers, 1933, Academy of Motion Picture Arts and Sciences, Beverly Hills).

254 "Mr. Gilbert is described as a 'looker-on'" (*New York Sun,* August 8, 1933).

254 "Universal had called me about a couple of scripts" (*Modern Screen,* November 1933).

255 "I didn't believe a word of it" (ibid.).

255 "Everyone but Ben Turpin" (Swenson, *Garbo,* 308).

256 "It was our intention when we signed John Gilbert for this part" (Eddie Mannix Papers, Academy of Motion Picture Arts and Sciences, Beverly Hills).

256 "Here I am. What are you going to do about me?" (*Modern Screen,* November 1933).

256 "so nominal that it would have seemed insulting to the old John Gilbert" (Gladys Hall Papers, 1933, Academy of Motion Picture Arts and Sciences, Beverly Hills).

256 "a seven-year contract"(*Modern Screen,* November 1933).

257 "sounded swell to me at the time" (Gladys Hall Papers, Academy of Motion Picture Arts and Sciences, Beverly Hills).

257 "It never occurred to me" (ibid.).

257 "We met again for the first time in two and a half years" (*Modern Screen,* November 1933).

257 "When they started to make publicity stills of us" (ibid.).

257 "Heavens, what did I ever see in him?" (Swenson, *Garbo,* 309).

257 "How could you ever get mixed up with a fellow like that?" (ibid., 313).

257 "We were both self-conscious and both felt awkward" (*Modern Screen,* November 1933).

259 "Oh, it is so damn beautiful" (ibid.).

259 "reports on his work in the picture indicate a real comeback" (*Los Angeles Times,* October 4, 1933).

259 "Mr. Gilbert is a married man now" (*Los Angeles Times,* September 13, 1933).

260 "I was nervous, shy, raw" (Gladys Hall Papers, December 4, 1933, Academy of Motion Picture Arts and Sciences, Beverly Hills).

260 "seemed like a man who had been floored by life" (Swenson, *Garbo,* 312).

260 "certainly makes it tough to determine" (ibid., 313).

260 "It should be a terrific scene" (Gladys Hall Papers, December 4, 1933, Academy of Motion Picture Arts and Sciences, Beverly Hills).

260 "I knew my job and, damn it, I cared about my job!" (ibid.).

261 "I started in to say thank you to him" (ibid.).

262 "They told me I'd been sitting around for months" (ibid.).

262 "I want to work" (ibid.).

263 "I had a grandmother who went broke" (Fowler, *Good Night, Sweet Prince,* 347–50).

263 "Then Barrymore put his hand on Gilbert's shoulder" (ibid.).

263 "It is certain there will never be reconciliation" (*Los Angeles Times,* January 31, 1934).
263 "drank heavily and abused Mrs. Gilbert" (*Los Angeles Times,* May 24, 1934).
264 "Why can't the screen's greatest lover be a success with love in real life?" (AP release, January 16, 1933).
264 "used profane language toward her" (*Los Angeles Times,* May 3, 1934).
264 "Our conversations became dramatic episodes" (*Photoplay,* April 1934).
264 "I don't believe any woman can ever really and truly make Jack happy" (*Movie Classic,* October 1934).
264 "It was my own fault, of course" (Gladys Hall Papers, June 26, 1934, Academy of Motion Picture Arts and Sciences, Beverly Hills).
264 "I forgot how young she is." (ibid.).
264 "It was living a tragedy to be with him" (Leatrice Fountain to Scott O'Brien, November 9, 2007).
265 "I don't expect to see him again" (*Photoplay,* September 1934).
265 "Metro-Goldwyn-Mayer will neither offer me work" (*New York Evening Post,* March 22, 1934).
265 "I have been on the screen for twenty years" (Gladys Hall Papers, June 26, 1934, Academy of Motion Picture Arts and Sciences, Beverly Hills).
266 "one of the largest automatic pistols I have ever seen" (Vidor, *A Tree Is a Tree,* 143).
266 "Suddenly he reappeared" (Moore, *You're Only Human Once,* 174).
266 "morose—he had a temperament like Edgar Allan Poe's" (*Galveston Daily News,* February 5, 1936).
266 "What am I to *do?*" (Gladys Hall Papers, June 26, 1934, Academy of Motion Picture Arts and Sciences, Beverly Hills).
268 "I read the script and turned it down" (ibid.).
268 "Everyone knew Jack could direct" (Fountain, *Dark Star,* 241).
269 "I know Jack very well" (Thomas, *King Cohn,* 100).
269 "if you keep your nose clean on this picture" (ibid.).
270 "good, clean fun" (*Los Angeles Times,* July 16, 1934).
270 "He was a quiet, strange man" (Eyman, *Speed of Sound,* 304).
270 "Hurry up" (Thomas, *King Cohn,* 101).
270 "When he wasn't drunk, he was being sick at home (Fountain, *Dark Star,* 244).
270 "Something went agley" (*New York Times,* November 29, 1934).
271 "It's too goddam bad" (Thomas, *King Cohn,* 100).
271 "I'd like to be sixty-seven instead of thirty-seven" (Gladys Hall Papers, June 26, 1934, Academy of Motion Picture Arts and Sciences, Beverly Hills).

Chapter Fifteen

272 "I think we failed to make a go of it" (AP release, January 12, 1935).
272 "I would rather have had Jack for the father of my baby" (*Photoplay,* November 1935).

272 "I am probably through with marriage" (Gladys Hall Papers, June 26, 1934, Academy of Motion Picture Arts and Sciences, Beverly Hills).
273 "was the gayest sort in his periods of real enjoyment of life" (*Los Angeles Times,* January 12, 1936).
273 "I wasn't with him" (*Modern Screen,* March 4, 1936).
274 "Love Face" (Riva, *Marlene Dietrich: Photographs and Memories,* 14).
276 "He just laughed and said it was indigestion" (AP release, January 10, 1936).
277 "He never gave the slightest hint" (*Galveston Daily News,* February 5, 1936).
277 "A fan letter, for God's sake!" (Fountain, *Dark Star,* 2).
277 "Leatrice would never let him see their little girl" (Drew, *Speaking of Silents,* 165).
278 "I have been very ill" (Fountain, *Dark Star,* 248–55).
278 "but he appeared to get better" (*Los Angeles Times,* January 10, 1936).
278 "tried to lift his hands as though to ask for something" (ibid.).
278 "one of her string of unsavory doctors" (Riva, *Marlene Dietrich,* 372).
279 "is certainly compatible with a heart attack" (Robert Pinals to author, August 3, 2011).
279 "Treating a heart attack at home was not unusual in 1936" (ibid.).
279 "He was beloved by all who knew him" (*Los Angeles Times,* January 10, 1936).
279 "A high-pitched voice" (*New York Times,* January 10, 1936).
280 "whose passing will be felt not only in the film world" (*Los Angeles Times,* January 10, 1936).
280 "Of course I am sorry he died" (ibid.).
280 "I still cannot think of his being gone" (Gladys Hall Papers, Academy of Motion Picture Arts and Sciences, Beverly Hills).
281 "I talked with Jack three weeks ago" (*Los Angeles Times,* January 12, 1936).
281 "hysterically" (*San Mateo Times,* January 11, 1936).
282 "The screen was his life" (*Galveston Daily News,* February 5, 1936).
282 "Jack was on the verge of a real comeback" (Fountain, *Dark Star,* 256).
282 "Thalberg was tormented by his failure" (Vieira, *Hollywood Dreams,* 300).
282 "That gold-digger Virginia Bruce" (Riva, *Marlene Dietrich,* 373–74).
283 "Articles of clothing which presumably had personal contact with the Gilbert torso" (United Press, August 26, 1936).

Afterword

284 "I retired at my height" (Watters and Horst, *Return Engagement,* 78).
284 "I truly, truly loved" (ibid., 79).
285 "She never played the star when she talked about Father" (Fountain, *Dark Star,* 3).
285 "My mom is a matriarch" (Lorin Hart to author, April 23, 2012).

285 “Shut up, you damned fool” (Swenson, *Garbo,* 394).
286 “Maybe I haven’t had it so tough” (Watters and Horst, *Return Engagement,* 91).
286 “All the money I am living on today is from the two annuities” (Leatrice Fountain to Scott O’Brien, January 19, 2007).
286 “Do you think when I’m gone, anyone will remember that I had awfully dreamy eyes?” (Watters and Horst, *Return Engagement,* 91).
286 “My mother kept us away from the Hollywood scene” (O’Brien, *Virginia Bruce,* 419).
287 “Angel—keep on loving me” (Riva, *Marlene Dietrich, Photographs and Memories,* 141).

Bibliography

Affron, Charles. *Lillian Gish: Her Legend, Her Life*. New York: Charles Scribner's Sons, 2001.

Ankerich, Michael G. *Broken Silence: Conversations with 23 Silent Film Stars*. Jefferson, NC: McFarland, 1993.

———. *The Sound of Silence: Conversations with 16 Film and Stage Personalities Who Bridged the Gap between Silents and Talkies*. Jefferson, NC: McFarland, 2011.

Bach, Steven. *Marlene Dietrich: Life and Legend*. New York: William Morrow, 1992.

Balio, Tino. *The American Film Industry*. Madison: University of Wisconsin Press, 1976.

Barrios, Richard. *A Song in the Dark: The Birth of the Musical Film*. New York: Oxford University Press, 1995.

Baum, Vicki. *It Was All Quite Different: The Memoirs of Vicki Baum*. New York: Funk & Wagnalls, 1964.

Beauchamp, Cari. *Without Lying Down: Frances Marion and the Powerful Women of Early Hollywood*. Berkeley: University of California Press, 1998.

Blum, Daniel. *A Pictorial History of the Silent Screen*. New York: Grosset & Dunlap, 1953.

———. *A Pictorial History of the Talkies*. New York: Grosset & Dunlap, 1958.

Brownlow, Kevin. *Hollywood: The Pioneers*. London: Thames Television, 1980.

———. *The Parade's Gone By . . . .* Berkeley: University of California Press, 1976.

Coffee, Lenore. *Storyline: Recollections of a Hollywood Screenwriter*. London: Cassell, 1973.

Crafton, Donald. *The Talkies: American Cinema's Transition to Sound, 1926–1931*. New York: Charles Scribner's Sons, 1997.

Crawford, Joan, with Jane Ardmore. *A Portrait of Joan: The Autobiography of Joan Crawford*. New York: Doubleday, 1962.

Dance, Robert. *Ruth Harriet Louise and Hollywood Glamour Photography*. Berkeley: University of California Press, 2002.

Dietz, Howard. *Dancing in the Dark*. New York: Quadrangle/New York Times Books, 1974.

Doherty, Edward. *The Rain Girl: The Tragic Story of Jeanne Eagels*. Philadelphia: MacRae-Smith, 1930.

Drew, William M. *At the Center of the Frame: Leading Ladies of the Twenties and Thirties*. Vestal, NY: Vestal, 1999.

———. *Speaking of Silents: First Ladies of the Screen*. Vestal, NY: Vestal, 1997.

Eyman, Scott. *Lion of Hollywood: The Life and Legend of Louis B. Mayer*. New York: Simon & Schuster, 2005.

———. *The Speed of Sound: Hollywood and the Talkie Revolution, 1926–1930*. New York: Simon & Schuster, 1997.

Fountain, Leatrice Joy. *Dark Star: The Meteoric Rise and Eclipse of John Gilbert*. New York: St. Martin's, 1985.

Fowler, Gene. *Good Night, Sweet Prince: The Life and Times of John Barrymore*. New York: Viking, 1944.

Fox, Charles Donald, and Milton L. Silver. *Who's Who on the Screen*. New York: Ross, 1920.

Fujiwara, Chris. *Jacques Tourneur: The Cinema of Nightfall*. Jefferson, NC: McFarland, 2011.

Gish, Lillian, with Ann Pinchot. *The Movies, Mr. Griffith, and Me*. Englewood Cliffs, NJ: Prentice Hall, 1970.

Hopper, Hedda. *From under My Hat*. New York: Doubleday, 1952.

Koszarski, Richard. *An Evening's Entertainment: the Age of the Silent Feature Picture, 1915–1928*. New York: Charles Scribner's Sons, 1990.

———. *Von: The Life and Films of Erich von Stroheim*. New York: Limelight, 2004.

Lahue, Kalton C. *Dreams for Sale: The Rise and Fall of the Triangle Film Corporation*. South Brunswick, NJ: A. S. Barnes, 1971.

Lambert, Gavin. *Norma Shearer: A Biography*. New York: Alfred A. Knopf, 1990.

Lewis, Philip C. *Trouping: How the Show Came to Town*. New York: Harper & Row, 1973.

Lillie, Beatrice. *Every Other Inch a Lady*. Garden City, NY: Doubleday, 1972.

Lowrey, Carolyn. *The First One Hundred Noted Men and Women of the Screen*. New York: Moffat, Yard, 1920.

Mann, William J. *Wisecracker: The Life and Times of William Haines, Hollywood's First Openly Gay Star*. New York: Viking, 1998.

Marion, Frances. *Off with Their Heads: A Serio-comic Tale of Hollywood*. New York: Macmillan, 1972.

Marx, Samuel. *Mayer and Thalberg: The Make-Believe Saints*. New York: Random House, 1975.

Millichap, Joseph. *Lewis Milestone*. Boston: Twayne, 1981.

Moore, Grace. *You're Only Human Once*. New York: Doubleday Doran, 1944.

Murray, Mae, with Jane Ardmore. *The Self Enchanted*. New York: McGraw Hill, 1959.

Newquist, Roy. *Conversations with Joan Crawford*. Secaucus, NJ: Citadel, 1980.

O'Brien, Scott. *Virginia Bruce: Under My Skin*. Albany, GA: BearManor, 2008.

Parris, Barry. *Garbo: A Biography*. New York: Alfred A. Knopf, 1995.

Riva, Maria. *Marlene Dietrich*. New York: Alfred A. Knopf, 1994.

———. *Marlene Dietrich: Photographs and Memories*. New York: Alfred A. Knopf, 2001.

Samuels, Charles. *The King of Hollywood—A Biography of Clark Gable*. New York: Coward-McCann, 1962.

Skal, David. *Dark Carnival: The Secret World of Tod Browning*. New York: Anchor Books/Doubleday, 1995.

Soares, André. *Beyond Paradise: The Life of Ramon Novarro*. New York: St. Martin's, 2002.

Swenson, Karen. *Garbo: A Life Apart*. New York: Charles Scribner's Sons, 1997.

Taves, Brian. *Thomas Ince: Hollywood's Independent Pioneer*. Lexington: University Press of Kentucky, 2011.

Thomas, Bob. *King Cohn: The Life and Times of Harry Cohn*. New York: Bantam Books, 1968.

———. *Thalberg: Life and Legend*. Garden City, NY: Doubleday, 1969.

Tornabene, Lyn. *Long Live the King: A Biography of Clark Gable*. New York: G. P. Putnam's Sons, 1976.

Vidor, King. *A Tree Is a Tree*. New York: Harcourt Brace, 1954.

Vieira, Mark A. *Hollywood Dreams Made Real: Irving Thalberg and the Rise of M-G-M*. New York: Harry N. Abrams, 2008.

Watters, James, with Horst. *Return Engagement: Faces to Remember Then and Now*. New York: Clarkson N. Potter, 1984.

Index

Page numbers in *italics* refer to photographs.

Monteith, Jeanette, 72

Screen Classics

Screen Classics is a series of critical biographies, film histories, and analytical studies focusing on neglected filmmakers and important screen artists and subjects, from the era of silent cinema to the golden age of Hollywood to the international generation of today. Books in the Screen Classics series are intended for scholars and general readers alike. The contributing authors are established figures in their respective fields. This series also serves the purpose of advancing scholarship on film personalities and themes with ties to Kentucky.

Series Editor
Patrick McGilligan

Books in the Series

Mae Murray: The Girl with the Bee-Stung Lips
Michael G. Ankerich

Hedy Lamarr: The Most Beautiful Woman in Film
Ruth Barton

Von Sternberg
John Baxter

The Marxist and the Movies: A Biography of Paul Jarrico
Larry Ceplair

Warren Oates: A Wild Life
Susan Compo

Jack Nicholson: The Early Years
Robert Crane and Christopher Fryer

Being Hal Ashby: Life of a Hollywood Rebel
Nick Dawson

John Gilbert: The Last of the Silent Film Stars
Eve Golden

Mamoulian: Life on Stage and Screen
David Luhrssen

My Life as a Mankiewicz: An Insider's Journey through Hollywood
Tom Mankiewicz and Robert Crane

Raoul Walsh: The True Adventures of Hollywood's Legendary Director
Marilyn Ann Moss

Some Like It Wilder: The Life and Controversial Films of Billy Wilder
Gene D. Phillips

Arthur Penn: American Director
Nat Segaloff

Claude Rains: An Actor's Voice
David J. Skal with Jessica Rains

Buzz: The Life and Art of Busby Berkeley
Jeffrey Spivak

Thomas Ince: Hollywood's Independent Pioneer
Brian Taves

Carl Theodor Dreyer and Ordet: My Summer with the Danish Filmmaker
Jan Wahl

CPSIA information can be obtained at www.ICGtesting.com
Printed in the USA
BVOW040133200613

323791BV00003B/7/P

9 780813 141626